Liberation Psychology

CULTURAL, RACIAL, AND ETHNIC PSYCHOLOGY BOOK SERIES

Liberation Psychology

Theory, Method, Practice, and Social Justice

Edited by Lillian Comas-Díaz and Edil Torres Rivera

 AMERICAN PSYCHOLOGICAL ASSOCIATION

Published by
American Psychological Association
750 First Street, NE
Washington, DC 20002
https://www.apa.org

Order Department
https://www.apa.org/pubs/books
order@apa.org

In the U.K., Europe, Africa, and the Middle East, copies may be ordered from Eurospan
https://www.eurospanbookstore.com/apa
info@eurospangroup.com

Typeset in Meridien and Ortodoxa by Circle Graphics, Inc., Reisterstown, MD

Printer: Sheridan Books, Chelsea, MI
Cover Designer: Mercury Publishing Services, Inc., Rockville, MD

Library of Congress Cataloging-in-Publication Data

Names: Comas-Díaz, Lillian, editor. | Torres Rivera, Edil, editor.
Title: Liberation psychology : theory, method, practice, and social justice /
   edited by Lillian Comas-Díaz and Edil Torres Rivera.
Description: Washington : American Psychological Association, 2020. |
   Series: Cultural, racial, and ethnic psychology | Includes bibliographical references
   and index.
Identifiers: LCCN 2020001927 (print) | LCCN 2020001928 (ebook) |
   ISBN 9781433832086 (paperback) | ISBN 9781433832093 (ebook)
Subjects: LCSH: Social psychology. | Liberty. | Social justice. | Race discrimination.
Classification: LCC HM1033 .L534 2020 (print) | LCC HM1033 (ebook) |
   DDC 302—dc23
LC record available at https://lccn.loc.gov/2020001927
LC ebook record available at https://lccn.loc.gov/2020001928

http://dx.doi.org/10.1037/0000198-000

Printed in the United States of America

10 9 8 7 6 5 4 3 2 1

We dedicate this volume to three liberation scholars/activists:
Paulo Freire, Ignacio Martín-Baró, and Maritza Montero.

CONTENTS

CONTRIBUTORS

Anushka R. Aqil, PhD, Johns Hopkins Bloomberg School of Public Health, Baltimore, MD

Nahaal Binazir, PsyD, LSU Heath Sciences Center, New Orleans, LA

Thema Bryant-Davis, PhD, Pepperdine University, Los Angeles, CA

Mark Burton, PhD, Independent Scholar–Activist, Manchester, England

Marlene L. Cabrera, MA, Pepperdine University, Los Angeles, CA

Carrie L. Castañeda-Sound, PhD, Pepperdine University, Los Angeles, CA

Alejandro Cervantes, MSc, New Mexico State University, Las Cruces, NM

Lillian Comas-Díaz, PhD, George Washington University, Department of Psychiatry and Behavioral Sciences; Psychologist in Independent Practice, Washington, DC

Jesica Siham Fernández, PhD, Department of Ethnic Studies, Santa Clara University, Santa Clara, CA

Daniel Gaztambide, PsyD, Independent Practice, New York, NY

Raquel Guzzo, PhD, Pontifícia Universidade Católica de Campinas, Campinas, Brazil

Chakira M. Haddock-Lazala, PhD, Independent Practice, Bronx, NY

Ouyporn Khuankaew, MA, International Women's Partnership for Peace and Justice, Chiang Mai, Thailand

Frederick T. L. Leong, PhD, Department of Psychology, Michigan State University, East Lansing

M. Brinton Lykes, PhD, Boston College, Chestnut Hill, MA

Shavonne J. Moore-Lobban, PhD, The Chicago School of Professional Psychology, Washington, DC

Kathryn L. Norsworthy, PhD, Rollins College, Winter Park, FL

Brean'a Parker, PhD, University of Georgia, Athens
Raúl Quiñones-Rosado, PhD, Independent Scholar–Practitioner, Cayey, PR
Daryl M. Rowe, PhD, Pepperdine University, Los Angeles, CA
Ester R. Shapiro (aka Ester Rebeca Shapiro Rok), PhD, University of
   Massachusetts, Boston
Anneliese A. Singh, PhD, University of Georgia, Athens
Gabriela Távara, PhD, Pontificia Universidad Católica del Perú, Lima
Falon Thacker, PhD, University of Central Florida, Orlando
Edil Torres Rivera, PhD, Department of Counseling, Educational Leadership,
   Educational & School Psychology, Wichita State University, Wichita, KS
Melba J. T. Vasquez, PhD, Independent Practice, Austin, TX; Former
   president, American Psychological Association

SERIES FOREWORD

As series editor of the American Psychological Association's (APA's) Division 45 (Society for the Psychological Study of Culture, Ethnicity, and Race) Cultural, Racial, and Ethnic Psychology Book Series, it is my pleasure to introduce the latest volume in the series: *Liberation Psychology: Theory, Method, Practice, and Social Justice*, edited by Lillian Comas-Díaz and Edil Torres Rivera.

The impetus for the series came from my presidential theme for Division 45, which focused on "Strengthening Our Science to Improve Our Practice." Given the increasing attention to racial and ethnic minority issues within the discipline of psychology, I argued that we needed to both generate more research and get the existing research known. From the *Supplement* to the *Surgeon General's Report on Mental Health* to the *Unequal Treatment* report from the Institute of Medicine—both of which documented extensive racial and ethnic disparities in our health care system—the complex of culture, race, and ethnicity was becoming a major challenge in both research and practice within the field of psychology.[1]

To meet that challenge, Division 45 acquired its own journal devoted to ethnic minority issues in psychology (*Cultural Diversity and Ethnic Minority Psychology*). At the same time, a series of handbooks on the topic were published, including Bernal, Trimble, Burlew, and Leong's *Handbook of Racial and*

---

[1]U.S. Department of Health and Human Services. (2001). *Mental health: Culture, race, and ethnicity, a supplement to mental health: A report of the Surgeon General.* Washington, DC; Smedley, B. D., Stith, A. Y., & Nelson, A. R. (Eds.). (2003). *Unequal treatment: Confronting racial and ethnic disparities in health care.* Washington, DC: National Academies Press.

Ethnic Minority Psychology.[2] Yet, we felt that more coverage of this subdiscipline was imperative—coverage that would match the substantive direction of the handbooks but would come from a variety of research and practice perspectives. Hence, the Division 45 book series was launched.

The Cultural, Racial, and Ethnic Psychology Book Series was designed to advance our theories, research, and practice regarding this increasingly crucial subdiscipline. It will focus on, but not be limited to, the major racial and ethnic groups in the United States (i.e., African Americans, Hispanic Americans, Asian Americans, and American Indians) and will include books that examine a single racial or ethnic group as well as books that undertake a comparative approach. The series will also address the full spectrum of related methodological, substantive, and theoretical issues, including topics in behavioral neuroscience, cognitive and developmental psychology, and personality and social psychology. Other volumes in the series will be devoted to cross-disciplinary explorations in the applied realms of clinical psychology and counseling as well as educational, community, and industrial-organizational psychology. Our goal is to commission state-of-the-art volumes in cultural, racial, and ethnic psychology that will be of interest to both practitioners and researchers.

I am particularly proud for our series to introduce this volume on liberation psychology. As Kuhn (1970)[3] has pointed out, scientific revolutions consist of dominant paradigms yielding to alternate paradigms when they can no longer account for all the phenomenon under question. I do not believe that mainstream psychology is about to be replaced by liberation psychology. Rather, my hope is that this volume will provide an opportunity for us to review one alternative paradigm for our field. Instead of paradigm shifts, I believe that we need multiple paradigms. Instead of studying only the privileged and middle-class, we need to understand and help the poor and the oppressed.

In this regard, Prilleltensky (1989)[4] provided an excellent analysis of the field of psychology and the status quo. Noting that the contemporary socioeconomic, cultural, and political trends had shaped the methods and content of our discipline, he also observed that "an alleged immunity to ideological influences within the profession has obstructed an in-depth examination of the interaction between social forces and psychology" (p. 795). This immunity has resulted in an uncritical acceptance of the status quo within psychology. A parallel theoretical development is that of critical race theory (Delgado and Stefancic, 2017),[5] which for a complex set of reasons has never received much attention in our field.

---

[2]Bernal, G., Trimble, J. E., Burlew, A. K., & Leong, F. T. L. (2003). *Handbook of racial and ethnic minority psychology.* Thousand Oaks, CA: Sage.

[3]Kuhn, T. S. (1970). *The structure of scientific revolutions* (2nd ed.). Chicago, IL: University of Chicago Press.

[4]Prilleltensky, I. (1989). Psychology and the status quo. *American Psychologist, 44,* 795–802. http://dx.doi.org/10.1037/0003-066X.44.5.795

[5]Delgado, R., & Stefancic, J. (2017). *Critical race theory: An introduction* (3rd ed.). New York, NY: New York University Press.

In reviewing this volume, I was reminded of Paulo Freire's (1970)[6] *Pedagogy of the Oppressed*, where he noted that

> No pedagogy which is truly liberating can remain distant from the oppressed by treating them as unfortunates and by presenting for their emulation models from among the oppressors. The oppressed must be their own example in the struggle for their redemption. (p. 54)

In addition to providing an alternative paradigm, I am also glad to see that this volume has given voice to the oppressed and allowed them to serve as "their own examples."

Let me end by thanking the members of the editorial board, who do the work of recruiting and reviewing proposals for the series: Guillermo Bernal, University of Puerto Rico, Rio Piedras Campus; Beth Boyd, University of South Dakota; Lillian Comas-Díaz, George Washington University and independent practice, Washington, DC; Sandra Graham, UCLA; Gordon Nagayama Hall, University of Oregon; Helen Neville, University of Illinois at Champaign–Urbana; Teresa LaFromboise, Stanford University; Richard Lee, University of Minnesota; Robert M. Sellers, University of Michigan; Stanley Sue, Palo Alto University; Joseph Trimble, Western Washington University; and Michael Zarate, University of Texas at El Paso. These leading scholars in psychology have graciously donated their time to help advance the field.

—Frederick T. L. Leong
Series Editor

---

[6]Freire, P. (1970). *Pedagogy of the oppressed*. New York, NY: Continuum.

FOREWORD: HOW APA HAS PROMOTED SOCIAL JUSTICE

As the United States becomes increasingly multicultural and diverse in various ways, so does psychology. The American Psychological Association (APA) is thus influenced in its evolving approaches to research, teaching and training, and practice. We also observe these influences in the APA's evolving mission and strategic initiatives enacted through its boards, committees, and directorates that influence policies, values, membership, and leadership of the association. APA has evolved to embrace one of the primary goals of social justice, which is to promote a common humanity of all social groups by valuing diversity and challenging injustice in all its forms (health, educational, economic, and political inequities). Social justice aims "to decrease human suffering and to promote human values of equality and justice" (Vasquez, 2012, p. 337). Liberation psychology, with its unique foci and innovative approaches, expands the understanding and inspires promotion of social justice in psychology.

At the time that Kenneth Clark became the first African American president of the APA (elected in 1969, served as president in 1971), APA and psychology in the United States had a historically dismal record on social justice. White men founded the APA in the late 19th century, and American psychology grew as both a laboratory-based and applied science, with laboratory science as a priority and its main credential for scientific legitimacy (Leong, Pickren, & Vasquez, 2017). Thus evolved the hierarchy of White men doing science, and women and Jews doing much of the less valued applied work (Winston, 2004). The development of psychological tests led to a sorting technology to note those who were "inferior," such as African Americans, Latinx, Native Americans, and recent immigrants (Fass, 1980; Guthrie, 2003).

However, the psychological oppression was challenged by African American and Latinx psychologists who, for example, disputed the application and interpretation of psychological tests with students and People of Color. They raised the importance of contextual issues such as social and educational disparities as contributing to differential academic achievement. These early scholars (Beckham, 1933; Canady, 1936, 1943; Fass, 1980; Long, 1935; Sanchez, 1932, 1934) contributed to the civil rights movements in the 1950s and 1960s, which then led to irreversible change in APA and American psychology (Guthrie, 2003; Padilla & Olmedo, 2009; Pickren, 2004). Guthrie (2003) documented how few racial or ethnic minorities had obtained doctorates in psychology before 1970 and how scientific racism had contributed to racial oppression, racial segregation, and White superiority.

The evolution of the mission and strategic initiatives of the APA has been influenced historically by the social challenges that have faced the United States over time. The activism of psychologists of color has been the primary force that has promoted a more inclusive psychology. The establishment of outside organizations such as the Association of Black Psychologists (ABPsi) and the Black Student Psychological Association (BSPA) led to changing the history of APA. ABPsi also inspired the development of other psychological associations, including the National Latinx Psychological Association (NLPA), the Asian American Psychological Association (AAPA), the Society of Indian Psychologists (SIP), and, more recently, the Association of Middle East and North African Psychologists (AMENA Psychologists), all of which have contributed to the diversification of research, scholarship, theory, and practice. These organizations and groups have influenced diversity and intersectionality across various other areas (including gender, sexual orientation, socioeconomic status, ability issues, and so forth) as well as the importance of civil and human rights.

A belief in universal human rights has simultaneously influenced APA's efforts, and those efforts have increased since the 1980s (Rosenzweig, 1988). The historical development of human rights in the United States can be tied to the Bill of Rights of the U.S. Constitution (1789) and to the Universal Declaration of Human Rights of the United Nations in 1948 (Rosenzweig, 1988). In his conclusions regarding APA's statements and efforts related to human rights, Rosenzweig (1988) noted that most involved civic and political rights; few involved economic, social, or cultural rights. The more recent multicultural psychology influences were inspired by the development of communities of color, as well as by feminist, womanist, and *mujerista* psychology.

Multicultural psychology and liberation psychology have a growing impact on mainstream psychology, and although similar, have different roots and emphases. The development and evolution of liberation psychology, as represented with this contribution, has also significantly contributed to the social justice applications in psychology. The influence of these groups is credited with influencing increased diversification in other areas.

Within APA, various boards and committees have been developed and evolved to address some of the pressing concerns of groups of psychologists committed to social justice, including institutional racism, status of women, sexual orientation concerns, socioeconomic status, ability issues, and aging, among others. The establishment of the Public Interest Directorate to support those structures is a reflection of commitment of considerable resources in APA. Various APA Divisions have also been established, driven by interests of the membership, to reflect the interests of those groups as well. A federally funded Minority Fellowship Program was established in the mid-1970s to attempt to increase the representation of racial and ethnic minorities in psychology, and those efforts continue. The APA Council of Representatives established and funded the Commission on Ethnic Minority Recruitment, Retention and Training in Psychology (CEMRRAT) in 2000, which still provides grants to energize, empower, and support enhancement of minority recruitment, retention, and training in psychology. A National Multicultural Conference and Summit (NMCS) is held every 2 years, the result of a project by Division leaders in 1999. In 2019, APA named its first chief diversity officer to build on and coordinate efforts to infuse equity, diversity, and inclusion throughout the association's work.

A more diverse and inclusive association with increased representation of various identity groups means that those with lived experiences of injustice are now more prevalent in the discipline of psychology, the APA, and its leadership and related associations. They and their allies are thus more able to develop and promote an understanding of the psychological science to face the challenges in society. Continuing challenges include health disparities, violent extremism, and ongoing social inequality (Leong et al., 2017).

Liberation Psychology: Theory, Method, Practice, and Social Justice is an excellent example of a significant contribution to promote progress in those problem areas. With its roots in Latin America, it applies its innate antioppression of low socioeconomic class perspective to a broader audience. This amazing contribution, edited by Comas-Díaz and Torres Rivera, helps to advance multicultural psychology and social justice in general by expanding the field's research and applications.

—Melba J. T. Vasquez
Independent Practice, Austin, Texas
Former President, American Psychological Association

REFERENCES

Beckham, A. S. (1933). A study of the intelligence of colored adolescents of differing social-economic status in typical metropolitan areas. *Journal of Social Psychology, 4,* 70–91.

Canady, H. G. (1936). The effect of rapport on the "IQ." *Journal of Negro Education, 5,* 209–219.

Canady, H. G. (1943). The problem of equating the environment of Negro–White groups for intelligence testing in comparative studies. *Journal of Social Psychology, 17,* 3–15.

Fass, P. (1980). The IQ: A cultural and historical framework. *American Journal of Education, 88,* 431–458.

Guthrie, R. V. (2003). *Even the rat was White: A historical view of psychology* (3rd ed.). Boston, MA: Allyn & Bacon.

Leong, F., Pickren, W., & Vasquez, M. J. T. (2017). APA efforts in promoting human rights and social justice. *American Psychologist, 72,* 778–790. http://dx.doi.org/10.1037/amp0000220

Long, H. H. (1935). Some psychogenic hazards of segregated education of Negroes. *Journal of Negro Education, 4,* 336–350.

Padilla, A. M., & Olmedo, E. (2009). Synopsis of key persons, events, and associations in the history of Latino psychology. *Cultural Diversity & Ethnic Minority Psychology, 15,* 363–373. http://dx.doi.org/10.1037/a0017557

Pickren, W. E. (2004). Between the cup of principle and the lip of practice: Ethnic minorities and psychology, 1966–1980. *History of Psychology, 7,* 45–64. http://dx.doi.org/10.1037/1093-4510.7.1.45

Rosenzweig, M. R. (1988). Psychology and United Nations human rights efforts. *American Psychologist, 43,* 79–86. http://dx.doi.org/10.1037/0003-066X.43.2.79

Sanchez, G. I. (1932). Group differences in Spanish-speaking children: A critical view. *Journal of Applied Psychology, 16,* 549–558.

Sanchez, G. I. (1934). Bilingualism and mental measures. *Journal of Applied Psychology, 18,* 765–772.

Vasquez, M. J. T. (2012). Psychology and social justice: Why we do what we do. *American Psychologist, 67,* 337–346. http://dx.doi.org/10.1037/a0029232

Winston, A. S. (Ed.). (2004). *Defining difference: Race and racism in the history of psychology.* Washington, DC: American Psychological Association. http://dx.doi.org/10.1037/10625-000

ACKNOWLEDGMENTS

I, Lillian, would like to acknowledge Mariana Bracetti, Ramón Emeterio Betances, Luisa Capetillo, William E. B. Du Bois, Pedro Albizu Campos, Albert Memmi, Frantz Fanon, Lolita Lebrón, Gustavo Gutiérrez, Dolores Huerta, Edward W. Said, and Ada Maria Isasi-Díaz for their contributions to the struggle against oppression. I am deeply grateful to the contributors to this edited book, whose chapters weaved an *arpillera* of liberation. I thank my coeditor, Edil Torres Rivera, for his *acompañamiento* throughout this remarkable journey. Moreover, I thank Melanie Domenech Rodríguez, who asked me to develop a training workshop on liberation psychology at a National Latinx Psychological Association (NLPA) conference. I am fortunate that Edil accepted my invitation to cofacilitate such NLPA workshop. Last, but not least, I thank my husband, Frederick M. Jacobsen, who after participating in the NLPA workshop, suggested to me the idea of a book on liberation psychology.

Just like Lillian, I, Edil, would like to acknowledge and echo her acknowledgment of all of those important people in their struggles against oppression. I also would like to acknowledge Eugenio Maria de Hostos, Doña Julia de Burgos, and the people who struggle everyday to have their voice heard, in particular, those of the public housing projects in Puerto Rico. I want to thank the women in my life: my mother, Iris Rivera Galarza; my daughter, Taina D. Torres; and my partner, Ivelisse Torres Fernández. I also thank my brothers, Robert and Basilio, who are always there for me. Finally, I want to thank Lillian for including me in this journey, and the contributors of the chapters— they really made a difference in this work.

We (Lillian and Edil) thank Frederick T. L. Leong, editor of the American Psychological Association's (APA's) Division 45 (Society for the Psychological Study of Culture, Ethnicity, and Race) book series on Cultural, Racial, and Ethnic Psychology, who enthusiastically embraced the idea of this volume. Deep thanks go to Susan Reynolds, APA acquisitions editor, for her invaluable guidance. Special thanks to Katherine Lenz, APA reference project editor, for her superb editorial suggestions. Many thanks also go to Ann Butler, APA production editor, for her helpful assistance. Moreover, we are indebted to APA for the selection of this book's cover—a picture that powerfully portrays the spirit of liberation psychology. Finally, we honor the memory of Tod Sloan, an advocate of critical psychology who due to his untimely death was unable to finalize his chapter for this edited book.

Liberation Psychology

Introduction

Edil Torres Rivera and Lillian Comas-Díaz

No one is free when others are oppressed.

—AUTHOR UNKNOWN

We invite you to expand your perspective on oppression, power, and liberation. In this edited book, we discuss liberation psychology, a discipline that encourages empowerment, healing, and transformation. *Liberation psychology* refers to the use of psychological approaches to understand and address oppression among individuals and groups (Martín-Baró, 1994). Liberation psychologists view oppression as the interaction of intrapsychic factors with systemic factors, such as sociopolitical injustice (Comas-Díaz, Hall, & Neville, 2019). They foster awareness of discrimination and inequality, fortify individuals' strengths, affirm cultural identities, and promote change to attenuate human suffering and improve people's lives (Martín-Baró, 1994; Montero & Sonn, 2009). If you are new to liberation psychology, you will find in this edited book ways to address oppression through psychological theory, method, practice, and activism. On the other hand, if you are already familiar with this approach, you will find new applications of liberation psychology. For example, given that liberation psychology has its beginnings in Latin America's community psychology, its uses in the therapeutic field are not well known.

To communicate with you, we use a testimonial voice (whether implicit or explicit) in several chapters, a liberation psychology method that relates in a more personal and intimate manner (Brabeck, 2003; see Chapter 7, this

http://dx.doi.org/10.1037/0000198-001
Liberation Psychology: Theory, Method, Practice, and Social Justice, L. Comas-Díaz and E. Torres Rivera (Editors)

volume). We believe that liberation psychology is relevant to most people because the majority of us have areas of oppression and areas of privilege. Given that we are caught in a matrix of oppression, we can benefit from liberation approaches. For instance, the Brazilian Paulo Freire (1970, 2005), who developed the pedagogy of the oppressed, suggested that the oppressed carry an internalized oppressor, an aspect of the self that is also in need of liberation. Freire (1970) indicated that oppressed people experience (a) powerlessness, (b) disunion, (c) prevention from realizing their full potential, (d) internalization of the oppressor's consciousness, (e) conditioning by dominant thinking and behavior, and (f) unawareness of being manipulated and exploited. Conversely, those with privilege (a) have power, (b) are unaware of their privilege, (c) feel unified, (d) believe that the status quo is "the way things are," (e) use their power to preserve their position, and (f) exploit the powerless without acknowledging this behavior (Butts & Rich, 2015). Consistent with this argument, liberation practitioners work in a collaborative and participatory manner with oppressed people and populations. They place individuals in multiple contexts, including cultural, historical, gender, sexual orientation, sociopolitical, geopolitical, and other intersecting factors. In this way, liberation psychologists recognize the impact of the confluence of context, history, social location, and power–powerlessness on health and well-being.

Liberation psychology originated from several emancipatory movements in Latin America. We find sources of liberation in Freire's (1970) pedagogical process, an approach that promotes *conscientización* (the Spanish word for critical consciousness), dialogue, and collaboration between educator and student in the struggle against oppression. Freire (2005) coined the term *concientizacao* (the Portuguese word for critical consciousness) to educate individuals in understanding their world to develop an awareness of social and political contradictions and to take action against oppression.

Liberation theology is another significant source of liberation psychology. This is not surprising given that the architect of liberation psychology, Ignacio Martín-Baró, was both a priest and a community psychologist. In the Spanish tradition, we place a hyphen between Ignacio's last two names to separate his paternal surname (Martín) from his maternal surname (Baró). Integrating Christian theology and socioeconomic analyses, liberation theologians focus on the emancipation of marginalized and oppressed communities (Gutierrez, 1973). Indeed, liberation theologians predicate a preferential approach for the poor and the oppressed. Similarly, liberation psychologists aim to address the needs of those who suffer from historical, cultural, systemic, and sociopolitical oppression.

We believe that liberation psychology can benefit you, in addition to the people with whom you work. Indeed, we developed this edited book as a resource for psychologists, researchers, educators, clinicians, counselors, trainees, and other mental health practitioners, as well as for social justice activists and other interested individuals. This book is particularly intended to provide the theoretical framework that is missing in the social justice movement in psychology and therapeutic settings, as well as to infuse applications to mental health practitioners that go beyond advocacy (Torres Rivera, 2019).

In this fashion, we follow liberation psychology's value of inclusivity. Because the field originated in Latin America, many liberatory conceptual terms are in Spanish and Portuguese. We recommend that you become familiar with these terms by using the glossary in this book. Likewise, we suggest that you consider the powerful influence of language, particularly when working with individuals whose first language is not English. Notwithstanding its Latin American origins, Liberation psychology has been practiced in many areas of the world, including the Philippines, Thailand, the United Kingdom, Ireland, England, South Africa, and others (see Chapter 1). Thus, the list of countries embracing liberation psychology is growing.

Numerous psychologists practice liberation approaches in the United States. These practitioners tend to be affiliated with diverse branches of psychology, such as social, community, multicultural, feminist, critical, African American, Latinx, Indigenous, international, Asian American, Native American, and other psychologies. Consequently, many U.S. psychologists have applied liberation psychology to People of Color and Indigenous people (POCI; Comas-Díaz, 2007), including African Americans (Thompson & Alfred, 2009); Latinx (Chavez-Dueñas et al., 2019); Indigenous individuals (Duran, Firehammer, & Gonzalez, 2008); immigrants (Torres Fernandez & Torres Rivera, 2014); Women of Color (Bryant-Davis & Comas-Díaz, 2016); lesbians, gays, bisexuals, transgender and queer people (LGBTQ; Singh, 2016); and White women (Lykes & Moane, 2009). Along these lines, the American Psychological Association (APA; 2018) *Revised Guidelines for Psychological Practice With Girls and Women* incorporated liberation psychology's elements. For example, the guidelines encourage psychologists to understand structural discrimination affecting girls and women and their legacies of oppression, in addition to engagement in activism (Guideline 3); use affirmative, strength-based, gender, and culturally relevant interventions (Guideline 4); engage in psychological practice that promotes agency and critical consciousness (Guideline 6); understand girls' and women's sociopolitical and geopolitical contexts (Guideline 8); when appropriate, use indigenous and complementary alternative healing (Guideline 9); and work to change institutional, systemic, and global discrimination affecting girls and women (Guideline 10).

Even though a number of psychologists have incorporated elements of liberation psychology into dominant psychological approaches, there is still a need to liberate psychology. This is essential to counterbalance psychology's monocultural orientation.

LIBERATING DOMINANT PSYCHOLOGY

To do liberation psychology requires first, to liberate psychology.
—IGNACIO MARTÍN-BARÓ

Martín-Baró (1994) reminded us that notwithstanding liberation psychology's acceptance in the United States, dominant psychology still needs to be liberated.

For instance, dominant psychology tends to be Eurocentric and linear and is perceived as universal psychological theory, science, and practice. This ethnocentric perception has limitations. To illustrate, psychology in the United States is characterized by being decontextualized and ahistorical. As a Western-based discipline, it is infused with individualist worldview values, such as meritocracy and self-determination (Pyke, 2010). Moreover, dominant European American psychology tends to support the status quo, resulting in the marginalization of POCI (Comas-Díaz, 2007), low socioeconomic status people, women (Lykes & Moane, 2009), LGBTQ people (Russell & Bohan, 2007; Singh et al., 2011), and other disenfranchised groups (Martín-Baró, 1994). Furthermore, dominant psychology can result in cultural imperialism (Afuape, 2011). Therefore, to liberate dominant psychology requires an infusion of diverse psychological and interdisciplinary approaches. We believe that liberation psychology is one of these approaches.

Liberation psychology emerged as a reaction to dominant Eurocentric psychology's limitations to impart collectivistic, holistic orientations and social justice activism into psychological knowledge, research, and practice. In this way, liberation psychology expands dominant psychology's lens. Consequently, liberation psychologists advance dominant psychology by offering pluralistic perspectives, recognizing the multiple contexts of reality, nurturing critical thinking, cultivating creative solutions, and fostering emancipatory actions. They honor multiple ways of knowing and integrate Indigenous, decolonial, postcolonial, antiracist, ethnic, and transnational approaches into psychology. Decolonial approaches are needed because a history of colonization, oppression, and subordination persist, permeating the culture and psychology of the colonized (Maldonado-Torres, 2007). These approaches address coloniality of power—how colonizing systems of control, power, and privilege prevalent during colonization continue to negatively impact individuals with a colonization history, affecting their culture, knowledge, and systems of hierarchies (Quijano, 2000). Liberation psychologists aim to decolonize dominant psychology's knowledge, research, and practice. Similarly, liberation psychologists use postcolonial approaches to combat neocolonialism (see Chapter 8) among marginalized individuals, groups, and communities.

In addition to decolonial methods, liberation psychologists endorse interdisciplinary approaches, such as philosophy, sociology, theology, anthropology, politics, arts, humanities, cultural studies, and others. In fact, there is no single liberation psychology. Instead, there are several liberation psychologies (Watkins & Shulman, 2008). Some of these include feminist (Lykes & Moane, 2009; Moane, 2010), womanist (Bryant-Davis & Comas-Díaz, 2016), *mujerista* (the term *mujerista* can be translated as Latinx womanist, i.e., that womanist and *mujerista* psychologies are conceptually and spiritually allied; Comas-Díaz, 2016), and transnational (Norsworthy, 2017) approaches, among other liberatory psychologies (see Chapter 1, this volume).

Liberation psychologists foster personal and collective agency by encouraging people to make things happen, as opposed to having things happen to them. This empowering process is based on the belief that everyone, regardless of intelligence, ability, or talent, needs to engage in the world to survive and help to transform it. Moreover, liberation psychologists believe that personal liberation leads to collective liberation. According to Freire (1970), healing and emancipation emerge for both the oppressed and the oppressor after the oppressed begin their liberation process.

Liberation psychologists engage in progressive action. For instance, they incorporate creativity, spirituality, mythology, *sabiduría popular* (popular wisdom), indigenous beliefs, and multiple ways of knowing into their work. Anchored in an interdisciplinary foundation, liberation psychologists embrace change, progress and evolution. Within this context, liberation psychology functions as Thomas Kuhn's (1970) concept of paradigmatic shift, where liberation psychology "moves" mainstream psychology into new paradigms—and thus, into progressive developments. According to Kuhn, outsiders to a specific science or field act as the promoters of the discipline's "scientific revolutions." As outsiders–insiders, liberation psychologists facilitate dominant psychology's development into its next paradigm.

CRITICISM OF LIBERATION PSYCHOLOGY

Liberation psychology is not without criticism. To illustrate, Afuape (2011), a woman of Nigerian descent born in England, stated that liberation ideas could harm when psychologists resort to an "expert" role and do not collaborate with clients or participants. As liberation practitioners, we can engage in micro-aggressions during therapy when we define oppression for clients, instead to listening to our clients' definitions of oppression. To avoid clinical microaggressions, Afuape recommended that we engage in radical humility and practice authentic collaboration. In other words, we need to become aware of how we can harm when we fail to accompany clients by not developing collaborative and or participatory relationships. Moreover, previous criticisms of liberation psychology highlighted its lack of attention to women (Lykes & Moane, 2009), and LGBTQ+ individuals (Singh, 2016). Therefore, women liberation psychologists gave birth to several female affirmative liberation psychologies. Some of these include feminist liberation psychology (Lykes & Moane, 2009; Moane, 2010), womanist, and *mujerista* psychologies (Bryant-Davis & Comas-Díaz, 2016).

A LIBERATION PSYCHOLOGY PATH

We believe that regardless of your theoretical and professional orientation, you can incorporate liberation psychology into your work. The cornerstone of liberation psychology is that it is about action. As an illustration, the contributors to this book enact liberation psychology principles in numerous aspects of their professional lives, such as teaching students, organizing community groups, supervising trainees, conducting research, engaging in clinical work, creating artivism or art for social justice purpose (Sandoval & LaTorre, 2008), engaging in social justice action, and training the next generation of psychologists. Moreover, you can potentially incorporate a liberation perspective into your personal life by engaging in creative endeavors, as well as committing to social justice action. In fact, this volume offers diverse forms of knowledge, method, practice, and activism to enhance your effectiveness as a psychologist, nurture your social justice consciousness, and promote your (and other people's) liberation. In this edited book, we aim to advance dominant psychology by expanding its focus, scope, inquiry, and application. We offer liberation psychology's innovative applications while envisioning future developments. This volume is composed of six main parts: Introduction (this chapter), Theory, Method, Clinical Practice, Special Populations, and Social Justice. We include our Conclusion chapter in the Social Justice section to expand liberatory social justice into diverse contexts. In the following section, we introduce the book's chapters, as a path to liberation psychology.

LIBERATION PSYCHOLOGY THEORY

Liberation psychology presents alternatives to Western-based dominant psychology by offering an emancipatory approach. Liberation psychologists anchor their knowledge in the *vivencia* (lived experience), *lo cotidiano* (everyday reality), and the recovery of the historical memory of oppressed individuals and communities.

In Chapter 1, Mark Burton and Raquel Guzzo present a historical overview of liberation psychology. They examine its antecedents in the anticolonial work of Frantz Fanon and Paulo Freire. They also cover parallel developments in several continents and review the growth and diversification of the liberation psychology in the 21st century. In Chapter 2, Edil Torres Rivera examines the roots of liberation psychology focusing on the principles and concepts dealing with its epistemology and ontology. Additionally, he presents liberation psychology's principles and research as they relate to the practice of mental health interventions. Because racism is a major source of oppression, Raúl Quiñones-Rosado (Chapter 3) discusses liberation psychology's antiracist perspective. He states that more than an ideology, racism is a worldview, an intersubjective lens on reality deeply embedded in economic and political institutions, and a paradigm that, after more than 500 years of coloniality, continues to shape colonized identities and guide our ways of relating.

LIBERATION PSYCHOLOGY METHOD

The contributors in this section examine liberation psychology methods and research. Liberation psychologists aim to conduct research from the bottom up, as a way of involving community members and framing the research in the context of benefit for the community. They use quantitative and qualitative research methods to explore evidence for practice. Within the liberation framework, we understand that research is not neutral. In fact, research is not even objective because it is historically embedded in the culture of privilege, where privileged groups exert dominance and power over marginalized groups (Smith, 2012). Consequently, liberation psychologists commit to the oppressed individuals' participation in conceptualizing and conducting research. In other words, members of the studied community participate and collaborate in the definition of the problem, the methods used to study the problem, and means of distributing the findings (Smith, 2012). Within participatory action research (PAR), a liberation psychology research method (see Chapter 6), community members act as coresearchers and examine the results in view of the needs of the community studied. In short, community members *own* the research findings.

Drawing on new research on the progressive origins of psychoanalysis, Daniel Gaztambide (Chapter 4) traces the psychoanalytic roots of liberation psychology through the works of Freud, Ferenczi, Memmi, Manoni, Fanon, and Freire. This "recovery of historical memory" is contextualized in contemporary psychoanalysis' increasing perspective into issues of race, class, and culture in the therapeutic space. Gaztambide identifies psychoanalysis as a liberatory psychological method. In Chapter 5, Jesica Siham Fernández describes how PAR aligns with *acompañamiento*. Within a liberation framework *acompañamiento* refers to an intentional act of working with, being with, and experiencing people impacted by systemic oppression. *Acompañamiento* (accompaniment) is identified as a key value that undergirds the role of the researcher and that facilitates liberation psychology processes toward transformative justice by and with oppressed communities. Last, in Chapter 6, M. Brinton Lykes and Gabriela Távara draw on their respective experiences as feminist participatory action researchers working in conflict and postconflict Latin American contexts to identify epistemological and methodological resources that have fostered the values and upheld the principles of liberation psychology.

LIBERATION PSYCHOLOGY CLINICAL PRACTICE

Liberation psychologists engage in clinical practice to heal individuals and groups. They honor clients' inner strength and promote resilience. Liberation psychotherapists acknowledge the confluence of clients' internal world with the systemic sociopolitical forces affecting health and well-being. In this way, they integrate liberation psychological approaches such as *testimonio*, psychospiritual, decolonial, and postcolonial approaches into mainstream psychotherapy approaches. The chapters in Part IV illustrate examples of these approaches. For example, Alejandro Cervantes (Chapter 7) presents *testimonio*, a liberation psychology narrative approach in which individuals account their experiences with oppression, trauma, and marginalization (Cervantes & Torres Fernandez, 2016). He illustrates the use of *testimonio* in treatment. Alejandro Cervantes discusses how *testimonio* can alleviate individuals' psychological trauma due to structural violence, oppressive systems, and institutional racism. He focuses on how clients' internal and external processing of creating and sharing their *papelitos guardados* (memories or lived experiences suppressed, put away) and promote liberatory practices to both the therapist and client(s). Next, Chakira M. Haddock-Lazala (Chapter 8) discusses how postcolonial feminist theory may offer clinicians insight into developing more social conscious clinical theories and liberatory practices. Specifically, she discusses concepts such as power, oppression, intersectionality, decolonization, and liberation and explores how they may be applied to clinical work—particularly when addressing issues related to race, gender, and class. Finally, in Chapter 9, Lillian Comas-Díaz discusses liberation psychotherapy, a culturally, contextual, and sociopolitically embedded approach that focuses on individuals' lived experience. Anchoring liberation psychotherapy in psychospirituality, she discusses its clinical application. She highlights the uniqueness of therapeutic relationship in liberation psychotherapy.

LIBERATION PSYCHOLOGY'S APPLICATION
TO SPECIAL POPULATIONS

Liberation psychology emerged as a vehicle to address the sociopolitical oppression of disadvantaged and marginalized communities. Psychologists in the United States have identified oppressed populations that can benefit from liberation approaches. In this section, we present three of these populations: African Americans, LGBTQ+ communities, and transnational applications of liberations psychology.

In Chapter 10, Thema Bryant-Davis and Shavonne J. Moore-Lobban discuss the dynamics and impact of racism and oppression using the framework of liberation psychology, which provides a revolutionary and radical commitment to the humanity and sacredness of Black Americans. These contributors present how liberation psychology provides a fuller understanding of the impact of the continued traumatic stress of dehumanization, displacement, and interdisciplinary disregard of people of African descent. The authors discuss the growth and creativity integral to liberation psychology that manifests in communal life-affirming innovation among Black Americans. Moreover, they discuss a sociopolitical development theory for action. Next, Anneliese A. Singh, Brean'a Parker, Anushka R. Aqil, and Falon Thacker (Chapter 11) describe applications of liberation psychology to LGBTQ+ communities. They examine the colonization trajectories of People of Color communities and provide a strategy of conscientization in individual and community settings to reclaim experiences and stories of queer and trans people across the globe. In doing so, they highlight practices of resilience that queer and trans communities have developed over time to sustain themselves in the face of oppression, discrimination, and decimation, with a special focus on applying these practices to individual and community change efforts. Lastly, in Chapter 12 Kathryn L. Norsworthy and Ouyporn Khuankaew use feminist liberation psychology, decoloniality, and postcolonial frameworks to examine transnational border crossings. They discuss this framework in describing their collaboration with their Thai and

Burmese colleagues, in addition to local Thai and other South and Southeastern Asian groups.

LIBERATION PSYCHOLOGY SOCIAL ACTION

Liberation psychologists consider social justice action an imperative construct in their work. We define *social justice action* as behaviors that aim to diminish oppression and support fairness, equality, and justice. In promoting our clients' social justice action, we invite them to define what social justice means for them. We ask them to engage in those social justice actions that they feel comfortable with. As part of this process, some clients identified volunteering in a range of ways, including community organizations, visiting sick people in hospitals, creating art for social justice purpose, teaching racial and ethnic socialization, serving community meals on holidays, voting in local and national elections, and even running for public office.

Ester R. Shapiro (Chapter 13) discusses creative arts and arts-based activism, such as artivism (art for the purpose of activism; Sandoval & LaTorre, 2008) as compelling social justice methods. An example of artivism is the musical group Las Cafeteras (a Chicano band that fuses folk music such as *son jarocho* and Afro Mexican melodies with spoken word) (Tompkins Rivas, 2013) to infuse social justice issues into their music. These artistic methods support the development of ways of knowing that can catalyze power culturally and spiritually rooted knowledge capable of crossing even heavily guarded borderlands. Shapiro applies a cultural-developmental perspective on creativity and the arts to explore the catalytic role of creative arts in liberation psychology across national borders and academic disciplines. Last, the praxis of liberation psychology for students training to become psychologists can be elusive within the structure of accredited doctoral programs, due to the constraints of dominant social discourse and perspectives permeating the field. Therefore, in Chapter 14, Carrie L. Castañeda-Sound, Daryl M. Rowe, Nahaal Binazir, and Marlene L. Cabrera present the development of a multicultural specialty track for clinical psychology doctoral students who work with underserved communities. The curriculum development and pedagogy of the specialty track are grounded in African, Indigenous, Latinx, and *mujerista* liberatory paradigms.

In the Conclusion, we (Lillian Comas-Díaz and Edil Torres Rivera) present an analysis of liberation psychology discussing the chapters in this volume. We integrate the chapters' contents and comment on the similarities between them, as well as their uniqueness. Additionally, we envision potential future applications of liberation psychology. We hope this book inspires you to develop and strengthen your commitment to liberation psychology and invite you to join the growing number of psychologists who find liberation approaches beneficial in their work and life. In our experience, liberation psychology acts as a mirror for continuing reflexivity, a vehicle for critical awareness, a channel for healing, and a beacon for social justice.

REFERENCES

Afuape, T. (2011). *Power, resistance and liberation in therapy with survivors of trauma: To have our hearts broken.* New York, NY: Routledge.

American Psychological Association. (2018, February). *APA guidelines for psychological practice with girls and women.* Retrieved from https://www.apa.org/about/policy/psychological-practice-girls-women.pdf

Brabeck, K. (2003). *Testimonio*: A strategy for collective resistance, cultural survival, and building solidarity. *Feminism & Psychology, 13*, 252–258. http://dx.doi.org/10.1177/0959353503013002009

Bryant-Davis, T., & Comas-Díaz, L. (Eds.). (2016). *Womanist and mujerista psychologies: Voices of fire, acts of courage.* Washington, DC: American Psychological Association.

Butts, J., & Rich, K. L. (2015). *Philosophies and theories for advanced nursing practice* (2nd ed.). Burlington, MA: Jones & Bartlett Learning.

Cervantes, A., & Torres Fernandez, I. (2016). The use of *testimonios* as a tool to promote liberation and social justice advocacy with Latinas in counseling. *Latina/o Psychology Today, 3*(1), 25–29.

Chavez-Dueñas, N. Y., Adames, H. Y., Perez-Chavez, J. G., & Salas, S. P. (2019). Healing ethno-racial trauma in Latinx immigrant communities: Cultivating hope, resistance, and action. *American Psychologist, 74*, 49–62. http://dx.doi.org/10.1037/amp0000289

Comas-Díaz, L. (2007). Ethnopolitical psychology: Healing and transformation. In E. Aldarondo (Ed.), *Promoting social justice in mental health practice* (pp. 91–118). Hillsdale, NJ: Erlbaum.

Comas-Díaz, L. (2016). *Mujerista* psychospirituality. In T. Bryant-Davis & L. Comas-Díaz (Eds.), *Womanist and mujerista psychologies: Voices of fire, acts of courage* (pp. 149–169). Washington, DC: American Psychological Association. http://dx.doi.org/10.1037/14937-007

Comas-Díaz, L., Hall, G. N., & Neville, H. (2019). Introduction to the special issue: Racial trauma, theory, research and healing. *American Psychologist, 74*, 1–5. http://dx.doi.org/10.1037/amp0000442

Duran, E., Firehammer, J., & Gonzalez, J. (2008). Liberation psychology as a path toward healing cultural soul wounds. *Journal of Counseling & Development, 86*, 288–295. http://dx.doi.org/10.1002/j.1556-6678.2008.tb00511.x

Freire, P. (1970). *Pedagogy of the oppressed.* New York, NY: Continuum.

Freire, P. (2005). *Education for critical consciousness.* New York, NY: Continuum.

Gutierrez, G. (1973). *A theology of liberation.* Maryknoll, NY: Orbis.

Kuhn, T. S. (1970). *The structure of scientific revolutions.* Chicago, IL: University of Chicago Press.

Lykes, M. B., & Moane, G. (2009). Editors' introduction: Whither feminist liberation psychology? Critical explorations of feminist and liberation psychologies for a globalizing world. *Feminism & Psychology, 19*, 283–297. http://dx.doi.org/10.1177/0959353509105620

Maldonado-Torres, N. (2007). On the coloniality of being: Contributions on the development of a concept. *Journal of Cultural Studies, 21*, 240–270. http://dx.doi.org/10.1080/09502380601162548

Martín-Baró, I. (1994). *Writings for a liberation psychology: Ignacio Martín-Baró* (A. Aron & S. Corne, Trans. & Eds.). Cambridge, MA: Harvard University Press.

Moane, G. (2010). Sociopolitical development and political activism: Synergies between feminist and liberation psychology. *Psychology of Women Quarterly, 34*, 521–529. http://dx.doi.org/10.1111/j.1471-6402.2010.01601.x

Montero, M., & Sonn, C. C. (Eds.). (2009). *Psychology of liberation: Theories and applications.* New York, NY: Springer.

Norsworthy, K. L. (2017). Mindful activism: Embracing the complexities of international border crossings. *American Psychologist, 72,* 1035–1043. http://dx.doi.org/10.1037/amp0000262

Pyke, K. D. (2010). What is internalized racial oppression and why don't we study it? Acknowledging racism's hidden injuries. *Sociological Perspectives, 53,* 551–572. http://dx.doi.org/10.1525/sop.2010.53.4.551

Quijano, A. (2000). Coloniality of power, Eurocentrism and Latin America. *Nepantla, 1,* 533–580. http://dx.doi.org/10.1177/0268580900015002005

Russell, G. M., & Bohan, J. S. (2007). Liberating psychotherapy: Liberation psychology and psychotherapy with LGBT clients. *Journal of Gay & Lesbian Psychotherapy, 11,* 59–75. http://dx.doi.org/10.1300/J236v11n03_04

Sandoval, C., & LaTorre, G. (2008). Chicana/o artivism: Judy Baca's digital work with youths of color. In A. Everett (Ed.), *Learning race and ethnicity: Youth and digital media* (pp. 81–108). Cambridge, MA: The MIT Press.

Singh, A. A. (2016). Moving from affirmation to liberation in psychological practice with transgender and gender nonconforming clients. *American Psychologist, 71,* 755–762. http://dx.doi.org/10.1037/amp0000106

Singh, A. A., Hays, D. G., & Watson, L. S. (2011). Strength in the face of adversity: Resilience strategies of transgender individuals. *Journal of Counseling and Development, 89,* 20–27.

Smith, L. T. (2012). *Decolonizing methodologies: Research and indigenous peoples* (2nd ed.). London, England: Zed Books.

Thompson, C. E., & Alfred, D. M. (2009). Black liberation psychology and practice. In H. A. Neville, B. M. Tynes, & S. O. Utsey (Eds.), *Handbook of African American psychology* (pp. 403–494). Thousand Oaks, CA: Sage.

Tompkins Rivas, P. (2013, January 1). Las Cafeteras: Crossing genres to become agents of change. *Art Bound.* Retrieved from https://www.kcet.org/shows/artbound/las-cafeteras-crossing-genres-to-become-agents-of-change

Torres Fernandez, I., & Torres Rivera, E. (2014). Moving though trauma and grief in children impacted by the violence on the U.S.–Mexico border: A liberation psychology approach. In M. T. Garrett (Ed.), *Youth and adversity: Understanding the psychology and influences of child adolescent resilience and coping* (pp. 209–226). New York, NY: Nova Science.

Torres Rivera, E. (2019). *Deconstruyendo la universalidad de la justicia social: Una perspectiva multicultural hacia nuevos horizontes* (Deconstructing the universality of social justice: A multicultural perspective toward new horizons). *Revista Interamericana De Psicología/Interamerican Journal of Psychology, 53*(1), 1–7.

Watkins, M., & Shulman, H. (2008). *Toward psychologies of liberation.* New York, NY: Routledge. http://dx.doi.org/10.1057/9780230227736

LIBERATION PSYCHOLOGY THEORY

1

Liberation Psychology

Origins and Development

Mark Burton and Raquel Guzzo

In this chapter, we outline the history of liberation psychology from before it was given a name, up to the present. We use a broad canvas, tracing liberation psychology to its diverse roots in both psychology and other areas of praxis. Writing a history involves decisions about what is most important, and inevitably this means biases and exclusions. So, let's say something about the perspective that informs this history. We focus on the Latin American movement with special reference to the antecedents of liberation psychology, with particular reference to the contribution of critical pedagogy (Brazil) and Martín-Baró's work in El Salvador. However, we also discuss parallel developments (what Watkins & Shulman, 2008, called *liberation psychologies*, in the plural) in other continents and continue the story into the 21st century. This reflects our understand that the Latin American evolution of liberation psychology has been the most influential, comprehensive, and long-lasting current—indeed, it has defined the field of liberation psychology so that when liberation psychology is referred to without any qualification, it is generally be assumed that the reference is to Latin American liberation psychology. We see it as closely connected with what may be termed *Latin American praxis* more generally. That is, the body of theory and practice that comprises liberation philosophy, theology and psychology; popular pedagogy, militant sociology, decolonial theory, postdevelopment theory; as well as the theory in practice of a diversity of liberatory social movements. However, this does not mean that liberation psychology is exclusively or even necessarily a Latin American phenomenon

http://dx.doi.org/10.1037/0000198-002
Liberation Psychology: Theory, Method, Practice, and Social Justice, L. Comas-Díaz and E. Torres Rivera (Editors)

(Burton, 2013b, 2013c): Because oppression is not confined to one continent, neither is liberation nor its psychology, liberation psychology.

BEFORE LIBERATION PSYCHOLOGY

The term *liberation psychology* appears to have first been used in print in 1976, in its Spanish version, *psicología de la liberación*, in a book with that title published in Madrid by the Argentinian psychologists Caparrós and Caparrós (1976). However, they did not use it in the sense in which it came to be used later on, their project having more in common with the nonindividualistic Marxist framework of Lucien Sève (1978). The first systematic use of the term to identify a distinctive way of doing psychology, in the context of oppression, was in 1986 by Ignacio Martín-Baró (1986, 1996c) as we will see. It would be wrong to suggest that there was no psychological theory and practice that, with hindsight, we might call liberation psychology before then. For an early example, Afuape (2011, pp. 61–62) argued that the work of United States–based Black social scientist W. E. B. Du Bois anticipated some of the themes of liberation psychology, including the conception of education as transformative action in relation to the casting of Black people as "the other," stripped of their cultural consciousness by the historical experience of slavery. This led to a concept of the needed restoration of what he called *self-consciousness* but which we would now understand as *critical consciousness* of one's positioning in the social system: compare *conscientization* in contemporary liberation psychology. He also anticipated the analysis of fatalism among oppressed populations, exploring the consequences of what we now call structural and institutional racism. Finally, he celebrated the subaltern knowledge of Black peoples and their educational practices.

LIBERATION PSYCHOLOGY AS A DECOLONIAL APPROACH

Burton and Gómez (2015) argued that liberation psychology is best understood as belonging to a much wider family of decolonizing bodies of theory and practice. These approaches recognize the legacy and continuing reality of the colonization, exploitation, and domination of other places by Western Europe, a domination that has its material and ideological components in, for example, the systems of resource expropriation and the imposition of a Western systems of values and thought, respectively (Escobar, 2007; for an early statement in English, see Stavenhagen, 1971). Although there were deeper roots, identifiable in the work over nearly 500 years of activist individuals such as de las Casas (Caribbean), Guamán Poma de Ayala (Peru), Martí (Cuba), Mariátegui (Peru), Betances (Puerto Rico), there was something of an explosion of such perspectives from the 1960s, both in Latin America and beyond.

PRECURSORS OF LIBERATION PSYCHOLOGY ON OTHER CONTINENTS

Elsewhere, the works of Frantz Fanon and Albert Memmi in the context of liberation struggles in North Africa and of Syed Hussein Alatas in Malaysia are particularly relevant as contributions to the psychology of liberation. Fanon (1965, 1967), a psychiatrist from Martinique, showed how the violence of racism and colonization created violence in the oppressed that, in the absence of an organized liberation struggle to channel it, tended to be directed at others in the oppressed community rather than at the oppressors. A theme in his work was the distorted consciousness of the oppressed that led to a tendency to emulate the oppressor. Similarly, Memmi (1969) documented the way in which the consciousness of both oppressor and oppressed are intertwined in the colonial context. The oppressed come to emulate the oppressors despite being oppressed by them. This can ultimately be resolved by rejection of that consciousness, finding a new consciousness in the collective struggle for liberation, and overthrowing the oppressors. Alatas (1979/2013) focused specifically on the way that the peoples of Southeast Asia were seen as lazy by European colonizers. This view was expressed in various forms from the vulgar to the quasi-scientific, evolving from one that cast the native as indolent and treacherous to one of dependency and of needing assistance to develop. Alatas thereby anticipated some of the themes of Martín-Baró's analysis of the ideological concept of the "lazy Latino" (Martín-Baró, 1987/1996b). He also identified the need for social science that responded to the context in which it was to be applied (Alatas, 1972).

PRECURSORS OF LIBERATION PSYCHOLOGY IN LATIN AMERICA

A variety of related responses to oppression emerged in Latin America at around the same time. These were all part of what might be termed *Latin American decolonial praxis*, a wider movement that also included critical or popular pedagogy, militant sociology and its methodology of participative action research, the theology of liberation, the theory of economic dependency, liberation philosophy, as well as popular social movements that sought to achieve a greater control over the destiny of the actors, whether through community self-help organizations, land occupation, or insurrection. Three of them (critical pedagogy, participative action research, and liberation theology) were cited by Martín-Baró as key influences on and resources for the construction of a psychology for liberation. However, the social and political context was an additional influential factor. The dictatorships imposed on the Latin American countries provoked revolutionary movements and processes through which consciousness was raised in the face of domination and violence (Hur & Lacerda, 2017).

CRITICAL PEDAGOGY

Paulo Freire came from Recife in northeastern Brazil. This part of the country suffered the highest levels of poverty and was still organized in many ways as a feudalistic, colonial economy and society (de Castro, 1969). In a series of publications, Freire reflected on the methods he and others were developing to enable peasants and workers to "read the word and read the world." By starting with people's own lived knowledge of their situation—their poverty, hunger, fatigue, and day-to day-experience of oppression—it was possible to expand with them a shared understanding of the wider picture, the structural relations that caused and maintained their situation. In so doing, consciousness was extended, but critically, so was the possibility of hope, of what Freire called *untested viability* (*inédito viável*; Freire, 2004, pp. 206–207), the idea of an imagined set of better possibilities and hence the possibility of collectively acting on the world. This overall process was given the name conscientization (*conscientização*) by Vieira Pinto (1960). When Freire used the term *conscientization*, he emphasized the triad of culture–awareness–freedom, arguing that people learn in communities and proposing a national plan to eliminate illiteracy, based on the insight that people would only learn and maintain the ability to read if their literacy was part of a broader social literacy, "reading the world." This plan therefore had a main goal of liberating people from living effectively enslaved lives subjugated by a ruling class. He presented a method for adult literacy as "pedagogy of the oppressed" (Freire, 1972b). While he developed, refined, and elucidated his approach and the philosophy behind it over the years and through periods in Chile, Switzerland, Guinea Bissau, and ultimately back in Brazil, his approach remained essentially as we have described (Freire, 1972a, 1972b, 1978, 2004).

MILITANT SOCIOLOGY AND PARTICIPATIVE ACTION RESEARCH

At the beginning of the 1970s, a number of social scientists in various locations of the global South were increasingly concerned with the challenging life conditions in communities around them which called for a radical rethinking of social theory and practice. These intellectuals, in Tanzania, Mexico, India, Brazil, and Colombia (among other places), who had often left their universities, tried to construct actionable social scientific knowledge with community actors themselves, instead of on or about them (Fals Borda, 2001, p. 28). In Colombia, a group of sociologists set up an NGO, La Rosca de Investigación y Acción Social. *Rosca* is a Colombian term (of Catalan origin) that the group used to describe a circle of equals identified with the ideals of working for the community (Jiménez, 1994, p. 108). Through their first projects with peasants oppressed by the *latifundio* system on Colombia's Atlantic coast, they developed their idealized model of participative action research. As Fals Borda described it, with hindsight some years later, the approach combines research (the production of situated knowledge), adult education, and sociopolitical action (Fals Borda & Rahman, 1991). By coproducing serious, reliable, and liberating knowledge in a continuous process of life and work, the idea was (a) through projects, actions, and struggles, to enable the oppressed groups and classes to exert political leverage and (b) to develop sociopolitical thought processes with which the people could identify (Fals Borda & Rahman, 1991, pp. 3–4). In this, the concept of *vivencia*, meaning "lived experience," is central. A second principle is that of *authentic commitment*; the *animators* (i.e., the facilitators of collective knowledge production for action), whose knowledge and experience have different bases from those of community members, constantly relate their action to the shared goals of social transformation. This orientation is supposed to overcome the asymmetrical relationship of submission–dependence implicit in the standard research model with its subject–object distinction. Throughout, the knowledge and cultures of the people, so often eclipsed as a result of conquest, colonization, and postcolonial elite domination, were especially important given the emphasis on what contemporary social policy terms *place*—in Fals Borda's exposition, the concept of region—within the context of the social formation (Fals Borda & Rahman, 1991, p. 6).

It is at this scale that participative action research takes place, with a view to ultimately join local struggles with those at the national and international levels (cf. Kagan & Burton, 2000). In the establishment of people's countervailing power, Fals Borda (Fals Borda & Rahman, 1991, pp. 8–9) identified four methodological headings: collective research, critical recovery of history, valuing and applying folk culture, and the production and diffusion of new knowledge. All these ideas were reflected in the subsequent development of liberation psychology, as a result of both borrowing from the example of participative action research and, we suggest, the general diffusion of the broader paradigm of participative popular engagement.

LIBERATION THEOLOGY

Liberation theology has been described as

> a reflection on the praxis of the liberation of the oppressed by Christians who are politically committed. It is a theological ethic developed from the perspective of those from the periphery, the marginalized, the outcasts of the world. The praxis that undergirds this theological ethic is not merely a praxis of meeting necessities . . . but rather a praxis of liberation. (Dussel, 1981, p. 19)

Liberation theology is often attributed to the influence on Latin America of the Second Vatican council initiated by Pope John XXIII. This sought to better connect the Roman Catholic Church with lay society, exploring what the Church could bring to society as much as what society might give to the Church. The 1968 conference of Latin American bishops in Medellín, Colombia, sought to deepen this thinking, adapting it to the specific circumstances of the continent in which poverty stood out:

> The Latin American bishops cannot remain indifferent to the tremendous social injustices existing in Latin America, which keep the majority of our peoples in a painful poverty, inhuman in many cases. An unheard cry springs from the millions,

demanding from its pastors a liberation that fails to reach them anywhere. (Second General Conference of the Latin American Episcopal Congregation; quoted by de la Corte Ibañez, 2001, p. 45, our translation)

Consequently, they adopted the "preferential option for the poor." They also incorporated social scientific concepts to understand social problems, such as the "structures of sin" and "institutional violence," and committed to addressing them. This orientation was developed further at subsequent conferences, notably one in Puebla, Mexico, in 1970.

However, this was not merely an initiative of the bishops and Church hierarchy. There had already been grassroots movements such as the Brazilian base communities and the pastoral activities of many priests and congregations (this included some protestant churches too), working with the poor throughout the region. As Hinkelammert (1997) illustrated in the case of Chile, liberation theology was already present before 1970:

Liberation Theology had already risen in the previous years, especially during the late sixties. It did not arise primarily in the academic environment but through pastoral activity in the churches, for at this time mainly priests and pastors worked with the poor of Latin American countries. Their first publications appeared as mimeographed manuscripts and were distributed at meetings or by mail. At the end of the sixties the first books appeared. . . . This way of thinking rapidly influenced seminaries and theology departments and created a current of opinion in Latin America, was expressed most intensely after the electoral victory of the Popular Unity Party in 1970. (p. 28)

The liberation theology movement represented an impetus for the organization of social movements with advancement in the political consciousness in the countries of Latin America. Contrary to the practices that distanced the Church from the life lived by the people, the Theology of Liberation broke with the "colonial pact," pronouncing on the ethical character of political practices (Boff, 1981/2012). In the 1950s, with the emergence of an industrial bourgeoisie, the challenge was to overcome the backwardness, of colonial origin, that characterized Latin American societies, which led to a process of modernization by populist governments and trade union organizations. The Catholic Church actively participated in this developmental program, denouncing abuses of the capitalist system and marginalization of the poor. In the 1960s, in almost all Latin American countries there was a growing awareness of the real mechanisms of underdevelopment, as a dependent development associated with the development of the countries. Here the Theory of Dependency was influential. The Theory of Dependency has a number of different versions (Flores, 2009) but all attempted to understand the economic characteristics of Latin America, including its relative poverty in relation to the systems of exploitation between periphery (the Global South) and the core (principally Western Europe and North America) of the World System. Many young people identified with and joined the movements for the poor, for the defense of their cultures and sovereignty, and met with violent oppression by the dictatorships of the "States of National Security," beginning in Brazil with the coup of 1964. After the hardest period of repression, the people again embraced their own destiny, with the creation of "Christian base communities" and a personal and community strengthening to face oppression.

These grassroots Ecclesiastical Base Communities, rather than an instrument for evangelizing the people, were a way for people to perceive the power of communities, of popular participation, fighting against centralization and domination from a center of power, the exercise of real popular democracy on preparation for historical·challenges. Thinking and acting on the liberating horizon involving politics, economics, education, and psychology through critique of ideology implies a new state of consciousness (Boff, 1980). The methods developed by Freire in the Basic Education Movement were also used by many Christian base communities in North East Brazil (Dussel, 1981, p. 215).

Among those influenced were theologians such as Gustavo Gutierrez, who drew attention to the Church's historical alignment with the Western, White, dominant culture, drawing on the metaphor of de las Casas (2004): the native Americans as "the flogged Christs," applying this concept to the oppressed majorities of the continent (Gutiérrez, 1973). The idea of a flogged Christ, enslaved by a dominant culture, served as a metaphor for the image of a theology committed to the oppressed. Another influential theologian of liberation was Ignacio Ellacuria, who was later to die in the massacre of academics by a U.S.-trained squad of the Salvadorian Army at the Central American University. Among the eight victims was Ignacio Martín-Baró. Inevitably, given both the issues of concern and the Church's opening to outside ideas, social scientific methods and theories began to be employed as part of liberation theology, including concepts from Marxism. However, the adaptation of these ideas to the practical realities of Latin American societies meant a liberation of this current of thought from the straitjacket of Soviet Marxism. Marxian concepts were to play a significant role in the evolution of liberation psychology as an approach, including in Martín-Baró's work (Lacerda, 2010).

PHILOSOPHY OF LIBERATION

The philosophy of liberation, although it had earlier antecedents, can be identified with the generation of Latin American philosophers born after 1930, active from the late 1960s. Augusto Salazar Bondy's 1954 challenge to Latin American philosophers now reads like a founding statement for the orientation:

> it is necessary, then, to forge a thinking that both takes root in the socio-historical reality of our communities and conveys their needs and goals, and also serves to wipe out the underdevelopment and domination that typify our historical situation. (Salazar Bondy, 2004, p. 118)

In Argentina, Dussel, Scannone, and others (Dussel, 2003), worked with the idea that such a philosophy had to be orientated to the oppressed majorities. Other currents included the influence of Levinas (e.g., 1969) and the notion of ethical responsibility for the other, the exploration and critique of Marx, indigenous thought, popular wisdom, and ideological deconstruction, while concrete developments in the region (e.g., Cuban humanistic Marxism) were also taken into account. As Beorlegui (2004) noted, however, the most important characteristic "is that the philosopher identifies with the people in its project of liberation. A project that, lived by the people, the intellectual will have to conceptualize and make rationally explicit" (p. 699). That is, the call is for an engaged and committed philosophy where the intellectual takes their lead from the people rather than vice versa.

Among liberation philosophers, the Argentinian–Mexican philosopher Enrique Dussel is probably the most influential (Dussel, 2013; for an introduction for psychologists, see Burton & Flores Osorio, 2011). For Dussel, as for the other thinkers and activists of the "decolonial turn," the concern is with those whose exclusion, exploitation, and denial of the right to reproduce their lives— in all senses, not just the biological—is an integral part of the Western system of domination, and not only in the peripheral zones of the majority world (Dussel, 2000, p. 277). Yet rather than rejecting the European tradition of rationality (as fundamentalists and most postmodernists do), he proposed its correction by the critical interlocutor—the eclipsed other, thereby producing a new understanding, a new "transmodern" construction of reality, that goes beyond the dominant, Eurocentric terms of reference, introducing an exterior perspective in what he called an ana-dialectical or analectical synthesis (Burton, n.d.; Burton & Flores Osorio, 2011; Montero, 2014). As we will see, a similar conception is at the heart of Martín-Baró's proposal for a liberation psychology.

It is difficult to say whether liberation philosophy had an influence on the early formulation of liberation psychology, but it was present in the intellectual environment of the 1980s, both through its close connections with liberation theology and its influence on the network of social psychologists who were rethinking the discipline, some of whom, such as M. Montero and J.M. Flores, had completed advanced studies in philosophy. In the mature period of Latin American liberation psychology, the work of liberation philosophy has been more explicitly drawn upon, and Dussel himself gave a plenary lecture at the fourth International Congress of Liberation Psychology in Guatemala City in 2001.

LIBERATION PSYCHOLOGY AND THE CRISIS IN SOCIAL PSYCHOLOGY

At the beginning of the 20th century, psychology was consolidated as a profession that sought to position itself in the service of powerful interests in capitalist society and thus became an important resource for the dominant system in adapting people to this new way of life (Danziger, 1990). From this time on, with the expansion and consolidation of the capitalist mode of production and reproduction of life, psychology established itself in several countries, including those of Latin America, as a profession that made little or no commitment to the social situation of the majority of people in those countries. We could say, psychology reached the countries of Latin America as colonial knowledge and was consolidated as a powerful ideological tool at the disposal of capitalism.

By the 1970s, there emerged what is usually referred to as "the crisis of social psychology" (Armistead, 1974; Parker, 1989). It had manifestations in

Europe and the Americas and was characterized by three concerns or critiques (Burton & Kagan, 2005; de la Corte Ibañez, 2000):

1. Its social irrelevance—social psychology did not seem to be producing much practical knowledge to address major social problems.

2. A parochial context of discovery combined with pretension of universal validity—social psychology was overly dependent on investigations of particular populations in artificial settings, typically undergraduate students in formal experiments. Yet, following the hegemonic model of psychology, it attempted to suggest general social psychological principles that would apply to all human beings in all contexts.

3. Imitating scientific neutrality meant ignoring the moral dimension—a supposed value freedom.

Social psychology in the core countries of Western Europe and North America tended to end up embracing broadly postmodernist, idealist, and highly academic paradigms (the discursive turn), or returning to the empiricist fold. This happened in Latin America, but there was also a significant movement (in the context of intensifying social struggles with the rise of the dictatorships; Hur & Lacerda, 2017, p. 33) that Burton (2013a) called the *analectic turn*—an attempt to resituate social psychology in and for the community, engaging with the existential challenges facing the popular majorities of the continent. Manifestations were community social psychology (Jiménez, 2013; Montero, 1994, 2011) and liberation psychology, which are not identical but rather overlapping approaches (Montero, Sonn, & Burton, 2016). As Hur and Lacerda (2017, p. 40) pointed out, the hyperdevelopment of critical reflexivity, as found in European and North American "critical psychology," was insufficient for the construction of a truly liberatory psychology. Instead, they argued, the precedent of insurgent social movements (including the armed struggle) was a necessary example for action-orientated psychologies of liberation that addressed themselves to the oppressive social realities in the countries concerned.

IGNACIO MARTÍN-BARÓ

Martín-Baró was based at the Universidad Centro Americana "José Simeón Cañas" (UCA) San Salvador, El Salvador, and it was the context of poverty, oppression, and civil war in Central America that made his intervention so necessary. As he explained,

> The massive violations of human rights that have taken place over this period, in nearly all the countries of the region, have been the object of derision by the civilized world. The widespread killing of indigenous Guatemalans or of Salvadorians peasants, the continual recourse to the "disappearance" of workers and professionals, the murder of more than twenty priests, including an Archbishop, the proliferation of corpses, beheaded and flung into the public waste tips, are some of the chilling depths of this wave of repression by the Central American regimes,

faithful emulators of the doctrine of "National Security" practiced in South America. Forty thousand victims of political repression in just three years and in one country, like El Salvador, with a population less than 5 million, are testament to a new genocide, carried out under the cover of a hysterical anticommunism, a disguise for exploitative interests. (Martín-Baró, 1983, p. vii, 2014)

What Martín-Baró attempted was to put psychology at the service of the poor and oppressed majorities of the American continent. This meant encouraging psychologists to move away from the internal problems of psychological research and from practice oriented to a wealthy minority who could afford private services, and instead toward problems such as urban overcrowding, land reform, and violence. This practical reorientation required a second task, the reconstruction of psychology itself from the standpoint of the excluded majorities of Latin America and other countries of the global South. This meant careful searching through the dominant North American psychology for useful concepts and findings, but always with a critical eye for their limitations and their untrustworthy ideological content. Martín-Baró's two textbooks on social psychology from Central America, *Acción e Ideología* (*Action and Ideology*; Martín-Baró, 1983) and *Sistema, Grupo y Poder* (*System, Group and Power*; Martín-Baró, 1989b), written in the heat of the Salvadorian civil war, are remarkable works of reconstruction, integrating orthodox psychological theory with a more sociological and political analysis. For example, his chapter on power starts from the classic French and Raven analysis of five forms of power (coercive, reward, legitimate, referent, expert), both offering a critique and adding in concepts from outside psychology. Much critical psychology either rejects psychology itself or tries to create a new psychology from philosophical premises (Pavón-Cuéllar, 2017). Martín-Baró's project did something altogether different, repurposing existing psychology and, where necessary, correcting and augmenting it, rather like someone who upcycles unwanted or used artifacts, creating something radically new and different.

> It is a social psychology from Central America, that sets out to unravel the entangled social interests behind the actions and aims of persons and groups in these conflict-ridden societies, orientated to making manifest the ideology that materializes in everyday action. It intentionally assumes a critical stance, but without throwing out the available accumulated knowledge. There is in this book an effort to construct a social psychology that, taking from the best in the tradition, tries to provide a response to the pressing questions that are posed by the daily life experiences of the Central American peoples. (Martín-Baró, 1983, p. ix, 2014)

In his programmatic article, "Towards a Liberation Psychology," Martín-Baró (1986, 1996c) identified "three essential elements for the construction of a psychology of the liberation of the Latin American peoples: a new horizon, a new epistemology and a new praxis." Accordingly,

1) Latin American psychology must switch focus from itself, stop being preoccupied with its scientific and social status and self-define as an effective service for the needs of the numerous majority . . . which should constitute the primary object of its work. . . .

2) The objective of serving the need for liberation . . . requires a new form of seeking knowledge: the truth of the Latin American people is not to be found in its oppressed present, but in its tomorrow of freedom; the truth of the numerous majorities is not to be found but to be made. . . . The new perspective has to be from below, from the numerous oppressed majority. . . . Assuming a new perspective does not suppose, obviously, throwing out all of our knowledge; what it does suppose is its being made relative and critically revised from the perspective of the numerous majorities. Only from there will the theories and models demonstrate their validity or deficiency, their usefulness or uselessness, their universality or provincialism: only from there will the techniques that have been learned demonstrate their potential for liberation or subjugation.

3) All human knowledge is conditioned by the limits imposed by reality itself. In many respects' reality is opaque, and only by acting upon it, only by transforming it, is it possible for the human being to gain knowledge of it. What we see and how we see it is certainly conditioned by our perspective, by the place from which we look at history; but it is conditioned also by reality itself. So to acquire new psychological knowledge it is not enough that we base ourselves in the perspective of the people; it is necessary to involve ourselves in a new praxis, an activity that transforms reality, allowing us to know it not just in what it is but in what it is not, so thereby we can try to shift it towards what it should be. (Martín-Baró, 1996c, pp. 25–26)

These three points mirrored the three emphases of liberation theology, which Martín-Baró explicitly used as model, or template, for the engaged social science of liberation psychology (Martín-Baró, 1989/1998).

A major practical project was Martín-Baró's work on public opinion (Martín-Baró, 1989a). This illustrates the *bricoleur* (from the French for a multiskilled craftsperson: *bricolage* being the practice of putting together methods or frameworks from diverse sources) nature of his psychology, in this case using a standard empirical method, the opinion survey, as a tool for deideologizing reality (Martín-Baró, 1996a). By discovering and reporting what the Salvadorian people really thought about the war, he was able to expose how statements of both the Salvadoran and the U.S. governments misrepresented, for propagandistic purposes, the reality on the ground. It seems likely that it was this use of evidence in the public sphere that made him a target for murder by the army (Chomsky, 1998; de la Corte Ibañez, 2001).

PARALLEL LATIN AMERICAN DEVELOPMENTS

Cuban Psychology

As well as being an event that signaled a possible alternative socioeconomic trajectory to people in Latin America, the Cuban revolution attracted the interest of researchers and scholars, psychologists included, through its impact on social, political, and economic circumstances (Sánchez & Wiesenfeld, 1991). Cuban academic contacts were mainly with Venezuela and Mexico, according to González Rey (1995). From this point on, critical voices emerged and came together. They were opposed to the dominant, academically orientated individual psychology. This is what Martín-Baró and Dobles (Dobles, 1986) later called the liberation of psychology from its own moorings. Notwithstanding the different theoretical and methodological approaches, a consensus was reached on the distance between, on one hand, the education, training, practice, and the production of knowledge in psychology and, on the other, the social reality of Latin America.

The Cuban revolutionary government, according to Miranda (1995), was able to understand, from the existence of Soviet socialism, the importance of the correlation of forces in the process of liberation of Cuba. These heirs of Martí, Marinello, and others (de la Torre, 2001; Palmarola-Gómez, 2012) were disputing space in the liberating project, maturing the understanding of Marxist theory and method in the sense proposed by Engels and Lenin as a guide for action. Psychology in Cuba at first followed this model. However, a number of developments helped it take on a distinctive role in the evolution of critical psychological approaches within the region. Firstly, there was the unique development of health psychology, whereby psychology became a partner in the national project of improving the health of the population, initially through the provision of publicly provided universal health care, drawing on the Soviet Semashko model (a system of free public health care centered on the polyclinic; Burton, 2008) but subsequently emphasizing community development in health, building on the 1978 Almaty (Alma Ata) declaration with its community-embedded family doctor model (de la Torre, 2006; García-Averasturi, 1985; Melluish et al., 2011; World Health Organization, 2004). Secondly, Cuban psychologists extended the Vygotskian cultural historical approach, which, among other things, situated human development societally, going beyond both cognitive-individualistic and mechanistic interpretations (Western interpretations of Vygotsky on the one hand and, on the other, Leontievian activity theory, an influential derivation, or distortion that emphasizes the interactions between people, their activity and objects, mediated by a variety of concrete and conceptual tools; González Rey, 2016). Thirdly, in the 1980s, Cuban psychology increased its contact with colleagues from other parts of Latin America. It was the Faculty of Psychology at the University of Havana that led the development of Cuban psychology, and its opening to mutual influence with Latin America is attributed, in large part, to the work of Albertina Mitjans, at the time the dean of faculty. According to González Rey (1995, and personal communication, October 8, 2018), through meetings between researchers (including Fernando González Rey and other Cuban colleagues, including José Miguel Salazar and Maritza Montero from Venezuela, Sylvia Lane from Brazil, Bernardo Jiménez from Mexico, and Ignacio Martín-Baró) at the events of the Interamerican Society of Psychology in Venezuela, Mexico, Havana, and also in Miami, social psychology in Latin America began to deepen its criticism of the positivist model and acceptance of social problems. This movement became a key process for the development of the social, critical liberation psychology.

Community Social Psychology

In Latin America, community psychology largely developed as the initiative of social psychologists who were trying to make their work more relevant to the needs of the local populations; this contrasted with more clinical origins in North America. These developments emerged simultaneously in a number of centers, most notably Brazil, Puerto Rico, Mexico, and Venezuela. Community social psychology shared some influences with liberation psychology, including liberation theology, and critical social theory, militant sociology–participative action research, and critical, popular pedagogy. There was also overlap among some of the key people in pioneering these approaches, although as Portillo argues, Martín-Baró himself was somewhat wary of community psychology, having an "aversion towards models of community intervention of the USA type," and viewing the question of social change in El Salvador "primarily from its macro-social dimension in contrast to micro-social change produced by community action" (Portillo, 2011). Dobles (2015) disputes this interpretation, noting Martín-Baró's sustained contact and work with poor communities and his theoretical contributions that transcend the micro–macro divide. Nevertheless, Portillo is highlighting the limits of the typically ameliorative (*asistencialista*) North American community psychology from Martín-Baró's more radical liberation psychology perspective.

Montero et al. (2016) explored the connections between liberation psychology and community psychology (chiefly in its Latin American variants). While noting that liberation psychology is not a branch of psychology but rather the "psychological branch of the liberation paradigm," they identified a number of themes that tend to recur in both fields—namely, *praxis*, the unity of theory and practice; *critical engagement*, taking the critical perspective of, and from, the oppressed Other; *decolonization*, working to remove characteristics from the nexus of colonial domination, broadly understood, and to promote liberation; *affectivity*, the importance of emotional dimensions in community work aimed at liberation; *challenging power dynamics* in research and practice in relation marginality and social exclusion through shared action; *historical memory* as a resource in healing and empowering peoples and communities; a valuing of *cultural practice and enactment*; and the *role of (social) consciousness* and practices aimed at its enhancement.

After Martín Baró: The Evolution of the Liberation Psychology Movement

For approximately a decade after Martín-Baró's murder, there was little further development of liberation psychology as an explicit orientation to psychology, although as Montero (2000) noted that

> the idea of liberation in psychology, with or without the influence of Martín-Baró [could] be felt much in practice, above all in the community and political spheres . . . wherein lies its current strength, and also in parallel theoretical production. (p. 16)

From around the turn of the century, however, there has been a sustained, if uneven, interest in liberation psychology. Nearly 10 years later, an international congress was held in Mexico City. This became the first International Congress of Liberation Psychology, and since then, 12 more international conferences have been held across the Latin American region. In several cases, there has been an effort to make a strong link between the scholarly discussions and presentations and the struggles of social movements, both in the host country or region and more broadly (see list at "Liberation Psychology," 2018). The conferences in Guatemala (2001), Liberia (Costa Rica, 2005), and Chiapas (Mexico, 2008) were notable for this. Several of the conferences led to the publication of substantial collections of works based on some of the conference papers (Dobles, Baltodano, & Leandro, 2007; Guzzo & Lacerda, 2011; Vázquez, 2000). In this way, the production of scientific knowledge in the area matured, seeking solutions to social problems rooted in daily life, such as violence, social inequality, and exclusion. However, as González Rey (2009, 2016) has pointed out, although the revival of liberation psychology was intended as a revival of the critical, integrative, fertile road pioneered by Martín-Baró and certain contemporaries in the 1980s, it has come to represent something more like an "identity space" for psychologists who are still interested in change and social commitment and, unfortunately, for others who have used the label for self-promotion and search for a leftist identity. Certainly, although there has been impressive social commitment and useful empirical work, there has not been a great amount of new original theoretical development, although there are exceptions (e.g., in Colombia: Sacipa Rodríguez & Montero, 2014; Brazil: Góis, 2005; Ximenes, Amaral, & Rebouças, 2008; Guatemala: Flores, 2011, as summarized in English by Montero et al., 2016; and in Costa Rica: e.g., Dobles, 2009).

In Brazil, it was after 2003, when the VI International Congress of Liberation Psychology took place in Campinas, Brazil, that the works of Martín-Baró began to circulate in programs training psychologists in Brazilian universities. However, although liberation psychology was already incorporated into practices and actions and disseminated in the northeast of the country (Góis, 2003, 2005), the hegemony of psychology in the southeast of the country did not allow this critical rupture to advance the production of knowledge and its practice, even after the dictatorial period. For example, these important regional developments were absent from an influential review of community social psychology in Brazil (Freitas, 2011). Although most of the rest of the "Other America" south of the Rio Grande/Rio Bravo shares a common language, Spanish (or more properly Castilian/*Castellano*), Martín-Baró's work is not widely disseminated. His books, published by a small University publisher (UCA Editors in San Salvador) are not distributed widely, although they can be obtained by mail order. Curiously, the publisher seems to have little interest in promoting the wider dissemination and translation of these key texts. With the exception of a small collection edited by Adrianne Aron and Shawn Corne (1994), they remain unavailable in English. His many articles appeared in a variety of journals, some of them short-lived, and initiatives to make them available on the Internet come and go. Likewise, much of the other work appears in book form, published by small niche and local publishers (the books from the Argentinian publisher Paidós, now part of the Spanish-owned Planeta group, are an exception, with wide marketing in the Hispanic world). However, the increased presence of open-access Internet journal publications (e.g., via the Scielo portal) does help with the availability of material.

Parallel International Developments

As noted earlier, liberation psychology is not restricted solely to Latin America. In other regions there is, or has been, systemic oppression and a conscious response; where this is informed by a deideologized psychology, it can have characteristics similar to the liberation psychology of Latin America. In an article for the short-lived Chilean *The Ignacio Martín-Baró Latin American Journal of Social Psychology*, Burton (2013b) reviewed the presence of liberation psychology in South Africa (Seedat, 1997, 2014; Seedat, Duncan, & Lazarus, 2001), the Philippines (Enriquez, 1994; Pe-Pua & Protacio-Marcelino, 2000), New Zealand (O'Connor, Tilyard, & Milfont, 2011; Robertson & Masters-Awatere, 2008), Ireland (Moane, 2003, 2010, 2011), and the United Kingdom (Afuape, 2011; Afuape & Hughes, 2015; Burton & Kagan, 2009; Kagan et al., 2011), showing that there were psychologies that had the same characteristics as the liberation psychology of the American continent. He noted that his review was selective and could have included developments in Palestine, Italy, Turkey, Canada, Spain, Australia, or India, for example. Some of these developments (e.g., in the United Kingdom) were made with some knowledge of the Latin American tradition, but in the main, they seem to have been independent of it.

Taking the case of Palestine, the neocolonial realities of oppression by the settler State of Israel have led to a variety of collective practices of resistance, in the main nonviolent, often drawing on the arts and drama (Alrowwad, n.d.; Ashoka Foundation, 2006; Silwadi & Mayo, 2014). There has been a relatively recent development of a "context-bound, yet globally integrative model of critical community psychology for the Arab-Palestinian context" (Burton, 2015, p. 122; for a review, see Makkawi, 2015). It may draw lessons from liberating psychologies in other, typically postcolonial, contexts, but it is also very much a homegrown product. Mainstream community psychological concepts are reworked—for example, "sense of community" in terms of collective resistance, identity, and solidarity in the face of concrete manifestations of the occupation and continued encroachment on Palestinian lands and settlements. Concepts from Palestinian culture are creatively brought into the praxis—for example, Sumud, derived from the strategies of resistance to interrogation, in place of Western psychology's trauma, "to critically understand how and why colonial violence, in particular the violence of torture, is not necessarily experienced as a traumatic event to be treated by professionals" (Meari, 2015, p. 85). In contrast to trauma, Sumud entails active resistance to torture, despite the experience of pain and suffering: It is anchored in and nurtured by the collective experience of struggle. This exemplifies Martín-Baró's paradigm of rebuilding psychological constructs from the experience of the oppressed majority, in the specific context of application. Meari's analysis can be fruitfully compared and contrasted with that of the Chilean Instituto Latinoamericano de Salud Mental y Derechos Humanos (ILAS) collective, an organization that worked with the victims of torture under the Pinochet regime and their families, as well as subsequent work that built on it elsewhere (Lira, 2001; Lira & Weinstein, 2000). This body of work retained a concept of trauma. Meari criticized trauma as a Western liberal human rights concept connected to the idea of the passive yet autonomous individual. While using the concept, Lira and colleagues also indicated a nonindividualist, culturally embedded set of understandings of it and how it may be overcome—in their case, through a clear linkage between individual and collective therapy and political action. In Turkey, there has been use of, and debate about, the related concept of social trauma, in the context of political struggle related to the violence of the Turkish State against national minorities, principally the Kurds (TODAP, 2012). These examples illustrate the liberation psychology idea of seeking and adapting psychological principles relevant to a particular social context.

In the cases Burton discussed, knowledge of the Latin American movement was either limited or possibly nonexistent, and yet the similarities are clear, particularly the development of psychologies that draw on indigenous knowledge and practice (and often the recovery of historical memory) to reformulate concepts and models from Western psychology—a deideologization of the profession, and the explicit focus on liberation from oppression. Other dimensions of Latin American praxis are better known outside that region, particularly popular pedagogy, participative action research, liberation theology, and critical postdevelopment. Moreover, the common experience, on the ground, of confronting oppression, striving to understand how it affects the oppressed (and indeed the oppressors), and constructing countervailing power and influence would seem likely to lead to frameworks that show a kind of family likeness. Nevertheless, psychologists in other locations have adopted insights directly from the paradigmatic Latin American liberation psychology in their work, although often reworking concepts in the local or national context. An example is the recovery of historical memory, a central idea in Martín-Baró and a constant refrain (sometimes no more than that but often articulated through praxis with oppressed peoples) in Latin America, where it resonates with historical consciousness—for example, in relation to the legacy of conquest and colonization or of the experience of transatlantic slavery. In a country such as the United Kingdom, however, perhaps in part because of the enormous historical legacy of dispossession, urbanization, industrialization, and deindustrialization and hence a distance from a historical common culture, the concept does not have "recognition value," so it cannot merely be invoked but has to be discovered through praxis.

EVALUATION

Liberation psychology has come a long way from its earliest stirrings. There is now a movement of scholars and activists who identify with its ideas, dispersed across several continents. Yet liberation psychology remains marginal, even in its continent of origin. As an approach to psychology, rather than a school or subdiscipline, it has innovated in a number of ways, and the other chapters in this book give witness to that. It is our contention that its basic approach of reconstruction of psychological concepts and practices, from the standpoint of the oppressed and excluded—that is, liberation psychology as "really social, analectical, psychology"—remains as relevant as ever. Indeed, it is more relevant now with the global challenges of the ecological and climate emergency, the continued dominance yet crisis of neoliberalism, the growth of fascism, massive population displacement, epidemics of sexual and economic abuse and exploitation, the continued explosion of material flows through the world economy with the consequent and violent extractivism, and environmental and livelihood destruction, to name the principal ones. liberation psychology and associated approaches have been extended to fields such as disaster response, disability, cultures of violence and organized crime, and genocidal State crimes. For liberation psychology to demonstrate its value, though, it needs—in a way that echoes Martín-Baró's prescription, now more than 30 years old—to orientate itself to three concerns:

1. Turn outward again and consider how, as a primary definition of the purpose of a liberatory psychology, it can become a more effective "under labourer" (cf. Locke, 1690/1997, who suggested philosophy's subordinate role to that of science) in social movements and collective struggles in the areas of global challenge identified earlier.

2. Commit to a reworking of psychological concepts and methods from the perspective of the oppressed—not remaining content to rely on a restricted set of methods and ideas but drawing on the totality of social scientific theory and knowledge, with an emphasis on the social psychological as the key to the relation between persons and their social context.

3. Constantly reflect on and evaluate the development of theory and practice as guided by the previous two premises: liberation psychology must avoid becoming repetitive and rhetorical but seek a dialectically intertwined extension of knowledge and effective action.

If we understand psychology as an important tool in the service of the dominant ideology, then disputation over training and practice for this area requires a critical and political reading of the economic, political, and social circumstances present in the various countries. This formulation requires field professionals and researchers to take sides. They assume their place in the dynamics of the production and reproduction of both life and of psychological knowledge. As a political ethical project for psychology, it is up to us to ensure the visibility of these ideas and their realization through activism. This is a challenge that is always present, especially in countries that are still effectively colonized.

REFERENCES

Afuape, T. (2011). *Power, resistance and liberation in therapy with survivors of trauma.* London, England: Routledge.

Afuape, T., & Hughes, G. (Eds.). (2015). *Towards and beyond liberation psychology.* London, England: Routledge.

Alatas, S. H. (1972). The captive mind in development studies: Some neglected problems and the need for an autonomous social science tradition in Asia. *International Social Science Journal, 24,* 9–25. Retrieved from http://eprints.usm.my/8298/1/The_Captive_Mind_In_Development_Studies_Pt_1.pdf

Alatas, S. H. (2013). *The myth of the lazy native: A study of the image of the Malays, Filipinos and Javanese from the 16th to the 20th Century and its function in the ideology of colonial capitalism.* Routledge. (Original work published 1979)

Alrowwad. (n.d.). *Who we are.* Retrieved from http://www.alrowwad.org/en/?page_id=705

Armistead, N. (1974). *Reconstructing social psychology.* Harmondsworth, England: Penguin.

Aron, A., & Corne, S. (Eds.). (1994). *Ignacio Martín-Baró: Writings for a liberation psychology.* Cambridge, MA: Harvard University Press.

Ashoka Foundation. (2006). *Abdelfattah Abusrour.* Retrieved from https://www.ashoka.org/en-gb/fellow/abdelfattah-abusrour

Beorlegui, C. (2004). La generación de los años setenta: Las filosofías de la liberación [The generation of the seventies: The philosophies of liberation]. In *Historia del Pensamiento Filosofico Latinoamericano: Una busqueda incesante de la identidad* [History of Latin American philosophical thought: An incessant search for identity] (p. 661–803). Bilbao, Spain: Universidad de Deusto.

Boff, L. (1980). *Teologia do cativeiro e da libertação* [Theology of captivity and liberation]. São Paulo, Brazil: Circulo do Livro.

Boff, L. (1981). *Igreja: Carisma e poder* [Church: Charisma and power]. Petropolis, Brazil: Vozes.

Boff, L. (2012). *Church, charisma and power: Liberation theology and the institutional church.* Eugene, OR: Wipf and Stock.

Burton, M. (n.d.). *Dussel, Enrique.* Retrieved from http://globalsocialtheory.org/thinkers/dussel-enrique/

Burton, M. (2008). *The idea of the polyclinic.* Retrieved from https://web.archive.org/web/20130723095025/http://www.cubasol-manch.org.uk/The%20idea%20of%20the%20polyclinic.pdf

Burton, M. (2013a). The analectic turn: Critical psychology and the new political context. *Les Cahiers de Psychologie Politique, 23.* Retrieved from http://lodel.irevues.inist.fr/cahierspsychologiepolitique/index.php?id=2465

Burton, M. (2013b). ¿Existe la psicología de la liberación fuera de América Latina? [Is the psychology of liberation outside of Latin America?]. *Revista Latinoamericana de Psicología Social: Ignacio Martín-Baró, 2,* 158–170. Retrieved from https://www.academia.edu/2122428/_Existe_la_psicolog%C3%ADa_de_la_liberaci%C3%B3n_fuera_de_Am%C3%A9rica_latina

Burton, M. (2013c). A second psychology of liberation? Valuing and moving beyond the Latin American. *The Journal of Critical Psychology, Counselling and Psychotherapy, 13,* 96–106. Retrieved from http://libpsy.org/wp-content/uploads/2011/11/A-second-psychology-of-liberation.pdf

Burton, M. (2015). Community psychology under colonial occupation: The case of Palestine. *Journal of Community Psychology, 43,* 119–123. http://dx.doi.org/10.1002/jcop.21715

Burton, M., & Flores Osorio, J. M. (2011). Introducing Dussel: The philosophy of liberation and a really social psychology. *Psychology in Society*, 20–39. Retrieved from http://
www.scielo.org.za/scielo.php?script=sci_arttext&pid=S1015-60462011000100003&
nrm=iso

Burton, M., & Gómez, L. (2015). Liberation psychology. In I. Parker (Ed.), *Handbook of
critical psychology* (pp. 348–355). London, England: Routledge.

Burton, M., & Kagan, C. (2005). Liberation social psychology: Learning from Latin
America. *Journal of Community & Applied Social Psychology*, 15, 63–78. http://dx.doi.org/
10.1002/casp.786

Burton, M., & Kagan, C. (2009). Towards a really social psychology: Liberation psychology beyond Latin America. In M. Montero & C. Sonn (Eds.), *The psychology of liberation: Theory and application* (pp. 51–73). New York, NY: Springer. http://dx.doi.org/
10.1007/978-0-387-85784-8_3

Caparrós, A., & Caparrós, N. (1976). *Psicología de la liberación* [Liberation psychology].
Madrid, Spain: Editorial Fundamentos.

Chomsky, N. (1998). El contexto socio-político del asesinato de Ignacio Martín-Baró
[Spanish translation of "The sociopolitical context of the murder of Ignacio Martín-
Baró" paper presented in August 1990 at the American Psychological Association
conference, Boston, MA]. In A. Blanco (Ed.), *Ignacio Martín-Baró: Psicología de la liberación* [Liberation psychology] (pp. 343–355). Madrid, Spain: Trotta.

Danziger, K. (1990). *Constructing the subject: Historical origins of psychological research.*
Cambridge, England: Cambridge University Press. http://dx.doi.org/10.1017/
CBO9780511524059

de Castro, J. (1969). *Death in the northeast: Poverty and revolution in the northeast of Brazil*
(English ed.). New York, NY: Random House.

de la Corte Ibañez, L. (2000). La psicología de Ignacio Martín-Baró como psicología social
crítica: Una presentación de su obra [The psychology of Ignacio Martín-Baró as critical social psychology: A presentation of his work]. *Revista de Psicología General y Apli-
cada*, 53, 437–450. Retrieved from http://www.copmadrid.org/pspolitica/baro.htm

de la Corte Ibañez, L. (2001). *Memoria de un compromiso: La psicología de Ignacio Martín-
Baró* [Memory of a commitment: The psychology of Ignacio Martín-Baró]. Bilbao,
Spain: Desclée de Brouwer.

de la Torre, C. (2001). *Las identidades: Una mirada desde la psicología* [Identities: A perspective from psychology]. Havana, Cuba: Centro Juan Marinello.

de la Torre, C. (2006). Psychology in Cuba after 1959. *History and Philosophy of Psychology*,
8(1), 12–29.

de las Casas, B. (2004). *A short account of the destruction of the Indies* (N. Griffin, Trans.).
London, England: Penguin Books.

Dobles, I. (1986). Psicología social desde centroamerica: Retos y perspectivas: Entrevista
con el Dr. Ignacio Martín-Baró [Social psychology from Central America: Challenges
and perspectives: Interview with Dr. Ignacio Martín-Baró]. *Revista Costarricense de
Psicología*, 10, 71–76.

Dobles, I. (2009). *Memorias del dolor: Consideraciones acerca de las Comisiones de la Verdad en
América Latina* [Memories of pain: Considerations about the Truth Commissions in
Latin America]. San José, Costa Rica: Arlekín.

Dobles, I. (2015). Psicología de la liberación y psicología comunitaria latinoamericana:
Una perspectiva [Liberation psychology and Latin American community psychology:
A perspective]. *Teoría y crítica de la psicología*, 6, 122–139. Retrieved from https://
dialnet.unirioja.es/servlet/articulo?codigo=5895387

Dobles, I., Baltodano, S., & Leandro, V. (Eds.). (2007). *Psicología de la liberación en el contexto de la globalización neoliberal: Acciones, reflexiones y desafíos* [Psychology of liberation in the context of neoliberal globalization: Actions, reflections and challenges].
San José, Costa Rica: Universidad de Costa Rica.

Dussel, E. (1981). *A history of the church in Latin America: Colonialism to liberation (1492–1979).*
Grand Rapids, MI: Eerdmans.

Dussel, E. (2000). Epilogue. In L. Alcoff & E. Mendieta (Eds.), *Thinking from the underside of history: Enrique Dussel's philosophy of liberation* (pp. 269–289). Lanham, MD: Rowman and Littlefield.

Dussel, E. (2003). Philosophy in Latin America in the twentieth century: Problems and currents. In E. Mendieta (Ed.), *Latin American philosophy: Currents, issues, debates* (pp. 15–59). Bloomington: Indiana University Press. http://dx.doi.org/10.1007/978-94-017-3651-0_2

Dussel, E. (2013). *Ethics of liberation in the age of globalization and exclusion* (A. A. Vallega, Ed.). Durham, NC: Duke University Press.

Enriquez, V. (1994). *From colonial to liberation psychology: The Philippine experience*. Manila, Philippines: De La Salle University Press. Retrieved from http://eaststemcell.com/files/storage.cloud.php?id=OTcxNTQyNTg4Nw==

Escobar, A. (2007). Worlds and knowledges otherwise: The Latin American modernity/coloniality research program. *Cultural Studies, 21*, 179–210. http://dx.doi.org/10.1080/09502380601162506

Fals Borda, O. (2001). Participatory (action) research in social theory: Origins and challenges. In P. Reason & H. Bradbury (Eds.), *Handbook of action research: Participative inquiry and practice* (pp. 28–37). Thousand Oaks, CA: Sage.

Fals Borda, O., & Rahman, M. A. (1991). *Action and knowledge: Breaking the monopoly of power with participatory action-research*. London, England: Intermediate Technology Publications; New York, NY: Apex Press. http://dx.doi.org/10.3362/9781780444239

Fanon, F. (1965). *The wretched of the earth* (Vol. 390). New York, NY: Grove Press. Retrieved from https://www.marxists.org/urdu/MarxistWriters/PDFs/005-WEARTH.pdf

Fanon, F. (1967). *Black skins white masks*. New York, NY: Grove Press.

Flores, J. M. (2009). Praxis and liberation in the context of Latin American theory. In M. Montero & C. Sonn (Eds.), *Psychology of liberation: Theory and applications*. New York, NY: Springer.

Flores, J. M. (2011). *Psicología y praxis comunitaria: Una visión Latinoamericana* [Community psychology and praxis: A Latin American vision]. Cuernavaca, Mexico: Editorial Latinoamerica.

Freire, P. (1972a). *Cultural action for freedom*. Harmondsworth, England: Penguin.

Freire, P. (1972b). *Pedagogy of the oppressed*. Harmondsworth, England: Penguin.

Freire, P. (1978). *Pedagogy in process: The letters to Guinea-Bissau*. London, England: Writers and Readers Publishing Cooperative.

Freire, P. (2004). *Pedagogy of hope: Reliving pedagogy of the oppressed*. London, England: Bloomsbury Academic.

Freitas, F. (2011). Construcción y consolidación de la psicología social comunitária en Brasil: Conocimientos, prácticas y perspectivas [Construction and consolidation of community social psychology in Brazil: Knowledge, practices, and perspectives]. In M. Montero & I. Serrano García (Eds.), *Historias de la psicología en América Latina: Participación y transformación* [Stories of psychology in Latin America: Participation and transformation] (pp. 93–113). Buenos Aires, Argentina: Paidós.

García-Averasturi, L. (1985). Community health psychology in Cuba. *Journal of Community Psychology, 13*, 117–123.

Góis, C. W. L. (2003). *Psicologia comunitária no Ceará: Uma caminhada* [Community psychology in Ceará: A walk]. Fortaleza, Brazil: Instituto Paulo Freire de Estudos Psicossociais.

Góis, C. W. L. (2005). *Psicologia comunitária: Actividade e consciência* [Community psychology: Activity and awareness]. Fortaleza, Brazil: Instituto Paulo Freire de Estudos Psicossociais.

González Rey, F. (1995). Acerca de lo social y lo subjetivo en el socialism [About the social and the subjective in socialism]. *Revista Temas, 3*, 93–101.

González Rey, F. (2009). La psicología en América Latina: Algunos momentos críticos de su desarrollo [Psychology in Latin America: Some critical moments of its development].

Psicología Para América Latina: Revista de La Unión Latinoamericana de Entidades de Psicología, 17. Retrieved from http://www.psicolatina.org/17/america-latina.html

González Rey, F. (2016). Paths, development and discontinuity of some critical approaches to psychology in Latin America: What happened in that history? *Annual Review of Critical Psychology, 10*, 642–662. Retrieved from https://thediscourseunit.files.wordpress.com/2016/05/latin-america-i-642-662.pdf

Gutiérrez, G. (1973). *A theology of liberation*. Maryknoll, NY: Orbis.

Guzzo, R. S. L., & Lacerda, F. (Eds.). (2011). *Psicologia social para América latina: O resgate da psicologia e libertação* [Social psychology for Latin America: The rescue of psychology and liberation]. Campinas, Brazil: Editora Alínea.

Hinkelammert, F. J. (1997). Liberation theology and the economic and social context of Latin America. In D. Batstone, E. Mendieta, L. A. Lorentzen, & D. N. Hopkins (Eds.), *Liberation theologies, postmodernity, and the Americas* (pp. 25–52). New York, NY: Routledge.

Hur, D. U., & Lacerda, F. (2017). Ditadura e insurgência na América Latina: Psicologia da libertação e resistência armada [Dictatorship and insurgency in Latin America: Psychology of libertarianism and armed resistance]. *Psicologia: Ciência e profissão, 37*, 28–43. http://dx.doi.org/10.1590/1982-3703020002017

Jiménez, B. (1994). Investigación ante acción participante: Una dimensión desconocida [Investigation before participant action: An unknown dimension]. In M. Montero (Ed.), *Psicología social comunitaria* [Community social psychology] (pp. 103–137). Guadalajara, Mexico: Universidad de Guadalajara.

Jiménez, B. (2013). An interview with Silvia Tatiana Maurer Lane (1933–2006): Pioneer of the Brazilian critical and community social psychology. *Annual Review of Critical Psychology, 11*, 663–671.

Kagan, C., & Burton, M. (2000). Prefigurative action research: An alternative basis for critical psychology? *Annual Review of Critical Psychology, 2*, 73–87.

Kagan, C., Lo, S., Mok, L., Lawthom, R., Sham, S., Greenwood, M., & Baines, S. (2011). *Experiences of forced labour among Chinese migrant workers*. York, England: Joseph Rowntree Foundation. Retrieved from http://www.jrf.org.uk/publications/chinese-experiences-forced-labour

Lacerda, F. (2010). ¿Liberarse de qué? ¿Liberarse para qué? Notas sobre marxismo, anti-capitalismo y psicología de la liberación [Get rid of what? Free yourself for what? Notes on Marxism, anti-capitalism and liberation psychology]. In I. Dobles & S. Baltodano (Eds.), *Psicología: Dominación, compromiso y transformación social* [Psychology: Domination, commitment and social transformation] (pp. 201–208). Ciudad Universitaria Rodrigo Facio. San José, Costa Rica: Universidad de Costa Rica.

Levinas, E. (1969). *Totality and infinity: An essay on exteriority*. Pittsburgh, PA: Duquesne University Press.

Liberation psychology. (2018). In *Wikipedia*. Retrieved from https://en.wikipedia.org/w/index.php?title=Liberation_psychology&oldid=860832240

Lira, E. (2001). Violence, fear, and impunity: Reflections on subjective and political obstacles for peace. *Peace and Conflict: Journal of Peace Psychology, 7*, 109–118.

Lira, E., & Weinstein, E. (2000). La tortura. Conceptualización psicológica y proceso terapéutico [Torture. Psychological conceptualization and therapeutic process]. In I. Martín-Baró (Ed.), *Psicología social de la guerra* [Social psychology of war] (pp. 335–390). San Salvador, El Salvador: UCA Editores.

Locke, J. (1997). *An essay concerning human understanding*. New York, NY: Penguin Books. (Original work published 1690)

Makkawi, I. (2015). Community psychology enactments in Palestine: Roots and current manifestations. *Journal of Community Psychology, 43*, 63–75. http://dx.doi.org/10.1002/jcop.21714

Martín-Baró, I. (1983). *Acción e Ideología: Psicología social desde Centroamérica I* [Action and ideology: Social psychology from Central America I]. San Salvador, El Salvador: UCA Editores.

Martín-Baró, I. (1986). Hacia una psicología de la liberación [Towards a psychology of liberation]. *Boletin de Psicología (UCA), 22,* 219–231. Retrieved from http://www.uca. edu.sv/deptos/psicolog/hacia.htm

Martín-Baró, I. (1987). El Latino indolente: Carácter ideológico del fatalismo Latino-Americano [The indolent Latino: Ideological character of Latin American fatalism]. In M. Montero (Ed.), *Psicología política latinoamericana* [Latin American political psychology] (pp. 135–162). Caracas, Venezuela: Panapo.

Martín-Baró, I. (1989a). *La opinión pública salvadoreña* [Salvadoran public opinion] *(1987–1988).* San Salvador, El Salvador: UCA Editores.

Martín-Baró, I. (1989b). *Sistema, grupo y poder: Psicología social desde Centroamérica II* [System, group and power: Social psychology from Central America II]. San Salvador, El Salvador: UCA Editores.

Martín-Baró, I. (1996a). Public opinion research as a de-ideologizing instrument. In *Writings for a liberation psychology* (A. Aron & C. Corne, Eds.; pp. 194–195). Cambridge, MA: Harvard University Press.

Martín-Baró, I. (1996b). The lazy Latino: The ideological nature of Latin American fatalism. In A. Aron & C. Corne (Eds.), *Writings for a liberation psychology* (pp. 198–220). Cambridge, MA: Harvard University Press.

Martín-Baró, I. (1996c). Toward a liberation psychology. In A. Aron & C. Corne (Eds.), *Writings for a liberation psychology* (pp. 17–33). Cambridge, MA: Harvard University Press.

Martín-Baró, I. (1998). *Retos y perspectivas de la psicología latinoamericana* [Challenges and perspectives of the Latin American psychology; paper presented at University of Guadalajara, 1989]. In A. Blanco (Ed.), *Psicología de la liberación* [Psychology of liberation] (pp. 283–302). Madrid, Spain: Trotta.

Martín-Baró, I. (2014). Prologue [unofficial English translation]. In *Acción e ideología: Psicología social desde Centroamérica I* [Action and ideology: Social psychology from Central America I] (M. Burton, Trans.; pp. vii–x). San Salvador, El Salvador: UCA Editores. Retrieved from http://libpsy.org/wp-content/uploads/2014/11/Accion-y-Ideologia-translation-Prologue.pdf

Meari, L. (2015). Reconsidering trauma: Towards a Palestinian community psychology. *Journal of Community Psychology, 43,* 76–86. http://dx.doi.org/10.1002/jcop.21712

Melluish, S. J., Corral, R., Dominguez, N., Torralbas, A., Castro, M., & Burton, M. (2011). Psychology in Cuba: Symposium presented at the Cuba Research Forum Annual Conference, Nottingham, England, September 2010. *International Journal of Canadian Studies, 3,* 346–365.

Memmi, A. (1969). *Dominated man; notes toward a portrait.* Boston, MA: Beacon Press.

Miranda, O. (1995). El marxismo en el ideal emancipador cubano durante la república neocolonial [Marxism in the Cuban emancipatory ideal during the neocolonial republic]. *Temas, 3,* 44–57. Retrieved from http://temas.cult.cu/revista/3/la-cultura-marxista-en-cuba

Moane, G. (2003). Bridging the personal and the political: Practices for a liberation psychology. *American Journal of Community Psychology, 31,* 91–101. http://dx.doi.org/10.1023/A:1023026704576

Moane, G. (2010). Sociopolitical development and political activism http://dx.doi.org/10.1111/j.1471-6402.2010.01601.x. *Psychology of Women Quarterly, 34,* 521–529. Retrieved from http://pwq.sagepub.com/content/34/4/521.abstract

Moane, G. (2011). *Gender and colonialism: A psychological analysis of oppression and liberation.* Basingstoke, England: Palgrave Macmillan.

Montero, M. (1994). *Psicología social comunitaria* [Community social psychology]. Guadalajara, Mexico: Universidad de Guadalajara.

Montero, M. (2000). Perspectivas y retos de la psicología de la liberación [Perspectives and challenges of liberation psychology]. In J. J. Vazquez (Ed.), *Psicología social y liberación en América Latina* [Social psychology and liberation in Latin America] (pp. 9–26). Mexico City, Mexico: Universidad Autonoma de Mexico, Unidad de Iztapalapa.

Montero, M. (2011). *Historias de la psicologia comunitaria en America: Participacion y transformacion* [Stories of community psychology in America: Participation and transformation]. Buenos Aires, Argentina: Paidós.

Montero, M. (2014). Algunas premisas para el desarrollo de métodos analécticos en el trabajo psicosocial comunitario [Some premises for the development of analytical methods in community psychosocial work]. In J. M. Flores Osorio (Ed.), *Repensar la psicología y lo comunitario en América Latina* [Rethinking psychology and community in Latin America]. Tijuana, Mexico: Universidad de Tijuana. Retrieved from https://www.academia.edu/8424848/Repensar_la_psicologia_y_lo_comunitario_en_am%C3%A9rica_latina

Montero, M., Sonn, C., & Burton, M. (2016). Community psychology and liberation psychology: Creative synergy for ethical and transformative praxis. In M. A. Bond, I. García de Serrano, & C. Keys (Eds.), *APA handbook of community psychology* (Vol. 1, pp. 149–167). Washington, DC: American Psychological Association.

O'Connor, S., Tilyard, B. A., & Milfont, T. L. (2011). Liberation psychology: From Latin America to Aoteroa/New Zealand. *Journal of New Zealand Studies, 11*, 151–170.

Palmarola-Gómez, N. (2012). *El pensamiento pedagógico de Juan Marinello vidaurreta en la república neocolonial* [The pedagogical thought of Juan Marinello in the neocolonial republic]. *VARONA, Revista Científico-Metodológica, 55*, 4–11. Retrieved from http://www.redalyc.org/pdf/3606/360633907002.pdf

Parker, I. (1989). *The crisis in modern social psychology—And how to end it*. London, England: Routledge.

Pavón-Cuéllar, D. (2017). Latin-American Marxist critiques of psychology. In G. Sullivan, J. Cresswell, B. Ellis, M. Morgan, & E. Schraube (Eds.), *Resistance and renewal in theoretical psychology* (pp. 106–115). Concord, CA: Captus University.

Pe-Pua, R., & Protacio-Marcelino, E. (2000). Sikolohiyang Pilipino (Filipino psychology): A legacy of Virgilio G. Enriquez. *Asian Journal of Social Psychology, 3*, 49–71. http://dx.doi.org/10.1111/1467-839X.00054

Pinto, A. V. (1960). *Consciência e realidade nacional* [Awareness and national reality]. Rio de Janeiro, Brazil: Ministerio da Educação e Cultura, Instituto Superior de Estudos Brasileiros.

Portillo, N. (2011). Entre la discontinuidad y el protagonismo histórico: Apuntes sobre el desarrollo de la psicología comunitaria en El Salvador [Between discontinuity and historical prominence: Notes on the development of community psychology in El Salvador]. In M. Montero & I. Serrano García (Eds.), *Historias de la psicología en América Latina: Participación y transformación* [Stories of psychology in Latin America: Participation and transformation] (pp. 213–233). Buenos Aires, Argentina: Paidós.

Robertson, N., & Masters-Awatere, B. (2008). Community psychology in Aotearoa/New Zealand. In S. Reich, M. Reimer, I. Prilleltensky, & M. Montero (Eds.), *International community psychology: History and theories* (pp. 140–163). Boston, MA: Springer Science+Media.

Sacipa Rodríguez, F. S., & Montero, M. (Eds.). (2014). *Psychosocial approaches to peacebuilding in Colombia*. New York, NY: Springer.

Salazar Bondy, A. (2004). *Existe una filosofía de nuestra América* [Is there a philosophy of our America]? Siglo XXI. Retrieved from https://books.google.co.uk/books?id=rF5yFpwcqRgC

Sánchez, E., & Wiesenfeld, E. (1991). Community social psychology in Latin America [Special issue]. *Applied Psychology, 40*(2).

Seedat, M. (1997). The quest for liberatory psychology. *South African Journal of Psychology, 27*, 261–270. http://dx.doi.org/10.1177/008124639702700410

Seedat, M. (2014). *Liberation psychology: 25 years on. Imagining Ignacio Martín-Baró and Steve Bantu Biko in conversation.* Retrieved from http://libpsy.org/2014/11/16/liberation-psychology-25-years-on-imagining-ignacio-martin-baro-and-steve-bantu-biko-in-conversation/

Seedat, M., Duncan, N., & Lazarus, S. (2001). *Community psychology: Theory, method and practice, South African and other perspectives.* Cape Town, South Africa: Oxford University Press.

Sève, L. (1978). *Man in Marxist theory and the psychology of personality.* Sussex, England: Harvester Press.

Silwadi, N., & Mayo, P. (2014). Pedagogy under siege in Palestine: Insights from Paulo Freire. *Holy Land Studies, 13*(1), 71–87. http://dx.doi.org/10.3366/hls.2014.0078

Stavenhagen, R. (1971). Decolonializing applied social sciences (includes comments and author's reply). *Human Organization, 30,* 333–357. http://dx.doi.org/10.17730/humo.30.4.p1w7700v333n6871

TODAP. (2012, September). Third Critical Psychology Symposium, Diyarbakir, Turkey.

Vázquez, J. J. (Ed.). (2000). *Psicología social y liberación en América Latina* [Social psychology and liberation in Latin America]. Mexico City, Mexico: Universidad Autonoma de Mexico, Unidad de Iztapalapa.

Watkins, M., & Shulman, H. (2008). *Towards psychologies of liberation.* Basingstoke, England: Palgrave Macmillan. http://dx.doi.org/10.1057/9780230227736

World Health Organization. (2004). Declaration of Alma-Ata International Conference on Primary Health Care, Alma-Ata, Soviet Union, 6–12 September 1978. *Development, 47,* 159–161. http://dx.doi.org/10.1057/palgrave.development.1100047

Ximenes, V. M., Amaral, C. E. M., & Rebouças, F. G. (2008). *Psicologia comunitária e Educação popular: Vivências de extensão/cooperação Universitária no Ceará* [Community psychology and popular education: Experiences of university extension/cooperation in Ceara]. Fortaleza, Brazil: Universidade Federal do Ceará.

2

Concepts of Liberation Psychology

Edil Torres Rivera

Todo conocimiento humano está condicionado por los límites impuestos por la propia realidad [Human knowledge is conditioned by the limits imposed by its own reality].
—MARTÍN-BARÓ (1998, p. 298)

When Martín-Baró's book *Writings for a Liberation Psychology* (Aron & Corne, 1996) first arrived in the United States, many psychologists seemed to embrace this psychology as a legitimate approach to work against oppression. This chapter attempts to address the complexity of liberation psychology's concepts. The liberation psychology phenomenon has been called many names, from movement to an approach. In this chapter, I refer to liberation psychology as a theory given that it meets several criteria that define a theory, beginning with (a) having postulates or assumptions; (b) a set of definitions of concepts; (c) these concepts bear certain relationships to each other; and (d) finally, from these assumptions, definitions, and relationships, hypotheses are constructed.

It is important to acknowledge that the authors of the chapters in this book are familiar with the concepts and principles. It is also essential to mention that liberation psychology is dynamic, and as such, it is constantly evolving and as Maritza Montero stated, the influences of liberation psychology are many, ranging from Amilcar Cabral to Mauricio Gaborit (Cabral, Wood, & Rabaka, 2016; Gaborit, 2015; M. Montero, personal communication, October 21, 2016; Montero & Sonn, 2009).

http://dx.doi.org/10.1037/0000198-003
Liberation Psychology: Theory, Method, Practice, and Social Justice, L. Comas-Díaz and E. Torres Rivera (Editors)

In addition, it is essential to remind readers that many of the concepts mentioned here are also revisited in numerous chapters in this book. For example, the roots of liberation psychology are described in Chapter 1 (Burton & Guzzo). Nonetheless, this chapter intends to familiarize the reader with the most basic concepts of the theory or movement of liberation psychology. Additionally, as a Puerto Rican psychologist who is familiar with the work of Paulo Freire, Orlando Fals Borda, Ignacio Martín-Baró, Frantz Fanon, Albert Memmi, Amilcar Cabral, Michel Foucault, and other authors in the liberatory movement, I understand that the connection among different proponents of the liberatory movement is always clear and understood (Bulhan, 1985; Cabral, 1974; Fals Borda, 1999; Freire, 1996; Hook, 2012; Memmi, 2004). This chapter relies heavily on Maritza Montero's work on the state of the liberation psychology movement and its development in the past 20 years (Montero, 2016; Montero, Sonn, & Burton, 2017).

Liberation psychology was first articulated by Martín-Baró (1986) and has been further developed in significant ways by others, such as Montero from Venezuela (Montero & Sonn, 2009; Montero et al., 2017) and Gaborit, who is less well-known in the United States; nonetheless, social researchers and, in particular, psychologists consider their work an extension and continuation of Martín-Baró's (Gaborit, 2007, 2015). This is not to dismiss the work of many Black psychologists or the early work of eminent African Americans in the development of "Black liberation psychology" (Afuape, 2011; Jamison, 2013; Thompson & Alfred, 2009). The principles are presented and described in the work of Martín-Baró (see http://www.uca.edu.sv/coleccion-digital-IMB/seccion/archivo-academicos/ for a complete review of Martín-Baró's work), as well as subsequent academics and practitioners (Afuape, 2011; Afuape & Hughes, 2016; Kagan, Burton, Duckett, Lawthom, & Siddiquee, 2012; Moane, 2014; Montero & Sonn, 2009).

BRIEF REVIEW OF THE ROOTS OF LIBERATION PSYCHOLOGY

As previously stated, Burton and Guzzo (Chapter 1, this volume) described in detail the roots and origins of liberation psychology, which is not only a product of Latin America or the United States but a global movement developed by independent actors in different parts of the world working independently from each other but with very similar concepts. Fanon, Foucault, Enriquez, Memmi, Biko, and Cabral, to name a few, are associated with the concepts and principles of liberation psychology that unknowingly were using the principles and methods of liberation psychology in different parts of the world (Campbell, 2008; Enriquez, 1994; Fanon & Chevalier, 1965; Hook, 2011). Furthermore, more broadly, liberation psychology has been influenced by the following movements: (a) liberation pedagogy, (b) theology of liberation, (c) philosophy of liberation, (d) critical sociology, and (e) community psychology (Montero, Sonn, & Burton, 2017). Chapter 1 of this volume explains in detail each of these influences, thus to save space, I am simply restating their influence and then moving into the principles of liberation psychology.

ANTIOPPRESSIVE ONTOLOGY AND EPISTEMOLOGY

"Anti-oppressive theoretical approaches to research and practice consist of a set of theories that hold common epistemological and ontological assumptions" (Moosa-Mitha, 2015, p. 65). However, the bases for the interpretation and understanding of particular experiences of oppression and margination differ considerably (Moosa-Mitha, 2015). Nonetheless, liberation psychology, given its focus on the poor and those marginalized in society, can be considered an antioppressive theory. Thus, it is important to name some aspect of the ontology and epistemology of liberation psychology to provide a more useful understanding of how liberation psychology has evolved from a movement to a theory that has clinical application when working with oppressed populations and trauma (Torres Fernandez & Torres-Rivera, 2014). Using the blueprint of Moosa-Mitha (2015) and following my experiential knowledge as a person of color practicing liberation psychology, I present characteristics of liberation psychology that pertain to how people interpret their reality (ontology) and how people learn or gain knowledge (epistemology).

Liberation psychology is an antioppressive theory given that, from the beginning, it was intended to counteract oppression and marginalization. Additionally, liberation psychology contends that all knowledge is socially and politically constructed (Montero, 2016), meaning that it advances knowledge and also implies that knowledge does not just happen to be somewhere, nor is it discovered. Instead, knowledge is the product of interaction among people (Freire, 1996). That is, in accordance with Freire, people with differences concerning politics, gender, and class can and do create knowledge when they interact (Potts & Brown, 2015).

Therefore, as an antioppressive theory, the ontology of liberation psychology can be labeled as subjective, as can particular sociohistorical experiences that simultaneously take numerous positions (Moosa-Mitha, 2015). In other words, the specific and differential nature of oppression is recognized without losing the collective experience. The idea that social reality is dualistic is not only challenged but also deconstructed as a social reality that is viewed as multiple, fluid, and intersectional. Liberation psychology is also discursive and practical when understanding the power relationship that enables oppression. Further, it is collective, yet recognizes individual experiences of oppression, in that one experience does not dominate the other; rather, individual and collective experiences complement one another. For example, as a Puerto Rican man who has experienced discrimination in the army and in academia, my experience is not bigger or smaller that the Puerto Rican people in their relationship with the United States as colonial subjects. In fact, my individual experience supports and enhances the collective experience of discrimination and margination.

Similarly, the epistemology of liberation psychology is that knowledge can be understood as subjective, grounded in people's lived experiences. It is also situated and subjugated; that is, knowledge is understood depending on the personal privileges, oppression, and social position of the people involved. Knowledge is only partial because not everything can be known.

PRINCIPLES OF LIBERATION PSYCHOLOGY

In this section, the main principles of liberation psychology are presented, as well as some points on the epistemology and ontology of this particular theory. The main principles include (a) reorientation of psychology, (b) recovering historical memory, (c) deideologizing everyday experience, (d) denaturalization, (e) problematization, (f) virtues of the people, (g) conscientization, (h) power dynamics, and (i) praxis.

Reorientation of Psychology

This particular concept is also considered an essential principle of liberation psychology theory. It is based on the idea that psychology, and in particular, "Western" influenced psychology, had little to offer regarding the region's (Latin America) severe and oppressive circumstances (Martín-Baró, 1998). Therefore, for psychology as a field to be relevant to the mental health concerns it purports to address, it must change its goal toward the lived experience of those subjected to the most extreme oppression, discrimination, and poverty.

Additionally, the poor and oppressed of South America were victims of structural, sociopolitical oppression that was the primary cause of the region's social and individual psychological problems. As such, Martín-Baró proposed a psychology of liberation that would address these psychological maladies by concentrating on their sociopolitical etiology. This process begins with a historical analysis of what brought these structural problems to bear. In fact, Farmer (2003) mentioned a similar point concerning structural violence and power. Within this reorientation, liberation psychologists also seek to find new or old knowledge that comes from the masses, also known as the indigenous way of knowing (Grayshield & Mihecoby, 2010).

Recovering Historical Memory

Many oppressed populations, particularly those who have been subject to colonization by foreign societies and cultures, have had their history written from the perspective of the colonizer (Adams, Dobles, Gómez, Kurtiş, & Molina, 2015; Afuape, 2011; Akken & Taracena, 2007; Enriquez, 1994). This is an essential concept of liberation psychology because without an understanding of the actual etiology of the oppression and subsequent conditions, accurate understandings from the perspective of the oppressed cannot be attained.

The most critical aspect of this principle is that the investigation of societal structures and the recovery of historical memory needs to be conducted by those who are oppressed in partnership with social scientists and practitioners. From the multicultural literature, we also acknowledge that knowing and understanding a particular group's "real" history is a necessary component of effective interventions because it provides the person doing the intervention(s) with information on variables such as pride, values, fears, and beliefs (Sue & Sue, 2016) as well as strengths and weaknesses; these variables can and usually do provide a path to freedom and healing (Chavez, Torres Fernandez, Hipolito-Delgado, & Torres Rivera, 2016).

Deideologizing Everyday Experience

In his writing, Martín-Baró (1986, 1998) described what he called a "cultural stranglehold" on how such circumstances are studied and understood by social scientists, in particular, those with a U.S. orientation. Martín-Baró (1998) suggested that to reach a more balanced socially just and mentally healthy context for these people, the liberation psychologist must study and analyze the dominant messages in light of the experiences of those living on the margins (Tate, Torres Rivera, Brown, & Skaistis, 2013). Similarly, Montero (2009) explained this process as "the conscious construction and reconstruction of an understanding of the world one lives in, and if one has lived circumstances, as part of a totality" (p. 75). Therefore, when psychologists and oppressed people participate in the process of deideologizing, they begin to make sense of their present, real situation in light of recovered historical memory and an evaluation of everyday experience. Thus, in the process of deideologizing, oppressed people can construct their reality by critically questioning the imposed reality and by reflecting on the answers or lack of answers.

Denaturalization

This concept refers to the critical examination of notions, beliefs, and assumptions that we usually take for granted and do not question. That is, many mental health professionals normalize discrimination and oppression, when it should be the other way around—it should be denaturalized, not normalized. Therefore, engaging in denaturalization, we question the interests of power dynamics that lead to the creation of our assumptions. Denaturalization and deideologizing lead to problematization.

Problematization

Problematization is the process of critically analyzing life circumstances and the role(s) they play on the person(s), which questions the explanations and the usual considerations of the situation(s). This process is described as one in which people develop an understanding of the issues faced by oppressed populations directly from the perspective of the oppressed. This process of problematization is tied to conscientization (mobilizing the conscience), but although it includes a methodology to create change, it is not a single set of steps; instead, it is the process of discussing, questioning, and creating a critical reflection in everyday functioning or habits. Therefore, problematization places emphasis on what is recovered from the historical memory, an understanding that is beyond what is be imposed by the ideology (or deideologized) of present circumstances; it focuses on the knowledge of people's strengths related to a particular issue that a group of oppressed individuals are experiencing in a specific context or circumstance. Thus, professionals using liberation psychology approaches are looking to present problems related to inconsistencies between what was the lived experience of these individuals and their beliefs about how it should be. This process is the basis for creating critical thinking and change; without having moved through this process, any understanding of a given problem will remain rooted in oppressive and marginalizing philosophies and histories (Tate et al., 2013).

Virtues of the People

It is imperative to use the virtues of oppressed peoples when working to improve their lived experience. According to Martín-Baró (1998), the virtues of the oppressed people of El Salvador, the country where he lived, can be described as "their ability to deliver and to sacrifice for the collective good, their tremendous faith in the human capacity to change the world, [and] their hope for tomorrow that keeps being violently denied to them" (p. 31). Oppressed peoples have also displayed such strengths and resilience in the United States. This strengths-based approach allows the social scientist to rely on those who are oppressed to produce the tools and energy that may lead to liberation. Furthermore, the process of focusing on the virtues of oppressed peoples provides us with tools that have been used to cope with harsh circumstances for generations and transform them for use as an indispensable tool for liberation.

Conscientization

Working from a liberation psychology stance means the awakening of critical *conscientization* (i.e., critical consciousness) in the person and group. As noted earlier, conscientization is the continuous process of mobilizing the consciousness. In this movement, the person or group is able to liberate a character or characters from situations, facts, or relationships hitherto ignored or unnoticed. This newly gained knowledge or awareness will lead to action or to a move from what is real to what is possible. This is regardless of whether the situation could be considered negative. The term is broad because the purpose is to expand, not to limit. Additionally, critical consciousness not only entails becoming aware of an absolute fact, but instead, it is a process of change and action (Montero, 2016). That is, to become conscious of reality is to become aware of, and involved in, a process of continual discovery and action related to "truth."

In other words, through rediscovering historical memory, deideologizing under-standings of cultural truths, nurturing the virtues of the people, and applying this knowledge to specific contexts and lived experiences through problematiza-tion, the process of critical consciousness emerges and is maintained.

Montero and Sonn (2009) described liberation through conscientization as a process involving a social rupture in the sense of transforming both the con-ditions of inequality and oppression and the institutions and practices produc-ing them. According to the authors, it has a collective nature, but its effects also transform the individuals participating, who, while carrying out material changes, are empowered and develop new forms of social identity.

> It is also a political process in the sense that its point of departure is the conscienti-zation of the participants, who become aware of their rights and duties within the society, developing their citizenship and critical capacities while strengthening democracy and civil society. (Montero & Sonn, 2009, p. 1)

Conscientization is also never complete but instead "brings with it the possibility of a new praxis, which at the same time makes possible new forms of con-sciousness" (Martín-Baró, 1998, p. 40). Therefore, the ongoing process of liber-atory praxis between theory and action provides the foundation for liberation psychology.

Power Dynamics

Liberation psychology focuses on challenging the power dynamics in research and practice—in particular, the dimensions of marginalization and exclusion (Montero et al., 2017). Power is pivotal in attaining wellness, promoting libera-tion, and resisting oppression. Contrary to fragmentary disciplinary discourses, power is never political or psychological; it is always both. The same goes for wellness, liberation, and oppression: They are never political or psychological; they are always both (Prilleltensky & Prilleltensky, 2006). Therefore, power is an important domain that liberation psychologists must consider when working with clients using this theory.

Martín-Baró presented the idea that power was the imposition of A over B to incorporate a social system view (Kagan et al., 2012). Montero expanded on Martín-Baró's definition by adding ideas from the work of Max Weber (Montero et al., 2017) in which power is the probability of one's own will even if resistance is present. In addition, Serrano-Garcia and Lopez Sanchez (1990) presented another concept of power, describing a dissonance between experiences and consciousness, which is also influenced by history and wealth. Nonetheless, the analysis of power in liberation psychology has to do with practicality. This means that it must be able to create change and allows community involvement.

Praxis

As a core foundational construct of liberation psychology, *praxis* is the con-nections between the theory and the action, or, in simpler terms, theory and practice cannot be separated—theory without application has limited use. Therefore, using this as a blueprint, theory cannot exist without practice and vice versa. The product of reclaiming one's history, deideologizing understandings of cultural truths, discovering the virtues of the people, and using this process as a method for making sense of current oppressive circumstances is critical consciousness. Critical consciousness is not only making one's own reality but also becoming awake (Tate et al., 2013). This relationship between a critical view of the past and a creative view of the future develops tension. Watkins and Shulman (2008) defined this tension as

> one motion is deconstructive and critical, looking backward at what we have been doing and thinking that is dysfunctional, dissociative, and destructive; the other motion is moving forward, toward new capacities for imagining, voicing, connecting, empathizing, and celebrating self and others in community. (pp. 28–29)

This understanding and conceptualization of praxis, reflection, and action together is also a manner to describe the truth personified at the present moment.

CONCLUSION

Underlying the concepts of liberation psychology and keeping in mind that "in Freire's terms concepts are action-words: They lead to modes of praxis, in which cognition, politics, epistemology, ontology, and ethics are intertwined in consciousness" (Montero et al., 2017, p. 150). It is essential to mention that, according to Martín-Baró, to liberate someone, psychologists themselves need to be liberated at a personal level. Fals Borda (1999) provided a framework that, if liberation psychologists adopt it, there is no objective observer or removed theorist. In other words, to become awake, congruent, and "real," we must come from the involved, praxis-based angle of the people liberation psychology purports to describe and help. This requires that the psychologist becomes a witness, a partner, the one walking beside, the mirror, and the vessel of faith for the process through which those who have been silenced can discover their full potential for recall of their historical memory, undergo critical analysis, and move toward social action and change (Watkins & Shulman, 2008). This means that all social science research and practice should move toward social change, quality of life, and the improvement of the difficult circumstance for clients. Such change should be driven by the experience, understandings, and actions of these very people (Tate et al., 2013).

The idea and purpose of liberation psychology are to facilitate and guide social change, action, and engagement with oppressed populations. Although the influence of Western psychology can be felt worldwide, liberation psychologists call into question the pragmatic "publish-or-perish" push of that influence, instead focusing primarily on clients' well-being and the quality of life of their communities. They do this by placing the poor and the oppressed first.

This is not to take anything away from scholarship and those whose primary purpose is scholarship but to encourage scholars to produce work that has practical purpose. We know that without scholarship on liberation psychology, furthering its use and development would be close impossible. Therefore, I hope that the contents of this book disseminate the application of liberation psychology to multiple populations and contexts. Martín-Baró was a fierce critic of the higher education system, which he saw as oppressive and narrow-minded because it forced psychologists and other social researchers to concentrate on credential-building at the expense of oppressed populations; this is a frequent criticism from People of Color in the United States, who have been the subjects of numerous studies without the advantage of the knowledge gained returning to benefit them in real life. Martín-Baró called for the creation of praxis-focus involvement, with oppressed populations as a starting point to liberate the academic system. And finally, Freire's bases of reflection–action–reflection dynamics illustrate the fundamental principle of liberation psychology: When working with oppressed or vulnerable populations, a theory that does not have practical application is useless.

REFERENCES

Adams, G., Dobles, I., Gómez, L. H., Kurtiş, T., & Molina, L. E. (2015). Decolonizing psychological science: Introduction to the special thematic section. *Journal of Social and Political Psychology, 3*, 213–238. http://dx.doi.org/10.5964/jspp.v3i1.564

Afuape, T. (2011). *Power, resistance and liberation in therapy with survivors of trauma.* London, England: Routledge.

Afuape, T., & Hughes, G. (Eds.). (2016). *Liberation practices: Toward emotional wellbeing through dialogue.* New York, NY: Routledge.

Akken, R. V., & Taracena, L. P. (2007). *La visión Indígena de la conquista* [The Indigenous vision of the conquest]. Guatemala City, Guatemala: Serviprensa.

Aron, A., & Corne, S. (Eds.). (1996). *Ignacio Martín-Baró: Writings for a liberation psychology.* Cambridge, MA: Harvard University Press.

Bulhan, H. A. (1985). *Frantz Fanon and the psychology of oppression.* New York, NY: Plenum Press.

Cabral, A. (1974). National liberation and culture. *Transition, 45*, 12–17. http://dx.doi.org/10.2307/2935020

Cabral, A., Wood, D., & Rabaka, R. (2016). *Resistance and decolonization.* London, England: Rowman & Littlefield International.

Campbell, C. (2008). Review of Foucault, psychology and the analytics of power [Review of the book *Foucault, psychology and the analytics of power*, by D. Hook, Ed.]. *Journal of Community and Applied Social Psychology, 18*, 645–646. http://dx.doi.org/10.1002/casp.994

Chavez, T. A., Torres Fernandez, I., Hipolito-Delgado, C. P., & Torres Rivera, E. (2016). Unifying liberation psychology and humanistic values to promote social justice in counseling. *The Journal of Humanistic Counseling, 55*, 166–182.

Enriquez, V. G. (1994). *From colonial to liberation psychology: The Philippine experience.* Manila, Philippines: De La Salle University Press.

Fals Borda, O. (1999). Orígenes universales y retos actuales de la IAP (investigación acción participativa) [Universal origins and current challenges of the IAP (participatory action research)]. *Peripecias, 110*, 1–15.

Fanon, F., & Chevalier, H. (1965). *Studies of a dying colonialism.* New York, NY: Grove Press.

Farmer, P. (2003). *Pathologies of power: Health, human rights, and the new war on the poor*. Berkeley: University of California Press.

Freire, P. (1996). *Pedagogy of the oppressed* (Rev. ed.). New York, NY: Penguin Group.

Gaborit, M. (2007). Recordar para vivir: El papel de la memoria histórica en la reparación del tejido social [Remember to live: The role of historical memory in the repair of the social fabric]. *ECA: Estudios Centroamericanos, 740*, 203–218.

Gaborit, M. (2015). Recalibrando la mirada al pasado: Reconciliación y perdón en el posconflicto [Recalibrating the look to the past: Reconciliation and forgiveness in the post-conflict]. *ECA: Estudios Centroamericanos, 740*, 87–105.

Grayshield, L., & Mihecoby, A. (2010). Indigenous ways of knowing as a philosophical base for the promotion of peace and justice in counseling education and psychology. *Journal for Social Action in Counseling and Psychology, 2*(2), 1–16.

Hook, D. (2011). Retrieving Biko: A Black consciousness critique of Whiteness. *African Identities, 9*(1), 19–32. http://dx.doi.org/10.1080/14725843.2011.530442

Hook, D. (2012). *Critical psychology of the postcolonial: The mind of apartheid*. London, England: Routledge. http://dx.doi.org/10.4324/9780203140529

Jamison, D. F. (2013). Amos Wilson: Toward a liberation psychology. *The Journal of Pan African Studies, 6*(2), 9–23.

Kagan, C., Burton, M., Duckett, P., Lawthom, R., & Siddiquee, A. (2012). *Critical community psychology*. Manchester, England: BPS Blackwell.

Martín-Baró, I. (1986). Hacia una psicología de la liberación [Towards a psychology of liberation]. *Boletin de Psicología, 22*, 1–11.

Martín-Baró, I. (1998). *Psicología de la liberación* [Liberation psychology]. Madrid, Spain: Editorial Trotta.

Memmi, A. (2004). *The colonizer and the colonized*. London, England: Routledge, http://dx.doi.org/10.4324/9781315065670

Moane, G. (2014). Liberation psychology, feminism, and social justice psychology. In J. Diaz, Z. Franco, & K. Nastasi, Bonnie (Eds.), *The handbook of social justice and psychology: Fundamental issues and special populations* (Vol. 1, pp. 115–132). Santa Barbara, CA: Praeger.

Montero, M. (2009). Methods for liberation: Critical consciousness in action. In M. Montero & C. C. Sonn (Eds.), *Psychology of liberation: Theory and applications* (pp. 73–91). New York, NY: Springer.

Montero, M. (2016). Psychology of liberation revised: A critique of critique. In B. Gough (Ed.), *The Palgrave handbook of critical social psychology* (pp. 147–161). London, England: Palgrave Macmillan UK.

Montero, M., & Sonn, C. C. (2009). *Psychology of liberation: Theory and applications*. New York, NY: Springer.

Montero, M., Sonn, C. C., & Burton, M. (2017). Community psychology and liberation psychology: A creative synergy for an ethical and transformative praxis. In M. A. Bond, I. Serrano-García, C. B. Keys, & M. Shinn (Eds.), *APA handbook of community psychology: Theoretical foundations, core concepts, and emerging challenges* (Vol. 1, pp. 149–167). Washington, DC: American Psychological Association. http://dx.doi.org/10.1037/14953-007

Moosa-Mitha, M. (2015). Situating anti-oppression theories within critical and difference-centred perspective. In S. Strega & L. Brown (Eds.), *Research as resistance: Revisiting critical, indigenous, and anti-oppressive approaches* (2nd ed., pp. 65–96). Toronto, Ontario, Canada: Canadian Scholars' Press.

Potts, K. L., & Brown, L. (2015). Becoming an anti-oppressive researcher. In S. Strega & L. Brown (Eds.), *Research as resistance: Revisiting critical, indigenous, and anti-oppressive approaches* (2nd ed., pp. 17–41). Toronto, Ontario, Canada: Canadian Scholars' Press.

Prilleltensky, I., & Prilleltensky, O. (2006). *Promoting well-being: Linking personal, organizational, and community change*. Hoboken, NJ: John Wiley.

Serrano-Garcia, I., & Lopez Sanchez, G. (1990). Una perspectiva diferente del poder y el cambio social para la psicología social-comunitaria [A different perspective of power and social change for social-community psychology]. *Revista de Ciencias Sociales, XXIX*, 349–382.

Sue, D. W., & Sue, D. (2016). *Counseling the culturally diverse: Theory and practice* (7th ed.). Hoboken, NJ: Wiley.

Tate, K. A., Torres Rivera, E., Brown, E., & Skaistis, L. (2013). Foundations for liberation: Social justice, liberation psychology, and counseling. *Revista Interamericana De Psicología/Interamerican Journal of Psychology, 47*, 373–382.

Thompson, C. E., & Alfred, D. M. (2009). Black liberation psychology and practice. In H. A. Neville, B. M. Tynes, & S. O. Utsey (Eds.), *Handbook of African American psychology* (pp. 483–494). Thousand Oaks, CA: Sage.

Torres Fernandez, I., & Torres-Rivera, E. (2014). Moving through trauma in grief in children impacted by the violence in the U.S.–Mexico border: A liberation psychology approach. In M. T. Garrett (Ed.), *Youth and adversity: Psychology and influences of child and adolescent resilience and coping* (pp. 209–226). New York, NY: Nova Science.

Watkins, M., & Shulman, H. (2008). *Toward psychologies of liberation*. New York, NY: Palgrave Macmillan.

3

Liberation Psychology and Racism

Raúl Quiñones-Rosado

Racism, like sexism, genderism, classism, colonialism, Eurocentrism, and all other forms of oppression, is a system of thought and behavior that is deeply entrenched in every aspect of culture (Hill Collins, 2000; Moane, 1999). Present in all spheres of human activity, racism shapes interpersonal dynamics and intergroup relationships, as well as institutional structures, policies, and practices. A legacy of advantage for White people and a history of oppression for People of Color, racism persists as a defining feature of modernity (Mignolo & Walsh, 2018; Quijano, 2000) and continues to pervade our society as an inescapable structural force that hinders human well-being at all levels.

Such a pervasive and powerful force could not have survived and endured the past 5 centuries since its emergence during Europe's trans-Atlantic colonial projects without also being deeply embedded within the psyche, both individual and collective. In effect, it is through the dynamic relationship between the personal and collective dimensions of life, between individuals and the institutions, that the culture of racism is transmitted across generations and the cycle of advantage and oppression, of dominance and subordination, of inclusion and exclusion, of superiority and inferiority is perpetuated.

In this chapter, I focus on some of many important psychological, social, and cultural aspects of racial identity from the perspective of a decolonial framework of human well-being. I also refer to *consciousness-in-action* (Quiñones-Rosado, 2007), a decolonial process model of conscientization for liberation and transformation, if only in broad strokes given the parameters of this chapter.

http://dx.doi.org/10.1037/0000198-004
Liberation Psychology: Theory, Method, Practice, and Social Justice, L. Comas-Díaz and E. Torres Rivera (Editors)

In doing so, I present basic concepts and premises concerning racism as it functions, primarily in the United States, as well as in Latin America, and, ostensibly, with applicability elsewhere across the globe.

TOWARD A DECOLONIAL MODEL OF WELL-BEING

The point of departure for conceptualizing a psychology of liberation (Martín-Baró, 1994; Montero & Sonn, 2009; Watkins & Shulman, 2008) in the context of racial oppression is not racism itself but a model of human well-being, conceptions, frameworks, and worldviews held by various original peoples of the Americas. The North American Lakota Medicine Wheel (Bopp & Bopp, 2001), a decolonial model of human well-being, is such a framework; it is also consistent with South American principles of well-being: *sumak kawsay* in Aymara, *suma kamaña* in Kichua, and *buen vivir* in Spanish (Gudynas, 2011, 2014). Common to these non-Western paradigms for well-being, human beings are conceived as integral to, and in a sustainable relationship with, all other beings, elements, the Earth itself, and beyond. Human well-being occurs in the context of, and is dependent on, an individual's personal and a people's collective ability to meet challenges and adversities in their environment through the intelligent, skillful, and ethical use of strengths and resources available to them. Person and community coexist—dynamically, interdependently, and integrally.

Integral well-being, through life's natural cycles in the face of ever-present challenges and adversities, is sustained by maintaining or restoring balance to and between the physical, mental, spiritual, and emotional aspects of being at the personal level, always within the context of collective life as organized through a community's economic, political, cultural, and social arrangements (Bopp & Bopp, 2001; Quiñones-Rosado, 2007). In contrast to Eurocentric linear, dichotomous, and hierarchical logic, the principle of balance implies that no aspect or dimension of living is first or last, bigger or smaller, more or less important than another.

Balance, as a functional application of will, volition, intention, and purpose, demands action. Healing or restorative actions, which may call for a specific personal (e.g., physical) or a general collective (e.g., economic) response, are ascertained and applied contextually as appropriate. Yet responsive (non-reactive) actions to maintain or restore balance are guided by another key principle of integral well-being. Although balance is consistent with the notion of equilibrium among all aspects and dimensions, harmony is about maintaining or restoring congruence between all aspects and dimensions. Harmony involves the intuitive directing of attention, awareness, consciousness, and wisdom; it requires pause and reflection necessary to disrupt unconscious reactivity. A person's responses, or the actions of a group, to restore balance must be harmonious, consistent, and congruous with the beliefs, values, and worldview shared within the culture if it is to (re)produce integral well-being. Otherwise, reactive behaviors that are internally (psychologically) or externally (socially) incongruent produce cognitive dissonance—not to mention economic inequities, political dissidence, cultural clashes, and social discord—that, unattended, produce disharmony, lack of balance, and hinder overall integral well-being.

Temporary states of integral well-being in which balance and harmony are attained and sustained over time and circumstances lead to growth through stages of development. Again, in contrast to Eurocentric conceptions of development as linear, fragmented, and hierarchical imposed by the colonial nature of knowledge, being, and power, this decolonial framework conceives development as growth, a process of maturation that emerges naturally through stages. Stages in a developmental process are not to be understood as isolated steps in a linear sequence, nor as mere objectives toward an ultimate goal, but as moments along an unfolding continuum. Development is not framed by notions of "progress" that would distance a person, a community, or a people from an original place or moment, far from physical rootedness or relational connection. From the perspective of this decolonial framework, growth and development emerge or unfold as one's capacity for maintaining balance and harmony increases within ever-challenging environments and contexts. Growth through the stages of development involves maintaining capacities of earlier stages while new capacities emerge and are tested in contexts of increased complexity. In this manner, one does not abandon perceptions, narratives, values, or identities of earlier stages of development, but rather includes and transcends them in subsequent developmental stages (Wilber, 1999). In this context, regression could be understood as a momentary and contextual contraction into an emotional state associated with earlier developmental stages, yet not a return to that earlier stage; the psychological tasks completed, capacities attained, and lessons learned are not lost but merely temporarily unavailable, as these can be accessed once again by restoring balance and harmony.

Development implies movement through time, and thus from this decolonial lens, nonlinear growth implies expansion of perspective (breadth, depth, and height), of transcendence (to include and move beyond), of our sense of "past," "present," and "future." Maintaining or restoring balance and harmony through the stages of development is facilitated by an ever-expanding awareness of the past–present–future continuum—that where we are (personally and collectively) in the present moment is as a result of where we (personally and collectively) have been in the past with implications for the future. This is not to say that our future is predetermined but that it is certainly inextricably linked to our personal and collective past. Besides this obvious conclusion, this notion of nonlinear time may connect us more intimately with our ancestors, with the relevance of our ancestral knowledge, and with the significance of our shared history.

The shared history that most directly frames our capacity for integral well-being today is the history of colonialism. The colonial projects of Europe in the Americas not only imposed a race-based economic system founded on patriarchic, distorted Christian fundamentalist and Euro-feudal politico-militaristic traditions, it also imposed Eurocentric epistemologies and axiologies (Ani, 1994; Dussel, 2000; Maldonado-Torres, 2007; Mignolo & Walsh, 2018; Quijano, 2014) that have, to this day, subordinated, if not kept hidden, worldviews, systems of knowledge, and ways of life that could be conducive to the integral well-being of all people.

It is in this context that racism, as a central force within that colonial project that persists to this day, continues to be an assault on humanity and a hindrance to *buen vivir*.

DEFINING RACISM

Although the notion that race can be biologically defined has been debunked by science for decades, after more than 500 years of dominant cultural narratives, oppressive social dynamics, exploitative economic relationships, and repressive political institutional structures guided by this social construct, the concept of race is as real today as ever. As baseless a concept as it has been proven to be, race remains the primary predictor of outcomes across a population: in health, wealth, and income; in education, employment, and housing; rates of arrests, convictions, sentencing, and incarceration; and representation in media and politics. By every measure of human well-being in the United States, Whites, collectively, fare far better than People of Color: Asians, Pacific Islanders, Latinxs, Indigenous Americans, and, most significantly, Blacks (Hayes-Greene & Love, 2018).

Racism, as a system of thought and behavior based on the presumed superiority of a White race (people of European origin) and the presumed inferiority of other races (people of origins elsewhere in the world), is the only reasonable explanation for the persistence and pervasiveness of this historical pattern of inequity and injustice (Ani, 1994; Kendi, 2016).

Although the structural and institutional nature of racism has been well established, the dominant narrative in our society—that racism is primarily, if not exclusively, about individual acts of cruelty and bigotry—is still widely shared across racial groups. All too often, racism is simply believed to be rooted in people's ignorance and race prejudices, thoughts, attitudes, and behaviors, motivated by disdain of people of a different color or, perhaps, even outright hatred of the racial "other." This commonly held view mistakenly reduces the complex systemic reality of racism to individualized psychological (cognitive, emotional, and behavioral) factors and interpersonal sociological (cultural, political, and relational) dynamics, phenomena presumed to affect only some individuals (Bonilla-Silva, 2010). Such limited understandings of racism—what it is, how and when it came into being, and why it still matters—leaves concerned citizens in all fields of endeavor, including the field of psychology, unable to address this enduring core societal problem effectively.

A critical study of history and culture of the Americas reveals that People of Color, as well as their land, labor, bodies, knowledge, and ways of life, came to be perceived, conceived, valued, and treated as mere resources to be controlled and exploited for the exclusive advancement of those who eventually came to refer to themselves as "White" (Dussel, 2013; Feagin, 2013; Zinn, 1980; see also Chapter 10, this volume). Although beyond the scope of this chapter, a historical analysis of the process of racialization is necessary to adequately understand the psycho–social–cultural impacts of racism. Functional definitions of racism that have been useful to racial justice movements and antiracism organizing founded on critical historical analyses include race prejudice plus power (Chisom & Washington, 1997) and the abuse or misuse of institutional power by White people (Barndt, 2007), or even "White supremacy enforced by the State" ("Facing the Truth"; Shemel, 2014). Expanding on a definition used by the racial justice education organization Dismantling Racism Works (2004/2017), the Racial Equity Institute proposes that racism is, first and foremost, a "system of advantage based on race" and, consequently, a "system of oppression based on race," both of which are grounded in "a White supremacy system supported by [and dependent on] an all-class collaboration called 'White' created to end cross-racial labor solidarity" (Hayes-Greene, Hunter, & Plihcik, 2018, p. 10). This analysis goes on to point out that the goal of racism, historically, was to create a system that produced and reproduced advantage for White people, and the oppression of People of Color was the strategy through which that goal was to be achieved. Meanwhile, White supremacy as an ideology would be the dominant cultural paradigm, psychologically embedded within individuals, ever-present in social interactions, and, most important, deeply entrenched within all of society's economic, political, cultural, and social institutions.

While these definitions of racism are contextual to the United States, given the historical parallels and moments of coincidence throughout the Americas, north and south, they are also relevant and, for the most part, applicable to societies in Latin America and the Caribbean (Godreau et al., 2013; Wade, 2010). Moreover, with the globalization of U.S. racism and, more broadly, the hegemonic pervasiveness of Eurocentric coloniality of knowledge, power, and being worldwide, these definitions and analyses may well be applicable or pertinent to other racialized societies as well (Duncan & Bowman, 2009; Moane, 1999). In defining racism, one must not overlook the significance of social and institutional power. Social and institutional power are the means through which persons, communities, and groups access and control the resources and opportunities required for well-being and development; they are the means through which to exercise the collective will of any organized society and, as such, are necessary for the survival and continuity of its people. White supremacy as a mere ideology could not have had its ongoing devastating impact on humanity without control of economic, political, cultural, and social institutions, whether in the United States, Europe, or their colonies around the world. It has been the misuse or abuse of social and institutional power, guided by White supremacy—compounded by patriarchy, genderism, capitalism, colonialism, Eurocentrism, and other oppressive ideologies within the matrix of domination—that continues to hinder integral well-being and development.

KEY CONCEPTS FOR AN ANTIRACIST DECOLONIAL LIBERATION PSYCHOLOGY

Without doubt, 5 centuries of systemic racism and other expressions of coloniality have produced a legacy of cumulative benefits that has advantaged White people, collectively, in the process producing exploitation, marginalization, and exclusion that has historically disadvantaged People of Color, collectively. Yet, beyond the dichotomous, linear, and hierarchical logic of Eurocentric thought, given how racism as a system of thought and behavior violates the principles of balance and harmony central to the notion of integral well-being and development, one may also observe, and conclude, that racism deeply harms and violates the inherent humanity of all people—both White people and People of Color. On this basis, a primary task for a psychology of liberation is to develop knowledge, methods, and practices for restoring integral well-being by supporting processes that liberate all people from racism. We must continue to create a psychology that decolonizes, breaks with Eurocentric patterns of thought and behavior that sustain racism and other expressions of coloniality (Maldonado-Torres, 2007; Mignolo & Walsh, 2018; Quijano, 2014), and replaces these with new knowledge and ways of being that foster our capacities for integral development, in the process producing a radical transformation of culture (Dussel, 2002; Maldonado-Torres, 2008).

Among many concepts central to the development of an antiracist decolonial liberation psychology, in this chapter, I briefly address these core concepts: racial identity development, psychocultural aspects of racial identity, and internalized racial oppression.

Racial Identity As a Developmental Process

Racism produces racial identity. Racial identity as an aspect of the self-in-society would not exist without race, which, in turn, would not exist without cultural and institutional racism. As racism continues to be reproduced through economic practices politically imposed through public policy, people today continue to be racialized. The race categories to which people are assigned not only largely determine a person's place or rank in economic, political, cultural, and social hierarchies, they also psychologically shape a person's sense of belonging, with which entire groups of people begin to identify (collectively), with which individuals begin to internalize as a core aspect of being, central to their sense of self and "I-am-ness" (Rowe, Bennett, & Atkinson, 1994; Worrell, Cross, & Vandiver, 2001). Therefore, children born and raised within cultures in which every person is viewed, ranked, and related to on the basis of the presumed superiority of White people develop an identity, an implicit sense of self, that is racialized in relationship to White people and to Whiteness. Who they are as a person, or rather, who they perceive, think, believe, and feel themselves to be is based on their racial group membership. Then, as an individual member of a racial collective, their racial identity is based on what it means to be—or not to be—White. Racial identity, then, is the result of a gradual process of reconstructing race psychologically, within the subjective sense of being, of individuals living within racist society. Understanding racial identity as a process of social identity development across stages can serve as a useful framework for liberation psychology.

Social identity development theory (Hardiman & Jackson, 1997), an adaptation of both Black and White identity development theories applied to other racial and social group identities, serves as a functional model because it describes patterns and characteristics generally shared across all social group identities. According to this developmental model, racial identity, like other social group identities, emerges progressively from one stage to the next, with each stage including and transcending the developmental lessons and perspectives of all previous stages. Patterns of thought and behavior (e.g., perspectives, narratives, beliefs, attitudes, feelings) of preceding stages are incorporated into subsequent ones, and although these patterns may have been outgrown and thus are no longer necessary to the current stage, they may still be consciously accessed or unconsciously triggered.

In this model, racial identity develops in stages along a continuum: from *naive* to *acceptance* to *resistance* to *redefinition* to *internalization*. At the *naive* stage, a child has no social consciousness, is unaware of racial narratives, and therefore has not yet developed a sense of self as a racial being. As they are exposed to social interactions and cultural narratives across racial difference and dynamics of power, the child enters the stage of acceptance. Still years away from developing any capacity for critical analysis, the child begins to accept dominant narratives of racial superiority and inferiority as a given. Whether in adolescence or much later, people enter the stage of *resistance* as they begin to experience cognitive dissonance and emotional distress within the social environment; they begin to question, challenge, or confront narratives, people, and relationships that conform to or comply with White supremacist culture. Once their passive observing or active questioning and challenging begins to produce answers that are more congruent with their experience and critical analysis, resistance expands into *redefinition*. At this stage new and positive narratives reframe the narratives of White supremacy, which in turn give rise to a new appreciation of one's own racial group and a more self-affirming racial identity. Eventually, as nurtured by a supportive social environment, the redefined racial identity becomes firmly rooted and largely unconsciously integrated into the sense of self-in-society, indicative of the stage of *internalization*. As a person's racial identity is firmly internalized, stage development along other social identities (e.g., class, gender, sexuality, nationally, religion) may be accelerated, as new cognitive–emotional–behavioral patterns and insights may be generalized across other or all dynamics of power—a synthesis of social identities into a stage of integration of self—liberated, transformed, and decolonized. Yet it would appear that this developmental process beyond the stage of resistance rarely, if ever, occurs spontaneously. A primary task of decolonial antiracist liberation psychology, then, is to actively foster and support racial identity development across all stages.

Cultural Aspects of Racial Identity

Within the first years of life, during the naive stage of racial identity, children begin to understand to which social groups they belong and to which they do not. Further, through implicit or explicit messages in the social environment, they begin to psychologically internalize what it means to be a member of their particular race, as well as their "place" within the racial hierarchy prescribed by White supremacist culture. Like structural racism, racial identity is a product of the coloniality of knowledge, being, and power and therefore expresses itself within the constraints of its hierarchical and dichotomous logic. This racial self in turn develops or emerges in relationship to core cultural aspects of self-identity within the social environment: self-image, self-concept, self-esteem, and self-love.

Racial self-image emerges as part of one's identity, or sense of I-am-ness, early in life, initially and primarily on the basis of perceiving traits—sights, sounds, smells, tastes, textures—associated with "race." Beyond sorting perceptually for sameness and difference, and later affectively sorting for belonging and not belonging, a child's image of self is shaped within and by the social milieu of White supremacy. Children's self-image develops or evolves as they compare and contrast themselves in accordance with a dominant cultural aesthetic, with that which is deemed by White culture to be "beautiful." Including, yet beyond, affirmations of their own beauty within the family context, a child's racial self-image is shaped by recurring exposure to both explicit messages and implicit racial/racist narratives of beauty. Because skin color, hair texture, facial features and body sizes were historically central to the social construction of race and remain central to racial narrative, these characteristics are among its most obvious defining parameters. It is in this context, compounded by the dichotomous logic of Eurocentric thought, that children psychologically internalize and cognitively imprint an image of self as either "beautiful" or "ugly" associated with permanent, physical aspects of their being.

Racial self-concept comes into being based on a person's racial self-image, on how they have learned to perceive themselves. Yet racial self-concept relates to the way in which they conceive (think, analyze, interpret, and describe) their identity as a racialized being: a person whose body (and behaviors) and patterns of thought (and language) are either similar to, or different from, those of other racialized peoples. Again, within White Eurocentric epistemological contexts, whether at home, school, or elsewhere in society, children begin to conceive of themselves in relationship to a racialized "truth," which determines, among many things, what is the "correct" answer to this question; which is the "right" way of thinking or the "proper" way of speaking; who is the "smart" person. And therefore, as a member of their particular racial group, are they "correct, right, proper, and smart?" Or the opposite? One might also say that if racial self-image is based on how racial groups are portrayed in the collective imagery, then racial self-concept, to a great extent, derives from how the racial self-image is described and articulated within the cultural narratives of White supremacy.

Racial self-esteem emerges as images of a racial self are seen through the lens of a White aesthetic, which are then interpreted through a Euro-dominant epistemology and pro-White racial narratives, on which one's worth within a Eurocentric axiology is determined. It is during this aspect of the psychocultural racial identity development process that people come to evaluate, judge, and rank themselves—and identify their self—in relationship to Eurocentric values and White cultural standards. A person's racial self-esteem reflects their answers to fundamental questions of who they are: What does it mean to be White, Black, Latinx, Asian, or Indigenous in a society where the Image of Beauty, the Concept of Truth (right–wrong), and the Judgment of the Good (vs. bad or evil) are predetermined by White culture; what is my worth in a society with a racial hierarchy that places White people as the model of humanity, the standard of beauty and intelligence, the ones who shape culture, who have the power to define reality itself, and who have come to represent the very face of God?

Racial self-love speaks to the extent to which a person's racial identity is rooted in a deep ontological awareness of their inherent value and sense of human dignity. In this context, self-love is the culmination of the dynamic, layered and textured self-image, self-concept and self-esteem as a racialized being and to what extent a person may consider themselves worthy of love and respect. Within the social environment of White dominant culture, personal self-identity that emerges through our collective racialization is a distortion of what might otherwise emerge within an environment aligned with the principles of *buen vivir*. Unsurprisingly, for People of Color, this process of socialization within White culture tends to produce negative self-image, limiting self-concept, low self-esteem, and a lack of self-love. Meanwhile, for White people, socialization within dominant culture tends to produce a self-image, self-concept, self-esteem, and self-love that, although seemingly positive and affirming of self, is also distorted, biased, and ultimately false.

Internalized Racism in the Social Environment

Internalized racism expresses attitudes or predispositions in thinking and feeling rooted in the coloniality of knowledge, being, and power in the social environment. As such, it reveals the psycho–social–cultural perspective or standpoint from which a person relates to others both within and across racial identities. Patterns commonly exhibited by White people are referred to as *internalized racial superiority* of the racially advantaged, while for People of Color these are known as *internalized racial inferiority* of the racially oppressed. *Internalized racial inferiority* comprises patterns of thought and behavior commonly observed and shared within and across racially subordinated groups. These patterns have generally emerged across generations as defensive mechanisms to contend with brutal historical realities of racial subjugation, abuse, violence, and death of People of Color by virtue of their racialization as beings presumed to be inferior, if not outright less than human. The legacy of this collective, historical, and unhealed psychological trauma, compounded by present-day acts or threats of racial violence, whether implicit or explicit, real, perceived, or imagined, internalized racial inferiority developed as a means—albeit distorted or dysfunctional—for personal and collective survival. As such, internalized racial inferiority expresses an acceptance by People of Color, individually and collectively, of the false premise of their presumed inferiority and belief in the false dominant cultural narratives of the presumed superiority of White people. For a People of Color, internalized racial inferiority, then, is a conscious or unconscious rejection of their own racial group, of their own racial identity, and ultimately of their own self (Bulhan, 1985; Fanon, 1952).

There are numerous behavioral manifestations of internalized racial inferiority, many of which reflect harmful psychosocial adaptations to White culture by People of Color, including lateral hostility within and across racial groups of color, or our collusion with White fragility, institutional tokenism, and White organizational culture at the expense of other People of Color. Among those pertaining more directly to aspects of racial identity is colorism (Chandler, 2017; Chavez-Dueñas, Adames, & Organista, 2014). Primarily associated with skin color and other physical traits, colorism is based on conceptions of beauty historically established and still generally prevalent within White supremacy culture. It reflects how a Person of Color is ranked, and thus ranks oneself, relative to other People of Color along a continuum within a hierarchy of beauty, with physical traits associated with Whiteness as the highest standard. Not merely subjective evaluations or emotional experiences at the intrapersonal level, colorism extends its negative impact to others because it undermines relationships at the interpersonal level (among family members, friends, colleagues, etc.) and across generations. This White-aesthetic ranking occurs within all subordinated racial groups—Black, Latinx, Asian, or Indigenous—where a light-skinned Person of Color, not deemed quite as beautiful as a White person, is typically considered more so than someone darker. Beyond skin tone, this ranking is further nuanced by hair texture, size and shape of nose, lips, eyes, and other facial and body features.

The logic and dynamics of colorism also extend within and across ethnic or national identity groups, between peoples from countries where a globalized, Eurocentric, racist coloniality of being has also been imposed. Not to be confused with xenophobia (fear, dislike, and distrust of people of another country or culture), *ethnocentric colorism* refers to race-based prejudice of people from one colonized nation against those from another colonized people—all of which have been racialized as non-White by European colonizers. Although often disguised as nationalistic preference, ethnocentric colorism, too, is rooted in anti-Black, anti-Indigenous, anti–dark skin and pro-White bias. Tensions between Puerto Ricans and Dominicans, or Dominicans and Haitians, or Chileans and Bolivians, or U.S. Blacks and Nigerians, or Chinese and Filipino—all of which have been racialized as People of Color is more likely rooted in each group's internalization of a hierarchical ranking and their self-perceived proximity to Eurocentric Whiteness and their self-assessed distance from colonial narratives of what it means to be "Asian," "Indian," or "Black" in the Americas.

Distancing refers to the process of creating psychological, if not also geographic, distance between self and one's family and community of color. It is often revealed when People of Color prefer and begin to adopt behavior patterns (e.g., language, speech, accents, fashion, cultural preferences, choice of friends, partners) typically associated with White culture. These preferences or choices are often explained or justified using the dominant culture's Eurocentric notions of progress, advancement and "moving up the ladder of success," or offered as evidence of "open-minded" or "postracial" attitudes concerning White people and White culture. Distancing as a personal strategy to seek social and economic status by moving into White communities, social spaces, educational environments and cultural contexts is often an expression of denial or rejection of one's own racial identity and racial narratives associated with those spaces. Even when not involving a literal, physical separation, distancing may be more of an attempt to counter racial shame than a strategy for securing personal survival or material advancement.

Like distancing, assimilation involves attempts, whether conscious or unconscious, to attain access to resources and opportunities historically reserved exclusively for White people by getting ever closer or becoming culturally similar to Whites. Yet beyond adopting ways of, and occupying spaces in proximity to, White people, assimilation refers to strategies to eradicate one's racial identity as a Person of Color and replace it with an assumed White racial identity. It reflects efforts to become *similar to*, although never quite the same as, White people by substituting one's cultural norms and standards with those of Whites. Although one may never be accepted as a bona fide member of the White racial collective, the goal of assimilation is to become—or, at minimum, be seen and ultimately treated—*as if* one were a member of the White collective. If perceptible markers of racial difference are unsurmountable (phenotype or accent), the assimilation impulse may employ other strategies for bringing future generations closer to Whiteness and, eventually, into White membership. Despite being rooted in survival strategies in the context of racism, assimilation as an expression of internalized racial inferiority reflects the deep cognitive–emotional–relational damage to self-identity caused by historical structural racism. In contrast, unsurprisingly, for White persons, being raised in the same culture that presumes the racial superiority of White people over other racial groups—albeit on the basis of myths, hidden histories, distorted narratives, stereotypes, and other socially constructed falsehoods—tends to result in the psychological *internalization of racial superiority*.

Internalized racial superiority is a predisposition that begins to express itself in White people during the acceptance stage of racial identity development. One common way this attitude expresses itself is as individualism: a sense of self as "an individual," separate and independent of membership in the White racial collective, as if inherently disconnected from community, somehow insulated from the social environment, and uniquely unaffected by the history of racism and the legacy of White supremacy. This pattern of White individualism is consistent with the dominant politico-economic ideology of liberalism and its belief in the inherent rights of the individual over the collective. Unaware of the historical advantage inherited through structural racism, individualism tends to foster in White people the naive belief that their achievements are fully based on their own merits. Yet when the experiences of racial others must be acknowledged, individualism becomes unconsciously collective in its embrace of the Eurocentric coloniality of knowledge, being, and power; the perspectives, worldviews, values, and experiences commonly shared by White people are implicitly or explicitly affirmed, if not imposed, as the standard, the "right way," what is "normal," and ultimately truth and reality itself. This internalized sense of racial superiority is often accompanied by *the right to comfort* and a *sense of entitlement* to privileged access to resources and opportunities—within a materialistic worldview premised on beliefs regarding the inherent scarcity of resources and the limited availability of opportunities. Like internalized racial inferiority, *internalized racial superiority* reflects a fundamentally distorted sense of self, one that generally leaves White people unaware of the personal implications of racism in their lives and, moreover, ill-equipped to deal with challenges concerning race in the social environment (Diangelo, 2018).

CONSCIOUSNESS-IN-ACTION

Both the psychocultural aspects of racial identity and the manifestations of internalized racism described in this chapter are expressed primarily during the acceptance stage of the racial identity development process. Much of the work of an antiracist decolonial liberation psychology, then, is to effectively reexamine and disrupt the narratives of White supremacy and interrupt and replace cognitive–emotional–relational patterns of internalized racial oppression in support of people's transition from acceptance into resistance and beyond into subsequent stages of racial identity development. *Consciousness-in-action* (Quiñones-Rosado, 2007), a term rooted in Freire's (2005) *conscientization*, refers to a process of fostering critical consciousness through ongoing cycles of action and reflection toward personal and collective liberation, beyond dichotomies of oppressor and oppressed. From the perspective of consciousness-in-action, liberation from the dynamics of advantage and oppression, on the basis of racial identity or any other social group identity, occurs when consciousness and will—awareness and volition, attention and intention—come together in deliberate, disciplined, and sustained ethical response.

Consciousness-in-action involves a sequenced cycle, the first step of which is to *perceive*, reexamine, or take a closer look at a problem. Examined from a diversity of perspective, one may then *(re)cognize* patterns of thought and behavior, then critically reinterpret events and reframe dominant narratives. Reframing for new, deeper meaning, however, also requires perceiving and recognizing cognitive dissonance that comes into clearer view in relationship to one's core values (beyond a Eurocentric axiology) and one's core identity (the self beyond one's multiple social identities). Such a reframing of meaning requires a person to *understand* in the context of moral self-reassessment. This reevaluating of an internalized Eurocentric worldview relative to other value systems may potentially result in a crisis of identity indicative of a transition into a subsequent developmental stage, a transition often characterized by unintended emotional–relational reactivity, a crisis necessary to cultivate the capacity to consciously *respond*. Response, then, involves the ability to catch ourselves in the midst of replicating old patterns of internalized advantage or oppression and pause long enough to interrupt the pattern, so that we may consciously choose a course of action that is, instead, ethically realigned with our core values and our deeper self.

A primary strategy of antiracist liberation psychology–informed interventions is to problematize structural, cultural, and internalized racism to subvert the dominant narratives of White supremacy culture and, in doing so, to reframe and decolonize racism at all levels. Regardless of the sphere of influence at which our work is directed—individual, family, community, institution, systemic— liberating interventions involve eliciting a person's will, or a collective's willingness and (re)directing their attention to perceive, recognize, understand, and respond to racism to disrupt and counter its effects in any—and ultimately all—of aspects and dimensions within the sphere of human activity.

An application of this process to support and foster an individual's racial identity development into "liberated" stages of growth might include helping them *perceive* and identify patterns of thought and behavior within themselves that are associated with internalized racial oppression. Willing to engage such self-exploration, the person can then begin to reexamine and *recognize* early socializing experiences or implicit racial biases supported by shared dominant-cultural narratives, an exploration further assisted by the study of historically accurate information and exposure to decolonial cross-racial perspectives. This process of self-reflective critical analysis of self-in-society and of I-am-ness in relationship to other racialized persons and groups then allows for deeper exploration of the core dissonance—lack of harmony and congruence—between their perceptions, ideas, beliefs, values, and behaviors: the conflict between who they, heretofore, have imagined themselves to be and who they, now, from an antiracism–decolonial perspective, more accurately understand themselves to be. Understanding is, then, a reassessment of values, of moral significance, of ontological meaning requiring a reconciliation of incongruent narratives or a synthesis of internal contradictions, which in turn allows, or demands, a more authentic expression of inherent human principles of balance and harmony in sustainable relationship with all people, other beings, and the planet.

To actualize this depth of insight and moral reassessment, one must express it through conscious action in the social environment. Breaking with lifelong (or historical) patterns of emotional reactivity, unconscious and largely normalized in the context of structural racism and the culture of White supremacy, requires ethical response. Response, unlike emotional reactivity, is conscious. In the context of consciousness-in-action, response refers to realignment of critical awareness and decolonized understanding: an act of will, attention, and intention aligned in ethical action for the purpose of *buen vivir* or integral well-being.

Ethical response does not occur in isolation but in authentic relationship with others in ways that transcend, without bypassing, the historical collective reactivity of racism and allows us to expand beyond. From a position of ethical response, we may continue the ongoing cycle of action and reflection, the unending spiral of consciousness-in-action toward liberation and transformation.

CONCLUSION

As racism—cultural, institutional, interpersonal, and psychologically internalized—is socially constructed, it can, and must, be deconstructed and dismantled. Developmental processes that help us reframe our racial identities, generate critical consciousness, and move into committed engagement toward liberation from racism in all its expressions may occur organically through one's life experiences. However, it is more likely these developmental processes will only occur through intentional antiracism actions: consciousness-raising educational programs, cultural events, political advocacy, social activism, and community organizing, as well as through a transdisciplinary array of interventions from an antiracist liberation psychology framework. Our guiding purpose within liberation psychology, then, must be to intentionally interrupt the cycle of racism anywhere within this complex system. Aware that the coloniality of knowing, being, and doing that is fundamental to White supremacy hinders the emergence of a true human identity, antiracist liberation psychologists must commit to decolonizing knowledge and developing practices that transform current cultural paradigms into ways of being that (re)produce integral well-being and development—*buen vivir*—for all people. Meanwhile, decolonial antiracist liberation psychologists must take our rightful place in collective efforts to free people from the dehumanizing effects of White supremacy, patriarchy, classism, and other forms of oppression that not only corrupt our very sense of self, but that undermine our capacity to relate and to connect in solidarity and love, further hindering our ability to jointly solve other social justice, environmental, and global urgencies.

REFERENCES

Ani, M. (1994). *Yurugu: An Afrikan-centered critique of European cultural thought and behavior*. Baltimore, MD: Afrikan World Books.

Barndt, J. (2007). *Understanding and dismantling racism: The twenty-first century challenge to White America*. Minneapolis, MN: Fortress Press.

Bonilla-Silva, E. (2010). *Racism without racists: Color-blind racism and racial inequality in contemporary America* (3rd ed.). New York, NY: Rowman & Littlefield.

Bopp, J., & Bopp, M. (2001). *Recreating the world: A practical guide to building sustainable communities*. Calgary, Alberta, Canada: Four Worlds Press.

Bulhan, H. A. (1985). *Frantz Fanon and the psychology of oppression*. New York, NY: Plenum Press. http://dx.doi.org/10.1007/978-1-4899-2269-4

Chandler, J. (2017). Confronting colorism. In L. L. Martin, H. D. Horton, C. Herring, V. M. Keith, & M. Thomas (Eds.), *Color struck* (pp. 143–156). Rotterdam, Netherlands: Sense. http://dx.doi.org/10.1007/978-94-6351-110-0_7

Chavez-Dueñas, N. Y., Adames, H. Y., & Organista, K. C. (2014). Skin-color prejudice and within-group racial discrimination: Historical and current impact on Latino/a populations. *Hispanic Journal of Behavioral Sciences, 36*(1), 3–26. http://dx.doi.org/10.1177/0739986313511306

Chisom, R., & Washington, M. (1997). *Undoing racism: A philosophy of international social change* (2nd ed.). New Orleans, LA: The People's Institute Press.

Diangelo, R. (2018). *White fragility*. Boston, MA: Beacon Press.

Dismantling Racism Works. (2004/2017). *What is racism? Racism defined.* Retrieved from http://www.dismantlingracism.org/racism-defined.html

Duncan, N., & Bowman, B. (2009). Liberating South African psychology: The legacy of racism and the pursuit of representative knowledge production. In M. Montero & C. C. Sonn (Eds.), *Psychology of liberation*. New York, NY: Springer Science + Business Media.

Dussel, E. (2000). *Ética de la liberación: En la edad de la globalización y de la exclusion* [Ethics of liberation: In the age of globalization and exclusion]. Madrid, Spain: Editorial Trotta.

Dussel, E. (2002). World system and "trans"-modernity. *Nepantla, 2*, 221–244.

Dussel, E. (2013). *Ethics of liberation: In the age of globalization and exclusion*. Durham, NC: Duke University Press.

Fanon, F. (1952). *Black skin, white masks*. New York, NY: Grove Press.

Feagin, J. R. (2013). *The white racial frame: Centuries of racial framing and counter-framing*. New York, NY: Routledge. http://dx.doi.org/10.4324/9780203076828

Freire, P. (2005). *Pedagogy of the oppressed*. New York, NY: Continuum International.

Godreau, I., Franco-Ortíz, M., Lloréns, H., Reinat-Pumarejo, M., Canabal-Torres, I., & Gaspar-Concepción, J. (2013). *Arrancando mitos de raíz: Guía para una enseñenaza antirracista de la herencia africana en Puerto Rico* [Breaking root myths: Guide to an antiracist teaching of African heritage in Puerto Rico]. Cayey, Puerto Rico: Instituto de Investigaciones Interdisciplinarias, University of Puerto Rico–Cayey.

Gudynas, E. (2011). *Buen vivir*: Today's tomorrow. *Development, 54*, 441–447. http://dx.doi.org/10.1057/dev.2011.86

Gudynas, E. (2014). El desarrollo como crítica y el buen vivir como alternative [Development as criticism and good living as an alternative]. In G. C. Delgado-Ramos (Ed.), *Buena vida, buen vivir: Imaginarios alternativos para el bien común de la humanidad* [Good life, good living: Imaginary alternatives for the common good of humanity]. Mexico City, Mexico: Universidad Autónoma de México.

Hardiman, R., & Jackson, B. W. (1997). Conceptual foundations for social justice courses. In M. Adams, L. A. Bell, & P. Griffin (Eds.), *Teaching for diversity and social justice* (pp. 16–29). New York, NY: Routledge.

Hayes-Greene, D., Hunter, W., & Plihcik, S. (Eds.). (2018). *Racial equity workshop: Foundations in historical and institutional racism*. Greensboro, NC: The Racial Equity Institute.

Hayes-Greene, D., & Love, B. (2018). *The groundwater approach: Building a practical understanding of structural racism*. Greensboro, NC: The Racial Equity Institute.

Hill Collins, P. (2000). *Black feminist thought: Knowledge, consciousness, and the politics of empowerment* (2nd ed.). New York, NY: Routledge.

Kendi, I. X. (2016). *Stamped from the beginning: The definitive history of racist ideas in America*. New York, NY: Nation Books.

Maldonado-Torres, N. (2007). Sobre la colonialidad del ser: Contribuciones al desarrollo de un concepto [On the coloniality of being: Contributions to the development of a concept]. In S. Castro-Gómez & R. Grosfoguel (Eds.), *El giro decolonial: Reflexiones para una diversidad epistémica más allá del capitalismo global* [The decolonial turn: Reflections for epistemic diversity beyond global capitalism] (pp. 127–167). Bogotá, Colombia: Siglo del Hombre Editores.

Maldonado-Torres, N. (2008). Secularism and religion in the modern/colonial world-system: From secular postcoloniality to post secular transmodernity. In M. Moraña, E. Dussel, & C. A. Jáuregui (Eds.), *Coloniality at large: Latin America and the postcolonial debate* (pp. 360–384). Durham, NC: Duke University Press.

Martín-Baró, I. (1994). *Writings for a liberation psychology*. Cambridge, MA: Harvard University Press.

Mignolo, W. D., & Walsh, C. E. (2018). *On decoloniality*. Durham, NC: Duke University Press. http://dx.doi.org/10.1215/9780822371779

Moane, G. (1999). *Gender and colonialism: A psychological analysis of oppression and liberation*. New York, NY: St. Martin Press. http://dx.doi.org/10.1057/9780230279377

Montero, M., & Sonn, C. C. (Eds.). (2009). *Psychology of liberation: Theory and applications*. New York, NY: Springer Science + Business Media.

Quijano, A. (2000). Colonialidad del poder y clasificación social [Coloniality of power and social classification]. In *Journal of World-Systems Research, VI*, 342–386.

Quijano, A. (2014). Colonialidad del poder, eurocentrismo y America Latina [Coloniality of power, Eurocentrism and Latin America]. In D. Assis Clímaco (Ed.), *Cuestiones y horizontes: De la dependencia histórico-estructural a la colonialidad/descolonialidad del poder* [Issues and horizons: From historical-structural dependence of coloniality/decoloniality of power] (pp. 777–832). Buenos Aires, Argentina: CLASCO.

Quiñones-Rosado, R. (2007). *Consciousness-in-action: Toward an integral psychology of liberation & transformation*. Caguas, Puerto Rico: Ilé.

Rowe, W., Bennett, S. K., & Atkinson, D. R. (1994). White racial identity models: A critique and alternative proposal. *The Counseling Psychologist, 22*, 129–146. http://dx.doi.org/10.1177/0011000094221009

Shemel, L. (Segment producer). (2014, May 21). Facing the truth: The case for reparations [Television series episode]. In G. Kim (Producer), *Moyers & Company*. New York, NY: Public Affairs Television, Inc./Public Broadcasting Service. Retrieved from http://billmoyers.com/episode/facing-the-truth-the-case-for-reparations

Wade, P. (2010). *Race and ethnicity in Latin America* (2nd ed.). New York, NY: Pluto Press. http://dx.doi.org/10.26530/OAPEN_625258

Watkins, M. & Shulman, H. (2008). *Toward psychologies of liberation*. New York, NY: Palgrave Macmillan.

Wilber, K. (1999). *The collected works of Ken Wilber: Vol. 4. Integral psychology*. Boston, MA: Shambhala.

Worrell, F. C., Cross, W. E., Jr., & Vandiver, B. J. (2001). Nigrescence theory: Current status and challenges for the future. *Journal of Multicultural Counseling and Development, 29*, 201–213. http://dx.doi.org/10.1002/j.2161-1912.2001.tb00517.x

Zinn, H. (1980). *A people's history of the United States*. New York, NY: HarperCollins.

LIBERATION PSYCHOLOGY METHOD

4

From Freud to Fanon to Freire

Psychoanalysis as a Liberation Method

Daniel Gaztambide

In preparing to write this chapter on psychoanalysis and liberation psychology, I recently found myself in the lecture room of the William Alanson White Institute for psychoanalytic training in New York City after a lecture by Pratyusha Tummala-Narra (2016), psychoanalytic psychologist and author of *Psychoanalytic Theory and Cultural Competency in Psychotherapy*. In the midst of talking to some friends and colleagues, I suddenly realized I was standing between a portrait of the founder of interpersonal psychoanalysis, Harry Stack Sullivan, and a portrait of Cultural School theorist and Frankfurt School don Erich Fromm. I was struck not only by the fact that I was standing between two giants of the contemporary psychoanalytic landscape, but as a Puerto Rican psychoanalytic psychologist also standing in for those whose contributions have been rendered invisible within the psychoanalytic "canon"—the ghosts of People of Color who have made outstanding contributions to psychoanalysis, liberation psychology, and their intersections with social justice.

For example, Ralph Waldo Ellison, the renowned Black novelist and essayist, was a clerk in Sullivan's private practice in the 1930s during the later phase of the Harlem Renaissance. Sullivan enlisted the young Ellison in reading and critiquing his writing, and the two enjoyed having lunch together, where they would talk about race, class, literature, and psychoanalysis (Rampersad, 2007). These dialogues left Ellison curious about how to integrate sociology, psychoanalysis, and the Black experience. He would go on to collaborate with Richard Wright on a series of publications on psychoanalysis and Blackness, and later

http://dx.doi.org/10.1037/0000198-005
Liberation Psychology: Theory, Method, Practice, and Social Justice, L. Comas-Díaz and E. Torres Rivera (Editors)

also with psychoanalyst Frederic Wertham to open the Lafargue Mental Hygiene Clinic in 1946 in Harlem, New York City (Ahad, 2010; Zaretsky, 2015).[1] Sullivan (1941), in turn, would conduct a series of psychoanalytic studies on the educational and emotional impact of segregation on Black youth. Erich Fromm also intersected with the tributaries of liberation psychology in Latin America, as he was a friend and ongoing dialogue partner of Brazilian educator Paulo Freire. Freire, whose work provided one of the foundations to Ignacio Martín-Baró's (1994) liberation psychology, developed a way of thinking about the pedagogical relationship that was itself embedded within a psychoanalytic mode of thinking that contextualized the teacher–student relationship within a wider social, cultural, and political context. During visits to Cuernavaca, Mexico, in the 1960s, Freire and Fromm would discuss the challenges of internalized oppression and how difficult it is to expunge the "oppressor within." It was during these dialogues that Fromm remarked that Freire's pedagogical method "is a kind of historical–sociocultural and political psychoanalysis" (Bingham, 2002; Freire & Faundez, 1989; Lake & Dagostino, 2013).

In psychoanalytic training and education, we often read Sullivan, Fromm, and Freud, as well as Ferenczi, Winnicott, and Klein. But what about Freire and Ellison, who thought and wrote psychoanalytically about economic and racial inequality in Latin and North America, respectively? Not to mention Albert Memmi in Algeria, Frantz Fanon in the Caribbean, Arthur Ramos in Brazil, or Enrique Pichón-Rivière in Argentina? What would it mean to read liberation psychology within the canon of psychoanalysis? What would it mean to read psychoanalysis as a tributary flowing into liberation psychology?

A related problem in this type of dialogue is the lack of knowledge regarding psychoanalysis' progressive origins. On the part of contemporary multicultural psychology scholars, it is often assumed that psychoanalysis is a conservative, reactionary, Western European product that is alien to the experiences of People of Color, and hence one should rightfully ask: what could psychoanalysis possibly contribute to discussions of social justice? (See the discussion of this question in Tummala-Narra, 2016.) Similarly, many contemporary psychodynamic practitioners and psychoanalysts are also unaware of this aspect of psychoanalysis' history. This chapter, by way of introduction, provides an abridged intellectual history of psychoanalysis, liberation psychology, and social justice, from Freud to Fanon to Freire. In so doing, it will serve as an entry point for psychoanalytic theorists, practitioners, and researchers, as well as scholars who identify with multicultural and liberation psychology, by engaging in what Martín-Baró (1994) called a *recovery of historical memory*.

To recover the historical memory of psychoanalysis and liberation psychology, I first describe the social and cultural context of psychoanalysis as a product of a predominantly marginal group in turn-of-the-century Europe: recently emancipated Jews. This fact of psychoanalysis's origins reveals a progressive

---

[1]Coincidentally, the clinic was named after Paul Lafargue, a French Afro Cuban socialist and Karl Marx's son-in-law (Zaretsky, 2015, p. 59).

history not often acknowledged in discussions of psychoanalysis and social justice. I briefly summarize Freud's on thinking on culture, society, and social justice and show how the themes begun in his work continue to run through the writings of two foundational thinkers in liberation psychology: Frantz Fanon and Paulo Freire. Having reviewed these connections, I address the limitations of the psychoanalytic forefathers of liberation psychology and "mark" those limitations to articulate a contemporary psychoanalytic psychology of liberation.

A final but important preface: Psychoanalysis in its history has been complicit in varied and intersecting forms of oppression. This chapter is not meant to gloss over the aptly documented history of the complicity of psychoanalysis in racism, sexism, and homophobia (e.g., among many others, Altman, 2009; Aron & Starr, 2012; Brickman, 2003). Rather, it is an attempt to shed light on a history too often forgotten—a history that suggests a different relationship between psychoanalysis and historically marginalized communities.

FREUD, RACE, AND THE BIRTH OF PSYCHOANALYSIS

To understand the place of social justice in the history of psychoanalysis, one must first situate it within its immediate cultural, social, and political context. One must also contextualize psychoanalysis within this simple fact: Sigmund Freud and the majority of the early psychoanalysts were Jews in a virulently anti-Semitic European milieu. They were members of a despised ethnic group that straddled the multiple positions of cultural, religious, sexual, and *racial* otherness in the imaginary of turn-of-century Europe. As stated by Sander Gilman (1993b), "The Jew defined what the Aryan was *not*. . . . The Jew became the projection of all the anxieties about control present within the Aryan" (p. 9). In the everyday anti-Semitism that served as a precursor to the horrors of the Shoah, Jews were seen as a non-White entity equivalent to African peoples, even defined as genetically related to them and imagined as being of African descent (in the racist literature of the time; Gilman, 1993a, 1993b). In addition, Jewish men were excluded from European ideals of masculinity and virility, seen as prone to hysteria through their perceived "femininity" and the specter of "passive homosexuality." Each of these racist, sexist, and homophobic discourses instilled in Jews, but especially in Jewish men like Freud and the early analysts, an incredible anxiety that informed both the progressive and reactionary aspects of psychoanalysis (Brickman, 2003; Gilman, 1993a, 1993b).

These racialized discourses, coupled with economic, social, and political disenfranchisement, led to ongoing oppression and marginalization with which Freud was all too painfully familiar. As an immigrant to Vienna, Freud and his family faced unstable housing, street harassment, and the ambivalence of a society that had only recently granted Jews civil rights. He experienced racial microaggressions in his early schooling at the Sperl Gymnasium in Vienna; later in life, he faced exclusion from a professorship at a university when the municipal government decided to "crack down" on the number of Jews attending and teaching at colleges. In regard to how his experience of marginality influenced his development of psychoanalysis, Freud (1925/1961a) stated that it is not a coincidence that its founder was a Jew: "To profess belief in this new theory called for a certain degree of readiness to accept a situation of solitary opposition—a situation with which no one is more familiar than a Jew" (p. 222).

Freud was painfully aware of how his positionality influenced not only the birth of psychoanalysis but also tensions within and outside of it. When non-Jews such as Carl Jung joined the psychoanalytic movement, this presented an opportunity for psychoanalysis to be seen as more cosmopolitan but also for greater exposure to the casual racism that its Jewish members would need to negotiate. Freud wrote in a letter to Karl Abraham,

> I nurse a suspicion that the suppressed anti-Semitism of the Swiss [Carl Jung] that spares me is deflected in reinforced form upon you. But I think that we as Jews, if we wish to join in anywhere, must develop a bit of masochism, be ready to suffer some wrong. Otherwise there is no hitting it off. Rest assured that if my name were *Oberhuber*, in spite of everything my innovations would have met with far less resistance. (as cited in Reijzer, 2011, p. 33)

Eli Zaretsky (2004), a noted historian of psychoanalysis and its influence on progressive politics, noted that the predominance of Jews in early psycho-analysis virtually guaranteed its marginality. As Jews, especially Jewish men, their marginalization from Aryan-White models of masculinity and sexuality made them all the more aware of the fear of vulnerability—and its association with "femaleness" and "homosexuality"—dissociated behind this ideal. "Under these conditions," Zaretsky (2004) wrote, "the Jewish composition of psychoanalysis guaranteed that all analysts regarded the dominant culture as hypocritical—an assumption shared by all oppressed or marginalized groups for obvious reasons" (p. 70).

"Such Treatments Will be Free": The Early Psychoanalytic Movement and Social Activism

In an evocative paper titled "Sigmund Freud and the Politics of Marginality," Rothman and Isenberg (1974) wondered whether "some of the motives associated with Freud's discovery of psychoanalysis had their sources in the same drives which led other Jews to Marxism, i.e., the desire to end marginality by undermining the bases of the dominant culture?" (p. 48). Elizabeth Danto (2005), in her now classic monograph *Freud's Free Clinics: Psychoanalysis & Social Justice, 1918–1938*, might answer with a resounding "Yes, but *both* psychoanalysis *and* Marxism." Danto (2005) outlined how in the same way that nearly all of Freud's early adherents were Jewish, so too did nearly all of them associate with leftist, progressive movements of the era. For example, "Erich Fromm, Otto Fenichel, and Wilhelm and Annie Reich identified as Marxists; Edith Jacobson and Marie Langer were Communists, while Paul Federn, Karen Horney, and Sigmund Freud were Social Democrats, to name a few" (pp. 18–19). The early psychoanalysts debated not only the nuances of psychodynamic theory and technique but also the impact of class inequality on the psyche, the relationship between anti-Black racism and anti-Semitism, and engaged in activism focused on the decriminalization of homosexuality (Danto, 2005).

A critical period in the history of psychoanalysis's engagement with social justice lies in the interwar period just after World War I. In the context of the vast devastation and worsening of existing economic and racial inequalities in turn-of-the-century Europe, Freud (1919) delivered a paper at the 1918 5th International Psycho-analytical Congress in Budapest entitled "Lines of Advance in Psychoanalytic Therapy" in which he declared,

> It is possible to foresee that the conscience of society will awake, and remind it that the poor man should have just as much right to assistance to his mind as he now has to the life-saving help offered by surgery; and that the neurosis threaten public health no less than tuberculosis, and can be left as little as the latter to the impotent care of individual members of the community. Then institutions and out-patient clinics will be started. . . . Such treatments will be free. (p. 165)

Freud's call for the conscience of society to awaken ignited the early psychoanalytic movement, whose members would go on to open psychoanalytic clinics in Berlin, Vienna, and Budapest providing free treatment for the poor and displaced, while also serving as training institutions for future generations of analysts. With this call, the early analysts became increasingly involved in public policy debates and activism on mental health, education, socialized medicine, and women's rights (Danto, 2005).

This period of activism and social consciousness would come to an end with the outbreak of the Second World War. With German occupation came the brutal Aryanization of the free clinics, as psychoanalysts were arrested and removed for being Jewish or Socialists (or often, both), and replaced with German (Aryan) therapists. Some leaders of the psychoanalytic movement struck a devil's bargain with the Reich, sacrificing its Jewish members in exchange for maintaining a psychoanalytic presence within its sphere of influence. Others did what they could to evacuate and flee, or procure the release of captured analysts and their families (Danto, 2012). Freud would lose four of his five sisters in concentration camps. Some, like Freud, would flee to England, others to the United States, others to Latin America. Trauma spread the seeds of psychoanalysis across the world. Depending on where they fell, this progressive tradition would either wilt or survive.

The Jewish and left-leaning psychoanalytic immigrants arrived in the United States post–World War II as refugees traumatized by persecution, loss, and genocide (Aron & Starr, 2012). For many, there would be no respite in their new "home." Some survived by assimilating into the dominant culture and "becoming White" (Altman, 2009). Others, who attempted to maintain their progressive values and identities as Marxists, Socialists, and Communists faced various levels of scrutiny and investigation by the Federal Bureau of Investigation, and ultimately renounced their beliefs to survive (Danto, 2012). Yet a few, including Otto Fenichel and a small circle of colleagues, maintained a letter correspondence in which they continued their dialogues on inequality, class, social justice, and psychoanalysis. Fenichel and his colleagues would pass copies of their letters among one another, with each member destroying theirs after being read to prevent discovery (Jacoby, 1986). Fenichel (1946), renowned in America as a clinical theorist and scholar, took up the relationship between anti-Blackness and anti-Semitism one last time, offering a psychoanalytic theory of racism before his death in 1946. Twenty years later, another paper of Fenichel's (1967) on how psychoanalysis can be integrated with Marxism to address the psychological and material conditions that maintain inequality would be published posthumously. But by then, American psychoanalysis had already lost its way and become disconnected from its progressive roots (Altman, 2009; Danto, 2005).

Russel Jacoby (1986), who in *The Repression of Psychoanalysis* documented Fenichel's secret letters with other activist psychoanalysts, argued that with his passing so too died the progressive history of psychoanalysis, which went hand in hand with cultural and economic trends of the time. At the turn of the century, the American Medical Association had enacted policies limiting the admission of African Americans and Jews to medical school, in turn restricting access for People of Color to psychoanalytic training (Danto, 2005). With the Americanization of psychoanalysis, Whiteness became centered instead of critiqued, in hand with increased commodification of psychoanalytic treatment, as something only accessible to those who were White and wealthy (Altman, 2009; Aron & Starr, 2012). People of Color and the poor were seen as not "psychologically minded" enough to receive psychoanalytic training or psychoanalytic treatment. Psychoanalytic theory in turn became further embedded in a milieu that privileged the intrapsychic, ignored the sociocultural, and became oriented toward adapting individuals to their social environment. It can be said that the death of psychoanalysis marked the birth of the American Freud.

But this is only part of the story. As Jewish and formerly leftist psychoanalysts turned toward Whiteness and away from their progressive values, People of Color turned toward psychoanalysis as a tool of social justice work in Harlem (Ahad, 2010; Zaretsky, 2015), throughout Latin America (Hollander, 1997), and in the Caribbean (for a more in-depth review, see Gaztambide, 2019). To chart the intellectual and psychoanalytic tradition that flows into liberation psychology, it becomes important to turn first to Freud's own writing. In it, we find a theory of oppression, internalization, and liberation that would go on to be further developed and elaborated in the pens of postcolonial psychoanalysis— pens whose ink would then flow into liberation psychology itself.

Freud's Thinking on Social Justice

The vibrancy of a social justice perspective in psychoanalysis was palpable not only in the activities of the early psychoanalysts but also quite cogently in Freud's written work. Due to space constraints, I will limit myself to reviewing some of his core ideas relevant to society, oppression, liberation, and social justice, with a focus on Freud's *Group Psychology and the Analysis of the Ego* (1921/1961d), *The Future of an Illusion* (1927/1961c), and *Civilization and Its Discontents* (1930/1961b).

Group Psychology and the Analysis of the Ego (Freud, 1921/1961d), when read against the backdrop of contemporary U.S. politics in a post-2016 world, takes on new life as a psychoanalytic account of right-wing populism and its discontents. Writing with the rise of Karl Lueger's own anti-Semitic populism in Vienna still fresh in his mind, Freud argued that mass movements submerge the individual's subjectivity in enthrallment to the authority of a "strong man" that impairs one's critical faculties, opening one up to falsehoods while at the same time instilling an "incontrovertible certainty" in its moral superiority and alternative reality. This type of right-wing populism demands strength and sees kindness "as a form of weakness. . . . It wants to be ruled and oppressed and to fear its Masters. Fundamentally it is entirely conservative, and it has a deep aversion to all innovations and advances and an unbounded respect for tradition" (Freud, 1921/1961d, pp. 10–11). The great leader is both the source of violence suffered by the masses and the one who commands the masses with the power of his words. Through his speech, the "strong man" lures the masses into losing their humanity through acts of violence toward an "other" that is seen as the "true cause" of their grievances, all the while they continue to be oppressed by those in power whose values they have internalized. Freud talks at length of the role of the "other," including the racial other, as a source of hatred and coherence for the masses, with racial difference leading "to an almost insufferable repugnance, such as the Gaelic people feel for the German, the Aryan for the semite, and the white races for the colored" (p. 33). Freud argued that the antidote to this unleashing of hatred between ingroup and outgroup is "love." He defined love as a force that can bind us within and despite our differences, a love whose first demand "is for justice, for equal treatment for all" (p. 52).

In *The Future of an Illusion* (Freud, 1927/1961c), Freud exhibited his most lucid reflections on power and society. He remarked that society reflects "something which was imposed on a resisting majority by a minority which understood how to obtain possession of the means to power and coercion" (p. 6). The powerful exhibit control over the distribution of wealth, and use external coercion to maintain systems of inequality. Freud argued that among the oppressed, this inequality breeds "intense hostility towards a culture whose existence they make possible by their work, but in whose wealth they have too small a share" (p. 12). To manage this rebellious hostility resulting from deprivation, the oppressors provide an alternative satisfaction through an ego ideal. The oppressors may offer the oppressed a common identity, against which an other is defined that is seen as the true source of their suffering. In this way, the oppressed come to identify with their oppressors. As Freud wrote, they "can be emotionally attached to their masters; in spite of their hostility to them they may see in them their ideals" (p. 13). The oppressed not only find in the oppressor their values but also come to desire to be like their oppressor.

Through compensatory illusions, internalized by the oppressed, the impulse to rebel against society is quelled. Two illusions that Freud (1927/1961c) expanded on in this text are "that the Indo-Germanic race is the only one capable of civilization" (pp. 30–31) and "White Christian Civilization." Although Freud certainly saw all religion as an illusion, and hence problematic, he did not cease in identifying the specific permutation of religion he criticized in *The Future of an Illusion*. He argued that religion in its White-Christian form was a system of psychological control that promised the oppressed a Kingdom in Heaven, in exchange for their toiling and exploitation on earth. He preempted an objection from the dominant classes—what if the masses reject religion and its satisfactions? What if they turn to violence to destroy society? Freud reasoned that if this is so, then either even greater repressive measures must be taken, or the relationship between society and religion needs to be reformed. He argued that oppression itself distorts the psyche of the oppressed and that if they free themselves from the illusions of religion, xenophobia, and inequality, they would transform society:

> As honest smallholders on this earth they will know how to cultivate their plot in such a way that it supports them. By withdrawing their expectations from the other world and concentrating all their liberated energies into their life on earth, they will probably succeed in achieving a state of things in which life will become tolerable for everyone and civilization no longer oppressive to anyone. (Freud, 1927/1961c, p. 50)

Freud believed that if the critical intellect of the oppressed were freed from society's illusions, they would create conditions under which the needs of all— rich and poor, Jew and Gentile, White and non-White—would be satisfied. This emancipatory vision, however, did not temper Freud's pessimistic view of human nature, nor his awareness of how prone humans are to engage in violence toward the "other."

Between *Group Psychology* (1921/1961d) and *Civilization and Its Discontents* (1930/1961b), Freud developed a psychoanalytic theory of social justice, one that serves as a bulwark against cyclical violence between oppressor and oppressed. He defined justice as a principle whereby society would not be founded on domination of the powerless by the powerful, but instead

> towards making the law no longer an expression of the will of a small community— a caste or a stratum of the population or a racial group—which, in its turn, behaves like a violent individual towards other, and perhaps more numerous, collections of people. The final outcome should be a rule of law to which all . . . have contributed by a sacrifice of their instincts, and which leaves no one—again with the same exception—at the mercy of brute force. (Freud, 1930/1961b, p. 95)

Justice requires a communal agreement in which all are treated equally and not privileged due to their race or class. As part of that communal pact, all members are to be protected from violence—including the brutality of the "strong man" who seeks to dominate. Similarly, Freud (1921/1961d) wrote, "Social justice means that we deny ourselves many things so that others may have to do without them as well. . . . This demand for equality is the root of social conscience and the sense of duty" (p. 53). His vision of social justice includes bearing witness to our aggressive impulses, including our vengeful desire to visit violence upon the other just as we have been subjected to violence, and renouncing those impulses in favor of an affective, libidinal (loving) tie to the other.

For Freud this is the quintessential ethic. In witnessing the violence that even poor, displaced Germans enacted toward other races, including poor, displaced Jews, he concluded that there is a cyclical or repetitive dimension to human violence in its desire for an other to violate and exploit—those who are oppressed are weaponized into becoming oppressors themselves. Social justice, then, involves experiencing and getting in touch with this desire, and renouncing it in favor of a new relationship with the other—one in which the other is recognized as an equal, as a human being who should not be victim to brutality. This theme—the relationship between internalized oppression, violence, and liberation—would consume the work of postcolonial psychoanalysis and its descendant, liberation psychology.

FANON AND THE BIRTH OF POSTCOLONIAL PSYCHOANALYSIS

The Martinican Black psychiatrist Frantz Fanon has oft been referred to as Freud's "most disputatious heir" (Said, 2003). I would argue that this is so in terms of not only style but also substance (see also Hook, 2012). Across *Black Skin, White Masks* (1952/2008) and *The Wretched of the Earth* (1963), Fanon (1952/2008) maintained "that only a psychoanalytical interpretation of the black problem can lay bare the anomalies of affect that are responsible for the structure of the complex" (p. 3) of internalized colonialism. Drawing on psychoanalytic concepts and tools, he showed how "White civilization and European culture have forced an existential deviation on the Negro" (p. 6), a split consciousness that divides the subjectivity of the colonized between the world of the oppressed and the desire of the oppressor—a desire to please, worship, and become like them. At the same time this desire, imposed from without, becomes a burden that restricts the freedom of the colonized. Hence Fanon (1952/2008) wrote, "Affect is exacerbated in the Negro, he is full of rage because he feels small" (p. 35). This anger manifests as hostility toward the oppressor, now a desire to become him to do to them what has been done *to* the oppressed. Fanon notes, however, how this hostility spills over in the relationship between the colonized and other colonized people, who are simultaneously seen as rivals and as objects for exploitation. The oppressed, then, becomes a "co-oppressor." It is this internalized and enacted oppression, this "poison," that Fanon stated "must be eliminated once and for all" (p. 44).

As a psychoanalytic practitioner, Fanon (1952) saw the purpose of his clinical work as helping his patients—often fellow Martinicans like himself—become "*conscious* of his unconscious and abandon his attempts at a hallucinatory whitening, but also to act in the direction of a change in the social structure" (p. 74). In relation to the dilemma faced by oppressed people—either submit to the oppressor or become like him by exerting power against him and other oppressed—Fanon argued that one has "to rise above this absurd drama that others have staged round me, to reject the two terms that are equally unacceptable, and, through one human being, to reach out for the universal" (p. 153). The oppressed takes a risk that is also a demand—to restore the humanity of the oppressor by offering recognition, while also demanding human behavior from them. Similar to Freud's model of recognition, Fanon argued for an intersubjective negotiation in which the oppressed takes the first step toward mutuality by renouncing cyclical violence and offering a human relation. This ethic, however, would shift for Fanon in the wake of the Algerian revolution. No longer able to witness the violence and torture enacted by the French forces as a psychiatrist working in a day treatment hospital, Fanon renounced his position and joined the Algerian National Liberation Front. His involvement in the war informed his most polemic and insightful text, *The Wretched of the Earth* (1963).

In the beginnings of *The Wretched of the Earth* (Fanon, 1963), there is no offer of recognition. There is instead an almost apocalyptic tenor in Fanon citing the classic biblical dictum, the rallying cry of many an interpretation of the Christian scripture from the point of view of the oppressed: "The last shall be first." For the "creation of new men," the restoration of the oppressed's humanity, there needed to be a great reversal that results in "a murderous and decisive confrontation" between colonizer and colonized (p. 3). The anger trapped inside the body of the oppressed needed to be discharged through revolutionary force. It important to note that Fanon is diagnosing a natural outcome of oppression—the hostility of the marginalized toward their oppressors (a la Freud). In diagnosing that outcome, Fanon again draws attention to the "spilling over" of that violence toward other oppressed, "it is not uncommon to see the colonized subject draw his knife at the slightest hostile or aggressive look from another colonized subject" (p. 17).

Fanon saw this dynamic as a necessary part of the emancipatory process. At the same time, there is another trend in Fanon, one that is reconciliatory and redemptive. He highlighted, for example, that the oppressed people of Africa and the Caribbean should join forces with the "European masses" in facing the rich and powerful few who dominate both Whites and People of Color. He also drew attention to the colonized's attempt to "copy" or draw inspiration from European models of subjectivity and how this attempt to be like the oppressor distorts the labor of liberation. "For Europe, for ourselves and for humanity, comrades," Fanon (1963) wrote, "We must make a new start, develop a new way of thinking, and endeavor to create a new man" (p. 239). This new creation reads differently from the "new man" forged through "murderous confrontation" against his oppressors. This "new way of thinking" carries echoes of Fanon's project in *Black Skins, White Masks* (1952/2008), in which he sought a way out of the dialectical impasse between oppressor and oppressed.

Like Freud, Fanon recognized the natural, even adaptive aggression that inequality evokes among oppressed people. Similarly, Fanon described the split "divide and conquer" strategies that pit one marginalized group (White European working class) against another, even more oppressed group (colonized people of Africa and the Caribbean), or within an oppressed community itself (colonized people toward one another). At the end of *The Wretched of the Earth*, Fanon (1963) suggested that a cross-racial act of recognition between colonized peoples and between colonized peoples and the White European working class would redirect their aggression toward the true source of the conflict: the White and rich whose wealth is made possible by their labor. This redirection of aggression is based on colonized people and the White European working class renouncing their identification with and desire to "copy" the powerful. This theory would be further elaborated close to 20 years later by Paulo Freire, a descendant of Fanon from Brazil.

FREIRE'S "HISTORICO-SOCIOCULTURAL AND POLITICAL PSYCHOANALYSIS"

Paulo Freire was a Brazilian educator who initially did literacy work with Indigenous and Afro-Brazilian people in the *favelas*, inner urban centers of Brazilian society all but forgotten by the dominant consciousness. His work shifted from simply raising literacy to collaborating with poor, Black and Indigenous communities to "read the word to read the world," raising political consciousness of their material conditions and organizing for basic human and civil rights. Freire's emphasis on "critical consciousness" was itself informed by a tradition of Afro-Brazilian psychoanalytic psychiatrists and psychoanalytically informed sociologists ranging from Juliano Moreira to Alberto Guerreiro Ramos (for a review, see Gaztambide, 2019). His synthesis of these traditions resulted in his exile to Chile, where he produced his major work, *Pedagogy of the Oppressed* (Freire, 1972). While in Chile, a political activist shared with him a copy of Fanon's *Wretched of the Earth*. "I was writing *Pedagogy of the Oppressed*, and the book was almost finished when I read Fanon," Freire later remembered. "I had to rewrite the book in order to begin to quote Fanon" (Horton & Freire, 1990, p. 36). Grounded in an Afro Brazilian psychoanalytic tradition, influenced by Fromm and equipped with Fanon, Freire would create a cornerstone for critical pedagogy, liberation psychology and later multicultural psychology. In this brief summary of his more developed thinking, I depend on his follow-up text, *Education for Critical Consciousness* (Freire, 1973).

For Freire (1973), to be human is to be born in a matrix of relation with others, "not only in the world but with the world" (p. 4). This matrix of relatedness holds a dialectical tension between adapting to the exigencies of reality, while maintaining "the critical capacity to make choices and to transform that reality" (p. 4). Taken to the extreme, a one-sided adaptation to the environment becomes a defense against self-assertion and self-definition, whereas one-sidedly demanding change from one's reality becomes a form of violence and domination. Freire defined the subjectivity of the oppressed and the oppressor as representing an exaggerated enactment of either polarity—different forms in which one loses their humanity. For the oppressor consciousness, the oppressed are "reduced to the status of objects at its disposal" (p. 44). The oppressed, in contrast, internalize a way of "being for another" that attaches their sense of self to the perspective of the oppressor. Within their conditions of psychological and material deprivation, the oppressed seek to restore their humanity. But at least initially, to be human is "to be *like* the oppressor." Paraphrasing Freud, Freire wrote: "The shadow of their . . . oppressor is still cast over them" (p. 31).

To begin the process of decolonizing their subjectivity, the oppressed must "discover their oppressor and in turn their own consciousness" (Freire, 1973, p. 47). Through a process of dialogue with an other, the oppressed become "conscious of, not only as intent on objects but as turned in upon itself in a Jasperian "split"—consciousness as consciousness of consciousness" (pp. 65–66). Being able to recognize the consciousness of self, other, and the "third" that grounds the two within a political space, forms part and parcel of what Freire termed *concientizacao* (*concientización* in Spanish)—critical consciousness. Freire argued that the dialogue that foments critical consciousness is grounded in love. A dialogue between polarities in tension, whether teacher–student, therapist–patient, oppressor–oppressed, leads to an intersubjective relation "between Subjects that know, with reference to a knowable object" (p. 136). Dialogue, then, turns what might collapse into a combat between dueling selves, into an exchange between two subjects that are mediated, perhaps even set against one another, by a contextual third—whether the broader system of inequality that frames the conflict between oppressor and oppressed, or the relation between oppressor and oppressed itself.

The alternative to this dialogue centered in love is a vertical relationship that requires both dominant and dominated—with each side cyclically trading positions, exchanging power through violence in the vein of the classic Puerto Rican reggaeton song, *Quítate tu pa' ponerme yo*—"Get out, so I can put myself there (in the position of power)." The way out of this impasse, for Freire (1973), "requires that the Subject recognize himself in the object (the coded concrete existential situation) and recognize the object as a situation in which he finds himself, together with other Subjects" (p. 96). A murderous encounter gives way to a dialogue about the fact that we find ourselves in a murderous encounter. Who set up this encounter? Who benefits from it? What powers structured this encounter in this way? This recognition that oppressor and oppressed are caught in a cycle together, a cycle that preceded them yet continues to define them in relation to each other, begins to restore the humanity both had lost. To engage in this dialogue, however, one or both members of the polarity must risk an "act of love." For Freire, this act of love may take the form of the teacher recognizing the desire of the student, and showing humility and vulnerability toward them (p. 51). But it may also take form in the oppressed taking this very risk, a risk that serves to liberate themselves and their oppressors as well (Freire, 1972).

Freire (1973) recognized that the oppressed, in their development of critical consciousness, may go through a series of stages. In the initial stage, the consciousness of the oppressed is "submerged" in the ideology of the oppressor— the oppressed and their culture are bad, the oppressor is the true, good, ideal human, for example. In this "intransitive" consciousness, the oppressed are disempowered in their belief that they are at fault for their condition in life and at the will of fate or God, unable to make change. As the oppressed begin to ascertain their condition of exploitation in relation to the oppressor, there develops an initial form of critical consciousness Freire termed *semitransitive*. In this stage, the oppressed experience a sense of empowerment and the belief in the possibility of change. However, their consciousness evidences a "reversal of terms" in relation to the oppressor. Now it is the oppressors who are all-bad and must be denigrated—in the extreme eliminated, typically through violence. It is in this stage, Freire noted that the oppressed are most vulnerable to identification with a "strong man" who either promises to create change (so they would not have to) or wills them toward revolt with the power of their words. In addition, the oppressed, in their desire to be like the oppressor, may turn against other oppressed people who are seen as traitors who do not follow the will of the strong man. They engage in what Freire termed *horizontal violence*, where instead of directing their energies against the system or even the oppressors, they enact a will to dominate other marginalized people. Although at this stage, there is an increased sense of agency and power on behalf of the oppressed, Freire argued that the development of critical consciousness remains incomplete.

"If the goal of the oppressed is to become fully human," Freire (1973) argued, "they will not achieve their goal by merely reversing the terms of the contradiction, by simply changing poles" (p. 38). Rather, the shift to the final stage of "transitive" critical consciousness is marked by the resolution of the contradiction of oppressor and oppressed, which yields the creation of a new subjectivity that is "neither oppressor nor oppressed, but man in the process of liberation" (p. 38). A fully realized critical consciousness, Freire argued, is capable of recognizing causality in human and societal relations, rather than locating blame primarily in individuals or specific groups without reference to the broader systemic context. Recognizing this shared social and systemic reality and inviting the other into a dialogue about it as a shared object serves to humanize both sides of the oppressor–oppressed conflict. Why is this world organized in this way? Who created it? Why does this world pull us toward conflict with one another? Whom does this division serve? Asking and addressing the question of what divides us, and who benefits from this division, results from a dialogue of mutual recognition that then transforms our aggression, and directs it toward enacting change in the world. Critical consciousness becomes "the loving encounter of people, who, mediated by the world, 'proclaim' that world. They transform the world and in transforming it, humanize it for all people" (p. 115).

AN INTEGRATIVE READING OF FREUD, FANON, AND FREIRE

Before attempting a synthesis of these ideas about oppression and liberation from Freud to Fanon to Freire, it is important to pause and take stock of the limitations, not to mention the injuries, that they are responsible for. Although American psychoanalysis post–World War II divorced itself from psychoanalysis's progressive origins, becoming an increasingly classist, White, sexist, and anti-LGBTQ institution (Altman, 2009; Aron & Starr, 2012; Danto, 2005,

2009, 2012; see also the preceding text of this chapter), it cannot be ignored that the excesses of American psychoanalysis do have an origin in racial, sexual, and gendered tensions inherent in Freud himself.

As stated earlier, Freud and the early psychoanalysts existed in a world that rendered them as "other" due to being Jewish. This created an anxiety for Jewish men like Freud in which they sought both to resist and to subvert White European, male, heterosexual subjectivity, while also seeking to access and be included within it (Aron & Starr, 2012; Brickman, 2003). Hence, depending on where and when one is reading Freud, one can either access a revolutionary, postcolonial psychoanalysis that criticizes and deconstructs oppressive ideologies and unconscious internalizations of social structures or a reactionary, conservative, and colonizing psychoanalysis that attempts to restore bourgeois notions of White, male, heterosexual normativity. Aron and Starr (2012) referred to this trend in Freud as a reflection of his "optimal marginality," able to apperceive the contradictions of society clearly as an outsider, yet still also operate within its norms as an insider. Read side by side, one can see how psychoanalysis emerges then as an emancipatory project that at the same time is prone to privileging White (implicitly Jewish), male, heterosexual subjectivity and also oscillates between restorative and negative portrayals of the subjectivity of women, LGBTQ people, and People of Color.

Turning to Fanon, although he rereads psychoanalysis through his own positionality as an Afro Caribbean man, he exhibits a similar trend. Although he is clearly a foundation for postcolonial psychoanalysis, and liberation psychology by association, his depiction (or lack thereof) of women and queer People of Color likewise centers the experience of Black, heterosexual men. In many respects, his work yields a comprehensive psychoanalysis of how Black male subjectivity internalizes different dimensions of oppression, while also treating women and homosexuals as denigrated categories to be avoided and transcended for the good of decolonization (of Black male subjectivity). Of the Woman of Color, he famously said, "I know nothing about her" (Fanon, 1952/2008, p. 138), exhibiting a pattern of thinking that, as Ahad (2010) stated, "is at best dismissive, and at worst disparaging" (p. 112). For Fanon, the Black male is a tragic victim of racism who desires to be humanized through the love of White women, whereas Women of Color are framed in his text as "race traitors" seeking Whiteness through the love of White men—an example of a racialized gendered double standard in his work. Nagel (2000) also examined Fanon's position that homosexuality is "an attribute of the white race," that is not "inherent" to the Caribbean because, according to Fanon, the African Diaspora does not experience Oedipal conflicts that lead to same-sex desire. As with Freud, so too with Fanon—the emancipatory project stops at the border of the cis-heterosexual, non-White male body, even as it treads over the bodies of women and those whose gender and sexuality do not conform to that ideal.

Lastly, although the influence of Freire in multicultural and liberation psychology cannot be understated, it is important to recognize that his major works were based on pedagogical interventions with poor indigenous and Black communities in Brazil. He devotes no clear or overt attention to issues of race in his early texts, rendering them invisible in relation to class. To be fair, Freire did address issues of race and gender in his later works and also acknowledged his indebtedness to Alberto Guerreiro Ramos's thinking on Black consciousness (see Gaztambide, 2019). Although Freire's more vague use of the terms *oppressor* and *oppressed* has allowed various communities and social justice traditions to "read themselves" into his theory and make use of it—from racial justice activists to economic justice, gender equality and queer activists—it is important to highlight that Freire's earlier political "colorblindness" reflects a broader trend in Latin American politics that risks the erasure of Black and Indigenous experiences.

If we read Freud against Freud, we find he did not, in effect, renounce the impulse to dominate and denigrate the racial, gender, and sexual other as *he* had been denigrated in favor of a higher ideal of social justice. This compromises the emancipatory potential of his work. If we read Fanon and Freud through Freire, we might say that they are both caught in the semitransitive stage of critical consciousness. They both begin to perceive the world and the system of oppression that surrounds them, but because they are enthralled by an attachment to the position of power—the position of the oppressor, they engage in horizontal violence against other oppressed and marginalized groups. In this oscillation, Freud alternates between intransitive and semitransitive consciousness (with moments of critical consciousness), whereas Fanon oscillates between semitransitive and critical consciousness proper. Fanon comes close to describing an emancipatory consciousness that reflects about the system of relations that create oppressor and oppressed to begin with, seeking a "new creation" outside of the dialectics of colonizer and colonized. It seems in fact that he yearns for such a third position. Early Freire, by contrast, might be recognized as adopting critical consciousness in relation to issues of class, but evidence intransitive consciousness with respect to race, rendering it invisible as an object of reflection.

CONCLUSION: A PSYCHOANALYTIC PSYCHOLOGY OF LIBERATION

Despite their limitations, Freud and Fanon together provided a necessary corrective to Freire's at times utopian vision of liberation. For Freire, what he called the semitransitive consciousness, the period during which the oppressed turn their aggression outward toward the oppressor and other oppressed, is a regrettable stepping-stone toward true critical consciousness. His hope is that oppressed communities will achieve a state of critical consciousness in which they are able to have a loving dialogue with the oppressor that restores both of their humanity. Although I appreciate the idea that those who are a part of oppressor classes also experience a distortion of their humanity and are wounded by systems of oppression in turn, it is also questionable not to include the role of affect, especially the experience of affect in the body, in the emancipatory process.

Freud outlined how oppression leads to a tacit hostility on the part of the oppressed toward their condition of deprivation, an aggression that is redirected by society through identification with the oppressor—the anger is directed inward, or toward other oppressed peoples. Fanon continued this line of reasoning by describing how the anger generated by oppression becomes embedded in the very viscera of the oppressed, which either destroys them from the inside or is discharged against other subalterns in turn. One possibility Fanon and Freud discuss is that the anger seeks discharge outward against the "true culprit," the oppressor. At first glance, Freire's model seems to sidestep the question of aggression altogether. But what if the liberating dialogue, the "act of love," is itself an attempt to vividly experience one's aggression toward the other, but—following Freud—this anger is sufficiently regulated so as to both set a demand upon the other—the demand to be treated humanely (Fanon)—and recognize their common humanity? For Freire, an act of vulnerability is important. For Freud, a renunciation of aggression in favor of an ideal of equity is paramount. For Fanon, he does not tire of calling for the liberation of one's repressed aggression and extending an appeal to the oppressor's humanity. To enact violence is easy. To disclose our anger at how the other has wounded us, to demand reparation, even as we see how the other also carries a wound—this takes real power. The power to survive vulnerability. Freire would say it takes the power of love. Fanon would say this is the love he has been waiting for. Freud (1930/1961b) would say it is precisely love that melts the walls set up to divide us, "to combine single human individuals, and after that families, then races, peoples and nations, into one great unity, the unity of mankind" (p. 122).

What are the practical methodological implications of this psychoanalytic liberation psychology? At the level of theory and political analysis, liberation psychology, from Freud to Fanon to Freire, argues that inequality and oppression are maintained through the creation of racial (and other) divisions that maintain the power structures of White bourgeois elites. As inequality and oppression naturally generate hostility and resentment, these affects and emotions need to be regulated in such a way as to protect the system. By redirecting the aggression and resentment of more privileged groups—working-class Whites, men, cis-heterosexual folks, and so on—toward historically marginalized groups—People of Color, women, LGBT folks—not only is the oppression of those groups maintained, but the very structures of inequality that also harm these suboppressor groups are reinforced.

In the U.S. context, for example, racial fears and resentments are mobilized through a combination of implicit racism and explicit dog-whistle politics that lead many Whites to vote for candidates who will "protect" them from encroaching "others"—People of Color, feminists, and LGBT people. These same politicians then enact policies that, while harming vulnerable communities, will also result in higher mortality rates and worse psychosocial outcomes for Whites. Metzl (2019) showed how the policies that result in defunding of schools, restricted health care systems, or proliferation of gun sales overwhelmingly harm communities of color and other marginalized communities, and also harm health and economic outcomes for Whites, while redistributing wealth upward. Speaking colloquially, when Whites then ask, "Who moved my cheese?" the powerful respond by extending a pointed finger while barely holding on to their hoarded wealth, "Well, *they* did."

At the level of praxis and political application, psychoanalytic liberation psychology suggests that a humanizing dialogue in which oppressor and oppressed can engage one another with empathy, recognizing each other's pain and wounding, can shift the dialectical tension from conflict and division toward solidarity and action upon the world. To put it another way, that oppressor and oppressed reflect jointly on this world that brings victim and perpetrator into being to begin with, understanding the causes for inequality and division. Within the field of psychology there are certainly models for intergroup dialogue which emphasize empathy, reflective listening and perspective taking as a way of regulating the powerful emotions that dialogue across race, gender, sexuality, and class can evoke for both privileged and underprivileged groups (Gurin-Sands, Gurin, Nagda, & Osuna, 2012). But psychoanalytic liberation psychology looks beyond group intervention as a source of political praxis. It clarifies a message and a perspective that takes race and class seriously and conjointly outside of small groups and in the political realm.

Lopez's (2019) research on dog-whistle politics, race, and class is analogous to this project. His work shows how dog-whistle politics—the subtle and not-so-subtle manipulation of racial resentment to access and maintain power—proves an especially effective tool in causing division among White people and People of Color in the United States. Lopez reviewed evidence showing that political messaging on the left that only emphasizes economic populism but fails to mention race, or that only mentions racism as something individual White people do to People of Color, is not convincing to either White people or the majority of People of Color. Conversely, a political message that communicates that (a) racism is used by the rich to divide us and maintain their wealth, (b) we need to join together across racial lines, and (c) build a society and government that works for everyone, was convincing to both the majority of People of Color and Whites in Lopez's study. Psychoanalytic liberation psychology draws on such insights to join together with other perspectives in psychology and the social sciences to develop tools, messages, and interventions at individual, group, and political levels. These methods, ultimately, are aimed at leading us to *renounce* our identification with power, and instead form links of solidarity with one another. *El pueblo unido*, White, Black, and Brown, *jamas sera vencido*.

At the clinical level of the psychotherapeutic relationship, psychoanalysis's attention to the subtle shifts in self-states and identity is crucial to understanding the role of race, class, gender, and sexuality in individual psychology and mental health. But psychoanalytic liberation psychology, following Fanon, would further that process by helping individuals reflect on and "link" their immediate experience of suffering to their social, cultural, and political context (Layton, 2006). Tummala-Narra (2016) similarly showed how psychoanalytic practice can help people from marginalized communities integrate multiple dissociated and split-off self-states that result from systemic oppression and race-based trauma. In another context, I have also discussed how the social divisions created by the powerful become internalized among communities of color, especially those most vulnerable and multiply traumatized (Gaztambide, 2018).

A psychoanalytic liberation psychology approach to clinical work involves careful and empathic exploration of the ways in which people from historically marginalized communities may internalize oppression in the form of a toxic self-state that is identified with the role of victim or perpetrator. Over the course of exploring and challenging these internalized self-states, however, it is inevitable that the therapist, even a socially conscious one, will enact those pernicious states in the therapeutic relationship. The therapist, after all, is no less a colonized subject than the patient. An ethic of radical openness to the truth the patient may hold about the therapist (Hart, 2017), and the therapist risking an act of love creates the space for humility and connection to emerge. The very kind of connection that subverts the position of oppressor and oppressed and points toward a broken world in need of transformation.

Liberation psychology, as described by Martín-Baró (1994), is a great lake into which many different tributaries flow (Watkins & Shulman, 2008). Recovering psychoanalysis as another such tributary means looking at what was lost as a result of trauma, while also discovering what was always already there, hidden in plain sight. As a Puerto Rican psychoanalytic psychologist, it means taking hold of a tradition that emerged from, and belongs to, marginalized peoples. It means recognizing that it has always belonged to us, while at the same time never ceasing to critique it to open up a new horizon toward liberation for all.

REFERENCES

Ahad, B. S. (2010). *Freud upside down: African American literature and psychoanalytic culture.* Chicago: University of Illinois Press.

Altman, N. (2009). *The analyst in the inner city: Race, class, and culture through a psychoanalytic lens* (2nd ed.). Hillsdale, NJ: Analytic Press.

Aron, L., & Starr, K. (2012). *A psychotherapy for the people: Toward a progressive psychoanalysis.* New York, NY: Relational Perspectives Book.

Bingham, C. (2002). On Freire's debt to psychoanalysis: Authority on the side of freedom. *Studies in Philosophy and Education, 21*, 447–464. http://dx.doi.org/10.1023/A:1020861224138

Brickman, C. (2003). *Aboriginal populations in the mind: Race and primitivity in psychoanalysis.* New York, NY: Columbia University Press.

Danto, E. A. (2005). *Freud's free clinics: Psychoanalysis and social justice, 1918–1938.* New York, NY: Columbia University Press. http://dx.doi.org/10.7312/dant13180

Danto, E. A. (2009). "A new sort of 'Salvation Army'": Historical perspectives on the confluence of psychoanalysis and social work. *Clinical Social Work Journal, 37*, 67–76. http://dx.doi.org/10.1007/s10615-008-0185-x

Danto, E. A. (2012). "Have you no shame"—American redbaiting of Europe's psychoanalysts. In J. Damousi & M. B. Plotkin (Eds.), *Psychoanalysis and politics: Histories of psychoanalysis under conditions of restricted political freedom* (pp. 213–231). New York, NY: Oxford University Press.

Fanon, F. (1963). *The wretched of the earth.* New York, NY: Grove Press.

Fanon, F. (2008). *Black skin, white masks* (C. L. Markham, Trans.). London, England: Pluto Press. (Original work published 1952)

Fenichel, O. (1946). Elements of a psychoanalytic theory of anti-Semitism. In E. Simmel (Ed.), *Anti-semitism: A social disease* (pp. 11–32). New York, NY: International Universities Press.

Fenichel, O. (1967). Psychoanalysis as the nucleus of a future dialectical–materialistic psychology. *The American Imago, 24,* 290–311.

Freire, P. (1972). *Pedagogy of the oppressed.* New York, NY: Continuum.

Freire, P. (1973). *Education for critical consciousness.* New York, NY: The Seabury Press.

Freire, P., & Faundez, A. (1989). *Learning to question: A pedagogy of liberation.* Geneva, Switzerland: World Council of Churches.

Freud, S. (1919). Lines of advance in psychoanalytic therapy. In (L. Strachey, Trans. & Ed.), *The standard edition of the complete psychological works of Sigmund Freud* (Vol. 17, pp. 157–168). London, England: Hogarth Press.

Freud, S. (1961a). *An autobiographical study.* New York, NY: Norton. (Original work published 1925)

Freud, S. (1961b). Civilization and its discontents. In J. Strachey (Ed. & Trans.), *The standard edition of the complete psychological works of Sigmund Freud* (Vol. 21, pp. 57–146). (Original work published 1930)

Freud, S. (1961c). *The future of an illusion.* New York, NY: Norton. (Original work published 1927)

Freud, S. (1961d). *Group psychology and the analysis of the ego.* New York, NY: Norton. (Original work published 1921)

Gaztambide, D. (2018). Treating borderline personality disorder in *el barrio*: Integrating race and class into transference-focused psychotherapy. In P. Gherovici & C. Christian (Eds.), *Psychoanalysis in the barrios: Race, class, and the unconscious* (pp. 203–220). New York, NY: Routledge. http://dx.doi.org/10.4324/9780429437298-13

Gaztambide, D. (2019). *A people's history of psychoanalysis: From Freud to liberation psychology.* Lanham, MD: Lexington Books.

Gilman, S. L. (1993a). *The case of Sigmund Freud: Medicine and identity at the fin de siecle.* London, England: John Hopkins University Press.

Gilman, S. L. (1993b). *Freud, race, and gender.* Princeton, NJ: Princeton University Press.

Gurin-Sands, C., Gurin, P., Nagda, B. A., & Osuna, S. (2012). Fostering a commitment to social action: How talking, thinking, and feeling make a difference in intergroup dialogue. *Equity & Excellence in Education, 45,* 60–79. http://dx.doi.org/10.1080/10665684.2012.643699

Hart, A. (2017). From multicultural competence to radical openness: A psychoanalytic engagement of otherness. *The American Psychoanalyst, 51.* Retrieved November 11, 2019 from https://apsa.org/apsaa-publications/vol51no1-TOC/html/vol51no1_09.xhtml

Hollander, N. C. (1997). *Love in a time of hate: Liberation psychology in Latin America.* New Brunswick, NJ: Rutgers University Press.

Hook, D. (2012). *A critical psychology of the postcolonial.* London, England: Psychology Press. http://dx.doi.org/10.4324/9780203140529

Horton, M., & Freire, P. (1990). *We make the road by walking: Conversations on education and social change.* Philadelphia, PA: Temple University Press.

Jacoby, R. (1986). *The repression of psychoanalysis: Otto Fenichel and the political Freudians.* Chicago, IL: University of Chicago Press.

Lake, R., & Dagostino, V. (2013). Converging self/other awareness: Erich Fromm and Paulo Freire on transcending the fear of freedom. In R. Lake & T. Kris (Eds.), *Paulo Freire's intellectual roots: Toward historicity in praxis.* London, England: Bloomsbury.

Layton, L. (2006). Attacks on linking: The unconscious pull to dissociate individuals from their social context. In L. Layton, N. Hollander, & S. Gutwill (Eds.), *Psychoanalysis, class, and politics: Encounters in the clinical setting* (pp. 107–117). New York, NY: Routledge. http://dx.doi.org/10.4324/9780203965139

Lopez, I. H. (2019). *Merge left: Fusing race and class, winning elections, and saving America.* New York, NY: The New Press.

Martín-Baró, I. (1994). *Writings for a liberation psychology* (A. Aron & S. Corne, Trans.). Cambridge, MA: Harvard University Press.

Metzl, J. (2019). *Dying of Whiteness: How the politics of racial resentment is killing America's heartland.* New York, NY: Basic Books.

Nagel, J. (2000). Ethnicity and sexuality. *Annual Review of Sociology, 26,* 107–133. http://dx.doi.org/10.1146/annurev.soc.26.1.107

Rampersad, A. (2007). *Ralph Ellison: A biography.* New York, NY: Vintage Books.

Reijzer, H. (2011). *A dangerous legacy: Judaism and the psychoanalytic movement* (J. K. Ringold, Trans.). Uitgeverij, Netherlands: Karnac Books.

Rothman, S., & Isenberg, P. (1974). Sigmund Freud and the politics of marginality. *Central European History, 7,* 58–78. http://dx.doi.org/10.1017/S0008938900010475

Said, E. (2003). *Freud and the non-European.* New York, NY: Verso Books.

Sullivan, H. S. (1941). Memorandum on a psychiatric reconnaissance. In C. Johnson (Ed.), *Growing up in the Black belt: Negro youth in the rural South* (pp. 328–333). Washington, DC: American Council on Education.

Tummala-Narra, P. (2016). *Psychoanalytic theory and cultural competency in psychotherapy.* Washington, DC: American Psychological Association. http://dx.doi.org/10.1037/14800-000

Watkins, M., & Shulman, H. (2008). *Toward psychologies of liberation.* New York, NY: Palgrave Macmillan. http://dx.doi.org/10.1057/9780230227736

Zaretsky, E. (2004). *Secrets of the soul: A social and cultural history of psychoanalysis.* New York, NY: Knopf.

Zaretsky, E. (2015). *Political Freud.* New York, NY: Columbia University Press. http://dx.doi.org/10.7312/columbia/9780231172448.001.0001

5

Liberation Psychology of and for Transformative Justice

Centering Acompañamiento *in Participatory Action Research*

Jesica Siham Fernández

rounded in the epistemological foundations of Latin American liberation psychology, as informed by the work of Ignacio Martín-Baró (1989, 1990, 1994), Paulo Freire (1970, 1999), Maritza Montero (2004, 2010; Montero & Sonn, 2009), and Catherine Walsh (2014), this chapter outlines the characteristics of a praxis of *acompañamiento* that aligns with participatory action research (PAR). Within a liberation framework of transformative justice, *acompañamiento* is defined as standing *with* people. It is an intentional act of being and experiencing social conditions alongside those who are impacted by these and interconnected systems of oppression (Goizueta, 2009; Sepúlveda, 2011; Watkins, 2015). By cobeing and colearning with people, researchers and community members develop intentional relations of mutuality that recognize and interrogate power inequities within research relationships and contexts. Together, yet guided and led by communities, we work to transgress and transform systems of power toward the fulfillment of liberation (Burton & Gómez Ordóñez, 2015; Comas-Díaz, Lykes, & Alarcón, 1998; Dobles, 2015; Lykes & Mallona, 2008). Centering acompañamiento as a praxis *of* and *for* liberation oriented toward transformative justice must be grounded, led, and determined by communities affected by systems of power and oppression.

A psychology for liberation, with and by those who are oppressed by historic and contemporary systems of power, underscores the potential of psychology to advance theory, research and practice that is synonymous with social justice and change (Nelson & Prilleltensky, 2010). Liberation psychology of and for

http://dx.doi.org/10.1037/0000198-006
Liberation Psychology: Theory, Method, Practice, and Social Justice, L. Comas-Díaz and E. Torres Rivera (Editors)

transformative justice uncovers, deconstructs, and alters relations of power that contribute to interlocking oppressions as forms systemic violence. *Transformative justice* is defined as "change that emphasizes local agency and resources, the prioritization of processes rather than preconceived outcomes and the challenging of unequal intersecting power relationships and structures of exclusion at both the local and the global level" (Gready & Robins, 2014, p. 340). By recentering the experiences, voices, and power of oppressed communities, transformative justice seeks to redress and deconstruct conditions of systemic violence and marginality at multiple structural levels within society.

Oriented toward the transmutation and emancipatory affirmation of communities wounded by systems of power, liberation psychology is characterized by an explicit intentional deconstruction of oppression in all of its manifestations. In line with liberation psychology's commitment to disrupt and interrogate power lies PAR as a paradigm that strives to engage communities affected by social conditions of oppression as experts and leaders in discerning, developing, and implementing solutions to problems that affect the quality of their lives. The epistemological origins and foundations of PAR are multidisciplinary, as are those of liberation psychology. Yet there are significant parallels between PAR processes and liberation psychology that align to foster the agency, determination, and power of individuals and communities institutionally marginalized. Comparing and contrasting PAR and liberation psychology is beyond the scope of this chapter. However, acompañamiento is presented as an ethically grounding common value, practice, and commitment. PAR collaborations, for example, can serve as valuable contexts to cultivate and engage with communities in a process of social change that is conducive to their thriving, liberation, and transformation. Within PAR and liberation psychology key values that undergird the role of the researcher and that facilitate liberation psychology processes toward transformative justice by and with oppressed communities is a praxis of acompañamiento. Therefore, through an autoethnographic reflexive analysis of my experiences within two separate PAR collaborations, I identify elements of acompañamiento.

A conceptual definition of acompañamiento, followed by a brief overview of liberation psychology and PAR foundations, sets the framework for the autoethnographic reflections I present and discuss in relation to two community-based PAR projects that strived to cultivate conditions of transformative justice. Three themes—interrogating power, counter-hegemonic storying, and collective healing—are described as PAR outcomes facilitated through a praxis of acompañamiento in community–researcher relationships. Through these autoethnographic reflections, I discuss how acompañamiento cultivated the development of these themes. Moreover, I describe how acompañamiento functioned as an important value in the embodiment of the (researcher's) self with the community, often perceived as "other." How acompañamiento is intentionally engaged in the development and implementation of PAR orients the researcher toward a psychology of liberation by, with, and from the perspective of the oppressed.

Acompañamiento, I argue, is critical to a liberation psychology oriented toward transformative justice because it is committed to the disruption of power asymmetries in knowledge production and disembodied research. Through an authoethnographic process, I reflect on my collaborations within two PAR projects to describe how acompañamiento facilitated the interrupting power, the producing of counter-hegemonic stories, and collective healing. This chapter invites community-engaged researchers and practitioners rooted or aligned with liberation psychology to consider the significance or presence of acompañamiento in their work and possibilities for putting acompañamiento into intentional meaningful practice.

DEFINING ACOMPAÑAMIENTO

Epistemologies of liberation psychology, also rooted in liberation theology, affirm the value of acompañamiento. Within critical psychologies such as liberation psychology, this is referred to as *psychosocial accompaniment* (Watkins, 2015). Consistent with acompañamiento, psychosocial accompaniment is identified as essential for liberation, decolonization, healing, and social justice (Adams, Dobles, Gómez, Kurtiş, & Molina, 2015). As a process that unfolds and evolves from standing with and alongside communities, through building relationships and everyday lived experiences of adaptation, assistance, compassion, and witnessing, acompañamiento implicates feelings of mutual vulnerability and struggle through cobeing (Sepúlveda, 2011, 2018). Latino theologian Goizueta (2009) posited that acompañamiento symbolizes the expression of humanity in its fullest: "To accompany another person is to walk with [them]. It is, above all, by walking with others that we learn to relate to them and love them" (p. 206). The love for the other that Goizueta (2009) described also characterizes Anzaldúa's (2015) theorizing on spiritual activism, which involves fostering an ethic of love anchored in an affirmation of one's humanity. Acompañamiento is not a passive process; on the contrary, it invites the recognition of mutual implacability in each other's lives toward the creation of social change. Defined as engagement with communities, acompañamiento serves as a foundation for a liberatory project that when combined with PAR, can facilitate conditions that allow for transformative justice.

Acompañamiento is being, doing, and feeling with and in the company of others. In circumstances of heightened inequities or injustices, building genuine relationships of solidarity and care with communities is a characteristic of acompañamiento. Shared experiences of cobeing cultivate accountability and a sense of care grounded in the experiential learning and growth of researchers and communities (Watkins, 2015). Walsh (2014) described these forms of acompañamiento as intentional forms of cobeing that involve *desaprendiendo* (unlearning), as well as *preguntando y caminando* (asking and walking). Thus, the process of unlearning, characterized by the reflexive and relational experiences of collaboration, invites researchers to interrogate or interrupt hegemonic forms of power to facilitate opportunities for community counternarratives and healing.

Similarly, Freire (1970) identified a praxis of acompañamiento as important when stating: "At all stages of their liberation, the oppressed must see themselves engaged in the ontological and historical vocation of becoming more fully human" (p. 52). Thus, it is through acompañamiento that social justice begins to sow seeds of authentic caring relationships of respect, dignity, and meaningful collaboration. The deep and critical empathy that characterizes acompañamiento is also fluid, culturally and contextually determined. Acts, expressions, and repertoires of acompañamiento are often performed within *borderlands* (Anzaldúa, 2015) of differential experiences and positionalities of power. Examples of these include, but are not limited to, the following: research collaborations with communities of Color with intersecting marginalized positionalities (Comas-Díaz, 2000; Fine & Torre, 2006; Howarth, 2006), countries torn apart by war and political unrest (Comas-Díaz, Lykes, & Alarcón, 1998; Lykes & Mallona, 2008; Rahman, 2004; Serrano-García & Vargas Molina, 1993), and young people advocating for education equity (Sepúlveda, 2011). Values of acompañamiento are used to a degree within each of these contexts and relationships. These expressions and orientations toward acompañamiento facilitate a critical praxis to engage in ethical socially responsive research, grounded in values of liberation psychology. Choosing acompañamiento over the disembodied and detached "objective" modes of research interrogates the pervasive hegemony inherent in some community-based research, or community–researcher collaboration, which despite their engagement in such contexts might not be led by and from the perspective of the community.

Relinquishing hegemonic power by letting go of hierarchical relational dynamics of control and influence is an important characteristic of acompañamiento. Without the leadership and contributions of those most affected by systems of power, transformative justice is not possible. The illusion that justice and liberation can be achieved without meaningful genuine community engagement reproduces epistemic injustice, along with other oppressions embedded within systems of power that are not immune to liberation psychology and PAR. Liberation in the name of those who are oppressed, without the oppressed, cannot be done. Acompañamiento therefore serves as mechanism by which to recenter the voices, lived experiences, and concerns of those who are on the margins. A praxis of acompañamiento is to embody authentic caring and critically compassionate relationships of collaboration, coexistence, and mutuality with the oppressed to accompany, or bear with them, the struggle and resistance in their pursuit of liberation of and for transformative justice.

A PSYCHOLOGY OF AND FOR LIBERATION

Liberation Psychology: A Latin American Perspective

Latin American liberation psychology evolved to address the social conditions of oppressed peoples, whose circumstances were best understood through a socio-historical and politically situated analysis of their lived realities as determined by the oppressed, not the psychologist. Liberation psychology functions as a tool for resistance and action toward transformative justice as the deconstruction of systems of power (Burton & Kagan, 2005; Dobles, 2015; Flores Osorio, 2009). By aligning itself with communities who are marginalized, liberation psychology interrogates the coloniality of power (Quijano, 2000), which is defined by interconnected practices of epistemic and sociocultural hegemony that maintain systems of oppression within the social order. The epistemological and methodological tools within liberation psychology are deployed strategically to deconstruct the coloniality of power with and from the perspectives of the oppressed. In the 1970s, cultural, economic, and political shifts were unraveling toward the sovereignty of Latin American nation-states that sought to reclaim or maintain their independence from Western Eurocentric influence. Liberation psychology emerged in Latin America within this unique sociopolitical moment (Serrano-García & Vargas Molina, 1993). The epistemic roots of liberation psychology emerged from core ideals that a psychology of and for liberation should begin and be led by oppressed communities. Traditional psychology was viewed as insufficient and inadequate in pursuing such ideals; hence, liberation psychology surfaced as a form of resistance to traditional psychology.

Psychology, heavily influenced by Western Eurocentric notions that prioritize individualism and objectivity over collective and subjective experiences, was criticized for its *ahistorical* and *apolitical* approach to social issues. The positivist orientation of traditional psychology, together with its assertion of neutrality and the universality of human development and behaviors, was viewed by critical psychologists as emblematic of the inherent hegemony of the discipline, which left the status quo intact (Dobles, 2015). Psychological theories, rather than generating knowledge and tools to address injustice and oppression, were informed by research conducted with predominantly White male groups, whose experiences became the "norm" by which marginalized groups with limited status and power would be compared (Burton & Gómez Ordóñez, 2015). Liberation psychology resisted these mechanisms of epistemic injustice by purporting its preferential option for the poor and oppressed (Burton & Kagan, 2005; Comas-Díaz, Lykes, & Alarcón, 1998). The development of a psychology from and informed by the social condition of the oppressed became the defining ethos of the field of liberation psychology.

The radical militancy and antihegemonic principles undergirding liberation psychology largely arose as a response to civil rights violations, political unrest, and sociocultural intergenerational trauma, which for decades characterized the social conditions of some Latin American countries (Serrano-García & Vargas Molina, 1993). U.S. economic and political influence contributed to the severe manifestations of civil unrest, war and military interventions in Latin America, specifically in El Salvador. In the struggle for justice, the restoration of peace, and the renewal of humanity and healing from trauma, Ignacio Martín-Baró (1994) conceived of a psychology of liberation that would animate the power, radical hope and well-being of oppressed peoples to reclaim their power in leading the path toward socially just change.

Martín-Baró's (1989, 1990, 1994) work was foundational to the formation of liberation psychology within Latin American. According to Martín-Baró (1994), liberation psychology "must turn away from the task of generalizing specific characteristics to whole populations. Instead, an attempt to understand the particularities of every community is in order" (p. 77). To understand these social conditions, several of Martín-Baró's (1994) concepts, such as *realismo-crítico*,[1] became foundational to the epistemological formation of liberation psychology. Realismo-crítico argues for a unique position on the construction of theory. That is, theory should not define social problems. Instead, it should be used as a guide to facilitate action. Theory is and must be informed by people's circumstances. A bottom-up community-centered grassroots process that begins with the questioning of reality must be a defining feature of theory.

In line with Martín-Baró's (1994) theorizing, allied scholars and practitioners also contributed to the formation of a psychology oriented toward the liberation of the oppressed. The writings by Flores Osorio (2009; see also Burton & Kagan, 2005) on dependency theory, Freire's (1970) notion of *conscientización*, Fals Borda's (1985, 2001, 2006; Fals Borda & Rahman, 1991) adaptation of participatory (action) research, and Montero's (2004, 2010) expanded theorizing of Martín-Baró's (1990, 1994) work, specifically, the concept of *deideologization*, contributed significantly to the development of liberation psychology. Each of these concepts sought to explain the underlying structural factors for social problems, while developing the critical consciousness and actions necessary to address them.

Dependency theory, for example, posits that "economic, political and cultural dependency are derived from colonial underdevelopment and thus structural dependency and exploitation in Latin American capitalism will only produce a substandard development" (Flores Osorio, 2009, p. 19). To transgress the conditions of structural dependency, conscientización, in line with liberation psychology and PAR paradigms, is characterized by iterative cycles of reflection–action–reflection (Fals Borda, 2006; Freire, 1970). These cycles strive toward the transformation of social conditions that Walsh (2014) described as decolonial pedagogies and Montero (2004, 2010) characterized as a process of deideologization. To deideologize is to develop a critical social analysis of how power and oppression surface and construct realities, and to interrogate these realities to deconstruct or transform them. In other words, to decolonize knowledge and the production of such discourses (Walsh, 2014) is to engage in a process of deideologization. All of these concepts have contributed to a psychology of and for liberation of the oppressed, and the emergence of allied disciplines and fields of study in the across the Global South and the West.

---

[1]*Realismo-crítico* literally translates to "critical realism"; however, this term is not to be equated with Ram Roy Bhaskar's (2013) philosophical use of the term to describe rational scientific inquiry. On the contrary, Martín-Baró's use of realismo-crítico differs in that it epistemologically posits that problems generate their own theories, and thus theory should not solely inform the conceptualization of a problem but rather should aim to uncover the root causes and mechanisms to address it.

The Beginnings of Liberation Psychology in the United States

Liberation psychology in the United States can trace its origins to the influential work of Martín-Baró (1994) and Freire (1970), as well as the social movements that catalyzed the formation of community psychology. As Watts and Serrano-García (2003) wrote,

> liberation psychology is different from U.S. community psychology because liberation psychology places emphasis squarely on the creation of just societies, strengthening self-determination, and healing the effects of oppression . . . new knowledge is acquired and deemed valuable in accordance with its contribution to the liberation process. The analysis of social power would be a central concern. (p. 74)

Liberation psychology's epistemological and methodological orientations are indeed different from community psychology; however, there are some shared values. Among these is a commitment to social justice, centering community experiences, and building the capacity of individuals and groups to create social change on their own terms (Nelson & Prilleltensky, 2010). Empowerment is also a key tenet of community psychology, which advocates for individuals and communities gaining access and control over the decision-making processes, resources, and institutions that affect their lives (Watts & Serrano-García, 2003). Instead of taking or claiming power within an inherently oppressive structure, liberation psychology advocates for the transformation of these systems and structures. Transformative justice is thus a central component, and mode of distinguishing liberation psychology from community psychology. Although parallels exist, there are significant differences that mark their divergent visions and approaches toward transformative justice.

The role of a psychologist, whose values align with liberation psychology, is to disturb and unsettle Western Eurocentric psychologies to forbid the discipline from becoming complacent and complicit in the perpetuation of oppressions. In the United States, this has been characterized by the development of critical psychologies and praxes that engage PAR as a tool to decenter the power and influence of the researcher over the research processes and outcomes. This process of decentering parallels that of delinking or, more specifically, decolonizing knowledge. In U.S. liberation psychology, decoloniality has become an important feature of the discipline as it strives to engage in a sociohistorical analysis of social problems and conditions of oppression (Adams et al., 2015). Decoloniality is characterized by a process of interrogating and deconstructing ways of knowing, doing and being that are rooted in or emerged from Eurocentric perspectives of colonial power, oppression and racialization (Maldonado-Torres, 2016). The permanence of injustice and inequity must be historically, socially, and politically situated in the communities whose lives have been affected by coloniality. Thus, liberation psychology implies the need to conceptualize problems with and from the sociohistorical and political subjectivities of the oppressed. To commit our work, and therefore sense of self, to the unveiling and destruction of conditions of oppression, injustice, and suffering is to engage liberation psychology as a praxis of acompañamiento in the pursuit of transformative justice.

PARTICIPATORY ACTION RESEARCH

The foundations of PAR, including the principles, ethics, and approaches that guide this paradigm, are reviewed and discussed in the sections that follow. Grounded in a brief overview of these foundations, the commitment to and orientation toward the liberation of the oppressed is made explicit, along with the use of autoethnography as a critical reflexivity tool to support PAR of and for liberation.

Foundations of PAR

The origins of PAR are unclear and nonlinear within the psychology literature. However, the values, ethics, and approaches that gave way to a PAR paradigm, broadly and most commonly known as community-based participatory research, emerged in response to social circumstances of systemic oppression. The significant threads that informed the development of PAR within the social sciences have multidisciplinary roots. Some of these are best characterized by the work of critical social scientists, such as Martín-Baró (1994), who used research as a tool for liberation and for the deconstruction of systems of power and oppression.

The democratization of knowledge and epistemic justice are perhaps two key defining features of PAR in the social sciences. In writing about the foundations of PAR, Montero (2006) stated that the name of PAR was introduced in 1970 by anthropologist Marja-Liisa Swantz (2008) in the context of her collaborative work with Tanzanian women and communities who were positioned as knowledgeable doers and contributors to the research process. Colombian sociologist, Orlando Fals Borda (1985), on the other hand, credits Bangladeshi scholar Anisur Rahman (1990, 2004) as the first to have coined the use of participation *and* action in relation to the word and work of research, hence the development of PAR. In general, the origins and conceptual definitions associated with PAR are attributed to these scholars, who engaged, developed, and advocated for community-centered approaches. Regardless of the discipline, a PAR paradigm can best be understood as an approach with a set of tools, values, and ethics that facilitate engagement by communities in leading efforts toward social change.

The social justice orientation of PAR within the Global South was also present in the U.S. context—namely, in the work of Kurt Lewin (1946), specifically, in his use of action research to address social issues with and through the contribution of communities affected by social problems. As Fals Borda (1985, 2001, 2006; Fals Borda & Rahman, 1991) has claimed, action research and PAR became interchangeable terms and legitimate modes of research and inquiry. PAR sought to build an epistemology oriented toward the deconstruction of positivist research that often reified dualistic or binary ways of thinking, and the positioning of subjects (e.g., people, communities) as objects of psychological investigation (Montero & Sonn, 2009).

At the 1977 Cartagena International Conference on Critical Research, the concept and practice of PAR became known, embraced, and developed by practitioners and scholars committed to birthing new ways of approaching and doing research with and from the perspectives of oppressed communities. This is often considered as the beginning of PAR in the academy. Yet it must be noted that practices of collaboration, meaningful participation, shared decision-making, and centering of local knowledge, culture, and histories were already key defining features of communities organizing themselves to redress social injustices, even before such PAR paradigms existed or were named. Indigenous communities, for example, practice elements of PAR among themselves through decolonial practices that emphasize and value local knowledge, mutuality, and relationality. A praxis of acompañamiento among several Indigenous communities is a defining experience and an embodiment of being and connecting to build toward transformative justice.

PAR Oriented to the Liberation of the Oppressed

PAR is a paradigm oriented to fomenting the liberation, agency, and power of communities engaged in the research process (Fine & Torre, 2006). Unlike other methodological paradigms, which prioritize the expertise of the researcher instead of the communities affected by social problems of inequity and injustice, PAR works from the bottom up. That is, it begins from the local needs, concerns, and experiences of communities, thereby centering the local knowledge, lived experiences and voices of communities. PAR situates the experiences of communities and views them as experts in their own lives with the capacity to effect change and lead the path toward transformative justice (Fals Borda, 1985, 2001; Swantz, 2008). The role of the researcher within a PAR process is one of a facilitator and ally to support the efforts and initiatives that communities want to lead. Unlike other paradigms, PAR is oriented toward social change and transformation instead of the production of theory for the sake of knowledge.

The prioritizing of community voice is central to a PAR process. Advocates of PAR have critiqued conventional or traditional research methodologies, which leave uncontested social structures and systems of power maintaining the status quo. As a means to disrupt the research dichotomies in knowledge and power, PAR strives to strengthen the agency and meaningful participation of communities in the research process. Through this paradigm, PAR aims to remedy inequities in knowledge production. In writing about research, Martín-Baró (1994) posited the following: "Practical knowledge acquired through PAR should lead toward the people gaining power, a power that allows for them to become the protagonists of their history and to effect change" (p. 30). Consistent with liberation psychology, PAR is guided toward a preferential treatment or engagement in the experiences and lives of oppressed communities.

The pursuit of liberation through a PAR process is characterized by three interconnected values, some of which align with liberation psychology principles. First, those who are directly affected by social problems must participate in the processes, research or otherwise, that allow them to address the social issues and conditions of injustice affecting them (Fals Borda, 2001, 2006; Fine & Torre, 2006; Montero, 2006). Democratizing power by placing it in the hands of communities affected by injustice and oppression is thus a key tenet of PAR. Community members are the experts; researchers are merely to position themselves as supporters or coconspirators in their pursuits for justice, transformation, and liberation for and by oppressed communities. As a paradigm that facilitates the liberatory conditions of transformative justice for those most on the margins, PAR engages community members as protagonists with the skills and capacity to critically analyze, interrogate, and confront social inequities of systemic oppression that constrain their power and thriving (Fals Borda & Rahman, 1991).

Second, knowledge is socially and contextually situated, as well as embedded within relations of power (Fals Borda, 2006; Gaventa & Cornwall, 2008). Thus, research paradigms like PAR that facilitate collective critical social analysis and engagement with people's lived experiences are most effective in deconstructing oppressive power relations that do not affirm the dignity, humanity, and sovereignty of communities. Local and Indigenous knowledge and culture must be centered in PAR; it must serve as a catalyst for the development of community-centered initiatives that restore and support the power and determination of communities.

Third, embodied and subjective experiences, rather than of being perceived as biased or compromising to the research process, are actually conceived as important and valuable to the research (Montero, 2006). As Selener (1997) wrote, "knowledge is deepened through a dialectical process of people acting, with others upon reality in order both to change and to understand it" (p. 74). PAR, like liberation, is an ongoing and continuous process that has no end point. Instead, PAR is a moving process of working toward liberation from the interlocking systems of oppression that overshadow or limit the enfranchisement of communities. To describe a process of engaging liberation psychology values through a praxis of acompañamiento within PAR, I turn to a brief description of autoethnography as a critically reflexive methodology.

Autoethnography: A PAR Critical Reflexivity Tool

As a community-engaged researcher, autoethnography has become the methodology through which I approach PAR collaborations and projects. Emerging out of critical race and feminist theories, including decolonial methodologies that underscore the value of stories and narratives to foment social change (Dutta, 2018), autoethnography is a method for documenting and deconstructing the culture of power that lies at the crux of research, theory, and practice. The researcher turns the gaze inward, looking into oneself to better discern the lived experiences, subjectivities and disquieting beliefs that inform power and positionality in relation to the research and, most important, the researched

(Denzin, 2003). *Autoethnography* is a methodological approach that centers the subjective, embodied, and situated experiences of the researcher within an ethnographic context (Fernández, 2018). As a qualitative research method, autoethnography is oriented toward engaging in critical reflexivity by and through the sociocultural, as well as the personal and political experiences of the researcher. Critical reflexivity undergirds the process of situating the researchers' positionalities, identities, and subjectivities at the intersections of power and coloniality, which inevitably surface at every phase of the research. Thus, a critical reflexive introspective evaluation and interrogation of power, in the context of research and research relationships, is necessary.

Autoethnography facilitates the development of a critically reflexive consciousness that aligns with liberation psychology mechanisms of deideologizing and problematizing social issues (Fernández, 2018). These mechanisms are central to a PAR process that specifically facilitates a praxis of acompañamiento. To further characterize the processes through which acompañamiento surfaces to advance a vision of transformative justice, I offer autoethnographic reflections of two PAR collaborations. Each reflection is organized along three themes, which I describe in relation to praxis of acompañamiento toward transformative justice: (a) interrupting power, (b) counter-hegemonic storying, and (c) collective healing. Through these reflections, I describe how acompañamiento as a form of praxis rooted in liberation psychology facilitated or sought to cultivate a vision of transformative justice for the communities with whom I collaborated. I discuss these themes as tenants of a psychology of and for liberation by and from the material realities of two distinct communities: student activists within the neoliberal university and Mexican immigrant mothers in a gentrifying neighborhood.

CENTERING ACOMPAÑAMIENTO IN PAR FOR TRANSFORMATIVE JUSTICE

Interrupting Power

When we have to think strategically, we also have to accept our complicity.... If we are not exterior to the problem under investigation, we too are the problem under investigation. Diversity work is messy, even dirty, work.

—SARA AHMED (2007)

Racialized incidents toward Students of Color are common at predominantly White institutions. Diversity efforts and initiatives have been the hallmark of such universities seeking to purport an image of inclusion and equity that is only superficial and performative (Ahmed, 2007). Given this climate, as a collective of Women of Color student activists and a faculty member, we formed the Sociopolitical Citizenship Participatory Action Research (SC-PAR) Collective, a student-led project that centers the voices, intersectional experiences, sociopolitical, and affective subjectivities of student activists engaged in the Unity IV movement at a small private Jesuit university in the Silicon Valley of California. Unity IV was catalyzed by the recurrence of racialized incidents and the inadequate administrative response by the university. These previous incidents, together with the poor transparency and accountability of the university to address issues of racism, colorblindness, and discrimination, catalyzed the student movement, which lasted approximately two academic years between spring 2015 through 2017.

Narratives of social justice affiliated with the university, along with the culture of entrepreneurialism that characterizes the Silicon Valley, were significantly tested by the campus climate of racism and colorblindness that most Black, African American, and Latinx students identified as oppressive and disempowering. The SC-PAR project sought to interrogate the practices and discourses of the university that championed diversity-related efforts that seemingly silenced and tuned out the concerns, experiences, and voices of the student activists at the forefront of the Unity IV movement. As a collective of four student activists and myself, we engaged in the SC-PAR project (for which I oversaw and acquired institutional research funding). Together, we developed aspects of the research process that aligned with their organizing strategies and goals. One of these strategies was documenting and disseminating the stories of students on the frontlines of the movement.

Acompañamiento within this specific project took the form of bearing witness to students' activism and their process of interrupting power through the development of an action project that involved student activists-coresearchers gathering stories, via an interview methodology, of students involved in Unity IV. Through this process, the SC-PAR collective engaged in a praxis of acompañamiento that involved students challenging discourses on diversity, which for them meant words with no action or institutional change to follow given the entrenched discourse of colorblindness within the university. In documenting the voices of students in the movement, student activist-coresearchers interrupted power by demanding a seat at the university administrators' table. In their meetings with administrators, student activists made recommendations for improving the curricula, implementing diversity-centered training for students, and recruiting Faculty and Students of Color, as well as the developing resources to support and retain Students of Color and first-generation college students, specifically those who are the first in their families to pursue higher education. The demands of their organizing also included establishing Ethnic Studies, as well as Women and Gender Studies Departments.

In line with the Jesuit values of companionship with the marginalized, acompañamiento as a praxis sought to validate students' experiences of oppression, specifically racism, as well as equip them with the research skills and tools to document and transform these conditions. Stories, as modes of discourse, are a form of power—and power, according to student activists, needed to be interrogated. My commitment to ensuring that the stories of student activists in the Unity IV movement lives on; they are reminders of what must not be tolerated and as affirmations of what can be done, grounded in a deep sense of acompañamiento with Unity IV student activists. Facilitating and supporting the development of student activists' research skills, specifically in ethnography and interview methodologies, allowed them to document and tell their own stories without censorship and in their own words. Walking alongside students, in their struggle to transform the racialized neoliberalization of the university leads me to remain vigilant of the university's attention to diversity. We, as the SC-PAR collective, accompany ourselves as allies and conspirators in interrupting the manifestations of power.

Counter-Hegemonic Storying

If we forget ourselves, who will be left to remember us?
—CHERRÍE MORAGA (2019, p. 6)

Power lies in spaces. Power also resides in the stories that people share across generations, transcending time and place. Stories inform a person's memories as these are attached or ascribed to communities. Thus, stories are a form of wielding power. Stories have the capacity to represent and produce, but they also contest and transgress conditions of oppression. Through the cultivation and affirmation of empowering narratives, I describe the process of storying (Goodson, 1998) that unfolded into a PAR collaboration with a group of Mexican immigrant *madres* (mothers), called *Madres Emprendedoras* (enterprising mothers). This autoethnographic reflection describes acompañamiento with the group Madres Emprendedoras in a low-income working-class community undergoing gentrification in the southernmost region of the Silicon Valley.

Located in very close proximity to downtown San José and less than a mile from the new Google megacampus, the Guadalupe-Washington community is considered a prime location for new housing and retail development that will serve the needs of the prospective technology industries. Although that is one narrative associated with the community, there are others concerning the families and long-term residents of the area. According to the San José Mayor's Gang Prevention Task Force, the Guadalupe–Washington area is recognized as one of several "gang hot spots" in the city. Uncharacteristic of other gang-affiliated areas, the community is referred by local law enforcement officials as "the triangle" because it is home to one of three rival gangs adjacent to each other. The Santa Clara County District Attorney's Office considers Guadalupe-Washington and its neighboring communities "ground zero" for street-level human trafficking and prostitution activity in the County (J. Fuentes, personal communication, May 2019). The labels attached to Guadalupe-Washington reflect a poor narrative of the community, one characterized by recurring high incidents of crime and a wavering sense of public safety.

Shifting the hegemonic narratives and associations of the Guadalupe-Washington community was an important goal of the Madres Emprendedoras. Our collaboration began as a college-level PAR course offered at no cost to a self-selected group of predominantly Mexican immigrant madres. In the context of this collaboration, I served as the instructor for the course, which was offered in Spanish in the community, as well as a resource and supporter of the madres' action-projects developed within the context of the course. I embraced a praxis of acompañamiento within the context of the PAR course because I saw it necessary to support the madres in their pursuit of challenging the disempowering and deficit narratives of their community. As an outsider to the community, yet viewed by the madres as the *maestra* (teacher) and therefore knowledgeable "expert," my praxis of acompañamiento was to reposition myself and shift the label of "expert" onto the madres because it was them who were most informed about the needs and concerns of their community.

To credit and affirm the madres in their knowledge or *sabiduria* (wisdom) of the community, research methodologies were modified to have these become a part of their daily activities. For example, in facilitating the madres' ethnographic research skills, each was tasked with journaling or audio recording what they saw, heard and felt in their community. Additionally, we engaged in *caminatas* (neighborhood walkthroughs) to better understand the impact of gentrification in the community. The caminatas allowed us to document the community while walking alongside, or in acompañamiento with each other. Our process of facilitating the madres' research skills, and collaborating with them on their action-projects, required them storying (i.e., telling stories) about and from the perspective of the community. Counter-hegemonic storying was an important practice of acompañamiento.

Many of the madres who participated in the CBPAR course and subsequent action-projects had resided in the area for more than a decade. The narrative the madres ascribed to the community was thus inconsistent with narrative of gangs and violence, as well as that of a prospective urban development zone. Neither of these narratives underscored the lived experiences of the madres and communities of Guadalupe-Washington. Narratives associated with low-income working-class communities, including communities of Color and immigrants, often reflect hegemonic knowledge and discourse. Counter-hegemonic storying as a practice of speaking back and against oppressive narratives that disenfranchise, disempower, and stigmatize the community, centers values of liberation psychology and transformative justice. Acompañamiento within this specific collaboration took the form of facilitating opportunities for the madres to tell their own stories, and to produce empowering narratives that were rooted in storying their hopes, dreams, and realities within the Guadalupe-Washington community.

A praxis of acompañamiento was thus characterized by a practice of active listening, witnessing, documenting, with and alongside the madres, and illustrating their stories in the creation of community-centered school-based mural, titled *Mosaicos de la Comunidad*. Leveraging institutional and cultural resources to amplify the stories of the madres whose voices were muffled by the noise of profit and crime aligned with a transformative justice approach toward liberation. Liberation among the madres was characterized by our mutual accompaniment to document the unfolding conditions of gentrification, displacement, and disenfranchisement in their community. Experiencing community life, through *platicas con café* (chatting over coffee), *caminatas* (walkathons), *fiestas* (parties), and *kermeses* (potlucks), as well as school and community-related events, such as neighborhood cleanups, constitute the sociocultural activities in the everyday lives of the madres. Acompañamiento was thus the will to coexist, to immerse myself in the lives, dreams, and vulnerabilities, but also the strength and agency of the madres and their community, and to listen to their stories of struggle and resistance.

Making Space for Healing

Pain is important: how we evade it, how we succumb to it, how we deal with it, how we transcend it.

—AUDRE LORDE (1984/2012)

Pain, as Lorde (1984/2012) stated, is important. Pain surfaces sensibilities to wounding from trauma that require healing and the restoration of one's being. Making space or even allotting a few minutes of time for such an intentional and necessary process is difficult to carve, however. This is especially the case among those who are engaged in activism and everyday forms of resistance. As a student activist stated: "Living is a struggle, healing is necessary to our survival, but it's a privilege I don't have the luxury for." The remark stayed with me; it has accompanied our SC-PAR collective through our work with student activists. Well-being is predicated on individual and community healing, and the restoration of a sense of humanity, dignity, and integrity. Healing facilitates conditions of self and collective love that transmute pain and suffering and are grounded in liberation. Yet how do we (or can we) make space for such meaningful forms of transformative justice at the personal, relational, and institutional levels?

To expand on this question, when approaching a community or group-centered research project or collaboration, to what extent do we as researchers consider the emotional, affective, and embodied wounds of peoples lived realities? Most often within the context of PAR the development of the research is approached through a question that centers on the examination or documentation of an issue or problem to redress it. The communities at the center of the problem become the conduits by which the issue is to be identified, documented, and remedied. Consideration for the social, intellectual, and even physical, as well as emotional, labor of the community, or coresearchers (including the researcher), is acknowledged to a modest degree. Yet the affective subjectivities and emotional labor that is expended remains on the periphery. Critical reflexive dialogues are an important practice within PAR, as is the development of narratives grounded in values that affirm the dignity and humanity of a community–researcher collaboration where liberation is meant to unfold. Healing can and must constitute an important element of the PAR process.

By intentionally engaging in a practice of acompañamiento that centers on making space for healing, individually or collective (or both), researchers alongside community members can open ourselves to change. We carve openings to the flow of new ways of cobeing, bridge-building (Anzaldúa, 2015), and solidarity that reflect a pedagogy of *sentipensante* (sensing, thinking; Rendón, 2012) that builds on deepening relationships in order to restore or device modes toward liberation. The curing of wounds in the pursuit of liberation involves the witnessing of our or others' pain and cocreating practices of care, critical compassion, and emotional emancipation. It must be noted, however, that healing is not a solitary process. Similarly, liberation is not individual processes with a determined clear-cut outcome. Healing is relational, a process with ebbs and flows, in the company and with the support of others. PAR oriented toward a liberation psychology of and for transformative justice is a praxis of acompañamiento that may also lend itself to forms of healing, love, and care. The SC-PAR collective is an example of this process given the collaborations that began with the personal and political dimensions of student activism, which then unfolded into identifying practices toward healing and care.

In the early stages of the project, we conceived of our research as merely a political strategy to preserve the integrity of the voices, contributions, and vision of Unity IV student activists, as well as to identify the factors that supported their academic thriving, political engagement, and sociopolitical citizenship as agents of change. We did not account for the emotional labor this process in itself would unearth for student activists-coresearchers, however. Clearly, questions in regard to our extent and abilities as researchers to make space for healing or account for the emotional labor of our coresearchers were not at the forefront of our project. Acompañamiento thus became an important mechanism through which we were able to assess the impact of our research and adjust our process to make intentional space for healing as determined by student activists themselves. The capacity for cultural humility, critical compassion, and relational solidarity therefore informed our process of acompañamiento. For me, it made salient the importance of putting aside any given research agenda and to interrogate my power and positionality within the research process and in relation to who, what, and why such issues were being engaged. Taking a step back to determine the trajectory of the research and remain present and mindful to what student activists-coresearchers determined as important and of value to them became another mode of acompañamiento conducive to healing on the terms and conditions led by the group of student activists-coresearchers in the SC-PAR collective.

Acompañamiento was not exclusive to my subjectivities as a researcher, however. In fact, student activists-coresearchers engaged acompañamiento through witnessing and listening to other student activists' stories. Student activists' desires to make space for their stories, as collective reflections of anger and pain, sought to cultivate a sense of liberation, collective power, and resistance to silence. Breaking the silence by telling their own stories would aid them in their healing. The interconnected emotional experiences that surfaced throughout the research, as well as our academic and community organizing contexts, led us to organize a 1-day healing retreat for Women of Color student activists. The retreat was informed by student activists' need to process the emotional toll of "doing the work of the university," as a student activist stated, and how this inflicted indignation and thus anger upon their bodies, minds, and hearts.

The Quest for Unapologetic Emotional Emancipation is Now! (QUEEN) retreat consisted of various self-care activities, such as journaling, reflections, meditations, and *limpias* (spiritual cleansing rituals), as well as community-building exercises, among them affirmation circles and vision boards. Making space for healing involved bearing witness to and facilitating conditions for collective liberation through acompañamiento, as well as mutual being and sharing. A praxis that attends to the spoken and unspoken challenges of engaging in liberatory projects through PAR aims to transform or create humanizing experiences of epistemic justice. The pursuit of liberation must therefore begin with healing—individual and collective. Furthermore, it must allow us to revel and unearth what causes affliction, friction, and pain to repiece the fragmentations of ourselves within and outside of the context of PAR. Transformative justice of and for liberation is guided and informed by the experiences of acompañamiento that invite syncretism into our body, mind, and heart and that incite transformative justice as a mode of liberation.

CONCLUSION: *ACOMPAÑANTES EN EL ANDAR* (ACCOMPANYING DURING THE WALK)

Liberation is not achieved alone as the autoethnographic reflections highlighted in this chapter within the context of PAR collaboration demonstrate. Liberation is a not an individual, solitary process; it is a relational, communal, and mutual project. There is no end point to liberation. One does not achieve or arrive at a point of liberation, but rather develops the critical consciousness and relational practices of solidarity to resist oppression and constantly strive for transformative justice in the company of others. Liberation can be characterized by an unending sense of struggle, yet the upending of oppression requires that structures and ideologies, including those that contribute to the logics of knowledge production and disembodied positivist objective research, be transgressed. The unsettling of structures in research necessitates that the researcher interrogate their complicity in these systems and, with intentionality and cultural humility, learn with, from, and in accompaniment of communities.

Liberation is a collective, community-driven process. As Black feminist scholar Audre Lorde (1984/2012), reminded us: "Without community, there is no liberation . . . but community must not mean a shedding of our differences, nor the pathetic pretense that these differences do not exist" (p. 111). Indeed, we must recognize these differences and the power within our differing positionalities, as well as how this can be leveraged toward community liberation. These words underscore those of Indigenous activist and artist Lilla Watson, who claimed that liberation is a collective, bounded process, not an individual pursuit, stating: "If you have come here to help me, you are wasting your time. But if you have come because your liberation is bound up with mine, then let us work together" (Invisible Children, n.d.). We are bound by to each other, and it is through acompañamiento that we can forge, build, and imagine radical change. We are *acompañantes en el andar*, companions in this walk; we build the road by walking alongside each other, learning through every mistake and wrong turn, and how we can rise, revise, and root ourselves in the integrity and dignity of our mutual companionship, coexistence, and acompañamiento.

REFERENCES

Adams, G., Dobles, I., Gómez, L. H., Kurtiş, T., & Molina, L. E. (2015). Decolonizing psychological science: Introduction to the special thematic section. *Journal of Social and Political Psychology, 3*, 213–238.

Ahmed, S. (2007). "You end up doing the document rather than doing the doing": Diversity, race equality and the politics of documentation. *Ethnic and Racial Studies, 30*, 590–609. http://dx.doi.org/10.1080/01419870701356015

Anzaldúa, G. (2015). *Light in the dark/Luz en lo oscuro: Rewriting identity, spirituality, reality*. Durham, NC: Duke University Press. http://dx.doi.org/10.1215/9780822375036

Bhaskar, R. (2013). *A realist theory of science*. London, England: Routledge. http://dx.doi.org/10.4324/9780203090732

Burton, M., & Gómez Ordóñez, L. H. (2015). Liberation psychology: Another kind of critical psychology. In I. Parker (Ed.), *Handbook of critical psychology* (pp. 248–255). London, England: Routledge.

Burton, M., & Kagan, C. (2005). Liberation social psychology: Learning from Latin America. *Journal of Community & Applied Social Psychology, 15*, 63–78. http://dx.doi.org/10.1002/casp.786

Comas-Díaz, L. (2000). An ethnopolitical approach to working with people of color. *American Psychologist, 55*, 1319–1325. http://dx.doi.org/10.1037/0003-066X.55.11.1319

Comas-Díaz, L., Lykes, M. B., & Alarcón, R. D. (1998). Ethnic conflict and the psychology of liberation in Guatemala, Peru, and Puerto Rico. *American Psychologist, 53*, 778–792. http://dx.doi.org/10.1037/0003-066X.53.7.778

Denzin, N. K. (2003). Performing [auto] ethnography politically. *Review of Education, Pedagogy & Cultural Studies, 25*, 257–278. http://dx.doi.org/10.1080/10714410390225894

Dobles, I. (2015). Psicología de la liberación y psicología comunitaria latinoamericana: Una perspectiva [Liberation psychology and Latin American community psychology: A perspective]. *Teoría y Crítica de la Psicología, 6*, 122–139.

Dutta, M. J. (2018). Autoethnography as decolonization, decolonizing autoethnography: Resisting to build our homes. *Cultural Studies, Critical Methodologies, 18*, 94–96. http://dx.doi.org/10.1177/1532708617735637

Fals Borda, O. (Ed.). (1985). *The challenge of social change*. London, England: Sage.

Fals Borda, O. (2001). Participatory (action) research in social theory: Origins and challenges. In P. Reason & H. Bradbury (Eds.), *Handbook of action research* (pp. 27–37). London, England: Sage.

Fals Borda, O. (2006). The North–South convergence: A 30-year first-person assessment of PAR. *Action Research, 4*, 351–358. http://dx.doi.org/10.1177/1476750306066806

Fals Borda, O., & Rahman, M. A. (Eds.). (1991). *Action and knowledge: Breaking the monopoly with participatory action research*. New York, NY: Intermediate Technology Publications/Apex Press. http://dx.doi.org/10.3362/9781780444239

Fernández, J. S. (2018). Toward an ethical reflective practice of a theory in the flesh: Embodied subjectivities in a youth participatory action research mural project. *American Journal of Community Psychology, 62*, 221–232. http://dx.doi.org/10.1002/ajcp.12264

Fine, M., & Torre, M. E. (2006). Intimate details, participatory action research in prison. *Action Research, 4*, 253–269. http://dx.doi.org/10.1177/1476750306066801

Flores Osorio, J. M. (2009). Praxis and liberation in the context of Latin American theory. In M. Montero & C. C. Sonn (Eds.), *Psychology of liberation: Theory and applications* (pp. 11–36). New York, NY: Springer.

Freire, P. (1970). *Pedagogy of the oppressed*. New York, NY: Herder and Herder.

Freire, P. (1999). *La importancia de leer y el proceso de liberación* [The importance of reading and the release process]. Coyoacan, Mexico: Siglo XXI.

Gaventa, J., & Cornwall, A. (2008). Power and knowledge. In P. Reason & H. Bradbury (Eds.), *The Sage handbook of action research: Participative inquiry and practice* (2nd ed.; pp. 172–189). London, England: Sage.

Goizueta, R. (2009). *Christ our companion: Toward a theological aesthetics of liberation.* Maryknoll, NY: Orbis Books.

Goodson, I. F. (1998). Storying the self: Life politics and the study of the teacher's life and work. In W. Pinar (Ed.), *Curriculum: Toward new identities* (pp. 3–20). New York, NY: Garland.

Gready, P., & Robins, S. (2014). From transitional to transformative justice: A new agenda for practice. *The International Journal of Transitional Justice, 8,* 339–361. http://dx.doi.org/10.1093/ijtj/iju013

Howarth, C. (2006). Race as stigma: Positioning the stigmatized as agents, not objects. *Journal of Community & Applied Social Psychology, 16,* 442–451. http://dx.doi.org/10.1002/casp.898

Invisible Children. (n.d.). *The origin of "Our liberty is bound together."* Retrieved from https://invisiblechildren.com/blog/2012/04/04/the-origin-of-our-liberty-is-bound-together/

Lewin, K. (1946). Action research and minority problems. *Journal of Social Issues, 2,* 34–46.

Lorde, A. (2012). *Sister outsider: Essays and speeches.* Berkeley, CA: Crossing Press. (Original work published 1984)

Lykes, M. B., & Mallona, A. (2008). Toward a transformational liberation: Participatory action research and activist praxis. In P. Reason & H. Bradbury (Eds.), *The Sage handbook of action research* (pp. 260–291). Thousand Oaks, CA: Sage.

Maldonado-Torres, N. (2016). *Outline of ten theses on coloniality and decoloniality.* Retrieved from the Frantz Fanon Foundation website: https://fondation-frantzfanon.com/wp-content/uploads/2018/10/maldonado-torres_outline_of_ten_theses-10.23.16.pdf

Martín-Baró, I. (1989). *Sistema, grupo y poder* [System, group and power]. San Salvador, El Salvador: UCA.

Martín-Baró, I. (1990). La encuesta de opinión pública como instrumento desideologizador [The public opinion survey as a deideologizing instrument]. *Revista de Psicologia de El Salvador, 9*(35), 9–22.

Martín-Baró, I. (1994). *Writings for a liberation psychology.* Cambridge, MA: Harvard University Press.

Montero, M. (2004). Relaciones entre psicología social comunitaria, psicología crítica y psicología de la liberación: Una respuesta latinoamericana [Relationships between community social psychology, critical psychology and liberation psychology: A Latin American response]. *Psykhe, 13*(2), 17–28. http://dx.doi.org/10.4067/S0718-22282004000200002

Montero, M. (2006). La investigación-acción-participativa: Orígenes, definición y fundamentación epistemológica y teórica [Participatory action in research: Origins, definition and epistemological and theoretical foundation]. In M. Montero, *Hacer para transformer: El método en la Psicología Comunitaria* [Do to transform: The method in community psychology] (pp. 121–158). Buenos Aires, Argentina: Paidós.

Montero, M. (2010). De la ética del individualismo a la ética de la otredad: La noción de Otro y la liberación de la psicología [From the ethics of individualism to the ethics of otherness: The notion of other and the liberation of psychology]. *Postconvencionales, Escuela de Estudios Politicos y Administrativos, 1,* 83–97.

Montero, M., & Sonn, C. C. (Eds.). (2009). *Psychology o liberation: Theory and applications.* New York, NY: Springer Science + Business Media.

Moraga, C. (2019). *Native country of the heart: A memoir.* New York, NY: FSG Press.

Nelson, G. B., & Prilleltensky, I. (2010). *Community psychology: In pursuit of liberation and well-being* (2nd ed.). New York, NY: Palgrave Macmillan.

Quijano, A. (2000). Coloniality of power and Eurocentrism in Latin America. *International Sociology, 15*, 215–232. http://dx.doi.org/10.1177/0268580900015002005

Rahman, M. A. (1990). The case of the Third World: People's self-development. *Community Development Journal: An International Forum, 25*, 307–314. http://dx.doi.org/10.1093/cdj/25.4.307

Rahman, M. A. (2004). Globalization: The emerging ideology in the popular protests and grassroots action research. *Action Research, 2*, 9–23. http://dx.doi.org/10.1177/1476750304040495

Rendón, L. I. (2012). *Sentipensante (sensing/thinking) pedagogy: Educating for wholeness, social justice and liberation.* Sterling, VA: Stylus.

Selener, D. (1997). *Participatory action research and social change.* Ithaca, NY: The Cornell Participatory Action Research Network, Cornell University.

Sepúlveda, E., III. (2011). Toward a pedagogy of acompañamiento: Mexican migrant youth writing from the underside of modernity. *Harvard Educational Review, 81*, 550–573. http://dx.doi.org/10.17763/haer.81.3.088mv5t704828u67

Sepúlveda, E., III. (2018). Border brokers: Teachers and undocumented Mexican students in search of acompañamiento. *Diaspora, Indigenous, and Minority Education, 12*, 53–69. http://dx.doi.org/10.1080/15595692.2017.1408584

Serrano-García, I., & Vargas Molina, R. (1993). La psicología comunitaria en América Latina: Estado actual, controversias y nuevos derroteros [Community psychology in Latin America: Current status, controversies and new paths]. *Papeles del Psicólogo, 55*, 6.

Swantz, M. L. (2008). Participatory action research as practice. In P. Reason & H. Bradbury (Eds.), *The Sage handbook of action research: Participative inquiry and practice* (2nd ed., pp. 31–48). London, England: Sage. http://dx.doi.org/10.4135/9781848607934.n8

Walsh, C. E. (2014). Pedagogías decoloniales caminando y preguntando: Notas a Paulo Freire desde Abya Yala [Decolonial pedagogies walking and asking: Notes to Paulo Freire from Abya Yala]. *Entramados. Educación y Sociedad, 1*, 17–30.

Watkins, M. (2015). Psychosocial accompaniment. *Journal of Social and Political Psychology, 3*, 324–341. http://dx.doi.org/10.5964/jspp.v3i1.103

Watts, R. J., & Serrano-García, I. (2003). The quest for a liberating community psychology: An overview. *American Journal of Community Psychology, 31*(1–2), 73–78. http://dx.doi.org/10.1023/A:1023022603667

6

Feminist Participatory Action Research

Coconstructing Liberation Psychological Praxis Through Dialogic Relationality and Critical Reflexivity

M. Brinton Lykes and Gabriela Távara

Mental health is a dimension of the relations between persons and groups more than an individual state, even though this dimension may take root differently in the body of each of the individuals in these relations, thereby producing a diversity of manifestations ("symptoms") and states ("syndromes") . . . we want to emphasize how enlightening it is to change the lens and see mental health or illness not . . . as the result of an individual's internal functioning but as the manifestation, in a person or group, of the humanizing or alienating character of a framework of historical relationships. *We cannot be satisfied with treating post-traumatic stress . . . it is of primary importance that treatment address itself to relationships between social groups, which constitute the "normal abnormality" that dehumanizes the . . . oppressor and the oppressed, soldier and victim, dominator and dominated, alike.*
—MARTÍN-BARÓ (1994, pp. 109–111, EMPHASIS ADDED)

As this book goes to press, many around the world have recently commemorated the 30th anniversary of the Salvadoran Army's Atlacatl Battalion's brutal assassination of Ignacio Martín-Baró, five of his Jesuit brothers, and Julia Elba Ramos and her 13-year-old daughter, Celina Maricet Ramos, on November 16, 1989 (Lassalle-Klein, 2014; Whitfield, 1994). The battalion was trained by the U.S.-funded School of the Americas (now the Western Hemisphere Institute for Security Cooperation), and troops trained there are responsible for many more assassinations and disappearances among the hundreds of thousands now documented to have occurred in Latin America during the 1980s. Some of us who had been collaborating with Ignacio in a

http://dx.doi.org/10.1037/0000198-007
Liberation Psychology: Theory, Method, Practice, and Social Justice, L. Comas-Díaz and E. Torres Rivera (Editors)

four-country, community-based psychosocial intervention remember well the horrific announcement that upended our first Internet-based dialogue planned for the morning of the 16th. Our envisioned critical interrogation of psychologists' stance vis-à-vis disappearances of children in Argentina and youth forced into exile in Chile shifted as we repositioned ourselves as activists, pressing psychological associations to join us in demanding justice and accountability from the Salvadoran and U.S. governments for these horrific crimes against humanity.

In 1997, not quite a decade after those events and after nearly that long working in rural Guatemala, I (MBL) generated what I suggested were "guidelines" for facilitating participatory action research (PAR) with communities emerging from armed conflict and gross violations of human rights. Drawing on that earlier four-country experience as well as a decade of work in rural Guatemala, they emphasized PAR's compatibility and complementarity with existing resources and priorities of *el pueblo* (the people)—that is, the local communities with whom one planned to work. PAR sought to enhance the possibility of the work's sustainability; its ease of participation, irrespective of literacy or language; and the development of action-based responses to identified problems. Additionally, I suggested that the PAR process seek to facilitate an action–reflection dialectic in which new ways of thinking or alternative cultural practices emerge; the sharing of multiple, frequently differing Indigenous beliefs and practices; participants' meaningful re-presentations of their priorities to activists, policymakers, and potential funders who could support their responses to the effects of war, state-sponsored violence, and institutionalized poverty; and a process that minimized risks to the participants, particularly those who live in a context of continuing violence or a fragile peace (see Lykes, 1997). I have continued to find these guidelines helpful as referent points for my own work, and they informed my accompaniment of Gabriela as she began to articulate her activist scholarship through PAR.

Thirty years later, I (MBL) continue to weave a sometimes-circuitous path alongside local survivors, victims, and protagonists of gross violations of human rights in Guatemala and beyond. They continue to demand truth, justice, and reparations, as I—and new generations of activist scholars—seek to accompany them in their journeys toward redressing harm as together we struggle to (a) hold those responsible for Ignacio's murder accountable (for a summary, see https://cja.org/what-we-do/litigation/the-jesuits-massacre-case) and (b) craft a praxis that "changes the lens," focusing on social relations that sustain or rupture the "normal abnormality" of the ongoing limit situations in which many live despite the cessation of armed conflict. This chapter argues for a praxis of feminist PAR (FPAR), one that reflects an intentional threading of Martín-Baró's (1974, 1994) liberation psychology and intersectional, feminist, antiracist, and decolonizing theories and methods (e.g., Collins & Bilge, 2016; Combahee River Collective, 1983; Crenshaw, 1989; Mohanty, 2003; Tuhiwai Smith, 2012) to inform "psychosocial accompaniment" (Watkins, 2019) and activist scholarship in the Global South in the context of ever-present and persistent colonization and neoliberal capitalism.

This chapter recounts some of the FPAR (Lykes & Crosby, 2014; Reid & Frisby, 2008) processes that we have developed through our accompaniment of and in solidarity with Indigenous women in the wake of war. Our praxis was deeply informed by the three tasks that Ignacio argued might contribute to "liberating psychology" from its positivist mooring, that is, "recovering historical memory, de-ideologizing common sense and everyday experience, and utilizing the virtues of the people" (Martín-Baró, 1994, p. 30) and is grounded in critical reflexivity through which we name and interrogate our positionalities as economically, educationally, and racially privileged activist scholars, one of whom is a White United Statesian and the other of whom is a Peruvian Mestiza. Thus, the FPAR processes discussed here are informed by liberation psychology (Martín-Baró, 1994), intersectional theory (Crenshaw, 1989), and Indigenous scholars' decolonizing epistemologies (Mohanty, 2003; Tuhiwai Smith, 2012). We draw on them to identify and document interlocking and intersectional circulations of power that constrain and facilitate Indigenous women's lives, including, among others, those due to gender, racialization, social class, nationality, and education (Riessman, 2015; Strega & Brown, 2015). We argue that through "pragmatic solidarity" (Farmer, 1999) with and "psychosocial accompaniment" (Watkins, 2019) of Indigenous women, we engage together in "dialogic relationality" (Crosby & Lykes, 2019) through which Indigenous participants develop praxis to redress some of the multiple effects of armed conflict and design actions in search of transformative change. Finally, we draw on critical reflexivity and deideologization to craft a more cautionary tale for activist scholars who are situated at the interstices of multiple privileges proffered by their identities and positionalities and who, like ourselves, seek to accompany communities emerging from armed conflict and human rights violations.

WEAVING LIBERATION PSYCHOLOGY AND FPAR IN SITU

From its roots in the scholarship of Ignacio Martín-Baró, liberation psychology has emphasized the importance of situating psychological praxis within history. Martín-Baró urged psychologists to develop their knowledge "from the bottom-up," that is, from the point of view of those all too frequently "othered" by positivist methodologies or marginalized from access to power and decision-making. This praxis facilitates processes through which all involved—community participants as well as "outsider" or university-based researchers—critically reflect on and deideologize everyday experiences, gaining a deeper, more critical understanding of social reality as well as of the circulations of power and dispossession that permeate all social relations. In a similar vein, PAR seeks to construct knowledge(s) that are situated in, and emerge from, a particular sociohistorical context that aims to redress inequities and injustices through participatory methodologies. FPAR infuses the latter with processes through which participants or coresearchers engage in a critical interrogation of gendered and intersectional power dynamics that all too often subordinate them, contributing to ongoing racialized and gendered violence against them and their families. Just as important, through critical reflexivity, researchers from outside of the communities with whom they are collaborating, such as ourselves, seek to deideologize our underlying assumptions frequently rooted in privileges of the dominator state (Strega & Brown, 2015). Through FPAR, local women and PARers collaborate in the dialogic, coconstruction of knowledge(s) that facilitate increased agency or protagonism (Crosby & Lykes, 2019; Lykes & Crosby, 2014) through which they advocate for a better life.

Guatemala and Peru in Brief

The praxis discussed in this chapter takes place in two Latin American countries with large Indigenous populations, Guatemala and Peru. Although these countries have different social and political dynamics, they are alike in multiple ways. The territories and peoples of what are now called Guatemala and Peru were both colonized by Spaniards. A significant part of the population is Indigenous or of Indigenous descent, tracing their roots back to millenary civilizations such as the Maya and the Inca and pre-Inca. Despite long-standing militarized occupation and ongoing colonization processes including occupations of lands and extractive industries destroying their environments, 22 ethnic and linguistic groups in Guatemala (Grandin, Levenson, & Oglesby, 2011) and 47 in Peru (Ministerio de Educación, Perú, 2013) have not only survived but are increasingly defending themselves and their rights (Comas-Díaz, Lykes, & Alarcón, 1998).

Among the pernicious legacies of colonization that persist in these countries are ongoing dynamics of socioeconomic and political inequality that exclude and marginalize a majority of the Indigenous populations. Guatemala and Peru are also countries with weak nation-states wherein most of the economic and political power is controlled by private oligarchs or transnational corporations (Bastos & de León, 2015; Vélez-Torres & Ruiz-Torres, 2016). These power dynamics are reflected in highly centralized governance and in the limited presence of state resources and services (e.g., education and health) in rural areas. Finally, and most important, Guatemala and Peru are both countries that have been deeply affected by armed conflicts (*Comisión para el Esclarecimiento Histórico* [CEH], 1999; *Comisión de la Verdad y Reconciliación*, 2003). Although different in their origins, Indigenous populations in both countries were targeted or impacted disproportionately, with Indigenous women frequently targeted through racialized sexual violence. Moreover, these modern armed conflicts have deep roots in long-standing racialized economic policies and practices.

Liberation Psychology Informs FPAR

These historical and contemporary hegemonic systems of racialized and gendered power operate within each country. Central to Martín-Baró's (1994) liberation psychology is the grounding of psychological knowledge in historical memory, processes through which local communities and those who accompany them develop new ways of knowing that are grounded in past experiences as well as in the communities' previously suppressed but now recovered knowledges. Despite multiple differences between these rural Mayan and Andean communities, the FPAR discussed herein drew from similar strategies through which local participants reencountered their historical narratives and resisted present-day marginalization. We analyze these with the intent of clarifying liberation psychology's contributions as well as some of the challenges of sustaining critical reflexivity in our everyday praxis. More specifically, we reflect on our experiences with (a) processes of *concientización* (that is, a process through which people identify and then analyze their oppression, apprehending their situation as a historical reality susceptible to transformation; Freire, 1970) and "deideologizing everyday experience" with the aim of generating knowledge from below. We also reflect on (b) the dialogic coconstruction of knowledge within the "recovery of historical memory" and (c) transnational relationality that "utilizes people's virtues" within and despite ongoing inequities of power wherein women in minoritized communities in the Global South continue to be marginalized and those of us from or educated in the Global North continue to benefit in diverse ways from these collaborations. We draw on critical reflexivity (Riessman, 2015; Strega & Brown, 2015) to clarify both the strengths and some of the contradictions or limitations of our experiences, insights through which we reposition ourselves in these long-term processes of accompaniment (Watkins, 2019).

Coauthors In Situ

In this section, we briefly describe experiences through which we weave this analysis. Brinton's experiences are drawn from her nearly three decades of FPAR in the Ixil area of the Guatemalan Highlands, site of more than two thirds of the 600-plus massacres carried out by the Guatemalan military during the first decades of the 1980s, the most brutal period of a 36-year armed conflict (CEH, 1999; *Oficina de Derechos Humanos del Arzobispado de Guatemala*, 1998). Gabriela's are from a more recent FPAR in a rural town in Ayacucho, Peru, wherein the Shining Path, an armed subversive group, recruited collaborators through the local high schools, and the town suffered horrific violence at its hands as well as at the hands of the Peruvian military. We entered each context after the worst years of these gross violations of human rights, seeking to accompany women who had survived these armed conflicts and were reestablishing personal, familial, and community ties. We revisit this work to clarify some of the contributions of Ignacio Martín-Baró's liberation psychology as we have been reiterating it alongside Indigenous women in contexts wherein our praxis has been informed by antiracist, decolonial, and feminist activist scholarship.

HISTORICALLY CONTEXTUALIZING OUR ENTRY INTO COMMUNITY

In 1992, I (MBL) traveled to the rural Ixil town of Chajul for the first time. A former member of this community whom I had befriended in Mexico had invited me to meet with a small group of women there hoping that I could facilitate a series of creative participatory workshops, similar to those I had been coordinating with rural community-based health promoters during the Guatemalan armed conflict (Lykes, 1994). Once there, I met a small group of Ixil women; some had descended from the Communities of Populations in Resistance; others had returned from exile in Mexico or internal displacement in Guatemala City; others were former guerillas; and others had spent days, sometimes weeks, hiding in the town where the army controlled all movements from their military base that was at first in the town's center and later on its outskirts.

Some of the women of Chajul wanted to build a corn mill. When I tried to explain that I was a psychologist, not a development worker, they noted that the corn mill was a "mental health project." Over many months and multiple visits, I facilitated creative workshops through which they re-presented their everyday lives through drawings, collages, dramatizations, image theater, and creative storytelling, and together we crafted a journey through which I learned that building and running a corn mill was indeed "good for their mental health." Little by little, I understood how the centrality of corn to their material and symbolic well-being, as well as the processes through which they demonstrated that they could care for their children, contributed to their self-esteem, healing, and overall well-being—that is, their mental health. Over time, I introduced the women of Chajul to *Visual Voices: 100 Photographs of Village China by the Women* (1995), a photovoice project through which local rural Chinese women took pictures of their lived experiences, commenting on them with the goal of informing policymakers of needed changes in childcare, education, and health (Wang & Burris, 1994). Drawing on this work, we generated an FPAR project with photographs, a photoPAR. PhotoPAR integrated ongoing FPAR processes and picture-taking as resources through which the women of Chajul photographed daily life, documented stories of those whose pictures they took, and then analyzed the photographs plus narratives (or phototexts) to generate their community's story of the Guatemalan armed conflict and their "survivance" (Vizenor, 2008)[1] as Maya Ixil and K'iche' women (Women of PhotoVoice/ADMI & Lykes, 2000).

The FPAR process in Peru took place in a town in Ayacucho, an area of the central-southern Andes impacted by the Peruvian armed conflict. Many thousands of *campesinxs* (peasants) lost their lives and the limited material possessions they had, while some engaged in complex ways with the Peruvian military, the Shining Path, or both (Theidon, 2013). The postconflict period has entailed multiple complex challenges for Andean communities who continue to struggle to make ends meet in a context of ongoing impoverishment.

I (GT) was introduced to a group of Andean women in Ayacucho who were forming a knitting association by a community relations staff of the

---

[1]Gerald Vizenor (2008), U.S. scholar and an enrolled member of the Minnesota Chippewa Tribe, White Earth Reservation, uses the construct *survivance* to refer to some of the ways in which Indigenous peoples and communities have learned to move "beyond our basic survival in the face of overwhelming cultural genocide to create spaces of synthesis and renewal" (as cited in Tuck, 2009, p. 422).

Peruvian mining company working in the area. These women sought to confront the ongoing economic violence that affected them as *campesinas* through their knitting association. Some noted that their initial gatherings had revealed a lack of trust among women in the town, while others spoke of multiple experiences of gender violence, or, in their words, *machismo*. They used this term to refer to experiences through which men exercised control over them— over their activities and roles at home and in public spheres.

Drawing on findings from a pilot project with these women and informed by my positionality as a community-clinical and aspiring liberation psychologist, I proposed that we develop an FPAR project to explore how their knitting association might serve as a resource through which they faced gendered racialized violence and engaged with the legacies of the armed conflict, particularly vis-à-vis the community's social relations. Of the association's 40 members, 15 to 20 met in monthly creative workshops such as those described briefly in the preceding text. I envisioned the discussions engendered through the creative techniques as resources for strengthening the knitting association. I facilitated dialogues through which we identified challenges that they were encountering and developed strategies through which they might face and, ideally, resolve these problems. Individual interviews with some participants and ethnographic observations through my participation in local community events complemented the FPAR processes for a thicker description of everyday life and provided additional opportunities for critical dialogue.

WEAVING A NEW PRAXIS: LIBERATION PSYCHOLOGY AND FPAR

Engaging Conscientization Processes

Martín-Baró (1994) suggested that psychologists accompanying local communities are challenged to facilitate conscientization processes through which participants can better understand their everyday experiences of marginalization by first analyzing the circulations of power that all too frequently dispossess them and then developing action steps that could improve their lives. Yet as outsiders to these communities, we bring understandings grounded in our own lived experiences and professional training. My (MBL) previous work with Mayan communities during the Guatemalan armed conflict, antiwar protests of U.S. support of the Guatemalan oligarchy and military, and many years of feminist activism and undoing racism training and activism informed by positionality as a feminist community-cultural psychologist. My (GT) understandings of the meanings the knitters in Ayacucho made of their everyday experiences were informed by urban Peruvian gendered relations as well as by my academic studies of feminisms and antiracist and decolonial pedagogies. We perceived local Mayan and Andean women's marginalization to have been shaped by macrolevel patriarchal and racist structures and to be rooted in historical colonial relations that persisted through neoliberal capitalism. Reflecting on our positioning as university-based, privileged White and Mestiza activist scholars, we argue here that we all too often engaged in these FPAR processes from·a stance that seems to have presumed that we were "conscientized" while the Indigenous women with whom we were partnering were not (Blackburn, 2000) and that our challenge was to facilitate processes through which *they* deideologized their lived experiences to achieve critical consciousness. In what follows, we analyze some of the experiences through which we deideologized our understandings to move toward a new conscientization.

All Maya Ixil Women Are Not the Same

During my first decade in Guatemala, I (MBL) had developed a critique of dominant theorizing about the traumatic effects of war (Lykes, 2002) and drawn extensively on creative techniques grounded in local cultural beliefs and practices (Lykes, 1994) in community-based psychosocial interventions. As the worst years of the armed conflict receded, what had grown to be an 80-member women's association in Chajul sought to tell the story of the war from their perspective using photoPAR. These iterative action-reflection processes included dramatic multiplication and analyses of photographs they had taken through which they performed, documented, and interpreted multiple versions of what were previously thought to be singular stories documenting acts of repression (e.g., a Maya Ixil woman hanged in the town square; massacres). The photoPAR process also facilitated the development of phototexts through which the women documented their experiences of work and play, religion and ritual, and economic development and educational projects. As I scaffolded processes through which the Maya Ixil and K'iche' women analyzed and critically interrogated these everyday experiences, I documented their performances of previously taken for granted of understandings of rural poverty, racism, ethnic discrimination or gendered violence. The women identified the phototexts as descriptive of both causes and consequences of the armed conflict, while I noted diversity where before I had seen homogeneity.

I slowly realized that my assumptions that all of the women in the project were "poor" belied multiple levels of impoverishment that differed not only due to marital status but also generationally, affecting women's literacy and formal education as well as their current abilities to access education for their children and grandchildren. Similarly, despite the racism that all Maya have experienced since colonization, interethnic (e.g., Ixil, K'iche'), interreligious (e.g., Mayan, Catholic, evangelical), and political/ideological (e.g., Guatemalan army, civil patrollers [PACs], guerrillas) experiences generated complex, intersectional tensions and contradictions that were often silenced or minimized in their group processes, towards prioritizing commonalities as women who survived genocidal violence. Although the latter was an accurate rendering of their reality—and seemed strategic given the fractures of the war that continued to plague the wider community as well as national truth commission processes—documenting the women's deideologization of the everyday challenged me to critically interrogate my previous assumptions of homogeneity among the Maya that also overrode some of the aforementioned diversities and a discourse of gendered racialized violence. I also began to deideologize my activist framing and positionality (Sloan, 2015), informed by my U.S. nationality and historical situatedness, deconstructing a sometimes-singular focus on the 36-year armed conflict as reflective of Ladinx-Maya polarization rooted in colonialism and supported by U.S. imperial power.[2] Despite the usefulness of this framing for forging community among Ixil and K'iche' women with diverse histories and in pressing for justice and reparations for the Maya vis-à-vis their perpetrators, it risks overwriting multiple complex, intersectional particularities within this rural community that might contribute to different understandings of redress and transitional justice "from below" (Gready & Robins, 2014). The FPAR process recovered local Ixil women's stories of genocidal violence and of gendered protagonism and survivance, processes through which 20 women dared to break silence and to forge a shared story of their community. Yet the submergence of multiple diversities in the service of a common story later resurfaced in ways that contributed to the subsequent fracturing of the Mayan women's association.

Knitting for Material Survival in Ayacucho

When starting to work with the group of knitters, I (GT) understood their material poverty as one of the multiple results of a capitalist economic system and a historic process of colonization, both of which sought to concentrate power in particular groups to the disadvantage of majority populations including Andeans of Ayacucho (Quijano & Ennis, 2000). However, the women knitters frequently described their poverty as the result of not being able to insert themselves optimally within this capitalist system. Thus, by forming a knitting association, they sought to bring together their craft-making skills and produce goods that provided a source of income. I perceived my support of this endeavor as contradictory; I had envisioned FPAR as a resource facilitating participants' critical interrogation of the economic system, thereby facilitating their "becoming conscientized" and then "understanding"—and "resisting"—capitalism's injustices that marginalized and oppressed them.

As the workshops progressed and I listened more deeply to their concerns, I heard diverse perceptions and constructions of "women's work" and its value within this local Andean community. Through creative activities, they represented multiple ways in which, despite their hard work as *campesinas*, they saw little "fruto de nuestros esfuerzos" (fruit of our efforts). They spoke of how using their own hands to create something with monetary value in a market economy made them feel good about themselves. Although the women acknowledged that the current economic system was unfair, they quickly added that they needed to be a part of it to make a living. These group processes contributed to my growing recognition of their perception of the knitting

---

[2]In Guatemala, the terms *Ladina* (feminine), *Ladino* (masculine), or *Ladinx* (to denote the gender-neutral term) are the most commonly used to describe those who are not Maya (see Grandin, Levenson, & Oglesby, 2011, p. 121ff, for a discussion of the shifting meanings of the term historically). More recently, some Guatemalans have begun to use the terms *Mestizo, Mestiza,* or *Mestizx* to acknowledge their mixed "race" identities.

association and the local capitalist economy as more nuanced than my representations of it; I broadened my perspective of what knowledge constructed from
below might mean. Although the local economic system clearly operates in
ways that foster inequality, in the short term, the women's limited options and
their more productive insertion into that economy through the knitting association contributed to their sense of having gained something that enhanced their
own and their families' well-being. As the workshops progressed, our discussions shifted from the interrogation of the economic system that I had initiated
toward a context in which they increasingly questioned how they were insert-
ing themselves in that system as an association.

Thinking Reflexively Across Contexts

Conscientization is not a state of being but a dialectic process (Martín-Baró,
1994). Despite our embrace of a FPAR process that emphasized facilitating
knowledge from below, we sometimes situated ourselves and our discursive
constructions of women's gendered racialized oppression as frameworks for
explaining Mayan and Andean women's lived experiences rather than listening
deeply to their constructions. We brought knowledge and experiences crafted
elsewhere and initiated participatory processes implicitly envisioning the ade-
quacy of *our* women's ways of knowing, despite our explicit recognition of our
positions as "other" and privileged. Although we had begun to deideologize or
liberate psychology from its positivist moorings through FPAR and earlier critical
writing (e.g., Lykes, 2002), we often failed to prioritize the ongoing and iterative
need to deideologize our own assumptions rooted in privileged positionalities as
a highly educated White United-Statesian and an urban, Mestiza Peruvian. The
engaged and embodied learning through which local women performed their
meaning-making of their everyday experiences contributed to deepening our
understandings of the complex processes through which we as human beings
come to know ourselves within systems of oppression or privilege, both of which
constrain and facilitate diverse ways of engagement. As activist scholars, we
are challenged to enhance our self-understandings as well as our critical and
reflexive analyses of our own identities and lived experiences within the structures of privilege and oppression in the specific historical contexts in which we
accompany local women. Martín-Baró (1974) recognized that, as academics, we
are immersed in privileged spaces, divorced from the lived experiences of the
majority population and beneficiaries of disciplinary training that we may critique or reject but that continues to dominate our profession. As we "stand
under" these knowledge(s) (Panikkar, 1990) as well as those generated through
the praxis of those we accompany, we are challenged to facilitate multiple
learning–teaching spaces through which we can embrace their lenses to reflexively and critically interrogate our own ideologies (Strega & Brown, 2015).

Coconstructing Knowledge Through Creativity and Reflexivity

Liberation psychologists are challenged to construct a new epistemology by
centering people's knowledge, which is inherent in their everyday praxis

(Martín-Baró, 1994). Although liberation psychology seems to advocate for an unmediated representation of people's voices, it situates psychologists in communities, dialoguing with *el pueblo* about how they read their worlds (Martín-Baró, 1994). FPAR fosters dialogic processes grounded in and informed by participants' priorities. The creative techniques in workshops in Chajul and Ayacucho facilitated the emergence and documentation of participants' meaning-making of issues encountered in the everyday. As facilitators, we shaped these creative processes, organizing and synthesizing the information for analysis in subsequent sessions. Community participants and accompanying researchers together generate new knowledge(s) through dialogic praxis (Lykes, Terre Blanche, & Hamber, 2003; Montenegro Martínez & Pujol, 2003).

Creativity and Mayan Beliefs and Practices

In Chajul, the design of both the creative workshops and the photoPAR processes facilitated individual, small group, and large group dialogic processes. The diversity of techniques facilitated the scaffolding of descriptive and analytic processes consonant with the participants' informal educations and diverse linguistic skills. The processes were iterative, alternating rituals grounded in cultural and religious practices, embodied performances, and verbal analyses and reflections. The feminist photoPAR process involved women's recovery of memories of the armed conflict and of their Mayan cultural practices and beliefs, as well as the documentation of their current experiences as women. The phototexts facilitated the generation of individual and collective narratives about the women's photographs, processes through which they remembered and memorialized past experiences. I often synthesized and summarized work generated each day to revisit it the following day, facilitating the Mayan women's generation of additional analyses or their dramatic multiplication of contested meanings to deepen our understanding or resolve conflicts. Some key events (e.g., the story of the woman hanged in the town square) were remembered differently, and participants challenged each other's stories. Traditional deference to older members of the group was enacted and sometimes transgressed, contributing to the silencing of some stories including, for example, the rape of young girls. The latter sometimes emerged through the intimacy of individual interviews, evidencing limits to group memory-making processes.

Exploring Women's Knitting Through Creativity

I (GT) facilitated similar processes in Ayacucho. Although initially timid, participants felt increasingly comfortable to share, sometimes contesting each other's perspectives or mine as the facilitator. Women differed in storying failures of past community organizations, women's roles in the home and community, and in how to address painful memories of the armed conflict. Similar to experiences in Chajul, most resisted describing intimate experiences of the armed conflict in group sessions, opting for individual interviews as a space more conducive to such sharing. I was to learn over time that most local organizations included people who had positioned themselves differently during the armed conflict, that is, they had supported—in more direct or indirect ways—either the Shining Path or the government's military forces. These differences seemed to limit their willingness to divulge their experiences of, and perspectives on, the armed conflict in shared spaces. Despite these cautionary tales about group processes, the workshops exposed participants to the strongly held opinions of others in their community and to the diverse meaning-making processes during which they sometimes reached consensus. Other times conversation was suspended, and there was tacit agreement to disagree. However, throughout this process participants' ideas shifted as they were able to encounter other women's opinions and new information shared in the group. As a result, new understandings of issues relevant to them as Andean women knitters were generated.

Coconstructed Knowledge(s) Informed by Critical Reflexivity

Montenegro Martínez and Pujol (2003) argued that all knowledge emerges from a particular subject position and is, therefore, partial or *situated*. People engage with each other from diverse stances, creating new meanings and knowledge(s) through their interactions. Each participant brought a set of situated knowledge(s) to the group processes in Chajul and Ayacucho. Neither were homogenous groups of women, but rather individuals who, while sharing cultural, ethnic, and linguistic identities and deeply communitarian in daily praxis, had different lived experiences; positioned themselves differently politically, religiously, and along other dimensions; and frequently had differing opinions about the experiences being discussed. The FPAR methodology included multiple techniques and resources that were deployed to facilitate additional meaning-making processes through conscientization processes, as noted earlier, and to document participants' historically situated knowledge from below. Thus, the content documented through the workshops was neither theirs nor ours, but rather a coconstruction or mosaic of understandings that centers Mayan and Andean women's knowledge(s). The latter are contingent on their and our subject positions.

As researchers, we were challenged to critically and reflexively interrogate our positionalities and deideologize our underlying assumptions vis-à-vis our developing relationships with participants (Riessman, 2015; St. Louis & Barton, 2002). I (MBL) have written extensively about my privileged positionality as it informs my meaning-making and coconstructed knowledge(s) and how it is challenged living among the Maya (e.g., Lykes, 2010). I (GT) recognize some shared aspects of our identities in situating myself among the Andean women with whom I worked while also acknowledging vast differences due to, among other social privileges, education, *mestizaje*, and language. Furthermore, I reflected throughout the FPAR processes about how those differences informed (and constrained) how we approached and understood the issues we were discussing (Távara, 2018). Each of our positionalities—and the knowledge(s) coconstructed alongside women participants—is grounded in and derived from our individual and collective historical situatedness in our communities of origin and in the communities of the FPAR processes described herein. Despite the theoretical and methodological limitations documented here, these coconstructions reflect a dialogically constructed "third voice" (Lykes, Terre Blanche, & Hamber, 2003) through which we collectively aspire to liberatory and transformative change.

Dialogic Relationality and People's Virtues Within and Across Circulations of Power

Feminist psychologists have emphasized women's diverse ways of knowing (Belenky, Clinchy, Goldberger, & Tarule, 1986) and stressed the gendering and racializing of women's relationships within and across diverse communities of women. The Combahee River Collective (1983)—and, more recently, Crenshaw (1989) and Collins and Bilge (2016)—have critiqued the all-too-frequent homogenization of "women-as-White" within second-wave feminist hegemonic knowledge assumed to be universal. Contemporary feminists and more intersectional activist scholars challenge us to clarify the complexities of dialogic relationality through which we seek to construct knowledge and praxis. Liberation psychologists and PAR researchers have stressed the importance of reflecting critically on such relationships, particularly those that traverse borders. Some liberation psychologists describe them in terms of accompaniment or relationships that are close and continuous, through which we situate ourselves openly alongside or reciprocally (Watkins, 2019) with the people with whom we work. The dialogic relationality (Crosby & Lykes, 2019) established through FPAR processes includes multiple levels of reciprocity, closeness, and "just enough trust" (Maguire, 1987) to act together. In FPAR, these relationships are gendered, racialized, and embedded historically.

Entering Chajul "for the Long Haul"

As Reinharz (1997), among others, has written, our entry into communities facilitates and constrains multiple relationships and future engagements. Less discussed in this literature are the effects of previous experiences that we bring to that first entry. When I (MBL) traveled to Chajul for the first time, I was a tenured faculty member and therefore was differently positioned than some young scholars facing pressures to "publish or perish." My entry came through a woman from a family actively engaged in supporting revolutionary processes during the armed conflict. Much of her family had been forced to flee Chajul for nearly a decade and had recently returned. These relationships were preceded by previous political and professional positioning within Guatemala and facilitated some but constrained other relationships within this community. Although the worst of the armed conflict and genocidal violence had ended, peace accords had not yet been signed, and the military occupied a base on the outskirts of the town. The work that I have facilitated over nearly 3 decades is deeply informed by my U.S.-based university job as well as by multiple political and human rights transitions in Guatemala.

These dialogic relationships continue to evolve in ways that intrigue me. Although deeply aware of my own power and privilege in them—and increasingly attentive to the ways in which Mayan women exercise their power in our relationships (see my early inattention to this, documented in Lykes, 1989) and of my commitments to ensuring that our teaching–learning activities enhance their well-being and that the "products" of our work were resources for them and their communities—my own writing about these experiences has been much more limited. I have published extensively about FPAR and drawn on the work we developed together in Chajul, and we have coauthored articles and a book. But it was not until 2010 that I "extracted myself" from these collaborations through which I had coconstructed knowledge with the Maya to sole author an article about my work in Chajul—and that was only due to a colleague's urging me to step back to move forward and to write in a voice that more intentionally targeted an academic community of which I was part. Despite my hesitancy—and a manuscript currently in preparation that reflexively engages my decades-long experiences with Mayan women in Chajul and beyond—there is no doubt that I have benefited professionally and personally from the profound journey the Maya have allowed me to walk among them.

Ayacucho as My Entry Into the Academy

This chapter has afforded me (GT) an opportunity to reflexively explore some of the multiple ways in which this FPAR process informed the relationships ncountered and developed in Ayacucho. The journey—and dialogic relationships herein—was framed by and both facilitated and constrained my PhD dissertation and the financial resources I was able to secure to support that scholarship. As mentioned earlier, I was introduced to this group of women by a staff member of a mining company. This entry into Ayacucho—and the close relationship that he had previously established with the women who would later join the FPAR process—facilitated my own positive relationships with them. However, the fact that other women in the community as well as other members of the knitting association did not have a similarly positive opinion of the mining company or its staff probably negatively affected how they perceived me and the project. The "sponsors" through whom we enter a community or the site of our fieldwork always affect how we are perceived and with whom we are able to affiliate when we first enter (Reinharz, 1997).

The fact that this FPAR process was carried out within the context of my doctoral studies constituted another contextual element that influenced the relationships I developed. I felt and conducted myself throughout the FPAR process in ways that reflected its being an important requirement for the successful completion of my academic degree. At times I became very anxious about the participatory nature of the workshops, particularly because the process lacked a clear-cut plan typical of more traditional research methods. There were many elements beyond my control, including the need to negotiate the research focus and my ongoing contact with the participants. I was aware of and journaled about an embodied anxiety that limited my intellectually or methodologically grounded idea of introducing topics that I had hoped to engage with the women (e.g., the effects of the armed conflict) but that I feared they would reject or, even worse, that it would limit their ongoing participation. Fortunately, as the PAR workshops progressed along lines that I had anticipated and women continued to come to the workshops, I more effectively managed my feelings to facilitate the process. Nevertheless, anxiety and pressure were constant companions and inevitably informed our relationships and the dialogic knowledge that we were coconstructing.

The completion of the FPAR project and my doctoral degree has affected these relationships in other ways. Reflecting on gains the FPAR process brought me (securing a PhD with all the opportunities that entails), I continue to ask myself whether these gains are comparable to what this process contributed to the women of Ayacucho who joined me in this journey. In the last workshop, participants discussed what the FPAR process had meant to them. They described it as a space in which they were able to strengthen their ties, to learn more of what others in the association thought about a variety of issues, and to feel more comfortable expressing themselves in social spaces. Although I recognize these as positive personal benefits, I remain concerned that I have realized more tangible, material benefits—and the latter were front and center to participants' articulated needs and goals as we began the FPAR process. As researchers, the products resulting from our work with marginalized or disenfranchised communities frequently bring us professional (e.g., publications, higher degrees, or promotions) and personal gains. Despite the concrete outcomes of work such as the FPAR processes described herein, liberation psychology reminds us that this work is first and foremost a reflection of our commitment to liberate psychology and to root our praxis within the people and communities with whom we are working. It challenges us to cultivate humility as we seek to stand under their lived experiences and embrace the local community's virtues. It is only through accompaniment and the coconstruction of knowledge(s) with them that we might realize a more equitable and just world in which we all seek to live.

CONCLUSION

Martín-Baró (1994), among others, grounded his understanding of the awakening critical consciousness that he urged psychologists to undertake in Freire's (1970) construct of *conscientização* (conscientization). He argued that it would enable psychologists to approximate "a new horizon" by facilitating processes through which the majority population, *el pueblo*, critically interrogated their social situatedness to understand the underlying causes of their experiences of marginalization or disenfranchisement and to take actions for transformative change. Despite this promise and nearly 30 years since his assassination, those of us seeking to liberate psychology and engage in building a more equitable and just world in which we seek to live are challenged to think more deeply and critically about the experiences through which we have attempted to facilitate processes of conscientization within marginalized communities. Toward that end, we welcome the multiple contributions of a growing body of Indigenous scholars from different parts of the globe who share multiple Indigenous methodologies and ways of knowing that they are constructing and recovering (e.g., Grayshield & Mihecoby, 2010; Tuhiwai Smith, Tuck, &

Yang, 2019; Vizenor, 2008). This scholarship opens new opportunities for future generations—including the children of the women participants of these projects—through which they will share their stories of colonial oppression and, most importantly, of resistance.

As more Indigenous scholars and activists publish previously repressed stories and document lived experiences through Indigenous and decolonizing methodologies, we are challenged to deepen our understanding of multiple knowledge systems and to interrogate more critically the methodologies and meaning-making processes described herein. Despite these important contributions, the Indigenous women who participated in these FPAR processes continue to be marginalized from formal educational experiences and opportunities to disseminate their knowledge(s). In this chapter, we have discussed select experiences among Mayan and Andean women and some of what we are learning through interrogating our experiences at the interstices of feminist, decolonizing, and liberatory FPAR that have contributed to coconstructing knowledge through dialogic relationality. We suggest that there are multiple possible paths through which local communities come to make meanings of and critically engage their particular experiences of social oppression, marginalization, and survivance and that FPAR is one resource for disseminating that knowledge. Moreover, listening carefully to their diverse meanings has contributed to our questioning what we may have assumed to be our own conscientized knowledge, generating greater comprehension of the ways through which the people with whom we work interpret and act on their daily lives and its potential for a more locally grounded conscientization for FPAR coresearchers.

As university-based researchers we entered local communities, coming together in particular spaces through processes crafted dialogically for the purpose of the FPAR projects described herein. These are not naturally occurring experiences within these communities but are rather generated through the entry of outsider researchers. The latter bring ideas, interest, and values alongside those of local participants, all of which are informed by each coresearcher's subjective positionality within broader racialized, classed, and gendered systems. We have discussed some of our experiences of dialogic relationality, processes in which power is constantly fluctuating, suggesting new forms knowledge that were created in situ. Although liberation psychology emphasizes the importance of facilitating processes where knowledge emerges from the "bottom up," from the communities or the people with whom we work, our experiences suggest that the knowledge(s) that emerge from these encounters are dialogic coconstructions; that is, they are not unmediated expressions of any single individual or community voice. Results from our FPAR praxis are neither a transparent representation of communities' understandings nor our sole authored interpretations of a social reality in which we have shared for limited periods of time. Rather, they can be described as a third voice (Lykes, Terre Blanche, & Hamber, 2003), an interplay of multiple understandings where the whole is greater than the sum of its parts. In this chapter, we explored some of the processes through which these third voices were forged as well as our respective and changing positionalities throughout these processes. We analyzed some of the ways in which the interplay between our Western-informed knowledge and the knowledges of the Indigenous women with whom we worked gave place to particular understandings about these postconflict realities.

We have critically and reflexively interrogated the dialogic relationships we forged through these FPAR processes. The latter involve reflections about, and action toward, redressing the effects of armed conflict and gross violations of human rights. Strong ties can develop among community members and between community members and outsider researchers as we establish common goals and work toward achieving them. However, these relationships are fraught with complexities. As we discussed, entry and the actors through whom we were introduced (either external or internal to the community), as well as our personal, political, and professional positions, informed how we were perceived by others and the alliances initially established. Relationships with the communities with whom we work beyond the duration of a specific PAR project continue to evolve. The liberatory goals of FPAR and liberation psychology cannot be achieved through time-limited projects or interventions but rather require long-term, sustained commitments. As suggested herein, the quality and the strength of these relationships depend on our capacity to recognize their evolution as we, they, and the broader social and political contexts shift over time. Martín-Baró spoke about standing alongside the communities with whom we work during and beyond their struggles (Aron & Corne, 1994). As feminist PARers whose praxis is deeply informed by liberation psychology, we conclude these reflections, affirming our commitments to continue to accompany these communities of Indigenous women "over the long haul."

REFERENCES

Aron, A., & Corne, S. (1994). Introduction. In A. Aron & S. Corne (Eds.), *Writings for a liberation psychology: Ignacio Martín-Baró* (pp. 1–11). Cambridge, MA: Harvard University Press.

Bastos, S., & de León, Q. (2015). Guatemala: Construyendo el desarrollo propio en un neoliberalismo de posguerra [Guatemala: Constructing one's own development in postwar neoliberalism]. *Revista Pueblos y Fronteras Digital, 10*(19), 52–79. Retrieved from https://www.redalyc.org/html/906/90638786004/

Belenky, M. F., Clinchy, B. M., Goldberger, N. R., & Tarule, J. M. (1986). *Women's ways of knowing: The development of self, voice, and mind.* New York, NY: Basic Books.

Blackburn, J. (2000). Understanding Paulo Freire: Reflections on the origins, concepts, and possible pitfalls of his educational approach. *Community Development Journal, 35,* 3–15. http://dx.doi.org/10.1093/cdj/35.1.3

Collins, P. H., & Bilge, S. (2016). *Intersectionality.* Malden, MA: Polity Press.

Comas-Díaz, L., Lykes, M. B., & Alarcón, R. D. (1998). Ethnic conflict and the psychology of liberation in Guatemala, Peru, and Puerto Rico. *American Psychologist, 53,* 778–792. http://dx.doi.org/10.1037/0003-066X.53.7.778

Combahee River Collective. (1983). The Combahee River Collective statement. In B. Smith (Ed.), *Home girls: A black feminist anthology* (pp. 264–274). New York, NY: Kitchen Table: Women of Color Press.

Comisión de la Verdad y Reconciliación. (2003). *Informe final de la Comisión de la Verdad y Reconciliación* [Final report of the Truth and Reconciliation Commission]. Lima, Peru: Author.

Comisión para el Esclarecimiento Histórico. (1999). *Guatemala: Memory of silence Tz'inil Na'tab'al.* Guatemala City, Guatemala: Author.

Crenshaw, K. (1989). Demarginalizing the intersection of race and sex: A black feminist critique. *University of Chicago Legal Forum, 1,* 139–167.

Crosby, A., & Lykes, M. B. (2019). *Beyond repair: Mayan women's protagonism in the aftermath of genocidal harm.* New Brunswick, NJ: Rutgers University Press. http://dx.doi.org/10.2307/j.ctvscxr3t

Farmer, P. (1999). Pathologies of power: Rethinking health and human rights. *American Journal of Public Health, 89,* 1486–1496. http://dx.doi.org/10.2105/AJPH.89.10.1486

Freire, P. (1970). *Pedagogy of the oppressed.* New York, NY: Herder and Herder.

Grandin, G., Levenson, D. T., & Oglesby, E. (Eds.). (2011). *The Guatemala reader: History, culture, politics.* Durham, NC: Duke University Press. http://dx.doi.org/10.1215/9780822394679

Grayshield, L., & Mihecoby, A. (2010). Indigenous ways of knowing as a philosophical base for the promotion of peace and justice in counseling education and psychology. *Journal for Social Action in Counseling and Psychology, 2*(2), 1–16.

Gready, P., & Robins, S. (2014). From transitional to transformative justice: A new agenda for practice. *The International Journal of Transitional Justice, 8,* 339–361. http://dx.doi.org/10.1093/ijtj/iju013

Lassalle-Klein, R. (2014). *Blood and ink: Ignacio Ellacuría, Jon Sobrino, and the Jesuit martyrs of the University of Central America.* Maryknoll, NY: Orbis Books.

Lykes, M. B. (1989). Dialogue with Guatemalan Indian women: Critical perspectives on constructing collaborative research. In R. Unger (Ed.), *Representations: Social constructions of gender* (pp. 167–185). Amityville, NY: Baywood. [Reprinted in M. Gergen, & S. Davis (Eds.). (1996). *Toward a new psychology of gender: A reader.* New York, NY: Routledge.]

Lykes, M. B. (1994). Terror, silencing and children: International, multidisciplinary collaboration with Guatemalan Maya communities. *Social Science & Medicine, 38,* 543–552. http://dx.doi.org/10.1016/0277-9536(94)90250-X

Lykes, M. B. (1997). Activist participatory research among the Maya of Guatemala: Constructing meanings from situated knowledge. *Journal of Social Issues, 53,* 725–746. http://dx.doi.org/10.1111/j.1540-4560.1997.tb02458.x

Lykes, M. B. (2002). A critical re-reading of PTSD from a cross-cultural/community perspective. In D. Hook & G. Eagle (Eds.), *Psychopathology and social prejudice* (pp. 92–108). Cape Town, South Africa: UCT Press/JUTA.

Lykes, M. B. (2010). Silence(ing), voice(s) and gross violations of human rights: Constituting and performing subjectivities through PhotoPAR. *Visual Studies, 25,* 238–254. http://dx.doi.org/10.1080/1472586X.2010.523276

Lykes, M. B., & Crosby, A. (2014). Feminist practice of community and participatory and action research. In S. Hesse-Biber (Ed.), *Feminist research practice: A primer* (2nd ed., pp. 145–181). Thousand Oaks, CA: Sage.

Lykes, M. B., Terre Blanche, M., & Hamber, B. (2003). Narrating survival and change in Guatemala and South Africa: The politics of representation and a liberatory community psychology. *American Journal of Community Psychology, 31*(1–2), 79–90. http://dx.doi.org/10.1023/A:1023074620506

Maguire, P. (1987). *Doing participatory research: A feminist approach.* Amherst: Center for International Education, University of Massachusetts.

Martín-Baró, I. (1974). Elementos de conscientización socio-política en la currícula de las universidades [Elements of sociopolitical conscientization in the curricula of universities]. *Estudios Centroamericanos ECA, 29,* 765–783. Retrieved from http://www.uca.edu.sv/coleccion-digital-IMB/articulo/elementos-de-consciencitizacion-socio-politica-en-los-curricula-de-las-universidades/

Martín-Baró, I. (1994). *Writings for a liberation psychology.* Cambridge, MA: Harvard University Press.

Ministerio de Educación, Perú. (2013). *Documento nacional de lenguas originarias del Perú* [National document of Indigenous languages of Perú]. Lima, Perú: Author. Retrieved from http://www2.minedu.gob.pe/filesogecop/DNL-version%20final%20WEB.pdf

Mohanty, C. (2003). "Under Western eyes" revisited: Feminist solidarity through anti-capitalist struggles. *Signs: Journal of Women in Culture and Society, 28*, 499–535. http://dx.doi.org/10.1086/342914

Montenegro Martínez, M., & Pujol, J. (2003). Conocimiento situado: Un forcejeo entre el relativismo construccionista y la necesidad de fundamentar la acción [Situated knowledge: A struggle between constructivist relativism and the need to substantiate action]. *Revista Interamericana de Psicología, 37*, 295–307. Retrieved from https://www.redalyc.org/articulo.oa?id=28437209

Oficina de Derechos Humanos del Arzobispado de Guatemala. (1998). *Nunca más: Impactos de la violencia* [Never again: Impact of the violence]. Guatemala City, Guatemala: Litografía e Imprenta LIL, SA. [Also referred to as the REMHI Report]

Panikkar, R. (1990). The pluralism of truth. *World Faith Insights, 26*, 7–16. Retrieved from http://www.dhdi.free.fr/recherches/horizonsinterculturels/articles/panikkarpluralism.pdf

Quijano, A., & Ennis, M. (2000). Coloniality of power, Eurocentrism, and Latin America. *Nepantla: Views from South, 1*, 533–580. https://muse.jhu.edu/article/23906/summary

Reid, C., & Frisby, W. (2008). Continuing the journey: Articulating dimensions of feminist participatory action research (FPAR). In P. Reason & H. Bradbury (Eds.), *The Sage handbook of action research: Participative inquiry and practice* (2nd ed., pp. 93–106). London, England: Sage. http://dx.doi.org/10.4135/9781848607934.n12

Reinharz, S. (1997). Who am I? The need for a variety of selves in the field. In R. Hertz (Ed.), *Reflexivity and voice* (pp. 3–20). Thousand Oaks, CA: Sage.

Riessman, C. K. (2015). Entering the hall of mirrors: Reflexivity and narrative research. In A. DeFina & A. Georgakopoulou (Eds.), *The handbook of narrative analysis* (pp. 219–238). Malden, MA: Wiley Blackwell. http://dx.doi.org/10.1002/9781118458204.ch11

Sloan, T. (2015). Una carta a Ignacio con respeto a la tarea de la desideologiación [A letter to Ignacio about the task of deideologization]. *Teoría y Crítica de la Psicología, 6*, 6–11. http://www.teocripsi.com/ojs/

St. Louis, K., & Barton, A. C. (2002). Tales from the science education crypt: A critical reflection of positionality. Subjectivity, and reflexivity in research. *Forum Qualitative Social Research, 3*(3), 19. Retrieved from http://www.qualitative-research.net/index.php/fqs/article/view/832/1808

Strega, S., & Brown, L. (2015). Introduction. In S. Strega & L. Brown (Eds.), *Research as resistance: Revisiting critical, Indigenous, and anti-oppressive approaches* (2nd ed., pp. 1–17). Toronto, Ontario, Canada: Canadian Scholars' Press Women's Press.

Távara, G. (2018). *Reclaiming our hands: Feminist participatory action research with Andean women of Peru* (Doctoral dissertation). Retrieved from http://hdl.handle.net/2345/bc-ir:108124

Theidon, K. (2013). *Intimate enemies: Violence and reconciliation in Peru*. Philadelphia: University of Pennsylvania Press.

Tuck, E. (2009). Suspending damage: A letter to communities. *Harvard Educational Review, 79*, 409–428. Retrieved from http://hepg.org/her-home/issues/harvard-educational-review-volume-79-issue/herarticle/a-letter-to-communities. http://dx.doi.org/10.17763/haer.79.3.n0016675661t3n15

Tuhiwai Smith, L. (2012). *Decolonizing methodologies: Research and Indigenous peoples*. London, England: Zed Books.

Tuhiwai Smith, L., Tuck, E., & Yang, K. W. (2019). *Indigenous and decolonizing studies in education: Mapping the long view*. New York: Routledge.

Vélez-Torres, I., & Ruiz-Torres, G. (2016). Extractivismo neoliberal minero y conflictos socio-ambientales en Perú y Colombia [Neoliberal mining extractivism and social-environmental conflicts in Perú and Colombia]. *Ambiente y Sostenibilidad, 5,* 3–15. http://dx.doi.org/10.25100/ays.v5i1.4297

Visual voices: 100 photographs of village China by the women of Yunnan province. (1995). Yunnan, China: Yunnan People's Publishing House.

Vizenor, G. (Ed.). (2008). *Survivance: Narratives of Native presence.* Lincoln: University of Nebraska Press.

Wang, C., & Burris, M. A. (1994). Empowerment through photo novella: Portraits of participation. *Health Education Quarterly, 21,* 171–186. http://dx.doi.org/10.1177/109019819402100204

Watkins, M. (2019). *Mutual accompaniment and the creation of the common.* New Haven, CT: Yale University Press. http://dx.doi.org/10.2307/j.ctvhrcxwz

Whitfield, T. (1994). *Paying the price: Ignacio Ellacuría and the murdered Jesuits of El Salvador.* Philadelphia, PA: Temple University Press.

Women of PhotoVoice/ADMI & Lykes, M. B. (2000). *Voces e imágenes: Mujeres Mayas Ixiles de Chajul* [Voices and images: Mayan Ixil women of Chajul]. Guatemala City, Guatemala: Magna Terra.

III

LIBERATION PSYCHOLOGY
CLINICAL PRACTICE

7

Testimonios

Alejandro Cervantes

To be a witness to a *testimonio* requires solidarity, humility, and empathy. *Testimonios* are "a verbal journey of a witness who speaks to reveal the racial, classed, gendered, and nativist injustices they have suffered as a means of healing, empowerment, and advocacy for a more human present and future" (Perez Huber, 2009, p. 644). Testimonios empower individuals from the margins or the subaltern experience to reclaim their voice and recognize their resiliency (Delgado Bernal, Burciaga, & Flores Carmona, 2012). Historically, the purpose of testimonios was to document oppressed experiences and, more important, to challenge oppressive conditions (Carrillo, Ender, & Perez, 2018). Those of us with marginalized and oppressed identities must find opportunities to recenter our experiences if we are to challenge racism, heterosexism, patriarchy, genderism, ableism, sizeism, and other "isms." The extent to which testimonios are salient for marginalized communities depends on the access and space provided for collaborative consciousness-raising and critical dialogue (Latina Feminist Group, 2001). In the absence of access to testimonios or areas to share them, the memories become more challenging and painful for individuals' personal, emotional, and experiential being (Delgado Bernal et al., 2012). We, as clinicians, must be the agents of change in how we offer therapeutic services from a culturally responsive manner.

Given the empowerment premise of the genre, testimonios are a political approach that also incorporates cultural, social, historical, and political stories intersecting with an individual's life experience (Delgado Bernal et al., 2012). As our lived experiences continue to shape our being, we must recognize the

http://dx.doi.org/10.1037/0000198-008
Liberation Psychology: Theory, Method, Practice, and Social Justice, L. Comas-Díaz and E. Torres Rivera (Editors)

power of producing our stories. As a result, testimonios emerge as products through which we live that we share with others in our community and in our generation (Benmayor, 2012). This aspect of testimonios is imperative due to the psychological revealing of painful, traumatic, yet resilient identities of individuals from marginalized communities (Urrieta, Kolano, & Jo, 2015). Therefore, testimonios, like adages or sayings (*dichos/refranes*) and stories (*cuentos*), create an opportunity for cultural *sabiduría* (wisdom) to be shared via interpersonal methods so that the stories of our lived experiences are heard.

In this chapter, I tease apart the components of testimonios and describe how they cultivate a multicultural, holistic, and liberation practice in therapy. I provide information about the genre and then move into their praxis and liberation psychology. In this section on praxis, I combine the elements of testimonios and liberation psychology to demonstrate how both theoretical underpinnings complement one another. Then, I discuss how counselors can implement testimonios in therapy as culturally responsive interventions. I discuss research examples and practices such as testimonios with Latino male adolescents in group therapy. I end the chapter by discussing the importance of including testimonios in the field of psychology.

THE *TESTIMONIO* GENRE

The genre of testimonios has deep roots within Latin American oral culture and human rights struggles (Moraga & Anzaldúa, 1983). Testimonios were used to express the disempowerment people experienced from the persecution by their governments and other sociopolitical forces in Latin American countries (Aron, 1992; Behar, 1993; Burgos-Debray, 1984). The act of testimoniando (i.e., sharing testimonios with others) is witnesses' telling of narratives, with urgency, in an effort to expose an injustice (Yúdice, 1991). When individuals are testimoniando, they are eliciting social change by sharing stories of generational memories, aspirational possibilities, and geographic journeys (El Ashmawi, Hernandez Sanchez, & Flores Carmona, 2018; Yosso, 2005). Participants who engage in testimonio work are critically reflecting their personal experiences within sociopolitical realities. As Delgado Bernal and her colleagues (2012) stated, testimonio "is and continues to be an approach that incorporates political, social, historical, and cultural histories that accompany one's life experiences as a means to bring about change through consciousness-raising" (p. 364). Testimonios emphasize the legitimacy of experiential and lived knowledge (Brabeck, 2003). Concerning the Latinx community, they are opportunities for individuals to expose the intricacies of the Latinx experience (Espino, Vega, Rendón, Ranero, & Muñiz, 2012; Flores Carmona, 2014). Testimonios also emphasize the importance of examining the individual story within the larger collective to understand connections and tensions (Espino et al., 2012; Henze, 2000). In part, testimonios are cultural resources of social and political empowerment based on resilience and knowledge creation (Latina Feminist Group, 2001).

Testimonios, a method that originated in Latin America as a response to political oppression and that promotes resistance and social transformation (Cienfuegos & Monelli, 1983). Testimonio work is based on historical documentation, healing, and encouraging social justice principles to address sociopolitical and sociocultural problems (Carrillo et al., 2018). Cervantes-Soon (2012) described testimonios as counternarratives, confessions, and *consejos*, or advice, that help individuals document their experiences with oppression. In this manner, testimonios critique Western forms of knowledge to bring attention to the painful experiences and memories that highlight specific struggles of an individual's journey (Carrillo et al., 2018; Espino et al., 2012; Menchú, 1984). For example, testimonios have brought attention to the agency of immigrant mothers (González, 2006), high school students (Cervantes-Soon, 2012), and Latino male adolescents in group therapy (Cervantes, Flores Carmona, & Torres Fernández, 2018; Cervantes, Torres Fernandez, & Flores Carmona, 2019). As we see with the examples of populations using testimonios, an essential concept of this work is affirmation and limiting silence around one's experiences.

The Latina Feminist Group (2001) described testimonios as opportunities for individuals to form meaningful relationships, discuss similarities and differences, and, through this process, to find common ground. Because testimonios bring attention to the intersecting identities of those who practice them, they emerge as products of cultural liberation. As part of liberation practices, testimonios create opportunities for unique and complex experiences to develop with the hope of change at the individual and systems levels (Brabeck, 2003; Latina Feminist Group, 2001). As we continue to exist within our intersecting identities and move through cultural communities in hopes of being acknowledged, testimonios create opportunities to share, speak out, and empower against those structures that silence the experiences of the other.

Testimonios are gifts based on trust with the hope of recording, telling, and bearing witness to the injustices one experiences in their families, community, schools, and much more (Delgado Bernal et al., 2012; Mangual Figueroa, 2013; Urrieta et al., 2015). The internal battle of choosing whether to share one's experience emphasizes the difficulty of embracing testimonio work. Because testimonios are perceived to be sacred (Urrieta et al., 2015), empowering individuals to construct and share their testimonios must be a tender process (Latina Feminist Group, 2001), that is, one based on support, love, and compassion, which must be demonstrated by those hoping to engage others in the testimonio process (Latina Feminist Group, 2001). More specifically, if psychologists wish to include testimonio work as part of their repertoire of interventions, they must familiarize themselves with the injustices that have negatively affected Latinx individuals' mental health. Further, they need to research how systemic oppression and collective trauma affect the mental health of the Latinx community if they are to ask about their experiences and stories in therapy (Flores, 2013; Latina Feminist Group, 2001). Finally, psychologists must recognize power differentials (e.g., race and ethnicity, sex, sexual orientation, gender identity, ability status, size, religion) when they create and share their testimonios with clients and vice versa. The intention of testimonio work is to establish trust, build rapport, and facilitate a healing space based on equity and liberation (Aron, 1992; Cervantes et al., 2019; Comas-Díaz & Vazquez, 2018; Delgado Bernal et al., 2012; Latina Feminist Group, 2001). If the intention is not based on the etiology of testimonios or the intention moves away from the purpose of testimonio work, then psychologists risk perpetuating the institutional oppression our clients experience in other contexts (Cervantes et al., 2019). Thus, it is recommended the clinician consult with a peer or supervisor before implementing testimonios in therapy (Comas-Díaz & Vazquez, 2018). Additionally, liberation psychology as a practice and intervention combined with testimonios could assist clinicians in determining how to incorporate systems-based approaches when working with the Latinx population.

THE PRAXIS OF *TESTIMONIOS* AND LIBERATION PSYCHOLOGY

Ignacio Martín-Baró, a social psychologist and Jesuit priest originally from Spain who claimed El Salvador as his home, upheld liberation psychology as a framework to understand individuals living in oppressed communities. Furthermore, he contended that structural inequalities contributed to the sociocultural, sociopolitical, and sociohistorical alienation that most community members experienced (Martín-Baró, 1994). In other words, a reflection of the systemic oppression from a psychological perspective is necessary for societal transformation (Martín-Baró, 1994). When explaining the role of psychology, Martín-Baró (1994) stated that psychologists must redesign theoretical and practical tools that promote healing through the clients' sufferings, aspirations, and struggles. For example, Martín-Baró suggested that psychology should assist clients in understanding their mental health concerns in the context of the broader sociopolitical structures that they inhabit (Torres Rivera, 2013). Testimonios, when using liberation psychology as a framework, could be an excellent tool that increases empathy and decreases shame when providing spaces to speak against institutional and structural discrimination (Flores Carmona & Luciano, 2014; Latina Feminist Group, 2001).

Because liberation psychology focuses on oppression and liberation at the structural level, we could argue that the root causes of abuse cause oppressive social conditions (Moane, 2003). By examining harsh social conditions, psychologists could assist clients to move toward relational resiliency (Torres Rivera, 2013). In other words, psychologists working from a liberation psychology perspective help in valuing and legitimatizing the knowledge and experiences of the oppressed (Hernández-Wolfe, 2013; Martín-Baró, 1994; Moane, 2008; Montero, 2009; Torres Rivera, 2013). Cruz (2012) reported that for individuals to build resiliency, their stories need to be shared. Additionally, the role of relational resiliency is vital in knowing how a community could play a part in the individual's healing process (Cruz, 2012). Therefore, as we move from an individual framework to a collective context, as demanded in liberation psychology, relational resiliency is a component of testimonio work because testimonios build connection by validating one another's experiences (Aron, 1992; Comas-Díaz, 2006; Delgado Bernal et al., 2012; Latina Feminist Group, 2001).

The praxis of testimonios and liberation psychology merges antioppressive and empowering approaches to the field of counseling. Testimonios and liberation psychology as praxis could be defined as "a dynamic process that functions as the central component of psychological growth and self-empowerment, which emphasizes healing and strength in the immediate environment of the individual and their community" (Cervantes et al., 2018, p. 2). In this article, Cervantes and his colleagues (2018) urged therapists and educators to collaborate to decolonize Western thinking when providing educational and therapeutic services to Latinx students along the borderlands. Additionally, the article compared the principles of liberation psychology and testimonios as praxis to focus on decolonizing counseling methods with Latinx clients. Within the Cervantes and associates' (2018) article, the guiding principles of liberation psychology and testimonios are outlined in narrative form to underline the process of using both frameworks as praxis with Latino male adolescents at a high school along the borderlands between Mexico and the United States. Praxis, the way of acting and doing, becomes poignant when implementing liberation psychology and testimonios in either educational or mental health settings (Cervantes et al., 2018). Thus, as we merge these antioppressive genres, we are informing psychologists on how to act as catalysts for individual and collective change (Cervantes et al., 2018).

TESTIMONIOS AS A CULTURALLY RESPONSIVE THERAPEUTIC INTERVENTION IN THERAPY

Testimonios, when used as a cultural therapeutic intervention, affirm and represent the person creating the testimonio. Before discussing how testimonios can be a valuable tool for use in therapy, it is crucial to define what a culturally responsive intervention is. A *culturally responsive intervention* could be described as a counseling technique, strategy, or skill introduced in therapy that encompasses the cultural background and lived experiences of the client (Malott & Paone, 2013). To inform a culturally responsive intervention, clinicians need to consider how they will determine which interventions would best attenuate the concerns of racially and minoritized clients, how they can learn from clients of color, and what information is needed to assist these clients to achieve their therapeutic goals (Adames & Chavez-Dueñas, 2017). An intervention must address the overall functioning of clients of color, especially when determining which approaches to use in therapy. Like testimonios, a response that incorporates the cultural background and lived experiences of clients seeks to understand ecologically how they are affected by oppressive social conditions (Aron, 1992; Moane, 2003).

Aron's (1992) sociotherapy with Latin American women appears to be the seminal work with testimonios in the field of counseling. She was the first to introduce testimonios as a psychotherapeutic tool to address the mental health concerns of Latin American women experiencing oppression and discrimination in their community. Aron discussed how groups of women in Latin America survived psychological trauma under states of terrorism. She used testimonios as a cultural intervention to recover the speech, trust, and value of those with whom she worked to expose the injustices they encountered. She hoped to increase the recovery of the women's personal and social value to affirm their ability to challenge political militancy. Aron stated, "There is no doubt that the telling of one's story before a group of sympathetic listeners with the potential for becoming active in the struggle against injustice is of benefit to the audience" (p. 186). Opening the wounds to begin the healing process increases people's consciousness and assists them in identifying oppressive experiences, starting the healing process, and finding solutions (Latina Feminist Group, 2001). Aron posited that the use of testimonios in therapy appeared to be culturally relevant, useful, and transformative to the personal and collective experience of Chicana and Latina feminists.

Cervantes and his colleagues (2019) focused on the use of testimonios as a culturally responsive intervention with Latino male adolescents in group therapy. The young men wrote or drew their testimonios to express their thoughts and feelings around different lived experiences. After creating their testimonios, each shared his, and as a result, a family was built on transformation, healing, and understanding (Cervantes et al., 2019). Cervantes and his colleagues found testimonios to be impactful for Latino male adolescents, particularly when addressing family loss, male gender role socialization, and discussions of emotions. Furthermore, the authors argued for the use of testimonio with Latino male adolescents in group therapy because of its cultural implications and connection to *personalismo, familismo,* and *machismo. Personalismo* is the value of interpersonal relationships (Arredondo, Gallardo-Cooper, Delgado-Romero, & Zapata, 2014); *familismo,* the value of immediate and extended family (Baca & Hernandez, 2004); and *machismo,* the male behavior that demand Latinx male-identified people to be strong, self-reliant, and aggressive (Morales, 1996). As we continue to explore testimonio and its effectiveness in therapy, it is essential to discuss how to integrate this approach as an intervention when working with our clients. In the following section, I describe how to implement testimonios in therapy.

IMPLEMENTING *TESTIMONIOS* IN THERAPY

Before discussing how to introduce testimonios in therapy, we must consider which clients are appropriate for this type of intervention. Aron (1992) used testimonios with women from Latin America who experienced oppression, marginalization, victimization, and trauma. Also, testimonios were used as a cultural, therapeutic intervention with Latino male adolescents in group therapy (Cervantes et al., 2018, 2019) and have been described as a powerful healing tool when working with Latinx clients (Vazquez & Rosa, 2011). Outside of therapy, testimonios have been useful in urban classrooms (Cruz, 2012), with Latinx elementary students (Romero, DeNicolo, & Fradkin, 2016), during Chicana doctoral experiences (Espino et al., 2010), with undocumented undergraduate students (Romo, Allen, & Martinez, 2018), and with leadership in higher education (Martínez & Fernández, 2018).

When introducing testimonios in therapy, the clinician must consider the following factors. Clinicians who believe a client might benefit from using testimonio in treatment could trust their clinical judgment, consult with another clinician or their supervisor, or ask the client if a testimonio might be therapeutic in session. Assuredly, the clinician and client should have developed rapport before implementing testimonio in therapy. As the research shows, testimonios foster self-healing and help reduce symptoms of depression, anxiety, and posttraumatic stress disorder (Agger, Igreja, Kiehle, & Polatin, 2012; Comas-Díaz & Vazquez, 2018), and a testimonio could be an opportunity to improve clients' psychological well-being. First, it is critical to define and explain to the client what a testimonio is (e.g., the definition at the beginning of the chapter), and how it could be beneficial to their presenting concerns by providing psychoeducation of how testimonios could be healing in therapy.

Clinicians must also inform clients about the vulnerability the testimonio process may elicit and explain that, at any point, they may stop creating or sharing their testimonio. Finally, clinicians must explain the purpose of testimonios. Perhaps clients are discussing a painful memory or trauma and how it is impacting their psychological functioning; here, the purpose of introducing testimonios could be for clients to externalize their experience because a testimonio could be therapeutic (Aron, 1992; Benmayor, 2012; Cervantes et al., 2019; Latina Feminist Group, 2001). If clients agree to create a testimonio, the clinician should ask what type they would like to produce (e.g., written or drawn). Also, the clinician should determine whether their making a testimonio would benefit the therapeutic experience. Simply asking clients if they would like for the therapist to participate is recommended. However, therapists must consider power differentials, their intention in making people share their testimonios, and the working relationship (Cervantes et al., 2018, 2019). If at any point clinicians believe making a testimonio would not benefit the therapeutic and healing experience, they should refrain from creating and sharing it. As stated earlier, consultation between the clinician and a supervisor or colleague is crucial when a clinician introduces testimonios to their clients. The impact of the clinician's sharing their testimonio with the client could strengthen the working relationship, normalize the client's experience, and equalize the relationship (Cervantes et al., 2018, 2019; Cervantes & Torres Fernández, 2016). The client then chooses how to create a testimonio, the clinician will provide the materials to the client, and they jointly participate in a brief mindfulness exercise to ground the client. Clinicians will inform the client that they will be there in silence as the client prepares the testimonio and that the client can ask questions or stop at any time. Once the client completes the testimonio, the clinician will process the experience with the client by using the SIFT (Sensations, Images, Feelings, and Thoughts) mindfulness-based practice. This exercise involves labeling emotions accurately as they surface. After processing the experience with the client, the clinician invites them to share the testimonio. As the client is sharing the testimonio, the clinician pays attention to both the client's verbal and nonverbal expressions to witness the holistic experience and honor the witness to the testimonio (Cervantes & Torres Fernández, 2016; Latina Feminist Group, 2001). Finally, once clients complete their testimonio, if they agree for the clinician to create a testimonio with them, the clinician will share a testimonio as well, and both will gently process the experience.

To understand the roots of testimonio, liberation psychologists' critical reflexivity on their personal and political experiences, and their potential influence on the counseling field, an example is warranted. As such, I now outline an example of using testimonios as a cultural, therapeutic intervention when working with Latino male adolescents in group counseling (this group was designed by the author, his advisor, and a dissertation chair member, then implemented by the author). For this chapter, I discuss some of the group sessions while highlighting the implementation of testimonios with young Latino men. When determining what topic to introduce, it was essential to research how to address issues congruent with the lived experiences of Latinx adolescents—more specifically, Latino male adolescents. The research regarding group therapy with Latino male adolescents is limited, and thus it was essential to include other works to assist with group planning (Malott & Paone, 2013; Millán & Chan, 1991; Torres Rivera et al., 2014). According to the Centers for Disease Control and Prevention (2017), Latino male high school adolescents and non-Latino Whites are just as likely to report suicidal thinking (10.7% vs. 10.5%), and more prone to attempt suicide (6.9% vs. 4.6%). Because culturally relevant interventions such as *cuento therapy* (Villalba, Ivers, & Ohlms, 2010) and the focus of lived experiences of Mexican American adolescents in group therapy (Malott & Paone, 2013) were helpful, testimonios appeared to be a good fit for Latino male adolescents hoping to improve their mental health. Specific psychotherapy modalities such as group therapy could help them to address their concerns while feeling validated in their experiences (Cervantes et al., 2019).

This group consisted of 24 sessions that took place over one semester. Each session was 30 minutes. The first session was focused on introducing and explaining testimonios to the young men. Before describing the concept to them, I, as the group facilitator, shared a written testimonio about what it meant to be Chicano. Although I mentioned earlier the importance of first building rapport with clients before implementing testimonio work in individual therapy, the sharing of the facilitator's testimonio during the first session in this group therapy context assisted with building rapport between the counselor and the group members (Cervantes et al., 2019). As indicated by the Latina Feminist Group (2001), sharing a testimonio is about witnessing your pain and welcoming others to hear it. Thus, healing begins when we collectively understand one another's suffering (Comas-Díaz & Vazquez, 2018; Espino et al., 2012; Latina Feminist Group, 2001). I discussed what it meant to grow up Chicano, not speaking Spanish, disliking my brown skin, and my mother abandoning me at the age of 2. This process was designed to introduce testimonios, its intentions in being created and shared, and ignite discussions around lived experiences such as what it meant to be Chicano/Latino/Hispanic. As the group facilitator, modeling vulnerability through testimonio work is critical in demonstrating the power of self-disclosure (Cervantes et al., 2018; Comas-Díaz & Vazquez, 2018; Delgado Bernal et al., 2012; Latina Feminist Group, 2001; Vazquez & Rosa, 2011). After sharing my testimonio, I joined in the silence with the group members. Silence allows for moments to reflect on the testimonio. Discussions began as it related to my testimonio, and after the members asked their questions or shared their reactions to the testimonios, an important question to ask members was, "What feelings did you have after hearing my testimonio?" This question shifts the focus from the "I," or in this case, the individual perspective, to that of a collective story (Benmayor, 2009; Comas-Díaz & Vazquez, 2018). In other words, when the members were expressing their emotions, they were also integrated into their lived experiences as a Chicano/Latino/Hispanic in the United States. As such, they were testimoniando—sharing their testimonios as a means to connect and build solidarity.

During subsequent sessions, it was the participants' turn to create and share their testimonios. As the therapist, it is essential to recognize the power you have in asking others to share their testimonios. As the group facilitator, asking clients to create and share their testimonio is a task that must be done compassionately and respectfully. For example, because the group members in this case were young Latino men, normalizing the creating and sharing process of testimonio work as well as being culturally aware and sensitive were salient when asking members to share experiences that might be painful (Arredondo et al., 2014; Malott & Paone, 2013; Millán & Chan, 1991; Torres Rivera et al., 2014). As the group facilitator attempting to use testimonios as an intervention with clients, I needed to be aware of my intersecting identities and how they might influence the working alliance between the members and myself. Therefore, as reported by the Latina Feminist Group (2001), the group facilitator must engage in a reciprocal process. To demonstrate a mutual process, therapists must participate in creating their testimonio and possibly share their testimonio, as experienced in the first session just described. The act of creating and sharing your testimonio with the members signifies your participation in the process and also demonstrates that you are part of the collective experience (Latina Feminist Group, 2001; Ortega, 2016). In this process, testimonio becomes a mass resistance against the power differential between the therapist and group members and enhances the materialization of solidarity for everyone participating in the group (Brabeck,

2003). During subsequent sessions, I shared my testimonio, but I made sure to share last to allow more time for the members to share and process their experiences with telling their testimonios.

During the fourth session, the topic was for group members to discuss their experiences and relationships with their families. *Familismo*, a cultural value, is essential to consider when conceptualizing and treating Latinx clients (Baca & Hernandez, 2004). I introduced the topic to the members and asked them if they would like to write or draw their testimonio as it relates to their family. As the members were writing or drawing their testimonios, so was I to demonstrate the reciprocal process of testimonio work (Latina Feminist Group, 2001). After about 10 minutes, the members finished, and I opened the group by asking, "Would anyone like to share their testimonio with the group?" It is crucial to refrain from asking questions while individuals are sharing their testimonio. Allowing the person to share without interruption affirms the individual as the storyteller and asserts the power that person has over their experience. Having this discussion with either the group or an individual client is critical if testimonios are to be used in the therapeutic process.

As Cervantes et al. (2019) reported, one group member drew a testimonio about his family experience. In his testimonio titled "Lots of Stuff," he drew himself, on the right, slouched over on the table. On the left, he created pictures of alcohol bottles, and at the bottom right of the page, he drew his family, with him pictured alone. As he was sharing his testimonio, he discussed how lonely his experience was in his family and how he believed his family did not care about him. He further stated how he wished to be in a family where they asked how he was doing. Finally, he hoped for his parents to stop drinking on the weekends so that they recognize how their alcoholism affected his self-esteem. After he finished sharing, the group was quiet. Then, one member spoke and shared his testimonio about living in a family that he believed does not respect, support, or love him. Another member shared his testimonio about his father not being in his life. Feelings of isolation appeared to dissipate as the members' connection with each other increased by sharing testimonios. I witnessed the members not only sharing their testimonios but also encouraging one another to reach out to them if they were feeling alone or isolated. During this group session, I did not facilitate any conversations with the members, as they young men themselves were leading the discussions.

In our seventh group session, with the permission of a previous client, I shared with the group a written testimonio she had written. The purpose of introducing them to another person's testimonio was to build insight around how they could help others who might have similar experiences. I provided each of them a copy of the testimonio and asked them to read it, then share their thoughts and feelings about it. There were a few sessions when I did not ask them to write or draw their own testimonios. Instead, I asked them to have a dialogue with one another to assist them in moving toward a collective consciousness around empowerment and resistance (Brabeck, 2003). Members commented on how they related to the person's experiences with her family, especially with her mom abandoning her at an early age. As members coalesced around assisting the person, some discussed how the school should create more groups such as the one they were participating in for other students. Some members indicated wanting to speak to the principal about this matter. I explained that this was a process of them advocating for others and critiquing social contexts—in this case, their school. As a result, I further explained that they became experts in their school because they demanded change to transform the school that would help students from a mental health perspective (Ortega, 2016). As group facilitator or therapist incorporating testimonios in his work, I recommend other therapists who wish to do so understand that testimonios are built on praxis. In other words, *testimoniando* is a liberatory practice of acting and doing that helps increase critical consciousness and promote an interest in justice and social equity (Cervantes et al., 2018; Comas-Díaz & Vazquez, 2018). In this session, I wanted to be intentional in building insight into the power the group members had to change their school. Through this process, the practice of *testimoniando* becomes liberatory, empowering, and emancipatory (Comas-Díaz & Vazquez, 2018).

These illustrations demonstrate the possible implementation of testimonios as a cultural, therapeutic intervention with Latino male adolescents in group therapy. Although the example in the chapter was with young men participating in group therapy, testimonios as an intervention could be used across populations and contexts. As demonstrated in the example, the use of testimonios in treatment is unique in that allows for the client to be reflective and action-oriented (Tate, Torres Rivera, Brown, & Skaistis, 2013). Testimonio should be considered for inclusion in treatment because it is a collaborative process between the therapist and the client that moves away from the traditional practices of therapy, thus informing a liberatory practice built on transformation and healing (Comas-Díaz & Vazquez, 2018). Most important, testimonios document how we can struggle against and ultimately thrive amid oppression.

CONCLUSION

As a young scholar who pushes for culturally responsive interventions for Latino male adolescents in therapy, I am reminded of the influence that liberation psychologists teach me every day. As stated by Afuape and Hughes (2016),

> I began to understand that if our work as psychologists is not connected to the social circumstances of people's lives, we are likely to reinforce the idea that distress is the fault of the individuals, not a response to disempowerment. (p. 18)

I see testimonio*s* infused with liberation psychology as an opportunity to improve the personal, social, and emotional well-being of community members. The lessons I continue to learn from studying testimonios and liberation psychology highlight that, as a clinician, there is an immense amount of work we need to accomplish if we are to interrupt oppressive structures that negate the experiences of Latinx individuals. Together, we could promote the stories of Latinx individuals to ensure that we holistically treat our clients and improve their mind, body, and spirit.

REFERENCES

Adames, H. Y., & Chavez-Dueñas, N. Y. (2017). *Cultural foundations and interventions in Latino/a mental health: History, theory, and within group differences.* New York, NY: Routledge.

Afuape, T., & Hughes, G. (Eds.). (2016). *Liberation practices: Towards emotional wellbeing through dialogue.* New York, NY: Routledge/Taylor & Francis.

Agger, I., Igreja, V., Kiehle, R., & Polatin, P. (2012). Testimony therapies in Asia: Integrating spirituality in testimonial therapy for torture survivors in India, Sri Lanka, Cambodia and the Philippines. *Transcultural Psychiatry, 49,* 568–589.

Aron, A. (1992). *Testimonio,* a bridge between psychotherapy and sociotherapy. *Women & Therapy, 13,* 173–189. http://dx.doi.org/10.1300/J015V13N03_01

Arredondo, P., Gallardo-Cooper, M., Delgado-Romero, E. A., & Zapata, A. L. (2014). *Culturally responsive counseling with Latinas/os.* Alexandria, VA: American Counseling Association.

Baca, L., & Hernandez, P. (2004). Group therapy with Chicanas. In R. J. Velásquez, L. M. Arellano, B. W. McNeill, R. J. Velásquez, L. M. Arellano, & B. W. McNeill (Eds.), *The handbook of Chicana/o psychology and mental health* (pp. 251–263). Mahwah, NJ: Erlbaum.

Behar, R. (1993). *Translated woman: Crossing the border with Esperanza's story.* Boston, MA: Beacon.

Benmayor, R. (2009, January). Theorizing through digital stories: The art of "writing back" and "writing for." *Academic Commons.* Retrieved from http://www.academic commons.org/2009/01/theorizing-through-digital-stories-the-art-of-writing-back-and-writing-for/

Benmayor, R. (2012). Digital "testimonio" as a signature pedagogy for Latin@ studies. *Equity & Excellence in Education, 45,* 507–524. http://dx.doi.org/10.1080/10665684.2012.698180

Brabeck, K. (2003). Testimonio: A strategy for collective resistance, cultural survival and building solidarity. *Feminism & Psychology, 13,* 252–258. http://dx.doi.org/10.1177/0959353503013002009

Burgos-Debray, E. (1984). *I, Rigoberta Menchú, an Indian woman in Guatemala* (A. Wright, Trans.). New York, NY: Verso.

Carrillo, J. F., Ender, T., & Perez, J. T. (2018). Letters to our children: Narrating legacies of love, dissent, and possibility. *Journal of Latinos and Education, 27,* 238–251.

Centers for Disease Control and Prevention. (2017). QuickStats: Suicide rates for teens aged 15–19 years, by sex—United States, 1975–2015. Retrieved from https://www.cdc.gov/mmwr/volumes/66/wr/mm6630a6.htm

Cervantes, A., Flores Carmona, J., & Torres Fernandez, I. (2018). *Testimonios* and liberation psychology as praxis: Informing educators in the borderlands. *Journal of Latinos and Education.* Advance online publication. http://dx.doi.org/10.1080/15348431.2018.1534692

Cervantes, A., & Torres Fernandez, I. (2016). The use of testimonios as tool to promote liberation and social justice advocacy with Latin@s in counseling. *Latina/o Psychology Today, 3*(1), 25–29.

Cervantes, A., Torres Fernandez, I., & Flores Carmona, J. (2019). *Nosotros importamos* (we matter): The use of *testimonios* with Latino male adolescents in group counseling. *Journal of Creativity in Mental Health, 14,* 181–192. http://dx.doi.org/10.1080/15401383.2019.1568941

Cervantes-Soon, C. G. (2012). *Testimonios* of life and learning in the borderlands: Subaltern Juárez girls speak. *Equity & Excellence in Education, 45,* 373–391. http://dx.doi.org/10.1080/10665684.2012.698182

Cienfuegos, A. J., & Monelli, C. (1983). The testimony of political repression as a therapeutic instrument. *American Journal of Orthopsychiatry, 53,* 43–51. http://dx.doi.org/10.1111/j.1939-0025.1983.tb03348.x

Comas-Díaz, L. (2006). Latino healing: The integration of ethnic psychology into psychotherapy. *Psychotherapy: Theory, Research, & Practice, 43,* 436–453. http://dx.doi.org/10.1037/0033-3204.43.4.436

Comas-Díaz, L., & Vazquez, C. I. (2018). Latina feminist psychology: *Testimonio,* borderlands theory, and embodied psychology. In L. Comas-Díaz & C. I. Vazquez (Eds.), *Latina psychologists: Thriving in the cultural borderlands* (pp. 54–68). New York, NY: Routledge. http://dx.doi.org/10.4324/9781315175706-1

Cruz, C. (2012). Making curriculum from scratch: *Testimonio* in an urban classroom. *Equity & Excellence in Education, 45,* 460–471. http://dx.doi.org/10.1080/10665684.2012.698185

Delgado Bernal, D., Burciaga, R., & Flores Carmona, J. (2012). Chicana/Latina *testimonios*: Mapping the methodological, pedagogical, and political. *Equity & Excellence in Education, 45,* 363–372. http://dx.doi.org/10.1080/10665684.2012.698149

El Ashmawi, Y. P., Hernandez Sanchez, E., & Flores Carmona, J. (2018). Testimonialista pedagogues: Testimonio pedagogy in critical multicultural education. *International Journal of Multicultural Education, 20*(1), 67–85. http://dx.doi.org/10.18251/ijme.v20i1.1524

Espino, M. M., Muñoz, S. M., & Marquez Kiyama, J. (2010). Transitioning from doctoral study to the academy: Theorizing *trenzas* of identity for Latina sister scholars. *Qualitative Inquiry, 16*(10), 804–818. http://dx.doi.org/10.1177/1077800410383123

Espino, M. M., Vega, I. I., Rendón, L. I., Ranero, J. J., & Muñiz, M. M. (2012). The process of reflexión in bridging testimonios across lived experience. *Equity & Excellence in Education, 45,* 444–459. http://dx.doi.org/10.1080/10665684.2012.698188

Flores, Y. G. (2013). *Chicana and Chicano mental health: Alma, mente y corazon* [Soul, mind and heart]. Tucson: University of Arizona Press.

Flores Carmona, J. (2014). Cutting out their tongues: *Mujeres' testimonios* and the Malintzin researcher. *Journal of Latino/Latin American Studies, 6*(2), 113–124.

Flores Carmona, J., & Luciano, M. (2014). A student–teacher *testimonio*: Reflexivity, empathy, and pedagogy. In J. Flores Carmona & K. Luschen (Eds.), *Crafting critical stories: Toward pedagogies and methodologies of collaboration, inclusion and voice* (pp. 75–92). New York, NY: Peter Lang. http://dx.doi.org/10.3726/978-1-4539-1017-7

González, J. C. (2006). Academic socialization experiences of Latina doctoral students: A qualitative understanding of support systems that aid and challenges that hinder the process. *Journal of Hispanic Higher Education, 5,* 347–365.

Henze, B. R. (2000). Who says who says? The epistemological grounds for agency in liberatory political projects. In P. M. L. Moya & M. R. Hames-Garcia (Eds.), *Reclaiming identity: Realist theory and the predicament of postmodernism* (pp. 229–250). Berkeley: University of California Press.

Hernández-Wolfe, P. (2013). *A borderlands view on Latinos, Latin Americans, and decolonization: Rethinking mental health.* Lanham, MD: Aronson.

Huber, L. P. (2009, December). Challenging racist nativist framing: Acknowledging the community cultural wealth of undocumented Chicana college students to reframe the immigration debate. *Harvard Educational Review, 79*(4), 704–729. http://dx.doi.org/10.17763/haer.79.4.r7j1xn011965w186

Latina Feminist Group. (2001). *Telling to live: Latina feminist testimonios* [Latina feminist testimonials]. Durham, NC: Duke University Press.

Malott, K. M., & Paone, T. R. (2013). Mexican-origin adolescents' exploration of a group experience. *Journal of Creativity in Mental Health, 8,* 204–218. http://dx.doi.org/10.1080/15401383.2013.821913

Mangual Figueroa, A. (2013). °Hay que hablar [We have to talk]! *Testimonio* in the everyday lives of migrant mothers. *Language & Communication, 33,* 559–572. http://dx.doi.org/10.1016/j.langcom.2013.03.011

Martín-Baró, I. (1994). *Writings for a liberation psychology* (A. Aron & S. Corne, Eds.). Cambridge, MA: Harvard University Press.

Martínez, M., & Fernández, E. (2018). Moving toward a reconceptualization of Latina/o leadership in higher education. In C. Rodríguez, M. A. Martinez, & F. Valle (Eds.), *Latino educational leadership: Serving Latino communities and preparing Latinx leaders Across the P-20 pipeline* (pp. 97–120). Charlotte, NC: Information Age.

Menchú, R. (1984). *I, Rigoberta Menchú: An Indian woman in Guatemala* (E. Burgos-Debray, Ed., & A. Wright, Trans.). London, England: Verso.

Millán, F., & Chan, J. (1991). Group therapy with inner city Hispanic acting-out adolescent males: Some theoretical observations. *Group, 15,* 109–115. http://dx.doi.org/10.1007/BF01456793

Moane, G. (2003). Bridging the personal and the political: Practices for a liberation psychology. *American Journal of Community Psychology, 31*(1–2), 91–101. http://dx.doi.org/10.1023/A:1023026704576

Moane, G. (2008). Applying psychology in contexts of oppression and marginalization Liberation, psychology, wellness, and social justice. *The Irish Journal of Psychology, 29*(1–2), 91–101. http://dx.doi.org/10.1080/03033910.2008.10446276

Montero, M. (2009). Methods for liberation: Critical consciousness in action. In M. Montero & C. Soon (Eds.), *Psychology of liberation: Theory and application* (pp. 73–91). New York, NY: Springer. http://dx.doi.org/10.1007/978-0-387-85784-8_4

Moraga, C., & Anzaldúa, G. (1983). *This bridge called my back: Writings by radical women of color.* Brooklyn, NY: Kitchen Table: Women of Color Press.

Morales, E. (1996). Gender roles among Latino gay and bisexual men: Implications for family and couple relationships. In J. Laird & R. J. Green (Eds.), *Lesbians and gays in couples and families: A handbook for therapists* (pp. 272–297). San Francisco, CA: Jossey Bass.

Ortega, M. (2016). *In-between: Latina feminist phenomenology, multiplicity, and the self.* Albany, NY: State University of New York Press.

Romero, G., DeNicolo, C. P., & Fradkin, C. (2016). Exploring instructional practices in a Spanish/English bilingual classroom through *sitios y lenguas* and *testimonio*. *The Urban Review, 48,* 440–462. http://dx.doi.org/10.1007/s11256-016-0362-0

Romo, E., Allen, T. O., & Martinez, M. A. (2018). "It was kind of a dream come true": Undocumented college students' *testimonios* of cultural wealth in the college choice process. *Journal of Hispanic Higher Education, 18,* 389–409.

Tate, K. A., Torres Rivera, E., Brown, E., & Skaistis, L. (2013). Foundations for liberation: Social justice, liberation psychology, and counseling. *Revista Interamericana de Psicología, 47,* 373–382.

Torres Rivera, E. (2013). Is quality a culturally-based or universal construct? *Interamerican Journal of Psychology, 47*(1). Retrieved from http://journals.fcla.edu/ijp/article/view/82129

Torres Rivera, E., Fernández, I. T., & Hendricks, W. A. (2014). Psychoeducational and counseling groups with Latinos/as. In J. L. DeLucia-Waack, C. R. Kalodner, & M. T. Riva (Eds.), *Handbook of group counseling and psychotherapy* (2nd ed., pp. 242–252). Thousand Oaks, CA: Sage.

Urrieta, L. J., Kolano, L. Q., & Jo, J. O. (2015). Learning from the testimonio of a "successful" undocumented Latino student in North Carolina. In E. T. Hamann,

S. Wortham, & E. J. Murillo, Jr. (Eds.), *Revisiting education in the new Latino diaspora* (pp. 49–70). Charlotte, NC: Information Age.

Vazquez, C. I., & Rosa, D. (2011). *Grief therapy with Latinos: Integrating culture for clinicians.* New York: Springer.

Villalba, J. A., Ivers, N. N., & Ohlms, A. B. (2010). *Cuento* group work in emerging rural Latino communities: Promoting personal–social development of Latina/o middle school students of Mexican heritage. *Journal for Specialists in Group Work, 35,* 23–43. http://dx.doi.org/10.1080/01933920903463502

Yosso, T. J. (2005). Whose culture has capital? A critical race theory discussion of community cultural wealth. *Race, Ethnicity and Education, 8,* 69–91.

Yúdice, G. (1991). *Testimonio* and postmodernism. *Latin American Perspectives, 18*(3), 15–31. http://dx.doi.org/10.1177/0094582X9101800302

8

Urban Liberation

Postcolonial Intersectional Feminism and Developing a Socially Conscious Therapeutic Practice

Chakira M. Haddock-Lazala

Central to understanding the zeitgeist of contemporary psychology is its denial and avoidance of the "social" realm—more specifically, it struggles to attend to and conceptualize the importance of social context, social (in)justice, oppression, and their link to social identity and mental health. Ego psychology and its link to Western philosophies and individualism has been the driving force of modernity, and it has gone to great lengths to devalue affect, the fluidity of identity, human interconnection, and the impact of social context and material conditions on consciousness. By focusing on cognition and neurology and ignoring affect and the social realm, we have also inadvertently ignored issues related to embodiment, morality, ideology, politics, and issues related to power—particularly how these influence mental health.

In this chapter, I aim to provide guidance on how to conceptualize ourselves as a crossroads during a therapeutic encounter—how we can think of ourselves as intersections between consciousness, material conditions, and social context. I discuss the experience of social identity and how it is influenced by power, oppression, and conflict. I also highlight how intersectional feminism and postcolonial theory may help us attend to the complexities of social identity in therapy, such that individuals are always understood within a larger collective. I challenge our tendency to advocate for a multicultural psychology dissociated from the oppressive social

http://dx.doi.org/10.1037/0000198-009
Liberation Psychology: Theory, Method, Practice, and Social Justice, L. Comas-Díaz and E. Torres Rivera (Editors)

contexts, systems, and material conditions. As established in my 2016 doctoral dissertation,

> My ontological approach is one of critical realism and is influenced by Muxerista[1] feminist theory, discursive and postcolonial psychology and psychoanalysis. As a primarily English-speaking bilingual Puerto Rican born on the mainland U.S., I aim to use my unique standpoint as a U.S. citizen—as well as colonized subject—to present knowledge that is situated and perspectival (Hekman, 1997) and to present bodies that are "written with language (and) overwritten with signifiers" (Viego, 2009, p. 132). This position departs from the notion that "no perspective/standpoint is epistemologically privileged" (Hekman, 1997, p. 351) and challenges the illusion that ethnic-racialized subjects "can be reduced to calculable, well-worn proofs" (Viego, 2009, p. 139). As a colonized subject who straddles the borderlands of multiple nations, languages, genders and classes, I hope that my positionality allows me to generate useful conocimento[2] (Anzaldúa, 1987) via my own Latinx[3] subjectivity. (Haddock-Lazala, pp. 25–26)

My approach, which I call *urban liberation*, situates mental health praxis as occurring within a Western medical model in a capitalist stratified society—and seeks to resist this.

The reification of capitalist stratified social systems can be seen in our diagnosis criteria based on social functioning and our implicit conceptualizations that locate mature and healthy psychological development as being akin to the desire and attainment of employment, capital, and upward mobility. The general movements of therapeutic change within this mainstream medical model are the movement from primitivity to civility, from concrete to abstract, from action and behavior (enactment) to symbolization and verbalization (speech) and ultimately from enslavement to domination, from working class to ruling elite. In this framework, resistance and noncompliance may be understood as the client's pathological refusal to submit to the demands of

---

[1] *Muxerista* refers to a Latinx feminist perspective that constitutes "oppositional expressions to dominant feminism . . . by focusing on the centrality of community, mutual caring, and global solidarity; while aiming towards collective liberation and transformation" (Bryant-Davis & Comas-Díaz, 2016, pp. 9–10). The "x" in *Muxerista* (rather than the traditional term *mujerista* with a "j") aims at being inclusive of transgender and gender-nonconforming people who identify as women.

[2] *Conocimiento* refers to Anzaldúa's seven-stage methodology of consciousness-raising, self-analysis, and examination aimed at confronting and integrating unconscious aspects of the self that may perpetuate oppression. "As individuals explore every aspect of their intersectional identities, *conocimiento* can facilitate reaching these insights that lead from awareness to public, and many times, political actions" (Hurtado, 2015, p. 66).

[3] As defined in Haddock-Lazala (2016),

> The term Latinx provides a social identifier that aims to neutralize the sex–gender binary inherent in the Spanish language and thus, the ethnic category formally known as Latino. It offers an alternative to a) the general and masculine-centric ethnic term "Latino," b) the inherently gendered terms Latina/o, as well as c) the more recent gender inclusive but binary embedded term, Latin@. Its use elucidates the diversity of genders and sexualities of people who identify with Latinidad as an ethnic identity and is meant to connote inclusivity rather than exclusivity (not meant to be used exclusively as an identifier for gender-nonconforming or trans people of Latin American descent).

society and socialization via education and therapy. Urban liberation advocates for a movement toward envisioning the human subject as motivated by freedom, including freedom from the constraints and controls imposed on them by a mental health system that exists in the intersection of the state power (Montero, 2004), capitalism, and a strictly objective medical model.

This urban liberation approach challenges the subject–object split that plagues the medical model. From this more contemporary and socially conscious approach, the therapist, rather than maintaining a rigidly objective position, approaches the therapeutic encounter from a place of radical openness (Hart, 2017), curiosity, and awe (McWilliams, 2004) where knowledge and meaning is intersubjective and coconstructed with the client (the expert regarding the client's own truth). Together, the dyad seeks to eradicate delusion and distortion by seeking wisdom and truth, to eradicate helplessness and powerlessness by wielding power and enacting agency, to transform uncertainty and fear into courage and excitement and conflict into mercy and peace. From this approach, clients are not individual egos that are constitutionally defective (or passive victims of hereditary degeneracy) but rather are subjects whose complex bodies and lives depend on their ability to have independent minds, see reality clearly, make decisions, and connect to the world and the social. As Paulo Freire (1970/2000), whose work is the basis and presents the founding principles of liberation psychology, stated,

> the more radical a person is, the more fully he or she enters into reality so that, knowing it better, he or she can better transform it. The individual is not afraid to meet the people or enter into dialogue with them. This person does not consider himself or herself the proprietor of history or of all people, or the liberator of the oppressed, but he or she does commit him or herself, within history, to fight at their side. (p. 38)

Regarding mental health practitioners, we must remain vigilant and aware about our collusion with structures or systems of oppression, stand firmly on the side of truth and justice, and in service of those we seek to serve: the ill, the oppressed. This raising of social consciousness attempts to transcend traditional multicultural models of psychology that take a noncritical categorical approach to social phenomena such as race, ethnicity, gender, and culture. Simply put, traditional multicultural psychology has studied social identity while decontextualizing it from collective histories of power, oppression, slavery, and colonization. This urban liberation approach understands social identities and mental illness as emerging within oppressive contexts, the foundations of which are structured by imperialism and colonization. These internalized social dynamics can be conflictual (based on conquest, enslavement, domination, and subjugation), collaborative (connection, interdependence, peace, and justice), and transcendent (resistance, revolution, reconstruction, and transformation). The therapeutic space becomes the setting in which these unconscious oppressive enactments can become conscious and thus subject to true will and action toward change (from reactionary to revolutionary). It is worth noting that the aim of the true revolutionary subject, in the context of health and healing, is not to destroy, replace, and become the oppressive master, replicating the cycle of oppression, but rather to liberate themselves and their oppressor (Freire, 1970/2000) from the cycle all together and no longer be subjects and objects of violence.

POWER, OPPRESSION, AND INTERSECTIONALITY DEFINED

Power

For many, particularly those who identify as minorities, power has been considered "bad," perhaps because it has historically been associated with abuse, dominance, and oppression. Power can be understood as a construct of society and a product of the systems and institutions humans have created to maintain control of and order among the masses. According to Hunjan and Pettit (2011), power is conceptualized as the ability to achieve a desired change: "Power is dynamic, relational, and multidimensional, changing according to context, circumstance and interest. Its expressions and forms can range from domination and resistance to collaboration and transformation" (p. 5). This definition emphasizes the contextual nature of power. On the other hand, Tew (2006) defined power as a "social relation that may open or close off opportunities for individuals or social groups" (p. 40). Tew's definition identifies power as the ability to wield privilege or be prevented from wielding it. As mental health professionals, our power to dominate, control, oppress, and exclude, as well as our power to treat and institutionalize, is endowed by our state-sponsored education and licensing bodies. While working within an established mental health system, therefore, we are indeed agents of the state, serving the surveillance and policing systems of our government and potentially having a negative impact on clients. A good example of this is the therapist's role in assessing risk for violence and addiction and our pursuant interventions—systemic and institutional oppression and violence disguised as anger management and substance abuse treatment.

Oppression

Just as with power, oppression has been defined by a wide range of scholars in a variety of fields. Gil (1994) presented oppression as

> relations of domination and exploitation—economic, social and psychologic—between individuals; between social groups and classes within and beyond societies; and, globally, between entire societies. Injustice refers to discriminatory, dehumanizing, and development-inhibiting conditions of living (e.g., unemployment, poverty, homelessness, and lack of health care), imposed by oppressors upon dominated and exploited individuals, social groups, classes and peoples. These conditions will often cause people to turn to social services for help. Oppression seems motivated by an intent to exploit (i.e., benefit disproportionately from the resources, capacities, and productivity of others) and it results typically in disadvantageous, unjust conditions of living for its victims. It serves as

a means to enforce exploitation toward the goal of securing advantageous conditions of living for its perpetrators. Justice reflects the absence of exploitation-enforcing oppression. (p. 233)

In the past, the definition of oppression was limited to the tyranny of a ruling group but today, oppression can also be understood as the process through which a people are denied their full humanity by limiting access to language, education, and other opportunities.

Oppressive Dynamics and Acculturation–Assimilation

Oppressive systems demand that the less powerful adapt and assimilate to the status quo of the "host society," and they must do so in a way that functions in favor of maintaining the privileges of the more powerful and elite. This means that our notions of whether someone is deemed as mentally ill comes from the interpretation of how well the person is adapting and functioning within the stratified society. The message is "adapt or die" (or, more explicitly in authoritarian regimes, adapt or be killed). This adaptation process has been conceptualized as acculturation and assimilation (Berry, 1998).

Although the epidemiological literature has relied heavily on the construct of acculturation as a basis for understanding ethnic minority populations, the construct itself has been shrouded in controversy and critique (Bhatia & Ram, 2001; Siatkowski, 2007). As I have stated in the past,

> The critique has centered around it's individualistic, linear, decontextualized approached, it's universalist assumptions and bias towards adaptation. Although mainstream acculturation theory and subsequent findings have been well accepted by the psychological community, Bhatia & Ram's (2001) postcolonial critique of acculturation theory posits that it fails to explain the process by which it is achieved. (Haddock-Lazala, 2016, p. 22)

More importantly, as it relates to this chapter, the Berry acculturation model fails to address how issues of power, oppression, and colonization affect the "adaptation" process and the ethnic–racialized experience. Additionally, the theory relies heavily on ego psychological and social Darwinist values of individualism and the assumption that resistance to acculturation and assimilation is a maladaptive strategy, without taking into consideration the possibility that the host culture might be colonial, oppressive, perverse, an authoritarian dictatorial regime, or a combination thereof.

In contrast, I believe that to gain a more complex and contextual understanding of the mental health of People of Color and (im)migrant populations, we need to "think of selfhood as firmly intertwined with socio-cultural factors such as colonialism, language, immigration and racially based laws" (Bhatia & Ram, 2001, p. 5). As a result, I have suggested (Haddock-Lazala, 2016) that postcolonial and intersectional feminist theories offer a worthy alternative to understanding multiculturalism, ethnic–racialization, and acculturation within the mental health system by contesting Eurocentric ideologies that contribute to "othering" the people we claim to serve.

Postcolonialism

Postcolonial theory strives to account for the effects of European imperialism and colonization on most cultures and practices around the world and acknowledges that some peoples have been affected more than others—in fact, some people continue to live under colonial rule (e.g., Palestinians, Puerto Ricans). Cases like these recall that postcolonialism does not apply only to cultures in which the colonial powers have unoccupied the land (hence, the prefix *post*), but also neocolonial contexts in which issues of colonial domination and the struggle for liberation are very much alive and ongoing. I urge us to expand our understanding of in vivo colonial experience as well as pre- and postcolonial experiences. Postcolonial theory offers a discourse that runs in "opposition to the influential discursive practices of Europe and United States" (Bhatia & Ram, 2001, p. 2), and its consideration is essential when working with marginalized populations.

Postcolonial theory "with its emphasis on understanding the construction of self and identity in terms of colonial histories and present-day transnational migration, has tremendous relevance for understanding issues related to acculturation and immigrant identities" (Bhatia & Ram, 2001, p. 2), especially within the field of psychology. This kind of framework elucidates the colonized subjects' constant struggle for fundamental existence in a context of violence and oppression. "Such negotiations have not been adequately recognized or understood in many of the existing acculturation models" (Bhatia & Ram, 2001, p. 3), especially when it comes to our understanding of People of Color and the negotiations that take place throughout their mental health care experiences.

Imperialism and colonization influence our sense of identity and belonging—to a nation, to a people, and to their culture. The construct of nationality has also been notoriously understudied within psychological research; when it has been studied, it has been done simplistically (Haddock-Lazala, 2016). Bhatia and Ram (2001) pointed out that race, ethnicity, culture, and nationality have often been conflated. People of Color and (im)migrants' social positions and power within a political system is subject to how the state wants to exploit them socioeconomically. States often change exploitative labor, citizenship, and immigration policies in ways that benefit their immediate labor or military needs (e.g., the United States giving Puerto Ricans citizenship immediately before World War II as a means to satisfy their need for troops; current migrant workers in the United States). Puerto Rico and its people (who are U.S. citizens but often identify primarily as "Puerto Rican" as their nationality rather than "American") exemplify the ways in which colonization forces us to abandon nationality as a firm container for culture. In fact, the boundaries of a culture and sense of nationhood often extend far beyond the geographic and political boundaries of a nation. This process and the resulting colonized subject with overlapping identities may be described as *intersectionality* (Crenshaw, 1989) or an *intracategorical approach to complexity* (McCall, 2005) and is best exemplified by *mestiza* consciousness and the dialectics of the borderlands (Anzaldúa, 1987). For Anzaldúa, the *borderlands* refers to a geographic as well as psychological location in which hybridity and mixing (*mezcla*) is more likely to occur. Although in one sense, she was referring specifically to the U.S.–Mexico border, as we'll see, her definition is actually far more expansive and metaphorical:

> Borders are set up to define the places that are safe and unsafe, to distinguish us from them. A border is a dividing line, a narrow strip along a steep edge. A borderland is a vague and undetermined place created by the emotional residue of an unnatural boundary. It is in a constant state of transition. The prohibited and forbidden are its inhabitants. (Anzaldúa, 1987, p. 25)

She posited that a new kind of consciousness and person arises at the border, the place where two or more nations, cultures, or languages collide. This dialectic between bodies, subjectivity, and geographic context alludes to the notion that, for Anzaldúa, material conditions and context precede consciousness. The subjects produced under these conditions are defined by hybridity and being the mix of two or more ethnicities, races, and their respective cultures and languages. Terms such as *mestizaje* and *mulataje* exemplify the idea of a people arising from the miscegenation that results from colonization, slavery, and social dynamics related to the borderlands. More specifically, *mestizaje* refers to the process in which indigenous and European ancestry become mixed and create *mestizo* people; similarly, *mulataje* refers to the mixing of African and European ancestry, creating *mulato* people. Additionally, *zambos* refers to people of mixed indigenous and African ancestry. It should be noted that these terms should be understood within their colonial contexts of social stratification, White supremacy, and slavery. These mixed groups were and are located and valued within society according to their proximity to Whiteness and thus supposed level of superiority–inferiority. As such, they also represent the borderlands of a racist, stratified class system, being mixed and thus situated somewhere between being inferior to Europeans (e.g., Spaniards or Criollos-Spaniards born in the Americas) but superior to indigenous natives or African slaves. These social categories seek to capture and categorize the results of colonization and miscegenation and eventually become internalized as social identities. These hybrid social identifiers would come to be commonly associated with ethnic groups such as Latinos, Hispanics, or, more recently, the Latinx communities.

Intersectionality

In 2016, I began highlighting the often-overlooked association between borderlands theory and intersectionality:

> In her 1987 book *Borderlands/La Frontera—The New Mestiza*, Gloria Anzaldúa aimed at profoundly challenging how we think not just about identity, but also language and acculturation. For Anzaldúa, Chicanos (or currently, Latinxs) are not defined by the Spanish language but by "racial, ideological, cultural and biological crosspollination which ultimately produces a new mestiza consciousness . . .

a consciousness of the Borderland" (p. 99). As opposed to presenting people of color as acculturating to another culture, Borderlands Theory presents *mestiza consciousness* as the notion that Latinx[4] existing within multiple social worlds (and their respective languages) develop "the agility to navigate and the ability to challenge linear conceptions of social reality" (Hurtado, 2009, p. 33) within a space in which "antithetical elements mix, not to obliterate each other nor to be subsumed by a larger whole but rather to combine in unique and unexpected ways" (Hurtado, 2009, p. 183). In Anzaldúa's words, "To live in the Borderlands means you are . . . caught in the crossfire between camps, while carrying all five races on your back . . . you are the battle ground. . . . To survive the Borderlands, you must live *sin fronteras*, be a crossroads" (pp. 216–217). . . . As Hurtado (2009) explains, "Borderlands theory and intersectionality recognizes that Latinas, as well as other people of color, suffer subordination based not only on their gender, but also on other stigmatized social categories, primarily race, class, ethnicity, sexuality and physical ableness" (p. 172). (Haddock-Lazala, 2016, pp. 25–30)

Kimberlé Crenshaw (1989) presented intersectionality as the idea that social identities; related systems of oppression, domination, or discrimination; and multiple group identities intersect to create a whole that is different from the component identities. These intersecting identities are often contradicting and conflictual. The theory urges us to think of each element or trait of a person as inextricably linked to all the other elements to fully understand someone's identity and lived experience. Borderlands theory and intersectionality seek to be simultaneously deconstructive and generative and attend to the dialectical tension between the personal and political and the contradictions, conflicts, and complexities that emerge at these intersections. As such, our minds and bodies are the crossroads; the multiple languages, cultures, nationalities and their systems are the lands we straddle. This has important implications when studying populations such as Puerto Ricans who are "exemplified in the concepts of mestizaje and double or multiple consciousness resulting from centuries of cultural blending and conflict" and may be "living as a conquered people with ambiguous citizenship status" (Stefancic, 1997, p. 426). In understanding the ethnicracialized from a postcolonial and intersectional perspective, the borderlands become a "metaphor for all social crossings and the knowledge produced by being within a system while also retaining the knowledge of an outsider who comes from outside the system" (Hurtado & Cervantez, 2009, p. 182).

Mestiza consciousness is foundational to rethinking acculturation and presents the notion that the bilingual subjects can, for example, actively "narrativize himself in the cracks between Spanish and English" (Viego, 2009, p. 132). In other words, rather than understanding bilingual peoples' relationship to multiple languages as an either–or situation, it presents the "and–with" situation in which the linguistic phenomena of Spanglish and Haitian Creole, for example, emerge (Haddock-Lazala, 2016). Anzaldúa also theorized about the link between acculturation and socioeconomic status stating that People of Color suffer economically for not acculturating. She explored the notions that

---

[4]And other bilingual, multicultural, multiracial, or colonized subjects.

due to this pressure, acculturation is experienced as both voluntary and forced, creating a psychological conflict defined by alienation and a sense of dual identity. Although the general message of borderlands theory is strengths-based and encourages multiracial, multicultural, multilingual subjects to embrace *mestizaje* and *mulataje* and tolerate ambiguity and contradictions without conflict, the simultaneous notion that they "suffer" (particularly, socioeconomically) for not acculturating (for resisting) is something the literature has truly failed to unpack and explore (Haddock-Lazala, 2016). It is also worth reflecting on how lower class White urban subjects may benefit from liberatory praxis as they may suffer othering based on their own resistance to performing Whiteness and their explicit and implicit identifications with urbanism and non-Whiteness. Although mainstream multicultural and acculturation theory has set the basis for our current understanding of ethnic and racial identity, it also "provides racist discourse with precisely the notion of [ethnic-racialized] subjectivity that it needs in order to function most effectively" (Viego, 2007, p. 4).

URBAN LIBERATION—A PSYCHOTHERAPY *PARA EL PUEBLO*

Comas-Díaz and Jacobsen (1991), discussing the ethnopolitics of therapy, offered us a foundational framework to understand psychodynamics as occurring within their respective sociocultural and political context. This basic framework has set the stage for understanding the relationships among individual identity, social context, and collective history (and how these manifest in therapy).

Complex Contexts, Complex Identities, Complex Traumas, Complex Treatments

Intersectionality presents people as embodying multiple oppressed and privileged identities simultaneously. I posit that the more oppressed identities individuals have, the more they are repeatedly and consistently exposed to trauma, leading to the development of what the mental health field has been calling *complex trauma*: That is, the more complex the person's identity, the more complex the trauma, the more likely to be "triggered" and retraumatized. This statement is based on empirical research findings and extant literature in the field of social determinants of health and mental health.

Luhrmann (2007) summarized the most poignant findings as having "demonstrated that there is a social gradient to health: your body's basic health rises, on average, as you rise up through the social classes" (p. 142). Luhrmann compiled empirical evidence supporting the notion that social factors are fundamental in the incidence of mental illnesses such as schizophrenia and delineated how social factors such as race, class, and urban dwelling impact serious mental illness. The article provides evidence not only for the idea that the risk of schizophrenia increases as class declines but also that issues related to living in an urban context also have detrimental effects. For example, Luhrmann reported that the risk of schizophrenia "increases with what is called ethnic density: the incidence of schizophrenia among non-white people rises as their presence in their neighborhood begins to fall. If your skin is dark, your risk of schizophrenia rises as your neighborhood whitens" (p. 142).

This is what distinguished urban liberatory praxis from traditional liberation psychology: it emerges from and aims to address issues that arise from urban dwelling—issues such as gentrification, class struggle, and racial tensions that arise from living in a diverse urban setting. Urban liberation conceptualizes cities as being the ultimate modern borderlands, where not only different nationalities, cultures, classes, genders, and races collide, but organic biological matter collides with technology and industry. Urban liberatory mental health praxis understands that mental health disparities not only exist but are exacerbated by the oppressive and unjust conditions of urbanicity. Thus, mental health justice cannot be achieved without racial, gender, socioeconomic, and environmental justice. Simply put, health and well-being—living a good life—cannot be achieved in a context of social injustice and socioeconomic inequality. When working with oppressed and vulnerable people living in urban areas, we must enter the therapeutic space aware of and ready to be confronted by the violence (interpersonal, domestic, community, institutional, police, and state) these populations may endure. Although the vestiges of violent abuse might be easily recognizable by both therapist and client, experiences of emotional, physical, medical, educational, and financial neglect might not be. This type of neglect is not only enacted by those closest to the client but also by the state in the form of poverty and the denial of access to social resources and services. This state-sponsored violence has a detrimental and even mortal impact on the development and functioning of entire populations. These types of neglect can also be seen in the existing disparities in mental health care access, as well as policies that penalize (im)migrants for utilizing social services.

Another more insidious form of emotional-psychological abuse and neglect is the experience of invalidation of a person's or people's lived experiences. Models such as dialectical behavioral therapy for borderline personality disorder locate characterological psychopathology as resulting from developing within an invalidating environment (Linehan, 2015). Unfortunately, the dialectical behavioral therapy model is colorblind (Bonilla-Silva, 2014) and dismisses the role of power and oppressive dynamics in the borderline client's experiences and emotions (thus colluding in invalidation). It seeks to regulate, rather than make true meaning of, emotions such as intense fear, rage, hopelessness, feelings of deprivation or neglect, and the hate that clients might experience as a result of living in violent, unsafe, and disadvantaged environments. These emotions and experiences are stifled and regulated in service of helping clients adjust to these oppressive conditions. Clients often leave treatment feeling unheard and unseen. When discussing the erasure and invalidation of the suffering experienced by victims of systemic violence, Paul Farmer (2003) noted that it aims at "hiding this suffering, or denying its real origins, (and) serves the interests of the powerful" (p. 17). He went on to link how erasure and silence manifest in doctor–patient relationships:

> It is true that members of any subjugated group do not expect to be received warmly even when they are sick or tired or wounded. . . . They wouldn't expect the sort of courtesy extended so effortlessly to the privileged. The silence of the poor is conditioned. (p. 26)

Oppressed populations historically have struggled with issues of (in)visibility[5] and (mis)representation.[6] In a White supremacist, imperial, patriarchal context, internalized racism, sexism, and classism have distorted people's internal representations of self and other and often have internalized negative stereotypes as self-representations and to regain self-esteem may have also unconsciously identified with their oppressors. This can have a disastrous effect on the development of identity, healthy self-esteem, and body image. These negative internalized representations can play out in therapy in subtle and not so subtle ways, usually presenting as a shift in the affective field of the dyad—one that could go unnoticed by a colorblind therapist. Comas-Díaz and Jacobsen (2001) elucidated the concept of ethnocultural allodynia as

> an abnormally increased sensitivity to ethnocultural dynamics associated with past exposure to emotionally painful social and ethnoracial stimuli. Ethnic and sociocultural emotional injuries can cause profound changes in the sense of self, altering object relatedness through an increased sensitivity to loss . . . can result from both historical and contemporary racial trauma. (p. 246)

This ethnocultural allodynia is often one of the primary but often ignored aspects of treatment with oppressed populations. Liberation psychologists are tasked with the insight and courage to explore and normalize ethnocultural allodynia as affective experiences of unprocessed trauma related to oppression. As a matter of technique, liberation therapists are expected to lean into difficult interpersonal moments and process them as a signal to shift attention to possible oppressive interpersonal processes playing out in the transference between the various social identities in the dyad. A simple technique might be explicitly asking clients to signal to the therapist when they feel disrespected, misunderstood, misinterpreted, or microaggressed. This allows for in vivo process of intolerable affects, the working though of enactments, impasses, or ruptures and allows clients the opportunity to teach therapists about how they would like to be treated.

Intersectional Intersubjectivity—Therapeutic "Real"-ationships

Although it is important to meet clients where "they are at" in terms of their social identities and lived experiences, it is of utmost importance to also

---

[5]Having a person's humanity seen, recognized, and tended to.
[6]Not having a person's humanity compassionately and accurately represented in societal discourse.

understand our own social positionalities and intersecting identities as therapists. Aside from gaining insight into our identities by undergoing our own personal therapies, there are a variety of helpful tools that can help us in this process (e.g., Kliman, 2010). Tools such as these help us locate ourselves in relation to others regarding not only areas of similarities and difference but also of power and oppression. An urban liberatory praxis contextualizes the dyad in relation to their positions in society and the cultures their respective intersecting social identities represent.

Power Analysis—Positionality and Conflict

It is important to attend to how our social identities are a product of the internalization of our cultures and environments—how these are representations of "to whom and where we belong" in the world's larger sociopolitical systems and become prescriptions for how power might be unequally distributed within relationships. The identification and analysis of these asymmetrical power dynamics within therapy is called *power analysis* (De Varis, 1994). It is important to begin our power analysis by locating the mental health fields themselves as functioning from a position of privilege and power. When we identify with our professions as mental health practitioners, we are also wielding power, and thus, we must face the fact that many of our theories and tools have historically been used in service of maintaining an oppressive and repressive status quo. Indeed, Lynne Layton (2006) urged therapists to be cautious and aware of unconscious normative processes within our therapeutic spaces. Urban liberatory praxis is critical and cautious of colluding with the idea that the therapist (the supposed "powerful, civilized, and enlightened" one) is charged with using his or her power to control and "tame" the "primitive" with the aim of civilizing and thus, saving or curing the client.

When therapists don't collaborate by readily offering power to be negotiated, clients find themselves reactively asserting their wills by putting up resistance in hopes of reclaiming freedom and justice. This resistance can lead to conflict, impasses, and ruptures within the therapeutic relationship. Our analysis of intersectional social identities, powers, and positionalities are unpacked in service of helping us better understand and thus change whatever conflicts we may be experiencing. I propose that during times of social unrest in which one's survival depends on our identifications and sense of group belonging, it is important to conduct power analysis to interrupt these conflicts based on social identity and facilitate healing, solidarity, and community. This approach relies heavily on therapists' capacity for self-reflection and ability to check their power, countertransference, and biases in service of interrupting and processing unconscious oppressive dynamics as signaled by the client's resistance. More specifically, therapists would directly address issues related to domination and subjugation, (self)objectification, (self)commodification and exploitation, sadism and masochism, as well as issues related to boundary violations, agency, and locus of control. Therapists can also work at affirming and normalizing the clients' need for power and resistance and their need to have their complex subjective experiences affirmed rather than pathologized.

We can address intersectionality by allowing oneself to form relationships with each of the client's self-states and identities and what real parts of yourself become salient in relation rather than just interpreting as a transferential relationship based on fantasy. We must remember that these identities in the dyad represent the real social relationships have out in the real world. Therapists are complex intersectional beings as well. Although mental health fields primarily uphold the status quo, therapists as people with free will can choose to what degree they are going to resist or collude with oppression. We can consciously navigate what I call *double agency*: being aware that we are agents of the state (and status quo) or agents of social change and liberation simultaneously. Lightfoot (1971) spoke about his own double agency and explored how his Blackness as medical doctor during the U.S. civil rights era of the 1960s became a "double-edge sword" (p. 367). He explored how his Blackness became of use to the oppressive state (as without it he could not serve the State as "liaison with the community") while it also served his communities' struggle for liberation (as his "allegiance was to the causes and concerns of oppressed Black people everywhere"). By exploring this double agency in both the client and the therapist, together the dyad can become social change makers by using the whole power of their complex identities within the potentiality and power of the therapeutic space (with the intent of influencing intrapsychic, interpersonal, and social dynamics "on the outside"). For example, in therapy, clients can play around with "trying on" different and new ways of living and being that might be risky or dangerous before "coming out" into the public space (e.g., someone questioning their sexual orientation or gender identity can use therapy as a space to experiment with new identities and ways of embodying emotions and desires within a safe, nonjudgmental space without fear of persecution and violence).

To coconstruct this kind of safe space that is full of creative potential, therapists must not only check their biases and internalized bigotry but also "check their privilege" or, as Worell and Remer (2003) called it, locate their "seats of privilege" ("characteristics that enable individuals to access and benefit from a variety of community resources with relative ease," p. 30). This means recognizing areas of privilege in one's life and identities and confronting how these experiences may be contributing to biases and violent enactments. We can also do the same with our oppressed identities and experiences. I call this *checking our oppressions*, the goal of which is to help us work better with clients who are either more privileged than we are, as well as to help us empathize with the suffering of oppressed others. Worell and Remer (2003) conceptualized this process as understanding within ourselves and others

> the general characteristics that may present barriers in U.S. society and may lead to experiences of discrimination or disadvantage (oppression) for you. That is, these are characteristics that signal that you are less valued and less respected in some venues, such as education or employment, and may provide barriers to you in accessing valued community resources. (p. 30)

They developed a model using the acronym SEARCH that helps therapists "search" themselves for potential biases:

> SEARCH represents sexism, ethnocentrism, ableism and ageism, racism, classism, and heterosexism, but your search for external sources of oppression should extend beyond these seven variables. In the process of assessment, diagnosis, and interventions with clients, it is important for you to "search" for the influence of external pressures, as well as attend to the client's internal processes. (p. 33)

We need to be careful that our biases stemming from our positionalities don't lead us to overpathologize anger and resistance and inappropriately encourage passivity and compliance to unjust circumstances by teaching clients how to "play the game" and not "get in trouble." This stance may help clients adapt and achieve some sort of stability in their lives, but it also reinforces silence, passivity, complacency, and submissiveness (potentially contributing to victimization). One way is via the therapist colluding in the client's anxieties and inhibitions (e.g., censoring of authentic and creative self-expression) via our attempts at shaping behaviors related to "civilized" performances of class, race and gender, and so on. Therapies in which clients are judged and pathologized on the fluidity and idiosyncrasies of their identities and personalities can be retraumatizing as its experienced as silencing and erasure—as being colonized and Whitened. This colluding of the therapist with the erasing effects of Whiteness can manifest in various ways, for example:

1. Repression of non-English language: Our fields neglect of issues related to bilingualism and our tendency to privilege English in clinical settings. Our fields are notorious for lacking adequate bilingual services for clients who speak languages other than English. This is especially important for clients whose "first language" or their "maternal tongue" is not English as some theories locate this primary language as the site of one's most basic desires and emotions. As such, it is conceivable that an (im)migrant who is fully bilingual may, in deeply painful and emotional moments of regression, spontaneously switch and employ their native language to express themselves.

2. Repression of sexuality and gender expression: Therapists, via our historically sexist, homophobic and transphobic diagnostic categories and conceptualizations, may shame and inhibit our clients from exploring and creating new sexualities, genders, embodiments and ways of loving and living. This can range from explicit diagnosis to unconscious anxieties and hostilities enacted in treatment.

3. Repression of ethnic and racial expression: Like the repression of sexuality and gender, we may collude with oppression by either shaping the clients to meet racist stereotypes that meet our expectations or by inhibiting the client resisting stereotypes and finding their own personal expression of their ethnicracialized identities. Unconscious racist dynamics that repress and oppress ethnicracialized expression may come in the form of implicit or explicit suggestions to alter the way the look and speak (i.e., suggesting a

Person of Color straighten their hair, remove/avoid tattoos or piercings and avoid speaking in slang).

4. Repression, invalidation and denial of the client's negative affects such as anger, rage, frustration, powerlessness, and/or of their aggressive, perhaps even violent, fantasies: While it is our responsibility to report any behaviors that may position the client, therapist or society at risk of harm or violence, we should be cautious of silencing and repressing a client's negative and aggressive emotions because of our own unconscious fears. While this is in fact anxiety provoking territory in therapy, it is wise to allow the clients a space to verbally express these emotions in order to prevent any actual violence being acted out upon themselves or others.

5. Explicit and formal collusion with state and institutional violence and torture: Examples include psychologists who are employed by governmental intelligence agencies and the military industrial complex. A poignant example are psychologists who were employed at Guantanamo Bay and helped develop advanced interrogation techniques that negatively impacted detainees (Hoffman et al., 2015).

To counteract these repressive impasses, the dyad works towards *concientización* (Freire, 2000) with an emphasis on the affective expression and embodied emotional bond between therapist and client. Gaztambide (2014) succinctly defined *concientización* as

> a new praxis by which knowledge and research developed from the perspective of the oppressed then becomes used to empower them by developing critical consciousness regarding their psycho-social-political reality . . . in order that they may liberate themselves and change that reality. (p. 1023)

By privileging affect over cognition, urban liberatory praxis aims to reconnect the dyad to their bodies (conscious embodiment) in hopes of working through any dissociated and projected negative affects and encouraging the reclaiming of bodily integrity, autonomy, intersubjective pleasure, and social peace and justice. These goals are closely related to contemporary feminist theories of objectification and emerging theories of trans embodiment and sensuous knowledge[7] (Shotwell, 2009). By incorporating movement, mindful breathing and meditation techniques, therapeutic dyads can become more aware of (and thus gain control over) powerful feelings of fear and rage that are experienced as dissociation, hypervigilance and defensiveness, as well as feelings of sadness that may be experienced as deep sense of frustration, hopelessness and helplessness. Of utmost importance is to attend and not disavow any emotions such as hate of self and others within the therapeutic

---

[7] *Sensuous knowledge* refers to a type of knowing and doing that comes from being socially situated within a particular embodiment. According to Shotwell (2009), the knowledge gained from sensuous knowledge can be transformative not only on an individual level but on a societal level as well because it shows us different ways of being and living in our bodies within society. This knowledge contributes to the creation of social movements.

space. By allowing ourselves to claim these negative emotions and cope with them in a mindful, embodied, and contextualized way, we will ideally be able reclaim our safety and integrity as humans attempting to live in harmoniously in a shared space. This healing and breathing space is one in which we have real communication (both verbally and nonverbally)—where the wounded in the therapist speaks to the wounded in the client, the powerful in therapist speaks to the powerful in client, and the powerful in the therapist recognizes the powerless in the client; where the powerful in the client speaks in relation to the wounded healer. We attempt to bear witness to each other's humanity and vulnerabilities.

DECOLONIZE THIS SPACE! CONSTRUCTING LIBERATORY HEALING SPACES IN AND OUTSIDE THE CLINIC

Although the theories and techniques I have presented are applicable to modalities ranging from individual psychotherapy to groups, there are considerations that are particularly important when expanding one's practice to groups and communities and working toward creating "safe spaces" for self-expression and renarrativizing lived experiences. I have found that one of the most effective ways of establishing a safe space is openly acknowledging that there is no such thing as inherently safe space; safety is constructed and negotiated (as I have tried to demonstrate). They understand that people come into these spaces feeling scared and unsafe and that they do, in fact, live in a hostile and persecutory environment as they are, indeed, endangered and worthy of special protections. Liberation therapists extend their work to ensure their clients' safety within their communities by using our power to protect them from systemic, institutional and state violence and oppression (e.g., by participating in developing policies and systems that work toward the establishment and use of sanctuary cities, safety-net hospitals, and safe zones, or advocating for sexual, intellectual, and emotional freedoms). Some contextual and ideological considerations that help us in reflecting on how oppressive social contexts and conditions are affecting our work are as follows:

- Attending to the real material and economic conditions in which the therapy is occurring: Assisting the client in obtaining the social and human resources needed to navigate issues related to poverty, gentrification, displacement, and disenfranchisement. Being emotionally sensitive and flexible when issues relate to class and finances may interfere with the therapeutic process (accessing care and staying in treatment). Liberation practitioners are highly encouraged to provide pro bono, sliding-scale, low-fee services and bartering when clinically and ethically appropriate.

- Attending to issues related institutional and state violence via policing: for example, conducting therapy in the context of an authoritarian regime and police or state violence, in which expressing resistance, critique, or protest against the state is pathologized and criminalized, or where even the perceived membership and identification with an oppressed and persecuted group puts the clients at risk of incarceration, and even death.

- Attending to issues related to the struggle for civil rights, social movements, armed conflict, and the impact of war: for example, acknowledge and process the client's experiences of armed conflict, war, civil unrest, disobedience, riots, and revolution. Create a containing space where they can discuss their experiences of these. Help them make decisions regarding their participation and survival throughout these processes.

As demonstrated, this expanded framework encourages us to reconceptualize mainstream psychotherapeutic group and community interventions by actively engaging with the realities of social conflicts when they erupt, such as the effects of armed riots and war. At the group and community levels, interventions can be more explicitly geared toward community organizing, activism, healing, and meeting the needs of those affected by the violence. Clients can be helped in deciding to safely and appropriately serve their communities, including their countries' armed forces (e.g., enlisting in active service in national armies, becoming civil servants), as well as participating in marches, protests, and demonstrations for causes they feel passionate about. A less extreme or violent example of clients getting involved in social actions is a group intervention for urban adolescent girls who have experienced sexual harassment on the street. Therapists can join with community organizers and artist to develop an anti–street harassment training in which the girls not only process their traumatic experiences of sexual harassment and assault but also create protest signs and hold a public demonstration expressing their resistance. Clients can also be encouraged to get involved in local or national politics (e.g., running for office, joining councils and committees) and community organizing around issues affecting their communities—such as gentrification and police/community relationships—while also processing the risks of doing so.

By taking therapy off the couch and into the streets, the therapist has a better perception of how to help clients gain more family and community support and resources. This can range from working with social workers in accessing social services and benefits, conducting home visits and family sessions, to assisting clients in accessing complementary alternative treatments within their communities, such as non-Western and indigenous healing practices (e.g., Santería, spiritual healing, drumming circles, yoga, and meditation circles for queer People of Color). It is also important to incorporate the arts in our treatments and decolonizing our notions of art and music therapies. One example is the development of spoken-word poetry and rap workshops collaboratively led by therapists and community artist and professionals teaching clients how to use these urban arts as a means of telling their stories, finding shared meaning and experience, and healing from trauma. These types of interventions would take place in nontraditional clinical settings such as community homes, religious institutions, parks, bookstores, shops, and organizations. At the end of each workshop series, the groups may work together to find ways of publishing and selling their works (e.g., publishing and selling youth poetry books in collaboration with a local independent publishing house or recording a mental health–themed hip-hop mix tape at a local producer's recording studio). These types of therapeutic experiences help expose whole communities to mental health services in a way that is organic, destigmatized, and, ideally, fun.

This process of decolonizing mental health is intended to help our clients reintegrate the possibly disavowed and denigrated parts of themselves. It reintroduces clients and communities to their own strength, skills, talents, arts, and healing modalities from a strengths-based wellness model rather than from a deficit and pathological clinical and Western model. Even within individual psychotherapy in a hospital setting, individuals can introduce their own healing arts. For example, when working with a woman of the native Dakota tribe struggling with panic attacks, we worked together to create a woven, weighted blanket to help her find peace and comfort. We discussed how in her tradition, one of their medicines involves the use of traditional blankets during ceremony. During the therapy, not only did we incorporate blankets in and out of session, but also (with the collaboration of her psychiatrist) encouraged her use of crystals, vitamins, and herbs to supplement our mental health treatment. Group therapies and interventions can all aim at helping clients reconnect to nature and the outdoors by hosting sessions in local parks or taking strolls around the neighborhood and exploring. All of these are examples in which creativity, community empowerment, civic engagement, social activism, and therapy meet.

CONCLUSION

I reaffirm and urge mental health fields to develop theoretical and practical models that (a) understand (inter)subjectivity and ethnicracialization as a complex relational and social process; (b) understand identity as socially constructed, contextual, and intersectional; and (c) approach ethnicracialization, (de)colonization, and social justice as not only a worthy topic of interest and investigation but as a medical and public health necessity intended to decrease mental health disparities that emerge as a result of oppression. I encourage us to critically reengage with multicultural mental health praxis from an explicitly liberatory stance—a stance that believes a multicultural psychology decontextualized from oppression is not sufficiently socially conscious and that a socially conscious psychology without intersectionality, power analysis, and activism is not revolutionary.

I may now add that civilization is a process in the service of Eros, whose purpose is to combine single human individuals, and after that families, then races, peoples and nations, into one great unity, the unity of mankind.

—SIGMUND FREUD (1930/1961)

REFERENCES

Anzaldúa, G. (1987). *Borderlands/la frontera: The new mestiza*. San Francisco, CA: Aunt Lute Books.

Berry, J. W. (1998). Acculturative stress. In P. B. Organista, K. M. Cren, & G. Marin (Eds.), *Readings in ethnic psychology* (pp. 117–122). New York, NY: Routledge.

Bhatia, S., & Ram, A. (2001). Rethinking "acculturation" in relation to diasporic cultures and postcolonial identities. *Human Development, 44,* 1–18. http://dx.doi.org/10.1159/000057036

Bonilla-Silva, E. (2014). *Racism without racists: Color-blind racism and the persistence of racial inequality in America* (4th ed.). Lanham, MD: Rowman & Littlefield.

Bryant-Davis, T., & Comas-Díaz, L. (Eds.). (2016). *Womanist and* mujerista *psychologies: Voices of fire, acts of courage*. Washington, DC: American Psychological Association. http://dx.doi.org/10.1037/14937-000

Comas-Díaz, L., & Jacobsen, F. M. (1991). Ethnocultural transference and countertransference in the therapeutic dyad. *American Journal of Orthopsychiatry, 61,* 392–402. http://dx.doi.org/10.1037/h0079267

Comas-Díaz, L., & Jacobsen, F. M. (2001). Ethnocultural allodynia. *Journal of Psychotherapy Practice and Research, 10,* 246–252.

Crenshaw, K. (1989). Demarginalizing the intersection of race and sex: A Black feminist critique of antidiscrimination doctrine, feminist theory and antiracist politics. *University of Chicago Legal Forum, 140,* 139–167.

De Varis, J. (1994). The dynamics of power in psychotherapy. *Psychotherapy: Theory, Research, Practice, Training, 31,* 588–593. http://dx.doi.org/10.1037/0033-3204.31.4.588

Farmer, P. (2003). *Pathologies of power: Health, human rights, and the new war on the poor*. Berkeley: University of California Press.

Freire, P. (2000). *Pedagogy of the oppressed*. New York, NY: Continuum. (Original work published 1970)

Freud, S. (1961). *Civilization and its discontents* (J. Strachey, Ed. & Trans.). London, England: Hogarth Press. (Original work published 1930)

Gaztambide, D. J. (2014). Liberation psychology. In D. A. Leeming (Ed.), *Encyclopedia of psychology and religion* (pp. 1023–1027). Boston, MA: Springer. http://dx.doi.org/10.1007/978-1-4614-6086-2_812

Gil, D. G. (1994). *Confronting social injustice and oppression*. New York, NY: Columbia University Press.

Haddock-Lazala, C. M. (2016). *Life and breasts at the borderlands: The breast reconstruction decision-making experiences of Dominican and Puerto Rican Latinxs* (Doctoral dissertation). Retrieved from ProQuest (10163151).

Hart, A. (2017). From multicultural competence to radical openness: A psychoanalytic engagement of otherness. *The American Psychoanalyst, 51*(1). Retrieved from http://www.apsa.org/apsaa-publications/vol51no1-TOC/html/vol51no1_09.xhtml

Hekman, S. (1997). Truth and method: Feminist standpoint theory revisited. *Signs: Journal of Women in Culture and Society, 22,* 341–365. http://dx.doi.org/10.1086/495159

Hoffman, D., Carter, D., Viglucci Lopez, C., Benzmiller, H. L., Guo, A. X., Latifi, S. Y., & Craig, D. C. (2015). *Report to the Special Committee of the Board of Directors of the American Psychological Association: Independent review relating to APA ethics guidelines, national security interrogations, and torture*. Chicago, IL: Sidley Austin. Retrieved from https://www.apa.org/independent-review/APA-FINAL-Report-7.2.15.pdf

Hunjan, R., & Pettit, J. (2011). *Power—A practical guide for facilitating social change*. Dunfermline, Scotland: Carnegie UK Trust.

Hurtado, A. (2009). Multiple lenses: Multicultural feminist theory. In H. Landrine & N. Russo (Eds.), *Handbook of diversity in feminist psychology* (pp. 29–54). New York, NY: Springer.

Hurtado, A. (2015). Gloria Anzaldúa's seven stages of *conocimiento* in redefining Latino masculinity: José's story. *Masculinidades y Cambio Social, 4,* 44–84.

Hurtado, A., & Cervantez, K. (2009). A view from within and from without: The development of Latina feminist psychology. In F. A. Villarruel, G. Carlo, J. M. Grau, M. Azmitia, N. J. Cabrera, & T. J. Chahin (Eds.), *Handbook of U.S. Latino psychology: Developmental and community-based perspectives* (pp. 171–190). Thousand Oaks, CA: Sage.

Kliman, J. (2010). Intersections of social privilege and marginalization: A visual teaching tool. In *Expanding our social justice practices: Advances in theory and training* [Special issue]. *AFTA Monograph Series: A Publication of the American Family Therapy Academy, 6*, 39–48.

Layton, L. (2006). Racial identities, racial enactments, and normative unconscious processes. *The Psychoanalytic Quarterly, 75*, 237–269. http://dx.doi.org/10.1002/j.2167-4086.2006.tb00039.x

Lightfoot, O. B. (1971). To be used or useful. The question for Black professionals. Cairo, Illinois, USA, 1969. *Journal of the National Medical Association, 63*, 365–371.

Linehan, M. M. (2015). *DBT® skills training manual* (2nd ed.). New York, NY: Guilford Press.

Luhrmann, T. M. (2007). Social defeat and the culture of chronicity: Or, why schizophrenia does so well over there and so badly here. *Culture, Medicine and Psychiatry, 31*, 135–172. http://dx.doi.org/10.1007/s11013-007-9049-z

McCall, L. (2005). The complexity of intersectionality. *Signs: Journal of Women in Culture and Society, 30*, 1771–1800. http://dx.doi.org/10.1086/426800

McWilliams, N. (2004). *Psychoanalytic psychotherapy: A practitioner's guide*. New York, NY: Guilford Press.

Montero, M. (2004). *Introducción a la psicología comunitaria: Desarrollo, conceptos y procesos* [Introduction to community psychology: Development, concepts and processes]. Buenos Aires, Argentina: Editorial Paidós.

Shotwell, A. (2009). A knowing that resided in my bones: Sensuous embodiment and trans social movement. In S. Campbell & L. Meynell (Eds.), *Embodiment and agency* (pp. 58–75). University Park: The Pennsylvania State University Press.

Siatkowski, A. A. (2007). Hispanic acculturation: A concept analysis. *Journal of Transcultural Nursing, 18*, 316–323. http://dx.doi.org/10.1177/1043659607305193

Stefancic, J. (1997). Latino and Latina critical theory: An annotated bibliography. *California Law Review, 85*, 1509–1585. http://dx.doi.org/10.2307/3481065

Tew, J. (2006). Understanding power and powerlessness: Towards a framework for emancipatory practice in social work. *Journal of Social Work, 6*, 33–51. http://dx.doi.org/10.1177/1468017306062222

Viego, A. (2007). *Dead subjects: Toward a politics of loss in Latino studies*. Durham, NC: Duke University Press. http://dx.doi.org/10.1215/9780822390619

Viego, A. (2009). The life of the undead: Biopower, Latino anxiety and the epidemiological paradox. *Women & Performance, 19*, 131–147. http://dx.doi.org/10.1080/07407700903034113

Worell, J., & Remer, P. (2003). *Feminist perspectives in therapy* (2nd ed.). New York, NY: Wiley.

Liberation Psychotherapy

Lillian Comas-Díaz

Healing the self, healing the world.

Liberation psychotherapy is a healing approach grounded in the lived experiences of oppressed individuals and communities. A central goal in liberation psychotherapy is the promotion of social justice action through the integration of Indigenous cultural healing and emancipatory approaches into mainstream psychotherapy. This orientation promotes an understanding of historical, socioeconomic, and political contexts as factors affecting psychological experience. Liberation psychotherapists help clients to become protagonists, instead of spectators, in their lives by addressing the intersection of clients' personal, public, and contextual realities. Liberation psychotherapists believe that when they work with an individual, they are potentially helping groups of people. Indeed, Freire (1970/1994) stated that when the oppressed initiate liberation, they ignite liberation for other individuals. Simply put, when we heal individuals, we are healing the world.

I begin this chapter with a discussion of liberation psychotherapy theory and practice. I then examine the Indigenous liberation concept of *buen vivir*—a contemplative, decolonial, and emancipatory principle that grounds humans into their sociopolitical and ecological contexts. Next, I introduce different types of liberation psychospiritual healing as sources of liberation psychotherapy. Afterward, I analyze the uniqueness of the liberation therapeutic

http://dx.doi.org/10.1037/0000198-010
Liberation Psychology: Theory, Method, Practice, and Social Justice, L. Comas-Díaz and E. Torres Rivera (Editors)

relationship. I conclude the chapter with a case vignette illustrating the application of liberation psychotherapy.

LIBERATION PSYCHOTHERAPY THEORY AND PRAXIS

The purpose of education is to change people so they can change the world.
—PAULO FREIRE

Liberation clinicians believe that the purpose of psychotherapy is to change people, so that they can change the world. They build theory and practice from a "knower and being" perspective (Collins, 1986) honoring the experience of the oppressed. Consequently, liberation psychotherapy is eclectic, syncretistic, and holistic. Liberation theory—grounded in cultural, historical and sociopolitical contexts—informs the liberation practice. To illustrate, liberation psychotherapy is a practice-based approach, developed from the bottom up. Indeed, practice-based healing offers promising forms of prevention and treatment grounded in scientific literature (Pomerville & Gone, 2019) and in clinical data. For example, liberation psychotherapy validates the cultural and spiritual practices of the oppressed. Accordingly, liberation psychotherapists integrate alternative forms of knowledge into psychotherapy to nurture clients' survival, cultural resilience, healing, optimal development, and social justice action.

Liberation psychotherapists promote clients' connection to their cultural unconsciousness as a source of power, healing and liberation (Montero, Sonn, & Burton, 2016; Watkins & Shulman, 2008). Indeed, the recovery of historical memory is a significant source of knowledge because the oppressed have *conocimiento* (knowledge, ancestral wisdom; Lugones, 2003). Conocimiento refers to a holistic understanding developed through self-reflection, imagination, rational thought, and social justice action (Keating, 2006). As an illustration, many marginalized people enhance their conocimiento when they identify daily living as a source of knowledge and life lessons (McCabe, 2007). Unfortunately, conocimiento from marginalized people is frequently deemed to be inferior to the mainstream knowledge.

When the oppressed recover their historical memory, they are able to construct liberation schemas by deconstructing oppressive ones (Moraga, 1981). An illustration is the Latinx's appropriation of the Virgin of Guadalupe. Many oppressed Latinx (especially Mexicans and Mexican Americans) deconstructed the Virgin Mary's representation of the Spanish Catholic colonization, and transformed it into *la Virgen de Guadalupe*—the mother of the oppressed. The Goddess of the Americas, Guadalupe is a Black Madonna syncretized from an Aztec goddess (*Tonantzin*) to become an icon of resistance, empowerment, and liberation (Castillo, 1996).

The internalization of oppression is a product of the intersection of numerous systems of domination (Pyke, 2010). Therefore, liberation psychotherapy emphasizes clients' resistance and resilience, but it also addresses their accommodation and complicity with oppression (Pyke, 2010). Liberation psychotherapists recognize the effects of a legacy of colonization. For example, individuals with a history of colonization may experience *postcolonization stress disorder*—the effect of coping with cultural imperialism and the imposition and internalization of mainstream culture as superior (Comas-Díaz, 2000). Many People of Color are exposed to postcolonization stress disorder due to their racial victimization (Comas-Díaz, 2007). Given that racism is a method of subjugation, postcolonization stress disorder involves people's internalized and projected racism (Comas-Díaz, 2007). In this regard, liberation clinicians examine coloniality of power, or how the structures of control, dominance and privilege that emerged during European colonization continue to impose Eurocentric ideals over individuals with a history of colonization (Quijano, 2000). As a control agent, coloniality of power exposes people to neo-colonization (Comas-Díaz, 2016b). Therefore, liberation psychologists address clients' internalized colonization and oppression, helping them to deconstruct (neo)colonizing stories, reformulate personal and collective identities, develop a sociopolitical consciousness, and foster transformative changes (Comas-Díaz, 2007). To achieve these goals, they employ decolonial approaches to foster resistance against neocolonizing forces. Moreover, they subscribe to a postcolonial (see Chapter 8, this volume) approach—a critical consciousness analysis to examine the legacies of colonialism, imperialism, and colonial mentality. The belief that the colonizer is superior to the colonized (David & Okazaki, 2006), a colonial mentality reduces the agency and effectiveness of the oppressed (Moane, 1999). Postcolonial approaches follow the contributions of Frantz Fanon (1961/1963) and Edward Said (1993). Using a postcolonial lens, liberation psychotherapists engage in critical border thinking (Grosfoguel, 2008), analyze psychology from a sociopolitical perspective, and add a psychopolitical lens to their understanding of people. Even more, they address oppression trauma.

Oppression Trauma

Oppression is inherently traumatic. Oppression trauma originates in historical, socioeconomic, and geopolitical causes. For instance, ethnic victimization and racial victimization are examples of oppression trauma (Comas-Díaz, Hall, & Neville, 2019). People of Color are exposed to insidious, pervasive, and cumulative racial oppression in a sporadic, acute, and chronic basis (Harrell, 2000). Along these lines, practicing psychologists have been criticized for their tendency to pathologize the marginalized, instead of addressing the sociopolitical systems that oppresses the disenfranchised (Afuape, 2011). Indeed, oppression trauma differs from posttraumatic stress disorder (PTSD). As a clinical entity, PTSD does not capture the cumulative and daily impact of living with oppression (Comas-Díaz et al., 2019). Actually, the term *posttraumatic* implies that trauma is a single isolated event. In contrast, oppression trauma inflicts continuous suffering to individuals and groups. Similar to terrorism and torture victims, oppression trauma victims should not be considered "mental health patients" because they experience a normal reaction to sociopolitical conditions (Comas-Díaz, 2007). When we designate individuals' reactions to oppression as merely psychological and or psychiatric disorders, we medicalize a sociopolitical problem, ignoring the historical and sociopolitical causes. Certainly, oppression trauma is human made, sociopolitically motivated, and continuously inflicted (Comas-Díaz, 2007).

Many oppressed people cope with historical trauma in addition to oppression trauma. To illustrate, Duran (2006) defined soul wounds as the negative effects of collective oppression, such as genocide, colonization, slavery, and other historical traumas. Therefore, the consequences of historical trauma include ungrieved losses, internalized oppression, powerlessness, and learned helplessness, among other debilitating psychological effects (Duran, 2006). Historical trauma imparts an added degree of vulnerability to contemporary oppression. As a complex entity, oppression trauma affects people's self-esteem, agency, psychological, and physical health, as well as their sense of well-being. For instance, individuals living in poverty are exposed to multiple stressors resulting in emotional, physical, and spiritual effects. For these reasons, the oppressed require a healing approach that addresses emotional, physical, and spiritual aspects. Such approach needs to take into consideration culture, history, context, identity, and spirituality.

Spirituality

Liberation psychotherapy promotes the recovery of the marginalized discounted wisdom. As part of recovering historical memory and ancestral wisdom, liberation psychotherapy is grounded in oppressed people's spirituality. Therefore, liberation psychotherapists recognize the centrality of spirit among many marginalized communities (Comas-Díaz, Lykes, & Alarcón, 1998). Nonetheless, liberation psychotherapy has a spiritual nonreligious foundation. This foundation is based on the values of interconnectedness, communality, holism, solidarity, and transformation (Comas-Díaz, 2016a). Actually, Ignacio Martín-Baró (1994), the architect of liberation psychology, stated that spirituality empowers individuals to believe that the divine works though them to achieve liberation.

Spirituality's health benefits have been documented in research. For example, a study of participants from diverse religions found that spirituality, as opposed to religion, correlated positively with mental health (Johnstone et al., 2012). Likewise, Miller and her colleagues (2014) found that spirituality, but not attendance to religious services, was associated with a thicker cerebral cortex among individuals with a high risk for familiar depression, compared with counterpart participants who did not endorse spirituality. This finding is important because a thin cerebral cortex is associated with cardiovascular risks (Leritz et al., 2011) and with decrease in IQ scores (Burgaleta, Johnson, Waber, Colom, & Karama, 2014).

Spirituality has been associated with health and wellness among People of Color (Comas-Díaz, 2016b). Moreover, it has been connected with the promotion of posttraumatic growth among Latinxs (Comas-Díaz, 2016b). Indeed, spirituality provides the foundation for a participatory practice that helps the oppressed to connect with their ethnic communities (Comas-Díaz, 2016b). As an illustration, research showed that compared with White counterparts, People of Color who used spirituality to cope with life challenges, experienced more positive relationships, had better life quality, and enjoyed a sense of wellness (Kirk, 2011). In the next section, I discuss an Indigenous concept of wellness.

LIBERATION PSYCHOTHERAPY AND *BUEN VIVIR* ("LIVING WELL" OR "WELL-BEING")

To live well or fully, first you need to be well.

—AYMARA WISDOM

As a holistic practice, liberation psychotherapy fosters wellness. Therefore, an important concept in liberation community psychology is *wellness as fairness* (Prilleltensky, 2012). Grounded in a cultural strength paradigm, liberation psychotherapy is consistent with the Latinx cultural concept of *buen vivir*, literally "living well" or "well-being" (see Chapter 3, this volume). However, this collectivistic and communitarian concept grounds humans within their social, spiritual, and environmental contexts. On the basis of a precolonial Indigenous worldview, *buen vivir* promotes harmonious relationships between people, nature, environment, and cosmos. It predicates that everyone has the right to be healthy, free, and with opportunities to fulfill their capacities (Pedregal Casanova, 2013). This collectivistic worldview affirms an integration of Indigenous knowledge with universal progressive perspectives in a process of continuing decolonization (Acosta, 2010).

Buen vivir promotes conviviality. As a collective value, conviviality means that individual liberation is realized within an interdependence context (Comas-Díaz, 2007). Therefore, a buen vivir perspective affirms the evolution of community-based initiatives as endogenous forms of development (Peredo, 2019). Consequently, based on buen vivir, Indigenous decolonizing movements have emerged to propose alternative ways of life. These movements foster change under the aegis of cultural diversity, democratic patterns, solidarity, and respect for nature (Acosta, 2016).

A central aspect of buen vivir is the promotion of self-healing. Thus, liberation psychotherapists foster self-healing by helping clients to connect with the inner healer that resides in all of us (Comas-Díaz, 2012). To accomplish this function, liberation psychotherapists drink in the fountains of psychospiritual healing.

LIBERATION PSYCHOSPIRITUAL HEALING

In our hearts we live in the land of the spirits.

—RATU CIVO

Psychospiritual healing helps clients to identify potential solutions to problems, strengthens their resilience, and nurtures their spiritual development. These holistic approaches are practice based because they are cultural, linguistic, historical, and spiritually relevant to the sufferers. In helping clients to recover their historical memory, liberation practitioners integrate Indigenous and ethnic healing into psychotherapy. To illustrate, Cane (2000) found decreased trauma symptoms among Central Americans' victims of violence, when she integrated ethnic healing (e.g., visualization, breathwork, acupressure, body work, intuition) with liberation psychology. Moreover, Indigenous healing entails a holistic pan-relational orientation that includes ancestral, sacred and spiritual relations in healing. In this way, healing requires harmony between body, mind and spirit. The concept of spirit is defined as an ancestral, personal, cosmic, and or divine entity (Comas-Díaz, 2012). There are several forms of liberation psychospiritual healing. Following is a brief discussion of shamanism, *Ayeli, espiritismo,* and *Ntu* psychotherapy.

The oldest healing practice, shamanism involves a dialogue between the spirit (problem) and the healer to identify, understand, and cure the cause of the sufferer's ailment. In this modality, both healer and sufferer meditate to enter into a trance. Then, the healer interrogates the spirit (client's higher self) and the client suggests ways to solve the problem. The healer asks the "spirit" questions such as: Who are you? Where did you come from? Why are you here? Where are you going? What would you look like if the problem distress (sorrow, illness) were not here? What is it that you really meant to ask for? (Greer, 2017). The sufferer answers the questions while being immersed in an altered state of consciousness. This healing dialogue allows the client to experience catharsis, cleansing, and to release deep-seated traumas.

Ayeli, another spiritual approach, is a Cherokee healing that involves using the four directions in the dialoguing process. Within this empowering approach, the East is associated with belonging, South symbolizes mastery, West represents independence, and North is related to generosity (Garrett & Garrett, 1994). Ayeli healers ask the following questions: Where do you belong? Who is your family, tribe, community, and nation? (East); What do you do well? What do you enjoy doing? (South); What are your sources of strength? What limits you? (West); and; What do you have to offer? What do you receive? (North). These types of questions elicit sufferers' awareness of their healing needs, challenges, gifts, and life lessons.

Espiritismo (Spanish word for spiritualism in Latin America) is a healing, religious, and spiritual approach. Puerto Rican espiritismo was first used as a liberating movement against colonization (Olmos & Paravisini-Gebert, 2003). On the basis of Allen Kardec's methods, the *espiritista* (medium) communicates with spirits and, similar to conventional psychotherapy, engages in assessment, diagnosis, and treatment. Espiritistas use altered states of consciousness (i.e., spirit possession), rituals, prayers, meditation, intuition, and Indigenous medicine, among other methods (Comas-Díaz, 2012). As a syncretistic healing, espiritismo incorporates *Taíno* (Native American), Spanish (Christianity and *Mozárabe*/Iberian Moorish), and African healing. Espiritismo promotes sufferers' spiritual development and empowers them by affirming their ethnocultural and spiritual identities.

Ntu psychotherapy is based on African spirituality. A key concept in this healing is the belief that everything is energy and that all energy has consciousness and purpose. Ntu highlights the interconnectedness—a unifying spiritual energy that connects humans, nature. and cosmos (see Chapter 10, this volume). According to Phillips (1990), the aim of Ntu therapy is to help clients recover their natural alignment though a reconnection with this spiritual energy. Phillips described Ntu psychotherapeutic process, which is based on Kwanza principles, as (a) harmony (a therapeutic relationship with empathy and authenticity), (b) awareness (clarification and deconstruction of the client's problem), (c) alignment (congruence between client's internal and external realities), (d) actualization (client makes the necessary changes to obtain balance), and (e) synthesis (client's reflection on the therapeutic gains).

Liberation psychotherapy incorporates psychospiritual, Indigenous healing, and holistic approaches. This incorporation infuses the therapeutic relationship with distinctive elements. In the following section, I discuss the uniqueness of the liberation psychotherapeutic relationship.

LIBERATION PSYCHOTHERAPEUTIC RELATIONSHIP

Tú eres mi otro yo [You are my other me].

—L. VALDEZ (1973)

The liberation psychotherapeutic relationship is similar to the mainstream therapy relationship in the establishment of rapport, trust, congruence, positive alliance, working relationship, and the examination of the therapeutic relationship's elements, such as transference and countertransference. However, mainstream psychotherapy's monocultural bias limits its application to socially oppressed populations. Consequently, liberation psychotherapists connect with clients through radical humility, *accompaniment*, and by fomenting psychospiritual development and activism.

Radical Humility and Radical Empathy

Radical humility entails relating to clients from a human-to-human perspective. Hence, liberation therapists abandon their expert role to engage in a mirroring process reflecting their human condition (Afuape, 2011). Comas-Díaz

(2014) called this process *multicultural mirroring*, a radical empathy that fosters the healer's permeability, allowing the self to be reflected in the other. In other words, radical empathy is a capacity to "embody" the sufferer's distress (Koss-Chioino, 2013). Radical empathy conveys to clients that the psychotherapist is able to intuitively *feel their pain*. Of particular importance, radical empathy fuses the individual differences between healer and sufferer into a field of experience and feeling (Koss-Chioino, 2007). Therefore, liberation therapists cultivate a capacity to health through the embodiment of their client's suffering (Comas-Díaz, 2016a). To deeply connect with clients, liberation healers use sensorial modes of connection and other nonrational kinds of knowledge. Similarly, when liberation therapists exhibit radical humility, they manifest compassion, respect, altruism, and positive regard toward their clients (Koss-Chioino, 2007). Such a relational practice is consistent with liberation psychology's value that justice, equality, and love are inseparable (Martín-Baró, 1994).

Contrary to the perception of the therapist as a blank screen with the illusion of neutrality, liberation practitioners aim to be genuine and authentic in their clinical interactions. In addition to applying practice-based, evidence-based, and culture-based psychotherapy, they perceive themselves as vessels of healing. Within this conceptualization, they are aware that healing bears mutual effects. In other words, when liberation therapists facilitate clients' healing, they promote their own, as well as other people's, healing. In this fashion, liberation psychotherapists embody the principle of interconnectivity: *Tú eres mi otro yo* (You are my other me). This means that therapists *see* themselves in their clients. This mirroring fosters a real healing relationship imbued with mutuality, empowerment, solidarity, and conviviality.

Liberation therapists work to earn their clients' trust. In this way, they facilitate the creation of a safe and sacred therapeutic space, one that nurtures healing, liberation, and transformation. Moreover, they invite clients or sufferers to cocreate their healing. Instead of defining problems and developing treatment plans (following medicine's dictum), liberation practitioners elicit clients' stories, distress perspectives, and potential healing solutions. As an illustration, they use anthropological–mental health methods such as the explanatory model of distress (Kleinman, 1980) to explore clients' definition of emotional problems, as well as their expectations from treatment and therapist. To accomplish these goals, liberation psychotherapists respond to clients' needs by infusing flexibility into their professional role. In this manner, they anchor liberation healing in the Native American concept of *All Our Relations*. This means that liberation clinicians can function as teacher, mentor, advocate, therapist, counselor, witness, and *sibling* (relative), among other roles. Similarly, Gordon (1973) urged African American psychologists to complement their professional roles by acting as advocates, watchdogs, information resource people, and lobbyists to advance African Americans' collective well-being.

As previously noted, liberation psychotherapists do not adhere to the myth of therapist's neutrality. When appropriate, therapists self-disclose during therapy to cement the therapeutic alliance (Hill, Knox, & Pinto-Coelho, 2018).

Appropriate self-disclosure is consistent with the centrality of positionality within liberation psychology. Originated in epistemology, the concept of positionality was further developed by social scientists, specifically feminist and queer scholars, to designate how our social identities (e.g., gender, race, ethnicity, sexual orientation) and social position influence our understanding of our world, and our life (Alcoff, 1988). In brief, positionality requires the acknowledgment of our position(s), including contexts (internal and external) where we are situated to delineate our identity. Therefore, we bring our positionality into our roles as practitioners, educators, researchers, and advocates. In this capacity, liberation clinicians examine power differentials between their clients and themselves. This examination is essential in liberation psychotherapy due to the power differential inherent in all therapeutic interactions (Gelso, Kivlighan, & Markin, 2018). Hence, liberation psychotherapists use power differential analyses (Worrell & Remer, 2003) and other related methods to contrast their areas of oppression and privilege with those of their clients. When appropriate, they disclose power differential analyses' findings to their clients. Equally important, liberation psychotherapists engage in an ongoing self-reflection to examine their potential contributions to inequality and injustice. Within this context, they commit to examine their adherence to liberation values and their congruence and incongruence within their personal, professional, and public lives. Moreover, they aim to model service to humanity, social justice activism, and self-care. In other words, liberation practitioners engage in inner work (including personal therapy) as a self-care method.

Accompaniment and Dialoguing

A distinctive function of liberation therapists is *acompañamiento* (accompaniment) (see Chapter 5, this volume). To *accompany*, liberation psychotherapists stand along side the clients who need listening, witnessing, advocacy, critical thinking, and a space to develop conocimiento (Watkins, 2012). Displaying solidarity, they *accompany* clients who are at the margins of society. Additionally, liberation psychotherapists *accompany* clients by developing collaborative relations that acknowledge power inequality in relationships, as well as in society (Comas-Díaz, 2000). In this fashion, they bear witness, as they help clients recover their ancestral conocimiento, embrace resistance, and alchemize anger and suffering into transformation (Comas-Díaz, 2007). During accompaniment, therapists engage in radical empathy to deepen their attunement with their clients (Comas-Díaz, 2016a). What is more, the act of acompañamiento imparts a vision or annunciation that guides the journey of liberation (Freire, 1970/1994; Watkins, 2015). However, when liberation therapists *accompany* clients, they do not abandon the intrapsychic nor biological bases of psychological problems; instead, they use intersectional analyses and integrate these elements into a broad accompaniment model (Watkins, 2012). To illustrate, they integrate neurobiological aspects of trauma (van der Kolk, 2014) into holistic treatments.

Dialoguing occupies a central role in liberation psychotherapy. According to Martín-Baró (1994), engaging in authentic dialogue contributes to the process of *deideologizing* (replacing systemic oppressive views with hopeful ones; see Chapter 2, this volume). This process facilitates addressing the sociopolitical and psychological implications of oppression. Consequently, dialoguing in a heart-to-heart manner promotes *concientización* (critical consciousness). To engage in dialoguing, liberation psychotherapists ask critical questions such as the following: What? Why? How? For whom? Against whom? In favor of what? By whom? To what end? (Freire & Macedo, 2000). Indeed, dialoguing is an expanding awareness practice within spirituality (Greer, 2017). This process helps clients–sufferers to perceive their circumstances critically, analyze the causes of their oppression, and begin the decolonization and liberation processes.

Decolonization and Creativity

Dominant society imposes cultural values such as individualism, self-agency, internal locus of control, and meritocracy upon the oppressed. Such a cultural script tends to exclude and oppress the marginalized. Moreover, people with a history of colonization may be exposed to neocolonialism—a current form of colonization through the imposition of imperialistic cultures onto subaltern (subjugated) populations. Indeed, cultural imperialism (neo)colonizes the mind of the oppressed, increasing their powerlessness (Said, 1993). Therefore, liberation clinicians employ decolonization and postcolonial methods (see Chapter 8, this volume) to address clients' colonized mentality and or internalized colonization. As indicated previously, *colonial mentality* refers to the conscious or unconscious belief that individuals with a historical and or current colonization sustain that they are inferior to the colonizers (David & Okazaki, 2006). Because cultural imperialism subjugates the conocimiento of the oppressed, Pease (2002) redefined *empowerment* as an insurrection of subjugated knowledge. Consequently, liberation therapists actively support subjugated knowledge as a decolonization effort (Watkins & Shulman, 2008). To illustrate, therapists nurture clients' voices to foster their narratives and listen to their stories without judging them. Moreover, therapists *hold the place* and act as a container, while emphatically witnessing clients' painful narratives. Furthermore, liberation therapists invite clients to compose stories of resilience and liberation. To accomplish these goals, they suggest narratives such as testimonio—a form of life history that promotes resistance and transformation (see Chapter 7, this volume)—and autoethnography—a self-reflection exploring political, social, and cultural contexts of an autobiographical narration (Chang, 2008). Additional narrative tools include memoirs, journaling, a note to self, and notes to others. Indeed, creativity is a psychological, spiritual, and emancipatory endeavor. As a decolonizing method, creativity helps the oppressed to cope with adversity (see Chapter 13, this volume). Even more, it foments survivalist, resilient, and insurgent responses to oppression. Consequently, liberation therapists nurture clients' creativity as a social justice tool. For instance, clinicians invite clients to produce artivism (art for social justice; see Chapter 13), such as *autohistoria*, a creative process of integrating a fragmented identity (Anzaldúa, 2002), *arpilleras* (complex tapestries developed to protest systemic and state-sponsored oppression), spoken word, hip-hop psychology, and other transformative art forms.

Spirituality and Social Justice

As indicated previously, liberation psychotherapy is infused with a justice-oriented spirituality. A pervasive force in the lives of many oppressed people, this kind of spirituality is grounded in *lo cotidiano* (daily living; Isasi-Diaz, 1996). Unfortunately, mainstream psychology does not focus on a justice-based spirituality (Katz, 2017). Therefore, liberation therapists promote clients' spiritual development to engage in a journey of personal and collective transformation. However, they are aware that a spiritual congruence between therapist and client does not guarantee a successful therapeutic outcome (Johnson, 2016). Consequently, liberation psychotherapists explore clients' (including agnostic clients') sources of resilience, inspiration, and hope to address therapy from this perspective. Because hope is a sacred activism method (Harvey, 2009), liberation psychotherapists pay special attention to clients' sources of hope. Spirituality legitimizes alternative forms of critical cultural analysis (Hurtado, 2003). For instance, liberation therapists assess clients' spirituality when they ask questions such as: Who are you in connection with your parents and ancestors? What life lessons did they provide you? How important is spirituality, religion and or humanism in your life? Do you believe in a higher power, or not? Have you involved your spirituality and or religion in resolving your problem? (Comas-Díaz, 2012). Additionally, liberation clinicians explore clients' complementary spiritual and religious beliefs to distinguish their positive spiritual coping from negative spiritual coping (Comas-Díaz, 2016b). As part of a psychospiritual paradigm, liberation psychotherapists engage in intuitive inquiry—an analysis of objective and subjective data through data collection and reflection (Anderson, 2004). Along these lines, they nurture their clients' intuition. Given that oppressed individuals suffer in a society characterized by power inequality, intuition facilitates the awareness of power differentials to facilitate coping with oppression. For example, Anzaldúa (1987) defined *la facultad* as a spiritual intuition that allows the oppressed to see accurately through people, systems, and dynamics, especially power dynamics. Similarly, Collins (1986) stated that Women of Color's outsider-within status allows them to cope effectively with power differentials. Therefore, liberation therapists commit to advance their clients' psychospiritual development, as well as their own. Indeed, promoting clients' growth helps the therapist's well-being, and enhances relational resilience (Jordan, 2010).

When appropriate, therapists cultivate clients' spiritual gifts such as a prophetic voice. In a liberation psychology context, prophecy means to tell the truth and to speak on behalf of the poor and the oppressed (Comas-Díaz, 2016a). Consistent with this notion, therapists nurture their clients' development of spiritual gifts such as la facultad, prophetic vision, self-healing, and healing abilities. Equally important, liberation psychotherapists nurture clients' spiritual activism development. This practice refers to the engagement of social justice action with a spiritual vision (Anzaldúa, 1987). In this way, they foster their clients' awakening of their inner freedom fighter (Comas-Díaz, 2020). In the next section, I present a case vignette illustrating the application of liberation psychotherapy.

CASE ILLUSTRATION: AMPARO'S SONG

Our first teacher is our own heart.

—CHEYENNE WISDOM

Amparo (a composite of several clients), a 40-year-old AfroLatinx woman, came to see me because she was depressed due to losing a promotion at work. She complained of sudden changes in mood, sleep, and eating. Amparo was divorced and lived with Milagros, her 70-year-old mother, and Beatriz, her 12-year-old daughter. A public school teacher, Amparo applied for a position as school principal, having fulfilled all the qualifications. Unfortunately, she did not get the position. This was the third time that Amparo applied for a similar position.

"I'm a failure," Amparo said during our initial session. Copious tears fell on her cheeks. I handed her a box of tissues and moved my chair closer to hers. After a few minutes, Amparo stared at me and asked in Spanish, "Qué debo hacer?" (What should I do?). Using my intuition, I said, "The answer is inside you. I will help you find it." Amparo replied with a smile and dried her eyes with a tissue. During our second session, Amparo mentioned that she felt like being *contra viento y marea* (against all odds). This Spanish *dicho* (proverb) suggests that the person has been struggling against adversity for a long time. This incident gave me permission to use *dichos*, an ethnic flash therapy (Comas-Díaz, 2012). To earn Amparo's trust, I related to her in a radical empathic manner while witnessing her pain. To alleviate her suffering, I taught her self-soothing techniques such as butterfly hug and acupressure (Comas-Díaz, 2012). Butterfly hug is a yoga technique used in eye movement desensitization and reprocessing (Shapiro, 1995) that involves embracing yourself and moving your hands life a flying butterfly. Flor agreed to work within a holistic approach. Therefore, we used a mind, body, spirit approach, including breath work, guided imagery, progressive muscle relaxation, and visualization.

A lapsed Catholic, Amparo accompanied Milagros to church. She reported feeling more grounded. Amparo learned to meditate through a contemplative practice. Her depressive thoughts diminished, but she continued experiencing emotional pain. I introduced the concept of buen vivir during a session. Amparo said that her mother Milagros subscribed to this worldview. Soon after, Amparo engaged in a gratitude practice. At that time, I introduced the concept of power differential analysis. Amparo agreed to conduct her power differential analysis. This tool revealed that we shared similar areas of privilege, such as a high educational level, good physical health, and a collectivistic orientation. Amparo named her areas of oppression as being a single mother, having a low-paying job (teacher), and being AfroLatina. We identified a common area of oppression between us—being AfroLatinas. This racial ethnic identity exposed us to intersectional oppression due to race, gender, and ethnicity. The completion of the power differential analysis strengthened the therapeutic alliance. Afterward, I initiated promoting Amparo's critical consciousness' development. We examined her work history using liberation critical questions. At that time, Amparo became agitated. She stood up and rushed to the bathroom.

"I don't know what happened to me," Amparo said when she returned to my office. However, she wanted to continue with the conscientización process. Suddenly, Amparo began to cry. "A memory just came up for me," she said. She wiped her tears and continued: "When I was in second grade, the teacher told me that I had a learning disability because I was bilingual." Amparo cried for a few moments, and then continued: "She proceeded to treat me like a disabled child throughout the whole year. Since teachers are authority figures, I believed her, even though in my heart, I knew that she was wrong." Amparo placed her right hand over the left side of her chest, and said: "I did not listen to my heart. That is how I began to see myself as a failure." I replied with a *dicho*: *A donde el corazón se inclina, el pie camina* (where the heart leads, positive change emerges).

We analyzed this traumatic incident from sociopolitical, racism, and xenophobic perspectives. Amparo concluded that her White teacher was racist. Throughout Amparo's critical consciousness process, she became aware that her teacher targeted her for being a poor, bilingual AfroLatina. With this revelation, Amparo initiated her decolonization process. To facilitate this development, I invited her to write a journal to record this process. Amparo's journal entries became a testimonio. She joined a Latinx group working against anti-immigration policies in the U.S. Amparo read her testimonio to this group. She received a lot of support from the members. Inspired by this positive reception, Amparo focused more in developing her creativity. Since she loved singing, she began taking singing lessons. This process culminated in her joining her church's choir. Amparo moved to another school district, applied for a school principal position, and obtained it. Her depressive symptoms subsided. Amparo remained in therapy for a year and a half. During her last therapy session, she said: "I wrote a song. I called it *Liberación* (Liberation)." Amparo began singing her *Liberación* song.

CONCLUSION

We are not alone in our struggles, and never have been. Somos almas afines [We are related souls] *and this interconnectedness is an unvoiced category of identity.*
—GLORIA ANZALDÚA

Liberation psychotherapists help clients to recover their cultural memory; acknowledge their ancestral legacy; become critically conscious; change negative cognitions, emotions, and behaviors; and cultivate a desire for social justice action. To achieve these goals, liberation psychotherapists promote clients' development of a sociopolitical consciousness. Moreover, they *accompany* clients in their journey of recovery, healing, and transformation. Liberation practitioners foster solidarity with other oppressed people as they journey toward personal and collective liberation. They engage in social justice and spiritual activism. *As almas afines* (related souls), liberation psychotherapists work toward the emergence of a socially just society characterized by equality, conviviality, and buen vivir.

REFERENCES

Acosta, A. (2010). El buen vivir: Una utopía por (re)construer [The good life: A utopia for reconstruction]. In *Enfoques sobre Bienestar y buen vivir* (pp. 11–28). Madrid, Spain: Centro de Investigación para La paz (CIP-Ecosocial). Retrieved from http://www.fuhem.es/media/cdv/file/biblioteca/Dossier/Dossier_Enfoques_sobre_bienestar_y_buen_vivir.pdf p. 13

Acosta, A. (2016). Rethinking the world from the perspective of buen vivir. Retrieved from https://www.degrowth.info/en/dim/degrowth-in-movements/buen-vivir/

Afuape, T. (2011). *Power, resistance and liberation in therapy with survivors of trauma: To have our hearts broken.* New York, NY: Routledge.

Alcoff, L. (1988). Cultural feminism vs. post-structuralism: The identity crisis in feminist theory. *Signs: Journal of Women in Culture and Society, 13*, 405–436. http://dx.doi.org/10.1086/494426

Anderson, R. (2004). Intuitive inquiry: An epistemology of the heart for scientific inquiry. *The Humanistic Psychologist, 32*, 307–334.

Anzaldúa, G. (1987). *Borderlands/la frontera: The new mestiza.* San Francisco, CA: Spinster/Aunt Lute.

Anzaldúa, G. E. (2002). now let us shift . . . the path of *conocimiento* . . . inner work, public acts. In G. E. Anzaldúa & A. Keating (Eds.), *This bridge we call home: Radical visions for transformation* (pp. 540–570). New York, NY: Routledge.

Burgaleta, M., Johnson, W., Waber, D. P., Colom, R., & Karama, S. (2014). Cognitive ability changes and dynamics of cortical thickness development in healthy children and adolescents. *NeuroImage, 84*, 810–819. http://dx.doi.org/10.1016/j.neuroimage.2013.09.038

Cane, P. (2000). *Trauma, healing and transformation: Awakening a new heart with body, mind, and spirit practices.* Watsonville, CA: Capacitar.

Castillo, A. (Ed.). (1996). *Goddess of the Americas/la Diosa de las Américas: Writings on the Virgin of Guadalupe.* New York: Riverhead Books.

Chang, H. (2008). *Autoethnography as method.* Walnut Creek, CA: Left Coast Press.

Collins, P. H. (1986). Learning from the outsider within status: The sociological significance of Black feminist thought. *Social Problems, 33*, S14–S32. http://dx.doi.org/10.2307/800672

Comas-Díaz, L. (2000). An ethnopolitical approach to working with people of color. *American Psychologist, 55*, 1319–1325. http://dx.doi.org/10.1037/0003-066X.55.11.1319

Comas-Díaz, L. (2007). Ethnopolitical psychology: Healing and transformation. In E. Aldarondo (Ed), *Promoting social justice in mental health practice* (pp. 91–118). Mahwah, NJ: Erlbaum.

Comas-Díaz, L. (2012). *Multicultural care: A clinician's guide to cultural competence.* Washington, DC: American Psychological Association. http://dx.doi.org/10.1037/13491-000

Comas-Díaz, L. (2014). Commentary: The bridge of transformation. In M. Gallardo (Ed.), *Developing cultural humility: Embracing race, privilege and power* (pp. 133–154). Thousand Oaks, CA: Sage.

Comas-Díaz, L. (2016a). *Mujerista* psychospirituality. In T. Bryant-Davis & L. Comas-Díaz (Eds.), *Womanist and mujerista psychologies: Voices of fire, acts of courage* (pp. 149–169). Washington, DC: American Psychological Association.

Comas-Díaz, L. (2016b). Multicultural spirituality: A syncretistic approach to healing, liberation, and social justice. In J. M. Casas, L. Suzuki, C. M. Alexander, & M. Jackson (Eds.), *Handbook of multicultural counseling* (4th ed., pp. 282–293). Thousand Oaks, CA: Sage.

Comas-Díaz, L. (2020). Journey to psychology: A *mujerista testimonio*. *Women & Therapy, 43*, 157–169. http://dx.doi.org/10.1080/02703149.2019.1684676

Comas-Díaz, L., Hall, G. N., & Neville, H. A. (2019). Racial trauma: Theory, research, and healing: Introduction to the special issue. *American Psychologist, 74*, 1–5. http://dx.doi.org/10.1037/amp0000442

Comas-Díaz, L., Lykes, M. B., & Alarcón, R. D. (1998). Ethnic conflict and the psychology of liberation in Guatemala, Peru, and Puerto Rico. *American Psychologist, 53*, 778–792. http://dx.doi.org/10.1037/0003-066X.53.7.778

David, E. J., & Okazaki, S. (2006). Colonial mentality: A review and recommendation for Filipino American psychology. *Cultural Diversity and Ethnic Minority Psychology, 12*, 1–16. http://dx.doi.org/10.1037/1099-9809.12.1.1

Duran, E. (2006). *Healing the soul wound: Counseling with American Indians and other native people*. New York, NY: Teachers College Press.

Fanon, F. (1963). *The wretched of the earth*. New York, NY: Grove Press. (Original work in French published 1961)

Freire, P. (1994). *Pedagogy of the oppressed*. New York, NY: Seabury Press. (Original work published 1970)

Freire, P., & Macedo, D. (2000). *The Paulo Freire reader*. New York, NY: Continuum.

Garrett, J. T., & Garrett, M. W. (1994). The path of good medicine: Understanding and counseling Native American Indians. *Journal of Multicultural Counseling and Development, 22*, 134–144. http://dx.doi.org/10.1002/j.2161-1912.1994.tb00459.x

Gelso, C. J., Kivlighan, D. M., & Markin, R. D. (2018). The real relationship and its role in psychotherapy outcome: A meta-analysis. *Psychotherapy, 55*, 434–444. http://dx.doi.org/10.1037/pst0000183

Gordon, T. (1973). Notes on White and Black psychology. *Journal of Social Issues, 29*, 87–95.

Greer, C. (2017). *Change the story of your health: Using shamanic and Jungian techniques for healing*. Foray, Scotland: Findhorn Press.

Grosfoguel, R. (2008). Transmodernity, border thinking, and global coloniality. *Revista Crítica de Ciencias Sociais* [Journal of Critical Social Sciences]. Retrieved from https://www.eurozine.com/transmodernity-border-thinking-and-global-coloniality/

Harrell, S. P. (2000). A multidimensional conceptualization of racism-related stress: Implications for the well-being of people of color. *American Journal of Orthopsychiatry, 70*, 42–57. http://dx.doi.org/10.1037/h0087722

Harvey, A. (2009). *The hope: A guide to sacred activism*. Carlsbad, CA: Hay House.

Hill, C. E., Knox, S., & Pinto-Coelho, K. G. (2018). Therapist self-disclosure and immediacy: A qualitative meta-analysis. *Psychotherapy, 55*, 445–460. http://dx.doi.org/10.1037/pst0000182

Hurtado, A. (2003). Theory in the flesh: Towards an endarkened epistemology. *Qualitative Studies in Education, 16*, 215–225.

Isasi-Diaz, A. M. (1996). *Mujerista theology: A theology for the twenty-first century*. Maryknoll, NY: Orbis Books.

Johnson, W. B. (2016). Challenging clinically salient religion: The art of respectful confrontation. *Spirituality in Clinical Practice, 3,* 10–13. http://dx.doi.org/10.1037/scp0000099

Johnstone, B., Yoon, D. P., Cohen, D., Schopp, L. H., McCormack, G., Campbell, J., & Smith, M. (2012). Relationships among spirituality, religious practices, personality factors, and health for five different faith traditions. *Journal of Religion and Health, 51,* 1017–1041. http://dx.doi.org/10.1007/s10943-012-9615-8

Jordan, J. V. (2010). *Relational–cultural therapy.* Washington, DC: American Psychological Association.

Katz, R. (2017). *Indigenous healing psychology: Honoring the wisdom of the First Peoples.* Rochester, VT: Healing Arts Press.

Keating, A. (2006). From borderlands and new *mestizas* to *nepantlas* and *nepantleras*: Anzaldúan theories for social change. *Human Architecture: Journal of the Sociology of Self-Knowledge, IV,* 5–16.

Kirk, M. D. (2011). Investigating relationships between well-being, stress, coping skills and quality of life among African Americans, Native Americans, and Latinos. *Dissertations Abstracts International Section B: The Sciences and Engineering, 725-B,* 3084.

Kleinman, A. (1980). *Patients and healers in the context of culture: An exploration of the borderland between anthropology, medicine, and psychiatry.* Berkeley: University of California Press.

Koss-Chioino, J. (2007). Spiritual transformation, ritual, healing and altruism. *Journal of Religion & Science, 41,* 877–892.

Koss-Chioino, J. (2013). Religion and spirituality in Latino life in the United States. In K. I. Pargament (Ed.), *APA handbook of psychology, religion, and spirituality: Vol. 1. Context, theory, and research* (pp. 599–615). Washington, DC: American Psychological Association.

Leritz, E. C., Salat, D. H., Williams, V. J., Schnyer, D. M., Rudolph, J. L., Lipsitz, L., . . . Milberg, W. P. (2011). Thickness of the human cerebral cortex is associated with metrics of cerebrovascular health in a normative sample of community dwelling older adults. *NeuroImage, 54,* 2659–2671. http://dx.doi.org/10.1016/j.neuroimage.2010.10.050

Lugones, M. (2003). *Pilgrimages/*Peregrinajes*: Theorizing coalition against multiple oppressions.* New York, NY: Rowan & Littlefield.

Martín-Baró, I. (1994). *Writings for a liberation psychology* (A. Aron & S. Corne, Eds.). Cambridge, MA: Harvard University Press.

McCabe, G. H. (2007). The healing path: A culture and community-derived indigenous therapy model. *Psychotherapy, 44,* 148–160. http://dx.doi.org/10.1037/0033-3204.44.2.148

Miller, L., Bansal, R., Wickramaratme, P. Hao, X., Tenke, C. E., Weissman, M. M., & Peterson, G. S. (2014). Neuroatomical correlates of religiosity and spirituality: A study in adults at high and low familiar risk for depression. *JAMA Psychiatry, 71,* 128–135.

Montero, M., Sonn, C., & Burton, M. (2016). Community psychology and liberation psychology: Creative synergy for ethical and transformative praxis. In M. A. Bond, I. García de Serrano, & C. Keys (Eds.), *APA handbook of community psychology* (Vol. 1, pp. 149–167). Washington, DC: American Psychological Association.

Moane, G. (1999). *Gender and colonialism. A psychological analysis of oppression and liberation.* London, England: Palgrave.

Moraga, C. (1981). Entering the lives of others: Theory in the flesh. In G. A. Anzaldúa & C. Moraga (Eds.), *This bridge called my back: Writings by radical women of color* (pp. 85–90). Watertown, MA: Persephone Press.

Olmos, M. F., & Paravisini-Gebert, L. (2003). Creole religions of the Caribbean: An introduction from Voodoo, and *Santería*, to Obeah and *Espiritismo*. New York: New York University Press.

Pease, B. (2002). Rethinking empowerment: A postmodern reappraisal for emancipatory practice. *British Journal of Social Work, 3,* 135–147. http://dx.doi.org/10.1093/bjsw/32.2.135

Pedregal Casanova, R. (2013). Ecuador: *Que es el buen vivir* [What is *el buen vivir*]? Retrieved from http://www.resumenlatinoamericano.org/2017/03/19/ecuador-que-es-el-buen-vivir/

Peredo, A. M. (2019). El buen vivir (The well-being). In C. Fleming & M. Manning (Eds.), *Routledge handbook of Indigenous wellbeing* (pp. 143–155). London, England: Routledge. http://dx.doi.org/10.4324/9781351051262-14

Phillips, F. B. (1990). NTU psychotherapy: An Afrocentric approach. *Journal of Black Psychology, 17*(1), 55–74. http://dx.doi.org/10.1177/00957984900171005

Pomerville, A., & Gone, J. P. (2019). Indigenous culture-as-treatment in an era of evidence-based mental health practice. In C. Fleming & M. Manning (Eds.), *Routledge handbook of Indigenous well-being* (pp. 237–247). New York, NY: Routledge. http://dx.doi.org/10.4324/9781351051262-20

Prilleltensky, I. (2012). Wellness as fairness. *American Journal of Community Psychology, 49*(1–2), 1–21. http://dx.doi.org/10.1007/s10464-011-9448-8

Pyke, K. D. (2010). What is internalized racial oppression and why don't study it? Acknowledging racism's hidden injuries. *Sociological Perspectives, 53,* 551–572. http://dx.doi.org/10.1525/sop.2010.53.4.551

Quijano, A. (2000). Coloniality of power, Eurocentrism and Latin America. *Nepantla, 1,* 533–580. http://dx.doi.org/10.1177/0268580900015002005

Said, E. W. (1993). *Culture and imperialism.* New York, NY: Knopf.

Shapiro, F. (1995). *Eye movement desensitization and reprocessing: Basic principles, protocols, and procedures.* New York, NY: Guilford Press.

Valdez, L. (1973). *Pensamiento serpentino*: The law of in Lak'ech Alia K'in. *Chicano Theater One, 1,* 7–19.

van der Kolk, B. (2014). *The body keeps the score: Brain, mind and body in the healing of trauma.* New York, NY: Penguin.

Watkins, M. (2012, July 13). *Accompaniment: Psychosocial, environmental, trans-species, Earth.* Presentation at the 30th Anniversary Conference of Psychologists for Social Responsibility, Washington, DC. Retrieved from https://mary-watkins.net/library/Accompaniment-Psychosocial-Environmental-Trans-Species-Earth.pdf

Watkins, M. (2015). Psychological psychosocial accompaniment. *Journal of Social and Political Psychology, 3,* 324–341.

Watkins, M., & Shulman, H. (2008). *Toward psychologies of liberation.* New York, NY: Routledge. http://dx.doi.org/10.1057/9780230227736

Worrell, J., & Remer, P. (2003). *Feminist perspectives in therapy* (2nd ed.). New York, NY: Wiley.

IV

LIBERATION PSYCHOLOGY AND SPECIAL POPULATIONS

10

Black Minds Matter

*Applying Liberation Psychology
to Black Americans*

Thema Bryant-Davis and Shavonne J. Moore-Lobban

Liberation psychology is the freeing of minds from the psychological bondage of oppression (Martín-Baró, 1994). This chapter explores the need for liberation by examining the dynamics and effects of racism in the lives of Black Americans. Additionally, we examine the tenets of liberation psychology, generally and as it relates to Black people living within the realities of intergenerational trauma. Liberation psychology can address racism and intersectional oppression in the lives of Black people by empowering communities to recognize oppression in its multiple forms, as well as to resist internally and externally (Thompson & Alfred, 2009). Moreover, liberation psychology is not only about reacting to the threats of oppression but also about reclaiming one's identity and agency to live with purpose, meaning, community, and even joy.

THE NEED FOR LIBERATION: DYNAMICS AND EFFECTS OF RACISM IN THE LIVES OF BLACK AMERICANS

Racism is conceptualized an as ideological phenomenon wherein negative attitudes, beliefs, and actions lead to the mistreatment of others based on ethnic group affiliation, phenotypic, or cultural characteristics (Brondolo, Ver Halen, Pencille, Beatty, & Contrada, 2009; R. Clark, Anderson, Clark, & Williams, 1999). Like many isms, racism is perpetrated by members of a

http://dx.doi.org/10.1037/0000198-011
Liberation Psychology: Theory, Method, Practice, and Social Justice, by L. Comas-Díaz and E. Torres Rivera (Editors)

majority group (e.g., White people) and used in ways that demean, ostracize, and shun members of a minority group (e.g., People of Color, Black Americans). It can also be understood as "the ideological apparatus of a racialized social system" where "the existence of racism indicates the existence of a racial structure in society" (Bonilla-Silva, 1997, p. 2). In this way, racism involves institutional policies and structural arrangements that are biased against, disadvantage, and oppress People of Color.

Prejudice, stereotyping, and discrimination intertwine with racism. Dovidio and colleagues (2010) provided a comprehensive summary of these concepts, noting that *prejudice* is the negative attitude or belief toward a target group or individual member of the target group; stereotyping is the cognitive bias and overgeneralization of traits, attributes, or characteristics of a target group or its members; and *discrimination* is the behavioral component of inappropriate and unfair treatment of target groups and its members based on prejudice attitudes and stereotyped beliefs. Underlining each of these concepts is *intergroup bias*, where individuals within a group have a deep-rooted propensity to evaluate their within-group members more favorably than people outside of their group (Dovidio, Hewstone, Glick, & Esses, 2010). In this way, racism and related biases create systems of hierarchy in which People of Color are viewed as "less than" others who hold the power to set social norms, roles, expectations, and opportunities. Indeed, racism is a process by which consistent prejudice, discrimination, and biases negatively affect People of Color, in particular, Black Americans.

Throughout U.S. history, Black Americans have been forced to contend with the effects of racism. Black Americans have endured slavery, brutality, segregation, unequal access to basic human rights, controlled opportunities for growth and advancement, and much more. Such atrocities have not ended with the abolishment of slavery or the ending of Jim Crow. Instead, dogmatic beliefs of superiority and systems of inequality have persisted for generations of people and become entrenched within society. Consequently, dynamics of racism can be seen through many levels of social structures.

Jones (2000) developed a framework to conceptualize the experience of racism across three levels: institutionalized, personally mediated, and internalized. Within this framework, *institutionalized racism* is seen as structurally embedded into the customs and practices of society, including institutional policies and societal laws. It creates differential access to opportunities (e.g., employment, education), goods (e.g., home ownership), services (e.g., medical treatment, health care), and power (e.g., voting rights, state and national elected office positions, resources of wealth and organizational influence). *Personally, mediated racism* is fueled by prejudice and discriminatory acts that can be intentional or unintentional. Acts within this interpersonal level of racism may range from (a) crossing the street or clutching one's purse in the presence of Black Americans; (b) providing poor service to Black Americans within establishments, such as a restaurant; (c) name-calling and hostility toward Black Americans; (d) devaluing the intellect and abilities of African

Descent Americans; and (e) a general lack of respect and value for the lives of Black Americans. Last, *internalized racism* is a process in which members of a group begin to accept and believe society's negative and prejudiced beliefs about them (Jones, 2000). For example, within the American Black community, *colorism*—the notion that having lighter skin tone is superior to having darker skin tone—is a form of internalized racism (Hunter, 2002, 2007; Mathews & Johnson, 2015). In this way, Whiteness is viewed as the epitome of beauty and humanness and those with skin tones that are closer to Whiteness (e.g., Black Americans with lighter skin tone) are seen as better because of it.

These levels of racism overlap and intersect in complex ways. Part of the complexity involves the shift from egregious overt racism to more subtle covert forms of racism. For example, during the era of Jim Crow laws, institutional and personally mediated racism was supported through legalized segregation and societal practices of "Whites only" drinking fountains, restaurants, business establishments, schools, public transportation, and more. This kind of racism, prejudice, and discrimination against African Descent Americans was overt. It was clear, obvious, and normalized. Although the Civil Rights Act of 1964 outlawed such discrimination, on the basis of race, color, sex, and other categories, the prejudicial beliefs that sustained centuries of overt racism did not spontaneously end. In some ways, racism adopted a new standard within society and became more covert (although overt racism still exists as well). Sue and colleagues (2007) have described these experiences as *racial microaggressions*—"brief and commonplace daily verbal, behavioral, and environmental indignities, whether intentional or unintentional, that communicate hostile, derogatory, or negative racial slights and insults to the target person or group" (Sue et al., 2007, p. 274). Underpinning such overt and covert racism are beliefs and biases that Black people do not belong in a White society and that they do not deserve the equal treatment that their White counterparts are privileged to have. Recent examples of covert racism can be seen through situations in which Black Americans are (a) pulled over for driving nice cars in the "wrong neighborhood," (b) sentenced to jail and prison at higher rates and for longer durations than their White counterparts committing the same crime, or (c) killed by police or civilian brutality.

Increases in technology, and social media specifically, have allowed us to better understand the frequency of such experiences. Footage of Black Americans being killed for walking down the street with a hoodie on (Trayvon Martin), playing with a toy gun in a playground (Tamir Rice), selling loose cigarettes outside of a store (Eric Garner), riding in the passenger side of a car (Philando Castile), getting pulled over for a routine traffic stop (Sandra Bland), or sitting in a Bible study (nine members of Mother Emmanuel AME Church) have highlighted the ways in which prejudiced beliefs and racism have seeped into society and created strong, implicit biases that can cost Black Americans their lives (on the lethal effects of implicit bias, see Banks, Eberhardt, & Ross,

2006, and Sadler, Correll, Park, & Judd, 2012). Additionally, technology has allowed for greater dissemination of information about the everyday occurrences of racism in the lives of Black Americans. Most recently, there was a case in St. Louis, Missouri, in which a White woman followed a Black American man through an apartment building in which they both lived, asking to see his identification and proof of residency (Gomez, 2018). She followed him all the way to his apartment door and watched him enter the apartment, all while threatening to call the police because she believed he did not look like someone who belonged in that apartment building. In the aftermath of this situation and the subsequent media storm, the White woman has implied that this Black American man misunderstood her intentions.

These types of racist events leave Black Americans questioning the reality of their experiences, the validity of their feelings and responses, and the existence of these messages about them as true or untrue. These messages are further fueled through media, literature, and other forms of entertainment that portray Black Americans as dangerous, lazy, unintelligent, unemployed, ghetto, or simply inferior to other groups of people. One of many potential consequences of these experiences is internalized racism. As discussed earlier in the chapter, *internalized racism* is a process in which people begin to accept and believe the racist and prejudiced messages about them (Jones, 2000). Scholars have highlighted the damaging consequences of victims of racism beginning to adopt and internalize the oppressors' views of them (Lee, Kellett, Seghal, & Van den Berg, 2018; Pyke, 2010; Speight, 2007).

Largely, the consequences of racism for Black Americans are profound. Although some studies have found inconsistent associations between racism and health outcomes (Paradies, 2006), many others have consistently identified the negative impact of racism and racial discrimination on Black Americans' mental and physical health (Alvarez, Liang, & Neville, 2016; Borrell, Kiefe, Williams, Diez-Roux, & Gordon-Larsen, 2006; U.S. Department of Health and Human Services, 2001; Williams & Williams-Morris, 2000). The literature highlights the impact of racism on depressive symptoms or major depressive disorder (Brondolo, Ng, Pierre, & Lane, 2016; T. T. Clark, Salas-Wright, Vaughn, & Whitfield, 2015; Mereish et al., 2016; Pieterse, Todd, Neville, & Carter, 2012), anxiety (Graham, Calloway, & Roemer, 2015; Pieterse et al., 2012), substance use (T. T. Clark et al., 2015; Gibbons et al., 2010), lowered self-esteem (Mereish, N'cho, Green, Jernigan, & Helms, 2016), and more. Racism has also been conceptualized as traumatic (Bryant-Davis & Ocampo, 2005; Carter, 2007; Kirkinis, Pieterse, Martin, Agiliga, & Brownell, 2018), which may lead to a variety of posttraumatic reactions and responses.

In reviewing the ways in which racism impacts physical health, Wyatt and colleagues (2003) applied Jones's (2000) three levels of experienced racism (outlined earlier) to the development of cardiovascular disease. They noted,

> First, institutional racism can lead to limited opportunities for socioeconomic mobility, differential access to goods and resources, and poor living conditions that can adversely affect cardiovascular health. Second, perceived/personally

mediated racism acts as a stressor and can induce psychophysiological reactions that negatively affect cardiovascular health. Third, in race-conscious societies, such as the United States, the negative self-evaluations of accepting negative cultural stereotypes as true (internalized racism) can have deleterious effects on cardiovascular health. (p. 315)

Indeed, racism has been linked to many physical health outcomes, including birth outcomes (e.g., infant mortality, low birth rate), hypertension, diabetes, cancer, cardiovascular disease, and more (for review, see Kaholokula, 2016). One can see clearly that the impact of racism is pervasive. It affects important domains of an individual's life from in utero through older adulthood (Gee & Verissimo, 2016).

The American Psychological Association's (APA's; 2017b) recent report on stress and health disparities emphasized a life span approach to understanding how race, ethnicity, and socioeconomic status (SES) influence the experience of stress and the manifestation of mental and physical health issues, such as depression, cardiovascular disease, cancer, and more. The authors note the disproportionate nature of stress in the lives of Black Americans who are at higher risk for stress (especially as it relates to experiences of ongoing racism and discrimination), experience disparities in accessing resources that mitigate such stress, and over the course of their lifetime, are affected in terms of their ability to self-actualize (or be their best self; APA, 2017b).

Indeed, the intersectionality of multiple marginalized identity domains (e.g., race, ethnicity, identified gender, socioeconomic status, ability status, sexual orientation, nationality) is critically important to understanding the dynamics and long-term effects of racism in the lives of Black Americans. Essed (1991) explored this with specific attention to the intersection of racism and sexism and coined the term *gendered racism* to describe the everyday discrimination and oppression that occurs based on prejudiced beliefs about ones' race or ethnicity, and gender. Gendered racism has been explored in terms of impact on Black women's psychological distress, and the means by which they have to cope with it (Lewis, Mendenhall, Harwood, & Huntt, 2013; Szymanski & Lewis, 2016; Szymanski & Stewart, 2010; Thomas, Witherspoon, & Speight, 2008). Although typically explored from the position of Black women, gendered racism has also been considered for Black men (Wingfield, 2007) and can clearly be identified in the prison population system (Alexander, 2012).

Any person that has consistently been oppressed, mistreated, denied access to resources and opportunity, and who has suffered the negative con-sequences of such acts on their mental and physical health would mistrust individuals and systems that such oppressiveness derives from. Certainly, many Black Americans experience *cultural mistrust* of White people and the Whiteness of society (Whaley, 2001). There have been historical instances in which Black Americans have been lied to and betrayed by individuals and systems of power that were supposed to help them. Take, for example, the Tuskegee syphilis experiment, which can be viewed as personally mediated and institutional racism. For 40 years, beginning in 1932, the U.S. Public Health Service conducted a study in which 600 Black American men were told that they were being treated for "bad blood" (a common term at the time for syphilis) when in fact, the almost 400 men who actually had syphilis did not receive the available treatment (Bhopal, 2007). These men where not informed about the true nature of the study, the real consequences of their participation, or their option to leave the study at any time. Like many forms of racism that have already been reviewed in this chapter, the consequences of the racism in the Tuskegee study left Black American men and their families, with serious psychological and physical health concerns, including death. Their untreated syphilis was transmitted to their wives and subsequently their children, and the aftermath was extremely damaging to their lives. The U.S. Public Health Services took advantage of a vulnerable population and put their lives in danger.

Moreover, the U.S. Public Health Services enlisted Black professionals to show support for the study and build relationships with the men who were being misused. Smith (1996) explored the dynamics around their involvement and noted that Black professionals such as Robert Moton (head of the Tuskegee Institute) and Dr. Eugene Dibble (medical director of Tuskegee Hospital) supported the study and believed that it would be financially beneficial for their institution as well as educationally helpful for other Black professionals. One medical professional, Nurse Eunice Rivers Laurie, was employed as a liaison between the U.S. Public Health Services workers and the Black men who were being used in the study (Smith, 1996). More than any other Black professional, Nurse Rivers has been vilified and written about as the one who should have known better (Bernal, 2013). During a time when Black Americans had little trust in White government representatives, Nurse Rivers was used to create relationships with the men who were presumed to trust her, and subsequently trust the study, because of their shared Black identity. Like Mr. Moton and Dr. Dibble, Nurse Rivers never spoke up about what was happening during the 40-year duration of the study (Smith, 1996). In many ways, the roles of the Black professionals are complicated and layered by the history of racism and oppression in the United States. Consider their need for financial gain in a time when many Black people were poor, their desire to contribute to something that they may have believed would benefit their community from a perspective of better understanding health symptoms and treatment, their internalized racism in not considering the humanity of other Black people, their experienced oppressive beliefs that White people could not be challenged within a professional settings, among other questions. Consider the implications of gendered racism and how Nurse Rivers was used and portrayed. Regardless of the controversy of the Black professionals in the study, this study was another reminder to Black Americans that their lives are not equally valued within health care or government institutions, and it is an example of what leads Black Americans to mistrust these systems, including other Black people within the systems.

Such cultural mistrust may prohibit Black Americans from seeking help within traditionally understood avenues, such as within psychotherapy or primary care. Researchers have shown that within the health care system Black Americans experience (a) unequal and poorer treatment (Nelson, 2003); (b) overdiagnosing and overmedication of some disorders, such as schizophrenia (Delphin-Rittmon et al., 2015; Metzl, 2010); (c) underdiagnoses of other disorders, such as depression (Delphin-Rittmon et al., 2015; Payne, 2014); and (d) treatment delays for receiving care (Fedewa, Ward, Stewart, & Edge, 2010). Consequently, their willingness to seek help, use health care services, and engage in treatment can be hindered (Substance Abuse and Mental Health Services Administration, 2015; U.S. Department of Health and Human Services, 2001; Whaley, 2001).

When Black Americans do seek help, it is important for mental health care professionals to attend to the cultural context that surrounds them within this society (APA, 2017a). That context includes the racism that Black Americans have experienced over centuries, as well as the biases that are entrenched in society and that many clinicians intentionally or unintentionally hold. In 2003, the Council of National Psychological Associations for the Advancement of Ethnic Minority Interests developed recommendations for the psychological treatment of ethnic minorities. In it, Sue (2003) made an important point that "clinicians are not immune from inheriting the biases, stereotypes, and values of the larger society. They often unintentionally act out these biases in the treatment of their clients of color" (p. 5). Additionally, the latest Multicultural Guidelines developed by the APA (2017a) note that

> psychologists aspire to recognize and understand that as cultural beings, they hold attitudes and beliefs that can influence their perceptions of and interactions with others as well as their clinical and empirical conceptualizations. As such, psychologists strive to move beyond conceptualizations rooted in categorical assumptions, biases, and/or formulations based on limited knowledge about individuals and communities. (p. 4)

The guidelines further encourage psychologists to consider the historical and current experiences of power, privilege, and oppression of the client; the client's environment; and the clinical setting overall.

The Multicultural Guidelines (APA, 2017a) and the larger field of helping professionals also identify the importance of *cultural competence* in the delivery and provision of services. Cultural competence is about effectively working within the context of other groups to best provide group members with appropriate services. Campinha-Bacote (2002) proposed a model of cultural competence in the delivery of health care services and noted that cultural competence is not an event or something that is necessarily achieved, but rather it is a process whereby providers seek to have cultural awareness, knowledge, and skills, as well as cultural encounters with others and a desire to be engaged in the entire process. Further, cultural competence at the institutional level is also needed and can be effective in addressing the racial disparities and barriers for health care treatment mentioned earlier (Betancourt, Green, Carrillo, & Owusu Ananeh-Firempong, 2016).

It is equally important for providers to be open to the notion that the standard practices of intervening (e.g., strictly evidence-based treatments) that were developed for predominately White individuals may not be "standard" or always appropriate for Black Americans and other diverse populations. Cultural practices of healing and transformation are also important to explore. Soto and colleagues (2018) conducted two meta-analytic reviews, one on culturally adapted interventions and one on therapist cultural competence, to better understand the provision of mental health services for diverse racial and ethnic groups. Interestingly, they found that culturally adapted interventions tend to be more effective with clients of color, while therapist cultural competence may not be enough given that treatment outcome is not significantly correlated with therapist self-reports of cultural competence, and clients' reports of therapist cultural competence may be influenced by a number of confounding factors (e.g., general positive and negative therapeutic experiences). Thus, it is reasonable to believe that although providers of these services can expand their cultural competence and ability to build trusting relationships with their Black American clients, other means of healing may be found by applying culturally adapted practices, including liberation psychology.

LIBERATION PSYCHOLOGY

Liberation, or *liberation psychology*, is a psychology that acts on the individual and society such that all people can pursue unhindered wellness, purpose, and abundant lives by eliminating oppression, domination, exploitation, and exclusion (Prilleltensky, 1996). Liberation psychology seeks to go beyond breaking chains to building resources of compassion, justice, voice, and authenticity by acknowledging and building on the links among mental health, human rights, and the fight against injustice (Martín-Baró, 1994). Liberation psychology requires attending to voice, choice, culture, and context (Prilleltensky, 1996). Although many psychologies focus on assisting people to create good lives, the prerequisite of addressing societal and structural barriers to self-determination, agency, and liberation are systematically ignored. Liberation psychology, which has an emancipatory orientation and emancipatory action, is rooted in distributive justice and sociopolitical literacy of the psychologist and the client (Prilleltensky, 1996). Black liberation psychology is born from Black liberation theology, which is a contextual theology that recognizes the need for the scriptural and doctrinal interpretive lens to include the experience of the community and individual (Trout, Dokecki, Newbrough, & O'Gorman, 2003). Likewise, liberation psychology acknowledges the limitations of using a science not reflective of a community as an accurate measure of that community's wellness and development. On the contrary, the psychology of a people, by a people, and for a people must be rooted in the identity and contextual realities of the people. To enhance and strengthen a people, one must start with their sociocultural identity to determine the course of action that will be liberating.

Gutiérrez's (see Digby, 2011) model of liberation practice entails observing historical engagement with liberation by impoverished and oppressed communities, reflecting critically on these actions, reflecting on these efforts in light of theology (or in our case in light of psychology), designing action strategies for the community, and taking action for the liberation and growth of the community. Applying this model to Black Americans requires us to acknowledge and study the various pathways to liberation that Black Americans adopted. These acts of rebellion, resistance, and revolution are documented starting from the Middle Passage. Efforts toward freedom were diverse, with some manifesting in holistic liberation and others ending in destruction or surviving without fulfillment.

Acknowledge and Study Pathways to Liberation

Liberation engagement for Black people who were enslaved legally and who after governmental liberation were enslaved sociopolitically sought liberation by jumping overboard during the Middle Passage to send their freed souls back home to Africa; staging organized revolts on plantations; covert resistance by breaking plantation equipment; loving themselves and each other despite a dehumanizing process; escaping; seeking spiritual liberation; creating community; establishing businesses; pursuing literacy and educational advancement; securing and utilizing the right to vote; running for political office; boycotts; legal cases; marches; civil disobedience; working within organizations, institutions, and governments for transformation; creating their own institutions, such as denominations, schools, nonprofit organizations, and political bodies; celebrating their culture; hiding their culture; positive racial socialization of their children (rites of passage programs); expressive art; political analysis presented in comedy, writing our narratives and histories through literature and media; and creating culturally affirming psychologies and theologies (Gardullo, 2007; Spencer, 2006)

Critical Analysis

A critical analysis of the previously mentioned strategies reveals that they resulted in legal liberation. Black people in the United States were able to use these interdisciplinary strategies to obtain liberation; the right to literacy; civil rights and legal protection from discrimination; voter's rights; and increased representation in multiple fields, including media, government, commerce, and education (King, 2015). However, this same analysis reveals the persistence of racism, discrimination, stigma, unconscious bias, microaggressions, marginalization, unequal protection under the law, inequity in resource access, and unchanged hearts and minds of many (DeGruy, 2005; Dovidio, Gaertner, & Pearson, 2017; Nadal, 2018).

Analyze Psychologically

The cost of continued racism and intersectional oppression manifests psychologically, physically, and socially. Black people in America have paid a steep cost for both the wounds of oppression and the emotional labor of activists and others who work for change. The labor of resistance can result in burn out, rage, depression, suicidal ideation, difficulty trusting, dissociation, vicarious trauma, anxiety, panic attacks, posttraumatic stress disorder, difficulty focusing, insecurity, and in some cases death (Greer & Spalding, 2017; Kwate & Goodman, 2015).

Design and Reimagine Liberation Interventions

Liberation psychology interventions are not only psychological but also spiritual because they address the soul wounds of oppression; resist internalized oppression; and seek to bring liberation to individuals, families, communities, and society (Duran, Firehammer, & Gonzalez, 2008). We review selected culturally emergent liberating interventions for Black people as we work toward the decolonization of psychology through the centering of wellness and empowerment of Black people on our own terms.

Black psychologists (the Community Healing Network and Association of Black Psychologists) created Emotional Liberation Circles as an intervention to heal and overcome the lies of Black inferiority and dehumanization (Grills, Aird, & Rowe, 2016). Recognizing the impact of racism not only on the individual but also on the collective consciousness and memory, the intervention uses a group format to foster community, collaboration, and connection. It also uses the therapeutic value of voice, storytelling, and narrative therapy by breaking silence and shame as survivors tell their stories of oppression, discrimination, and stigma. The therapeutic, liberating aim is healing from historical and contemporary racism, complete freedom from the lie of Black inferiority, and acquisition of empowerment and identity. Within the circles, Black people share their stories, gain understanding of the impact of historical trauma, narrate a new story, cultivate self-care and community care skills, learn the roots causes of oppression, and from a foundation of affirmed identity organize to take community action.

Ntu psychotherapy, based in ancient African and Afrocentric principles, is a spiritually integrative, culturally emergent approach to liberation (Phillips, 1990). The aim is to bring balance to Black Americans psychospiritually to address the various ways that oppression has created individual and collective destabilization. Ntu psychotherapy seeks to bring liberation by exploring the following principles for wellness: harmony, balance, cultural awareness, interconnectedness, and authenticity. The therapist facilitates the process of guiding the client to the natural state of alignment, being consistent and purposeful mentally, physically, relationally, and spiritually. Spirituality is the basic force guiding the therapeutic process and the essence of the values, goals, and purpose. When clients are Ntu, they live in a state of clarity not in a combative mind-set. Liberation from an Afrocentric perspective honors an affective epistemology, which is awareness that our emotions are important sources of knowledge. Denial and repression of our affective experiences create further bondage and dehumanization, while feeling what we feel is an important path to liberation (Phillips, 1990).

Hip-hop psychology is another culturally emergent liberating intervention (Hadley & Yancy, 2012; Tyson, 2003). It uses the creation, expression, and reception of affirming hip-hop music to raise self-expression, cultural awareness, critical consciousness, empowerment, and interconnectedness to liberate Black people. Participants write lyrics, share their creation or narrative, and reflect on the narratives of others. The intervention is possible in individual therapy but is more collaborative and connecting when conducted in a group format. The creation of hip-hop music becomes therapy when facilitated by the therapist with intentionality and the intention is to affirm, heal, empower, connect, and liberate while consciously building on the legacy of those hip-hop artists and activists that came before us with an aim of liberating themselves and others (Hadley & Yancy, 2012).

Another cultural emergent intervention for liberation is movement, and one of the movement forms is liturgical dance. Liturgical dance, found in both Christian traditions and Indigenous Black religious traditions, is movement used in public, collective worship. Liturgical dance is a sacred practice that can include both choreographed movement and spirit-led, improvisational movement (Elisha, 2017). The participant adopts this holistic path to liberation that rejects notions of Black bodies as insignificant and instead offers them as a sacred, holy, and powerful. The therapist or sacred artist who facilitates liturgical dance as liberation therapy can guide the participants in various forms of liturgical dance, such as but not limited to celebration, warfare, prayer, prophetic, thanksgiving, and testimony or narrative. Liturgical dance therapists, including the first author, provide single workshops and series of sessions that may be time-limited or ongoing.

Black contemplative practices are also significant pathways to liberation. Bryant-Davis, Young, and Harrell (2018) explored Afrocentric principles of mindfulness, the path of embodied healing, and Young and Soulfulness, an Afrocentric approach to contemplative practice that uses music and affirmation. In the principles-based model, the clinician presents the client with culturally informed psychoeducation regarding compassion, nonjudgment, acceptance, being present, and connection to all living things and then invites the client(s) to engage in meditation. Bryant-Davis noted that being still is a radical act for Black Americans, whose unpaid and underpaid labor has been demanded since they were placed in bondage. In Harrell's Soulfulness, the client learns to live in flow and holistic wellness using meditation, music, movement, and affirmation. These culturally emergent approaches recognize the value in Black people learning the roots of contemplative and mindfulness practice that existed in ancient Black traditions and holistic ways of being.

Womanist psychology is the framework for a therapeutic intervention focused on the liberation and celebration of Black women (Bryant-Davis & Comas-Díaz, 2016). Womanist therapy uses storytelling, art, spirituality, and activism to counter the negative mental, physical, social, and spiritual consequences of intersectional oppression in the lives of Black women. This intersectional approach includes attending to psychospiritual costs of poverty, violence, racism, sexism, heterosexism, forced and consensual migration, cultural disconnection, dehumanization, and global issues facing Black and Diasporic women as well as Women of Color globally. While feminist psychology and Black psychology as liberating frameworks have often neglected or marginalized the experiences, needs, and value of Black women, womanist psychology centers Black women. Womanist therapy pursues not just the healing of Black women but liberation as demonstrated by growth, transformation, thriving, and optimal living. Thematically, womanist therapy liberates Black women by attending to their gendered cultural narratives while actively exploring self-definition, agency, community or social support, survival strategies, coping strategies, resistance strategies, growth, healing, resilience, and thriving. Womanist therapeutic approaches have been proposed and conducted for women and men, individually, within family therapy, and in group-based interventions (Sanchez-Hucles, 2016). This liberation approaches centers Black women's psychospiritual journey from the soul wounds of oppression to survival, wholeness, justice, empowerment, life enhancement, and connection. Liberated Black women embrace their voices, needs, agency, and power, while celebrating and honoring the value of other members of the community.

Bryant-Davis and Ocampo (2006) proposed a model for healing and liberating the minds, hearts, and spirits of Black Americans by directly addressing the wounds of racial trauma. The intervention is a themes-based approach in which clients explore their experiences by working through therapeutic constructs. The therapeutic process of liberation starts with acknowledging that racial traumas have occurred, and the next step is to share those experiences with the individual therapist or within a group. After the sharing, the client follows similar steps from Herman's model for healing from interpersonal trauma. Namely, they explore safety, self-care, and grieving the losses (what racism has taken from them and their community). In Herman's model, the next step is for clients to explore shame and self-blame, but in Bryant-Davis's model this next step is shame and internalized racism, exploring the ways clients have come to believe the lies they have been told about themselves as Black people. After addressing internalized racism, clients are free to explore their anger, including the ways in which they have dealt with it in the past, ranging from denial to rage. The next theme is healthy coping with an awareness of both unhealthy, self-destructive coping strategies as well as healthy, spiritually and culturally affirming practices. The final stage is absent from Herman's model and that is resistance. Liberation psychology affirms that we seek freedom to live fully as ourselves and we seek freedom to free others. Resistance involves working actively to combat intersectional oppression that manifests both toward us and toward Black people nationally and globally. Liberation involves gaining agency and voice to combat forces of White supremacy and every form of oppression that exists. People who are not attuned to their power and responsibility to resist oppression are not fully liberated.

CONCLUSION

Black liberation psychology is about transforming not only people but also systems, institutions, and even governments to eradicate oppressive actions and build a more just and beloved community. Balance and healthy development for Black Americans includes a sense of agency and critical consciousness that may manifest as collective action, service, empowerment, and political activation (Watts & Flanagan, 2007). Liberation psychology for Black Americans involves an awareness of historical and contemporary manifestations of racism, as well as a healthy vigilance and awareness of the realities of oppression in diverse forms (Adams, O'Brien, & Nelson, 2006). Culturally emergent approaches to liberation as well as traditional psychotherapy reformatted through a liberation psychology lens may serve as effective vehicles to liberation for Black people. Psychologists need to examine these practices both in terms of their capacity to transform individuals but also on the proposed ripple effect of their capacity to lead to transformation of systems, institutions, and governments. Liberating individuals will always be a reactive stance in the aftermath of oppression, but liberated peoples can engage in preventive justice work that eradicates oppressive forces that have the potential and purpose of wounding Black people. Liberation psychology recognizes and celebrates Black people and prioritizes their freedom from oppression, while spiritually, culturally, and psychologically equipping them to work toward the liberation of others.

REFERENCES

Adams, G., O'Brien, L. T., & Nelson, J. C. (2006). Perceptions of racism in Hurricane Katrina: A liberation psychology analysis. *Analyses of Social Issues and Public Policy, 6*, 215–235. http://dx.doi.org/10.1111/j.1530-2415.2006.00112.x

Alexander, M. (2012). *The new Jim Crow: Mass incarceration in the age of colorblindness.* New York, NY: The New Press.

Alvarez, A. N., Liang, C. T., & Neville, H. A. (Eds.). (2016). *The cost of racism for People of Color: Contextualizing experiences of discrimination.* Washington, DC: American Psychological Association. http://dx.doi.org/10.1037/14852-000

American Psychological Association. (2017a). *Multicultural guidelines: An ecological approach to context, identity, and intersectionality.* Retrieved from http://www.apa.org/about/policy/multicultural-guidelines.pdf

American Psychological Association, APA Working Group on Stress and Health Disparities. (2017b). *Stress and health disparities: Contexts, mechanisms, and interventions among racial/ethnic minority and low-socioeconomic status populations.* Retrieved from http://www.apa.org/pi/health-disparities/resources/stress-report.aspx

Banks, R. R., Eberhardt, J. L., & Ross, L. (2006). Discrimination and implicit bias in a racially unequal society. *California Law Review, 94,* 1169–1190. http://dx.doi.org/10.2307/20439061

Bernal, E. (2013, March). Rivers' role: A deeper look into nurse Eunice Rivers Laurie. *The Tuskegee News.* Retrieved from http://www.thetuskegeenews.com/news/rivers-role-a-deeper-look-into-nurse-eunice-rivers-laurie/article_47f97284-7a37-5b4b-b2e9-9566570b4dae.html

Betancourt, J. R., Green, A. R., Carrillo, J. E., & Owusu Ananeh-Firempong, I. I. (2016). Defining cultural competence: A practical framework for addressing racial/ethnic disparities in health and health care. *Public Health Reports, 118,* 293–302.

Bhopal, R. S. (2007). *Ethnicity, race, and health in multicultural societies: Foundations for better epidemiology, public health, and health care.* Oxford University Press. http://dx.doi.org/10.1093/acprof:oso/9780198568179.001.0001

Bonilla-Silva, E. (1997). Rethinking racism: Toward a structural interpretation. *American Sociological Review, 62,* 465–480. http://dx.doi.org/10.2307/2657316

Borrell, L. N., Kiefe, C. I., Williams, D. R., Diez-Roux, A. V., & Gordon-Larsen, P. (2006). Self-reported health, perceived racial discrimination, and skin color in African Americans in the CARDIA study. *Social Science & Medicine, 63,* 1415–1427. http://dx.doi.org/10.1016/j.socscimed.2006.04.008

Brondolo, E., Ng, W., Pierre, K.-E. J., & Lane, R. (2016). Racism and mental health: Examining the link between racism and depression from a social cognitive perspective. In A. N. Alvarez, C. T. H. Liang, & H. A. Neville (Eds.), *The cost of racism for People of Color: Contextualizing experiences of discrimination* (pp. 109–132). Washington, DC: American Psychological Association. http://dx.doi.org/10.1037/14852-006

Brondolo, E., Ver Halen, N. B., Pencille, M., Beatty, D., & Contrada, R. J. (2009). Coping with racism: A selective review of the literature and a theoretical and methodological critique. *Journal of Behavioral Medicine, 32*(1), 64–88.

Bryant-Davis, T., & Comas-Díaz, L. (2016). Introduction: Womanist and mujerista psychologies. In T. Bryant-Davis & L. Comas-Díaz (Eds.), *Womanist and mujerista psychologies: Voices of fire, acts of courage* (pp. 3–25). Washington, DC: American Psychological Association. http://dx.doi.org/10.1037/14937-001

Bryant-Davis, T., & Ocampo, C. (2005). The trauma of racism: Implications for counseling, research, and education. *The Counseling Psychologist, 33,* 574–578. http://dx.doi.org/10.1177/0011000005276581

Bryant-Davis, T., & Ocampo, C. (2006). A therapeutic approach to the treatment of racist-incident-based trauma. *Journal of Emotional Abuse, 6*(4), 1–22. http://dx.doi.org/10.1300/J135v06n04_01

Bryant-Davis, T., Young, S., & Harrell, S. (2018, June). *Inside out and outside in: Contemplative practices for healing, liberation, and transformation.* Presented at the Association of Black Psychology Annual Convention, Oakland, CA.

Campinha-Bacote, J. (2002). The process of cultural competence in the delivery of healthcare services: A model of care. *Journal of Transcultural Nursing, 13,* 181–184. http://dx.doi.org/10.1177/10459602013003003

Carter, R. (2007). Racism and psychological and emotion injury: Recognizing and assessing race-based traumatic stress. *The Counseling Psychologist, 35,* 13–105. http://dx.doi.org/10.1177/0011000006292033

Clark, R., Anderson, N. B., Clark, V. R., & Williams, D. R. (1999). Racism as a stressor for African Americans. A biopsychosocial model. *American Psychologist, 54,* 805–816. http://dx.doi.org/10.1037/0003-066X.54.10.805

Clark, T. T., Salas-Wright, C. P., Vaughn, M. G., & Whitfield, K. E. (2015). Everyday discrimination and mood and substance use disorders: A latent profile analysis with African Americans and Caribbean Blacks. *Addictive Behaviors, 40,* 119–125. http://dx.doi.org/10.1016/j.addbeh.2014.08.006

DeGruy, J. A. (2005). *Post traumatic slave syndrome: America's legacy of enduring injury and healing.* Milwaukie, OR: Uptone Press.

Delphin-Rittmon, M. E., Flanagan, E. H., Andres-Hyman, R., Ortiz, J., Amer, M. M., & Davidson, L. (2015). Racial-ethnic differences in access, diagnosis, and outcomes in public-sector inpatient mental health treatment. *Psychological Services, 12,* 158–166. http://dx.doi.org/10.1037/a0038858

Digby, N. T. (2011). Mindful, liberating social action: Gustavo Gutiérrez and Thich Nhat Hanh. In *Dissertation Abstracts International: Section A. Humanities and Social Sciences, 72*(4-A), 1328.

Dovidio, J. F., Gaertner, S. L., & Pearson, A. R. (2017). Aversive racism and contemporary bias. In C. G. Sibley & F. K. Barlow (Eds.), *The Cambridge handbook of the psychology of prejudice* (pp. 267–294). New York, NY: Cambridge University Press. http://dx.doi.org/ 10.1017/9781316161579.012

Dovidio, J. F., Hewstone, M., Glick, P., & Esses, V. M. (2010). Prejudice, stereotyping and discrimination: Theoretical and empirical overview. In J. F. Dovidio, M. Hewstone, P. Glick, & V. M. Esses (Eds.), *The Sage handbook of prejudice, stereotyping and discrimination* (pp. 3–29). London, England: Sage. http://dx.doi.org/10.4135/9781446200919.n1

Duran, E., Firehammer, J., & Gonzalez, J. (2008). Liberation psychology as the path toward healing cultural soul wounds. *Journal of Counseling & Development, 86,* 288–295. http://dx.doi.org/10.1002/j.1556-6678.2008.tb00511.x

Elisha, O. (2017). Proximations of public religion: Worship, spiritual warfare, and the ritualization of Christian dance. *American Anthropologist, 119,* 73–85. http://dx.doi.org/ 10.1111/aman.12819

Essed, P. (1991). *Understanding everyday racism: An interdisciplinary theory* (Vol. 2). London, England: Sage.

Fedewa, S. A., Ward, E. M., Stewart, A. K., & Edge, S. B. (2010). Delays in adjuvant chemotherapy treatment among patients with breast cancer are more likely in African American and Hispanic populations: A national cohort study 2004–2006. *Journal of Clinical Oncology, 28,* 4135–4141. http://dx.doi.org/10.1200/JCO.2009.27.2427

Gardullo, P. (2007). "Just keeps rollin' along": Rebellions, revolts and radical Black memories of slavery in the 1930s. *Patterns of Prejudice, 41,* 271–301. http://dx.doi.org/ 10.1080/00313220701431427

Gee, G. C., & Verissimo, A. D. O. (2016). Racism and behavioral outcomes over the life course. In A. N. Alvarez, C. T. H. Liang, & H. A. Neville (Eds.), *The cost of racism for People of Color: Contextualizing experiences of discrimination* (pp. 133–162). Washington, DC: American Psychological Association. http://dx.doi.org/10.1037/14852-007

Gibbons, F. X., Etcheverry, P. E., Stock, M. L., Gerrard, M., Weng, C. Y., Kiviniemi, M., & O'Hara, R. E. (2010). Exploring the link between racial discrimination and substance use: What mediates? What buffers? *Journal of Personality and Social Psychology, 99,* 785–801. http://dx.doi.org/10.1037/a0019880

Gomez, M. (2018, October 16). White woman who blocked Black neighbor from building is fired. *The New York Times.* Retrieved from https://www.nytimes.com/ 2018/10/15/us/hilary-brooke-apartment-patty-st-louis.html

Graham, J. R., Calloway, A., & Roemer, L. (2015). The buffering effects of emotion regulation in the relationship between experiences of racism and anxiety in a Black American sample. *Cognitive Therapy and Research, 39,* 553–563. http://dx.doi.org/ 10.1007/s10608-015-9682-8

Greer, T. M., & Spalding, A. (2017). The role of age in understanding the psychological effects of racism for African Americans. *Cultural Diversity and Ethnic Minority Psychology, 23,* 588–594. http://dx.doi.org/10.1037/cdp0000148

Grills, C. N., Aird, E. G., & Rowe, D. (2016). Breathe, baby, breathe: Clearing the way for the emotional emancipation of Black people. *Cultural Studies—Critical Methodologies, 16*, 333–343. http://dx.doi.org/10.1177/1532708616634839

Hadley, S., & Yancy, G. (Eds.). (2012). *Therapeutic uses of rap and hip-hop.* New York, NY: Routledge/Taylor & Francis. http://dx.doi.org/10.4324/9780203806012

Hunter, M. L. (2002). "If you're light you're alright" light skin color as social capital for women of color. *Gender & Society, 16*, 175–193. http://dx.doi.org/10.1177/0891243202016002003

Hunter, M. L. (2007). The persistent problem of colorism: Skin tone, status, and inequality. *Sociology Compass, 1*, 237–254. http://dx.doi.org/10.1111/j.1751-9020.2007.00006.x

Jones, C. P. (2000). Levels of racism: A theoretic framework and a gardener's tale. *American Journal of Public Health, 90*, 1212–1215. http://dx.doi.org/10.2105/AJPH.90.8.1212

Kaholokula, J. K. (2016). Racism and physical health disparities. In A. N. Alvarez, C. T. H. Liang, & H. A. Neville (Eds.), *The cost of racism for People of Color: Contextualizing experiences of discrimination* (pp. 163–188). Washington, DC: American Psychological Association. http://dx.doi.org/10.1037/14852-008

King, R. H. (2015). Introduction: The Civil Rights Movement, a retrospective. *Patterns of Prejudice, 49*, 435–439. http://dx.doi.org/10.1080/0031322X.2015.1103438

Kirkinis, K., Pieterse, A. L., Martin, C., Agiliga, A., & Brownell, A. (2018, August 30). Racism, racial discrimination, and trauma: A systematic review of the social science literature. *Ethnicity & Health*, 1–21. http://dx.doi.org/10.1080/13557858.2018.1514453

Kwate, N. O. A., & Goodman, M. S. (2015). Cross-sectional and longitudinal effects of racism on mental health among residents of Black neighborhoods in New York City. *American Journal of Public Health, 105*, 711–718. http://dx.doi.org/10.2105/AJPH.2014.302243

Lee, B., Kellett, P., Seghal, K., & Van den Berg, C. (2018). Breaking the silence of racism injuries: A community-driven study. *International Journal of Migration, Health and Social Care, 14*(1), 1–14. http://dx.doi.org/10.1108/IJMHSC-01-2016-0003

Lewis, J. A., Mendenhall, R., Harwood, S. A., & Huntt, M. B. (2013). Coping with gendered racial microaggressions among Black women college students. *Journal of Black American Studies, 17*(1), 51–73. http://dx.doi.org/10.1007/s12111-012-9219-0

Martín-Baró, I. (1994). *Writings for a liberation psychology* (A. Aron & S. Corne, Eds.). Cambridge, MA: Harvard University Press.

Mathews, T. J., & Johnson, G. S. (2015). Skin complexion in the twenty-first century: The impact of colorism on Black American women. *Race, Gender, & Class, 22*, 248–274.

Mereish, E. H., N'cho, H. S., Green, C. E., Jernigan, M. M., & Helms, J. E. (2016). Discrimination and depressive symptoms among Black American men: Moderated-mediation effects of ethnicity and self-esteem. *Behavioral Medicine, 42*, 190–196. http://dx.doi.org/10.1080/08964289.2016.1150804

Metzl, J. M. (2010). *The protest psychosis: How schizophrenia became a black disease.* Boston, MA: Beacon Press.

Nadal, K. L. (2018). *Microaggressions and traumatic stress: Theory, research, and clinical treatment* (pp. 53–70). Washington, DC: American Psychological Association. http://dx.doi.org/10.1037/0000073-004

Nelson, A. R. (2003). Unequal treatment: Report of the Institute of Medicine on racial and ethnic disparities in healthcare. *The Annals of Thoracic Surgery, 76*, S1377–S1381. http://dx.doi.org/10.1016/S0003-4975(03)01205-0

Paradies, Y. (2006). A systematic review of empirical research on self-reported racism and health. *International Journal of Epidemiology, 35*, 888–901. http://dx.doi.org/10.1093/ije/dyl056

Payne, J. S. (2014). Social determinants affecting major depressive disorder: Diagnostic accuracy for Black American men. *Best Practices in Mental Health, 10*(2), 78–95.

Phillips, F. B. (1990). NTU psychotherapy: An Afrocentric approach. *Journal of Black Psychology, 17*, 55–74. http://dx.doi.org/10.1177/00957984900171005

Pieterse, A. L., Todd, N. R., Neville, H. A., & Carter, R. T. (2012). Perceived racism and mental health among Black American adults: A meta-analytic review. *Journal of Counseling Psychology, 59*, 1–9. http://dx.doi.org/10.1037/a0026208

Prilleltensky, I. (1996). Human, moral, and political values for an emancipatory psychology. *The Humanistic Psychologist, 24*, 307–324. http://dx.doi.org/10.1080/08873267.1996.9986859

Pyke, K. D. (2010). What is internalized racial oppression and why don't we study it? Acknowledging racism's hidden injuries. *Sociological Perspectives, 53*, 551–572. http://dx.doi.org/10.1525/sop.2010.53.4.551

Sadler, M. S., Correll, J., Park, B., & Judd, C. M. (2012). The world is not black and white: Racial bias in the decision to shoot in a multiethnic context. *Journal of Social Issues, 68*, 286–313. http://dx.doi.org/10.1111/j.1540-4560.2012.01749.x

Sanchez-Hucles, J. V. (2016). Womanist therapy with Black women. In T. Bryant-Davis & L. Comas-Díaz (Eds.), *Womanist and mujerista psychologies: Voices of fire, acts of courage* (pp. 69–92). Washington, DC: American Psychological Association. http://dx.doi.org/10.1037/14937-004

Smith, S. L. (1996). Neither victim nor villain: Nurse Eunice Rivers, the Tuskegee Syphilis Experiment, and public health work. *Journal of Women's History, 8*, 95–113. http://dx.doi.org/10.1353/jowh.2010.0446

Soto, A., Smith, T. B., Griner, D., Domenech Rodríguez, M., & Bernal, G. (2018). Cultural adaptations and therapist multicultural competence: Two meta-analytic reviews. *Journal of Clinical Psychology: In Session, 74*, 1907–1923. http://dx.doi.org/10.1002/jclp.22679

Speight, S. L. (2007). Internalized racism: One more piece of the puzzle. *The Counseling Psychologist, 35*, 126–134. http://dx.doi.org/10.1177/0011000006295119

Spencer, S. A. (2006). An international fugitive: Henry Box Brown, anti-imperialism, resistance and slavery. *Social Identities, 12*, 227–248. http://dx.doi.org/10.1080/13504630600583411

Substance Abuse and Mental Health Services Administration. (2015). *Racial/ethnic differences in mental health service use among adults* (HHS Publication No. SMA-15-4906). Rockville, MD: Author.

Sue, D. W. (2003). Cultural competence in the treatment of ethnic minority populations. In Council of National Psychological Associations for the Advancement of Ethnic Minority Interests (Ed.), *Psychological treatment of ethnic minority populations* (pp. 4–7). Washington, DC: Association of Black Psychologists.

Sue, D. W., Capodilupo, C. M., Torino, G. C., Bucceri, J. M., Holder, A. M., Nadal, K. L., & Esquilin, M. (2007). Racial microaggressions in everyday life: Implications for clinical practice. *American Psychologist, 62*, 271–286. http://dx.doi.org/10.1037/0003-066X.62.4.271

Szymanski, D. M., & Lewis, J. A. (2016). Gendered racism, coping, identity centrality, and Black American college women's psychological distress. *Psychology of Women Quarterly, 40*, 229–243. http://dx.doi.org/10.1177/0361684315616113

Szymanski, D. M., & Stewart, D. N. (2010). Racism and sexism as correlates of Black American women's psychological distress. *Sex Roles, 63*, 226–238. http://dx.doi.org/10.1007/s11199-010-9788-0

Thomas, A. J., Witherspoon, K. M., & Speight, S. L. (2008). Gendered racism, psychological distress, and coping styles of African American women. *Cultural Diversity and Ethnic Minority Psychology, 14*, 307–314. http://dx.doi.org/10.1037/1099-9809.14.4.307

Thompson, C. E., & Alfred, D. M. (2009). Black liberation psychology and practice. In H. A. Neville, B. M. Tynes, & S. O. Utsey (Eds.), *Handbook of Black American psychology* (pp. 483–494). Thousand Oaks, CA: Sage.

Trout, J., Dokecki, P. R., Newbrough, J. R., & O'Gorman, R. T. (2003). Action research on leadership for community development in West Africa and North America:

A joining of liberation theology and community psychology. *Journal of Community Psychology, 31,* 129–148. http://dx.doi.org/10.1002/jcop.10043

Tyson, E. H. (2003). Rap music in social work practice with African-American and Latino youth: A conceptual model with practical applications. *Journal of Human Behavior in the Social Environment, 8*(4), 1–21. http://dx.doi.org/10.1300/J137v08n04_01

U.S. Department of Health and Human Services. (2001). *Mental health: Culture, race, and ethnicity—A supplement to mental health: A report of the Surgeon General.* Rockville, MD: U.S. Department of Health & Human Services, Public Health Service, Office of the Surgeon General.

Watts, R. J., & Flanagan, C. (2007). Pushing the envelope on youth civic engagement: A developmental and liberation psychology perspective. *Journal of Community Psychology, 35,* 779–792. http://dx.doi.org/10.1002/jcop.20178

Whaley, A. L. (2001). Cultural mistrust and mental health services for African Americans: A review and meta-analysis. *The Counseling Psychologist, 29,* 513–531. http://dx.doi.org/10.1177/0011000001294003

Williams, D. R., & Williams-Morris, R. (2000). Racism and mental health: The African American experience. *Ethnicity & Health, 5,* 243–268. http://dx.doi.org/10.1080/713667453

Wingfield, A. H. (2007). The modern mammy and the angry Black man: Black American professionals' experiences with gendered racism in the workplace. *Race, Gender, & Class, 14,* 196–212.

Wyatt, S. B., Williams, D. R., Calvin, R., Henderson, F. C., Walker, E. R., & Winters, K. (2003). Racism and cardiovascular disease in African Americans. *The American Journal of the Medical Sciences, 325,* 315–331. http://dx.doi.org/10.1097/00000441-200306000-00003

11

Liberation Psychology and LGBTQ+ Communities

Naming Colonization, Uplifting Resilience, and Reclaiming Ancient His-Stories, Her-Stories, and T-Stories

Anneliese A. Singh, Brean'a Parker, Anushka R. Aqil, and Falon Thacker

When we accepted the invitation to write this chapter about queer and trans communities and *psicología de la liberación*, we were both excited and nervous. We are four authors (one faculty and three doctoral students) who straddle the lines of academia and street activism as queer, nonbinary, cisgender, and straight people. We have each engaged in both scholar and campus activism, alongside university and community education, and we have each sought to uplift queer and trans people and communities as we have infused the tenets of liberation psychology across each of these artificial boundaries. We have also experienced successes and setbacks, as well as liberation and heartbreak in this process. We are excited because we can have a larger dialogue with you, the reader, about how we always do our work—queer and trans education, activism, empowerment, liberation, and more—with a firm grounding in the very queer and trans historical roots precolonization. Liberation psychology is not just something we write about—it is something we strive to live. Therefore, you will read a mixture of a *testimonio* voice—our personal liberation work (some of our primary sources of information are our lived experiences), as well as our academic voice (where it is important for us to cite the lineage of scholars who have come before us). We are also excited because we have a strong intersectional perspective in doing this work that is not in name only. We know not only that our race/ethnicities have influenced every single moment of our journeys of queer, trans, straight, and cisgender

http://dx.doi.org/10.1037/0000198-012
Liberation Psychology: Theory, Method, Practice, and Social Justice, L. Comas-Díaz and E. Torres Rivera (Editors)

liberation. For instance, we are strongly aware that our gender and sexual orientation identity journeys are influenced by societal racism that is strongly rooted in anti-Blackness. So, it is important that we uplift the Black feminist scholars (Bowleg, 2008; Collins, 2001; Crenshaw, 1991) who fought (and continue to fight) for the ideas of intersectionality, power, privilege, and oppression regarding gender, race/ethnicity, and social class to take root within a largely White and Western scholarship.

At the same time, we are nervous, because in writing this chapter, we must confront our own academic privilege—and the academic privilege that rests within liberation psychology itself—to ensure that as we actually *do* speak truth to power. For instance, many of our most beloved and effective queer and trans community organizers and freedom fighters in the Deep South, where we live and do liberatory work, will never use many of the terms we describe in this chapter. Instead, they are busy living out liberation tenets. At the same time, we see the larger possibility of liberation for all queer and trans people in this dialogue between these communities and liberation psychology. As we began to dig into our writing and reflected on our own experiences of queer and trans liberation and working toward a more just world for LGBTQ+ (lesbian, gay, bisexual, trans, queer, and more) communities, we realized that a larger dialogue bridging queer and trans academic communities and the queer and trans grassroots organizers could help liberate us all. In addition, we realized that queer and trans communities are perhaps the true originators of a lived experience of what we now call liberation psychology— the communities of ongoing queer and trans resilience, resistance, and freedom fighters, who find ways to live and thrive despite a larger postcolonial world that wants to erase our very bodies, minds, and spirits (Feinberg, 1996; Stryker, 2008). We realized that the attempts to erase our queer and trans communities have not only failed but that we have sustained these cis-heteronormative attacks to engage in queer and trans *concientización* (consciousness-raising) more fiercely and strengthen our communities more intelligently (Feinberg, 1996; Stryker, 2008). We have also each engaged in racial justice work within queer and trans communities, exploring the ways that racism has shown up in the ways we learn about queer and trans history and the ways that we continue to see and experience White supremacy within our queer and trans liberation movements.

So, in writing this chapter, we bring all of these emotions to our writing as we describe applications of liberation psychology (Martín-Baró, 1994) to queer and trans communities. In doing so, we examine colonization trajectories queer and trans People of Color and White communities have experienced as a strategy of *concientización* in individual and community settings to reclaim experiences and stories of queer and trans people across the globe. We highlight practices of resilience that queer and trans communities have developed over time to sustain ourselves in the face of oppression, discrimination, and decimation—with a special focus on applying these practices to individual and community change efforts (Singh, 2018). Drawing on Singh's (2016a, 2016b) challenge to mental health practitioners to move beyond trans-affirmative counseling to liberatory approaches to counseling trans people grounded in liberation psychology, we expand their call to counseling and psychological work with queer and trans individuals and communities, addressing how helping professionals and other social justice change agents can use liberation psychology tenets in their change work. As we do so, we unpack binary understandings of gender, interrogate internalized oppression of not only queer and trans people but also of straight and cisgender people to identify a holistic approach of liberation psychology.

WHY A LIBERATION PSYCHOLOGY FOR QUEER AND TRANS COMMUNITIES?

When we say queer and trans communities are the originators of living a liberation psychology, we do not seek to take anything away from Martín-Baró (1994) and other liberation scholars, such as Frantz Fanon and Michael Foucault. At the same time, we notice the silences in liberation psychology about queer and trans people in much of the liberation psychology literature (Nyland & Waddle's 2016 article, "Breaking Out of the Gender Binary: Liberating Transgender Prisoners," is a notable exception), which likely reflected an even deeper erasure of potential liberation that they and others at the time could, or would, name. It makes sense, therefore, that there are so few even conceptual explorations of liberation psychology for queer and trans people, much less empirical work (hence the importance of *testimonio* in our writing). So, to bridge Martín-Baró's work and queer and trans mental health is a potential liberation of even liberation psychology itself—and simultaneously the opportunity to correct this silence.

Why would there be silence within Martín-Baró's original work about queer and trans liberation? We believe this is due to the role and promise of Western and Christian colonization; colonizers sought to take over lands of Indigenous people and sought (often violently) to convert Indigenous communities (who were often embraced by their cultures as holders of the sacred rites and rituals of their tribes) to take on Christian values and practices, which included antiqueer and trans polemics (Akken & Taracena, 2007). Martín-Baró was born and raised in Spain, land of the original Christian and Western colonizers. He became a Jesuit priest, so it is more likely than not that he had no official training on or awareness of issues of concern to queer and trans people, as the church often has had little to no concern for our communities (see http://www.uca.edu.sv/coleccion-digital-IMB/biografia/).

As we have wrestled with this erasure of queer and trans communities within liberation psychology itself, we began to wonder what, if Martín-Baró were alive to speak and bridge this gap, would he say? What would this conversation "look like" if queer and trans street activists and community organizers, and our ancestors, joined the dialogue? We explored these wonderings in the framing of following key liberation psychology tenets (Martín-Baró, 1994).

Concientización

Martín-Baró (1994) centered concientización as a key foundation of liberation psychology. Leaning on Freire's (1970/2000) work *Pedagogy of the Oppressed*, Martín-Baró believed that historically oppressed communities could move toward social justice action once they had awareness and knowledge about both historical and current systems of oppression that created lived experiences of disadvantages for them in society. Concientización has been a crucial aspect of queer and trans resilience and resistance (both discussed in the next sections), because queer and trans people have long had to teach ourselves about ourselves (Singh, 2016a, 2016b). This teaching has included not just learning information that our LGBTQ+ identities are valid and exist (Chang & Singh, 2017) but also includes unlearning false binaries of gender and sexual orientation (Nyland & Waddle, 2016). Just as there are not only two genders, there is not just one sexual orientation. Instead, in queer and trans communities, we relearn and embrace (ideally, and it is still true that many of us don't survive and thrive long in this world because of extensive societal antiqueer and trans oppression) that gender and sexuality are fluid and that there are as many gender and sexual orientation identities as there are people on the earth. Every single person has a unique expression and embodiment of gender and sexuality (Singh, Meng, & Hansen, 2014).

Deideologizing Psychology

According to Martín-Baró's (1994) liberation psychology, psychology as a field had to be deideologized if it were to be in service of freedom and support of the rights of the oppressed. Deideologizing psychology refers to demystifying its practices. For Martín-Baró, there could be no psychological jargon, and instead a liberated psychology must insist on rooting out internalized oppression that was rooted in dominant power and control by the oppressor. In other words, there must be a deconstruction of the deficit-driven language used in psychology that is rooted in socialized internalized oppression peddled by the upholders of psychology—the mental health industrial complex—which includes all of us as mental health clinicians (Singh, 2016a, 2016b). In the ongoing work of concientización that queer and trans communities must do just to find ourselves as people and as communities, we have always had to deideologize ourselves and root out our internalized oppression to survive. When our families are living with colonized and oppressive ideas of who we "should" be instead of accepting us for who we are in our genders and sexual orientations, we have to leave our homes by choice, or because we are forced out, to find supportive communities to house us and remind us of our inner worth and sacredness. But we also get kicked out of our homes and families for being LGBTQ+. We often are taught to internalize dominant ideas that we are not worthy. As a result, many of us do not survive this internalized oppression and free our minds as the liberation psychology project of deideologizing demands. A survey of approximately 6,000 trans people suggested that more than 40% of the respondents had attempted suicide at least once, and that for trans People of Color, structural racism combined with antitrans stigma was a lethal combination for our community (James et al., 2016). A similar story exists with our young people, as queer and trans youth comprise the highest rate of suicide completion for the 16- to 25-year-old demographic cohort. What helps those of us who survive? Family acceptance, social support, ongoing resilience to anti-LGBTQ+ oppression, and advocacy are crucial aspects of our survival, thriving, and liberation (Singh, 2018). Literally, the only way we can survive is to externalize the oppression we were taught by those closest to us in our families, schools, religious institutions and more to believe.

Problematización

One of the ways that Martín-Baró (1994) proposed that psychology could move towards being a discipline actually supporting the liberation of the oppressed—as opposed to a mental health industrial complex that supports the dominant and status quo majority (in our discussion—cisgender and straight polemics)—is to question where the "problem" of psychology actually rests. In our mental health disciplines, we typically look to and engage with psychiatry to uphold the fifth edition of the *Diagnostic and Statistical Manual of Mental Disorders* (*DSM–5*; American Psychiatric Association, 2013). However, in doing so, we uphold the anti-liberation psychology idea that mental health disorders are located in individuals, as opposed to in society (Singh, 2016a, 2016b).

This has been true over time with how psychology and psychiatry have treated and diagnosed queer and trans people as having an "illness" because of our gender and sexual orientation identities as opposed to naming societal anti-LGBTQ+ bias as the root of colonized "disorders" that have been assigned to our community (e.g., the history of homosexuality being listed as a disorder and included under the paraphilias; the development of gender identity disorder and the continued inclusion of gender dysphoria as a mental disorder as opposed to a health need and concern). So, problematizing psychology (questioning who the goals and aims of psychology are truly written by and for) from a queer and trans perspective in liberation psychology is to demand that cisgender and straight conceptions of mental health be removed. We are angry that there is not a "Cisgenderism and Heterosexism Disorder Not Otherwise Specified" in the *DSM*, nor are there disorders naming the realities of racism, ableism, classism, and other oppressions that uphold the dominant status quo in our society. Therefore, problematizing for queer and trans people means that we do so in a specific manner—the aim of which must always be our own liberation from cisgender and straight narratives of mental health and developing our own true reality.

Realismo Crítico

Realismo crítico is the development of critical consciousness by people who have experienced oppression, injustices, and inequities. One of the most exciting components of Martín-Baró's (1994) *psicología de la liberación* is his focus on counterstories to oppression. He argued that once problems are challenged and deideologized, historically oppressed peoples and communities could then develop their own theories of solutions and liberations. There is a common chant you will hear among queer People of Color, leaning on the words and Black liberation work of freedom fighter Assata Shakur: "It is our duty to fight for our freedom. It is our duty to win. We must love each other and support each other. We have nothing to lose but our chains."

We bring these important words into the bridging of liberation psychology with queer and trans communities, but the actual reality and birthplace of both our LGBTQ+ communities and resistances/freedom movements are in People of Color communities. This is our realismo crítico. Precolonization on each continents, queer and trans people were often the holders of the sacred rites and rituals of their tribes. Their genders and sexualities were evidence of their value, markedly different from the colonization and postcolonization realities of LGBTQ+ communities. In addition, our modern LGBTQ+ rights movement was catalyzed by the riot at the Stonewall Inn bar in June 1969 and led by Latinx and Black activists—Sylvia Rivera and Marsha P. Johnson, respectively, among many others (discussed at more length later in the chapter). As a queer and trans community, we have had to look deeper underneath a colonized and White-washed telling of the Stonewall "gay" liberation movement to find our revolutionary trans women of color leaders (Riemer & Brown, 2019; Román, 2013).

In the next section, we explore these four liberation psychology tenets—concientización, deideologizing psychology, problematización, and realism crítico—to review the queer and trans resilience and coping research and note how LGBTQ+ communities have long taken up these principles in our struggle to live, resist, survive, and, ideally, thrive.

LIBERATION PSYCHOLOGY AND QUEER AND TRANS RESILIENCE AND COPING

To describe queer and trans resilience, we must return to the origins of resilience research, which dates back to the 1960s, and critique these conceptions. Resilience was originally defined as positive adaptation despite adversity (Luthar, 2015). Although this has been the more common understanding of resilience, it was in the 1980s that the field of resilience research expanded to create a place for multiple conceptualizations of resilience that went beyond individual capacities. One conceptualization is resilience as a social ecological process. Initially theorized for youth in the 1990s, resilience as a social ecological process is founded on two principles: (a) individuals rely on both their individual capacities and social ecologies to provide them with resilience-promoting resources and (b) resilience-promoting resources are context-dependent and unique to different populations (Ungar, 2011). Another conceptualization of resilience recognizes that resilience fluctuates and shifts over time and is not a fixed or a permanent state of being for anyone (Luthar, 2015). Given recent shifts in conceptualizing resilience, the current general consensus is that resilience is context dependent, not a specific trait (Masten, 2001; Tugade, 2011; Zautra, Affleck, Tennen, Reich, & Davis, 2005) and that resilience can and does occur at both the individual and community levels based on the context and adverse event (Bockting, Miner, Swinburne Romine, Hamilton, & Coleman, 2013; Breslow et al., 2015; Erich, Tittsworth, & Kersten, 2010; Figueroa & Zoccola, 2015; Hartling, 2008; Huang, 1995; Von Culin, Tsukayama, & Duckworth, 2014; Wilson et al., 2016). Resilience has also been studied as the processes used by historically marginalized groups to navigate oppression (Elsass, 1992); these resilience strategies for queer and trans people have included being involved in LGBTQ+ activist communities, cultivating hope, and intentional development of liberated communities (Singh, Hays, & Watson, 2011; Singh & McKleroy, 2011).

This comprehensive approach is key for understanding how queer and trans individuals and communities experience and enact resilience and resilience-related behaviors. It is useful, therefore, to distinguish resilience from coping given that historically the two concepts have often been conflated. *Coping*, however, is defined as individual adaptive behaviors (Folkman & Lazarus, 1980), while *resilience* is a multilevel process influenced by context. By separating the two processes, how individuals and communities survive and thrive with multiple influencing factors (e.g., environment, access and barriers to resources) can be comprehensively understood.

For queer and trans individuals and communities, and especially for queer and trans communities of color, research on resilience and coping has shown that additional considerations (e.g., examining systemic oppression and discrimination at individual and community levels) of how resilience operates are necessary given the multiple levels of oppression faced by these communities (e.g., antitrans bias, heterosexism, cissexism, racism). Meyer (2015), Singh and McKleroy (2011), and Singh et al. (2011, 2014) posed that given the intersecting experiences of these communities (e.g., gender identity, sexual orientation), resilience for queer and trans communities then exists on two levels: (a) at the individual level with self-acceptance and (b) at the community-level based on available tangible and intangible resources. This context- and community-specific conceptualization of resilience also aligns with liberation psychology's four tenets—concientización, deideologizing psychology, problematización, and realismo crítico—given that queer and trans communities engage and participate with the aforementioned principles to access and exhibit resilience.

For example, in researching how resilience occurs among LGBTQ youth, Asakura (2017) found that as youth worked on accepting themselves, they developed a critical consciousness. This self-reflection then pushed them to seek out like-minded individuals (often activist communities) and engage in a culture of "breaking the silence" and exposing systems of oppression. This practice exemplifies concientización as this community dives into examining the levels of oppression to identify mechanisms toward their own liberation. Others have written of mechanisms through which psychologists and other practitioners can emulate the principle of deideologizing psychology and foster resiliency within queer and trans communities by training a workforce that acknowledges power differentials based on social identity, engages in practices of critical reflection and understanding of contextual experiences, and builds affirming and accessible spaces (Goodman et al., 2004; Grothaus, McAuliffe, Danner, & Doyle, 2008; Moane, 2008). Within these practices, problematización is also encouraged to facilitate understanding of the historical context that has resulted in the marginalization of queer and trans communities and generating a will to challenge the status quo by focusing on social justice–centered mental health practice (Singh, 2016a, 2016b).

By engaging indirectly and directly with these four tenets of liberation psychology, queer and trans individuals and communities exhibit resilience as they see themselves and access spaces that are invested in their liberation while navigating oppressive structures and continued discrimination. Next, we delve deeper into our queer and trans individual and community resilience and coping into our history of LGBTQ+ liberation movements to integrate these tenets with our resistance, asking the question of what can we learn from queer and trans movements that relate to the practice of liberation psychology?

QUEER AND TRANS RESISTANCE AND LIBERATION MOVEMENTS

Queer and trans communities historically and currently use movements to address and resist the heteronormative, trans-antagonistic, and discriminatory policies and social systems within the United States (D'Emilio, 2014). These movements, documented as far back as the 1940s and 1950s with the Mattachine Society and the Daughters of Bilitis, aim to provide communal space of affirmation, coping, and healing for communities of people who shared sexual or gender identities, or both. These groups and organizations were created for various purposes, such as advocacy for queer and trans rights through political reform; addressing harassment and violence by the criminal justice system and other public institutions; providing resources for queer and trans youth; and promoting visibility of lived realities of people who agitate static sexual orientation and gender identity norms (D'Emilio, 2014; Gossett, Gossett, & Lewis, 2012; Morris, n.d.). These movements are often depicted as a current occurrence cited by instances of resistance to violence and intimidation, such as the famous Stonewall Inn riot, when police officers agitated and harassed queer and trans individuals who courageously fought back for their right to occupy public space and not be harassed by police (Schlaffer, 2016).

However, there are countless other mobilizations for queer and trans move-ments that centered myriad social equity and justice issues within urban cities and rural areas alike. As we have noted, liberation psychology provides us with four tenets, concientización, deideologizing psychology, problematización, and realismo crítico, that can guide us in moving away from traditional psy-chology promoting Western, White, and Eurocentric conceptions of wellness to a discipline more informed by how equity and justice relate to well-being (Tate, Torres Rivera, Brown, & Skaistis, 2013). Queer and trans movements are instrumental as a model that enacts the values of liberation psychology in real praxis. The following section seeks to answer the question: What can we learn from queer and trans movements that relate to the practice of liberation psychology?

LINEAGE OF QUEER, GENDER DIVERSE, AND TRANS RESISTANCE

Queer and trans people have been resisting within other movements since the beginning of time; however, historical records have focused too much on cisgender White people and communities when documenting the instrumental queer and trans activists and organizers of earlier revolutionary movements (Singh, 2016a, 2016b). For example, although most people associate non-violent protest for civil rights (e.g., bus boycotts, the March on Washington) with Dr. Martin Luther King, Jr., Bayard Rustin was instrumental in influencing Dr. King's adoption of nonviolent strategies. Despite his contributions of bring-ing Gandhi's nonviolent protest techniques to civil rights leaders and organi-zations, and impactful strategies to illuminate racist discrimination, violence, and inequality, Rustin was erased from the historical recollection of the Civil Rights Movement because he was openly queer (D'Emilio, 2014). More recently, Black Lives Matter founders, two who identify as queer women and one who identifies as straight, used social media platforms, along with countless grass-roots organizations and networks to promote the awareness of the movement for all Black lives. However, their major contribution, leadership, and Black queer identities are often erased in the narrative of the origin of the Black Lives Matter movement (Garza, 2016). Opal Tometi, Patrisse Khan-Cullors, and Alicia Garza have continued to dedicate their efforts to promoting the lives of all Black people, including those relegated to the margins or erasure: the undocumented, those who are or have been incarcerated, individuals with disabilities, people who are in unemployed or underemployed, and queer and trans individuals who experience violence and death by state-sanctioned violence. The intentional *straightening* of the narratives of activism is associ-ated with heteropatriarchy supporting the suppression of marginalized voices and the narrative of erasure of the invaluable impact queer and trans activists have contributed to liberation movements. Liberation psychology calls us to begin to unpack the history from the standpoint of the oppressed to understand the reality of lived experience, and we start here to understand the trajectory of queer and trans liberation movements within Indigenous land we now call the United States.

As mentioned previously, earlier movements for queer people were localized in both large urban cities and small rural towns as spaces for building relationships—having conversations about daily experiences of stigma, prejudice, and bias (Nadal, 2013; Stulberg, 2018; Watkins, 2017). In addition to finding affinity in shared spaces, gay rights social organizations such as the Mattachine Society and others, addressed the needs and barriers existing for queer and trans communities (Nadal, 2013). The Gay Activists Alliance and other lesbian and gay organizations began examining antigay policies and pushing for affirming political reform that would allow both visibility and access to societal opportunities regardless of sexual orientation (Bailey, 2018; Ellison, n.d.; Gossett et al., 2012). These spaces embodied opportunities to self-define, celebrate, and acknowledge the value and beauty within a shared identity countering messages that were fueled by hate and prejudice. In line with these societies throughout history queer and trans People of Color began organizing and looking to other movements that modeled effective mobilization, action, and resistance. Gay liberation activists observed and modeled their strategies after tactics of the Black Panther Party, who strategically called out racially motivated harassment by police, while instilling cultural value and positive messages to negate dominant messages of inferiority for Black communities.

In that same spirit, queer and trans People of Color began creating their own organizations and societies where they were able to discuss daily experience of intersectional oppression given marginalized racialized and citizenship identities in addition to their sexual identities. In these spaces, queer and trans People of Color were able to have critical conversations about how to promote visibility about intersectionality, that is, double or sometimes triple marginalization in a society and community that primarily focused on the single identity of sexual orientation (Alimahomed, 2010). Organizations such as Salsa Sistas, Familia, Trans Queer Liberation Movement, Black and White Gay Men Together, The National Coalition of Black Lesbians, Gays, Dykes Against Racism Everywhere, Black Lesbians, and the Feminist Combahee River Collective are just a few of the many groups that began examining the intersecting power structures of employment discrimination, police harassment and violence, and health care discrimination, as well as how intergroup biases played out within their organizations.

These organizations provided spaces to have critical dialogues, organize and mobilize demonstrations, and build coalitions to document the unique experiences of being queer and trans within the United States. In addition to the emerging queer movement, trans activists such as Marsha P. Johnson and Sylvia Rivera used riots and street activism to protest the violence, inhumane treatment, and discrimination the trans community experienced both within and outside of queer liberation movements. In addition to demonstrations, activist shared the struggles of being criminalized as street workers; stalked by law enforcement; and denied access to equal and affordable health care, employment, and housing (Morris, n.d.; Schlaffer, 2016; Simon, 2016). Trans People of Color leaders were motivated to develop their own resources in response to pervasive and structural societal challenges, such as housing insecurity, substance abuse, HIV/AIDS, and sanctioned police violence. For instance, STAR (Street Transvestite Action Revolutionaries) was an advocacy group that served as a shelter for queer and trans youth experiencing housing insecurity, where these young people could experience safety and a chosen family when their own families had disowned them. It is telling that decades later, the need for these organizations remains, which demonstrates the substantial ways public and social policies continue to fail queer and trans communities.

The purpose of queer and trans liberation movements has been to develop *concientización*. For instance, many queer and trans leaders within these movements were raising their own consciousness about the internalized anti-LGBTQ+ messages from society and family members labeling them as defective, immoral, and inherently bad. As a result, these organizations not only worked to illuminate the lived experiences with being on the margins of an antiqueer and antitrans society, they also found ways to celebrate their identity and existence despite their real-life struggles. Celebrations such as Black Ballroom culture, Pride parades, creating annual LGBTQ+ workshops and conferences, and publishing LGBTQ+ newsletters allowed queer and trans activists and members to begin to see themselves as members of a society that shunned them from public view (*Paris Is Burning*; Finch & Livingston, 1990). These spaces offered opportunities for queer and trans people to engage in political and personal work that fought for LGBTQ+-affirming reform that held institutions accountable for creating safe, inclusive, and equitable spaces for queer and trans youth and adults. The different identities within queer and trans resistance movements also provided the opportunity to have difficult dialogue around the racism and other forms of oppression within the LGBTQ community and how this microcosm of people who share sexual or gender identity (or both), reflected the prejudicial stance of the outside world (Gossett et al., 2012; Tate et al., 2013). These movements enlisted people with disability status, low socioeconomic backgrounds, and People of Color to lead conversations and initiatives that brought awareness, consciousness, and distinct narratives of the ways multiple forms of oppression lead to violence, psychological trauma, and inequitable treatment.

Queer and trans liberation movements are also important models for helping people who are straight and cisgender to reflect on social constructs of gender and sexual orientation and how these rigid social identities categories produce more harm than freedom. Also, through a multilayer organizational and mobilization tactics, many of the laws, policies, treatments, and progress that are currently in place have been in response to the tireless work and courageous involvement of queer and trans activists who were dedicated to shifting, overtly and covertly, the narrative of queer and trans community to one that valued the indigenous, multicultural, and intersectional voices of a community that has been able to define and trace the lineage of their resistance work and continued investment in removing the barriers and hardships for all people. In addition to queer and trans advocates and movements, counselors and psychologists are charged with the responsibility and expectation to support and advocate for the liberation of queer and trans communities in counseling and psychotherapy. The following section illustrates the four tenets of liberation psychology and how counselors can integrate liberation psychology in their practice to support and advocate for their clients.

QUEER AND TRANS LIBERATION PSYCHOLOGY: MOVING FORWARD WITH EMBODIMENT AND INTEGRITY

Liberation psychology draws attention to the systemic issues within society and their impacts on mental health (Afuape & Hughes, 2016). This requires the role of the counselor and psychologist to become that of a witness, coparticipant, and a mirror for a therapeutic process through those who have been oppressed so they may discover their own capacities for historical memory, critical analysis, and transformative social action (Tate et al., 2013). Mental health providers operating from a liberation psychology perspective are primarily focused on their clients and the transformation of themselves and their communities. Martín-Baró (1994) suggested that social scientists and practitioners critically reflect and act on the oppressive set of higher education structures and norms that prioritize building credentials over pursuing liberatory change for oppressed populations. The following sections illustrate how counselors can use liberatory practices in their work by employing the tenets of liberation psychology.

Concientización

For counselors to be effective using liberation psychology, they must develop a critical consciousness, to become aware of and involved in an action related to understanding truth (Martín-Baró, 1994). Liberation psychology training calls on counselors and psychologists to focus on and commit to clients and the transformation of both clients and their communities. Engaging in consciousness-raising experiences can help counselors avoid unintended harm to clients (Ratts & Greenleaf, 2017). Counselors and psychologists must connect their own experiences of liberation to the reasons why they work with their clients. Within and across differences, liberation is connected. As a profession, mental health providers are responsible for knowing and understanding how their liberation is connected to the liberation of their clients within and outside of counseling. This is accomplished through knowledge, application of their clients' identities, and advocacy skills (Singh, 2016b). One strategy used in a graduate program included encouraging students to reflect on their personal histories as they relate to each other; they are asked to focus reflectively on their reactions to the salient aspects of one another's identities, such as age, gender, race, ethnicity, class background, sexual orientation, religion-spirituality, physical ability or challenge, and experiences of privilege and oppression (Motulsky, Gere, Saleem, & Trantham, 2014).

Deideologizing Psychology

Martín-Baró (1994) argued that for psychology to be relevant to the mental health concerns it seeks to address, it must be reoriented toward the lived experience of those who experience the most extreme conditions of poverty and oppression. Martín-Baró also brought attention to history, noting that for oppressed populations in particular, it is written from the perspective of the oppressor. This is a critical component of liberation psychology in that, without an understanding of the actual etiology of oppression and subsequent conditions, true understandings from the oppressed cannot be attained.

To engage in the deideologizing of psychology, counselors and psychologists must practice how to name oppressive structures and systems within our society. Mental health providers must be comfortable broaching and naming power differentials, societal barriers, and other dynamics that may create hesitancy for clients to fully engage in the therapeutic process (Motulsky et al., 2014). Mental health providers can engage in role-playing as a part of courses or professional development as it give them an opportunity to practice and receive feedback from faculty and peers. For example, a White mental health provider who works with a client of color will need to name the power structures that exist around racial injustices in society and how they play out in counseling. Mental health providers must be able to communicate their commitment to countering injustices and how they wish to work alongside their client(s).

Problematización

A key step in achieving a socially just and mentally healthy context for oppressed groups is to investigate the dominant messages and embrace the lived experiences of the oppressed (Martín-Baró, 1994). Martín-Baró (1994) pointed out that it is crucial to use the virtues of oppressed peoples when working to improve their lived experiences; this strengths-based approach allows social scientists to depend on those who are oppressed to produce the tools and energy that may lead to liberation. Additionally, he considered problematization a critical aspect of his theory, which is best described as a method for understanding a particular issue faced by oppressed populations from their own perspective (Martín-Baró, 1994).

New perspectives expand the ability of mental health providers to identify necessary action as well as understand how these actions relate to their own experiences (Lewis, Ratts, Paladino, & Toporek, 2011). Mental health providers must look at the roots of systems of oppression that exist within society and around the world. Additionally, they must concurrently explore their own beliefs, norms, and structures of oppression that exist within and outside of their own communities. Doing so allows providers to develop further understanding of their own lived experiences of inequities within oppressive systemic structures while also learning about the experiences of other groups who have different cultural backgrounds and worldviews than them. This may be achieved by having mental health providers explore the stories of those who have been disadvantaged by oppressive systems over time and counter-narratives of people and marginalized groups (Singh, 2016b). Mental health providers should consider how their practice could change as a result of under-standing the stories and counter narratives of people, rather than have their approach be driven by dominant narratives (Singh, 2016a, 2016b).

Realismo Crítico

To become conscious of reality is to become aware of, and involved in, a process of continual discovery and action related to "truth." A liberation psychology perspective emphasizes that prevailing understandings of everyday experience are not the neutral or natural reflection of objective truth (Adams & Kurtiş, 2012). Liberation psychology takes a holistic approach and contextual perspective in which meaning, purpose, values, choice, spirituality, self-acceptance, and self-actualization help form the entire person who is able to take action (Chávez, Fernández, Hipolito-Delgado, & Torres Rivera, 2016). Mental health providers must learn to discuss and reframe what their clients' futures may look like (Chang & Singh, 2017). Mental health providers can do this by using a reflection process and asking themselves questions to explore deep personal experiences of liberation and oppression (Singh, 2016b). Examples of reflection questions include the following: When did I first become aware of my race? When did I first learn my own gender? What has been lost and found in the development of your identities (both privileged and marginalized)? Mental health providers can then begin to see how their own truth and liberation is inherently embedded and connected to their clients' truth and liberation.

CONCLUSION

Liberation psychology holds the vision that people should be liberated through counseling and psychotherapy and that counseling should focus on human potential and growth (Chávez et al., 2016). Martín-Baró (1994) developed liberation psychology in response to traditional psychology's perspective, which neglected the influence of social structures and historical contexts in understanding individual behavior and concerns. However, history tells us that the virtues of queer and trans folks were absent in the development of

Martín-Baró's work that is deeply rooted in Christianity and Christian principles. Therefore, liberation psychology is enriched when its attention is turned to queer and trans histories, identities, and trajectories. This chapter calls attention to this gap within liberation psychology and addresses how it can play a role in the healing and resilience of queer and trans communities. In doing so, it is clear that not only queer and trans people are important in liberation psychology; however, the questioning and interrogation of gender and sexuality is also crucial for the liberation of cisgender and straight people.

Finally, liberation psychology invokes an individual's inseparability from sociopolitical structures and asserts that the political has an impact on the psychological (Russell & Bohan, 2007). Using liberation psychology with queer and trans clients enhances the work of liberation psychology as an approach that can allow queer and trans clients to trust mental health providers because they historically have learned to distrust helping professionals who use traditional counseling and psychotherapy disaffirming or gatekeeping practices (Singh, 2016a, 2016b). This also enhances the practice of liberation psychology because it allows counselors to practice and use liberatory and affirmative practices in their work. Knowing this, mental health providers can use the strategies outlined in this chapter as a place to begin their practice of liberation psychology tools in their work with queer and trans clients.

REFERENCES

Adams, G., & Kurtiş, T. (2012). Collective memory practices as tools for reconciliation: Perspectives from liberation and cultural psychology. *African Conflict and Peacebuilding Review, 2*(2), 5–28. http://dx.doi.org/10.2979/africonfpeacrevi.2.2.5

Afuape, T., & Hughes, G. (Eds.). (2016). *Liberation practices: Toward emotional wellbeing through dialogue*. New York, NY: Routledge.

Akken, R. V., & Taracena, L. P. (2007). *La visión Indigena de la conquista* [The Indigenous vision of the conquest]. Guatemala City, Guatemala: Serviprensa.

Alimahomed, S. (2010). Thinking outside the rainbow: Women of Color redefining queer politics and identity. *Social Identities, 16*, 151–168. http://dx.doi.org/10.1080/13504631003688849

American Psychiatric Association. (2013). *Diagnostic and statistical manual of mental disorders* (5th ed.). Washington, DC: Author.

Asakura, K. (2017). Paving pathways through the pain: A grounded theory of resilience among lesbian, gay, bisexual, trans, and queer youth. *Journal of Research on Adolescence, 27*, 521–536. http://dx.doi.org/10.1111/jora.12291

Bailey, E. (2018, August 3). Shoulders to stand on: The LGBTQ resistance movement pre-Stonewall. *The Empty Closet*, 525. Retrieved from the Out Alliance website: https://outalliance.org/shoulders-to-stand-on-august-2018-the-lgbtq-resistance-movement-pre-stonewall/

Bockting, W. O., Miner, M. H., Swinburne Romine, R. E., Hamilton, A., & Coleman, E. (2013). Stigma, mental health, and resilience in an online sample of the U.S. transgender population. *American Journal of Public Health, 103*, 943–951. http://dx.doi.org/10.2105/AJPH.2013.301241

Bowleg, L. (2008). When Black + lesbian + woman π Black lesbian woman: The methodological challenges of qualitative and quantitative intersectionality research. *Sex Roles, 59*, 312–325. https://dx.doi.org/10.1007/s11199-008-9400-z

Breslow, A. S., Brewster, M. E., Velez, B. L., Wong, S., Geiger, E., & Soderstrom, B. (2015). Resilience and collective action: Exploring buffers against minority stress for transgender individuals. *Psychology of Sexual Orientation and Gender Diversity, 2,* 253–265. http://dx.doi.org/10.1037/sgd0000117

Chang, S., & Singh, A. A. (2017). Gender and sexual orientation diversity. In A. A. Singh & L. M. Dickey (Eds.), *Affirmative counseling and psychological practice with transgender and gender nonconforming clients.* Washington, DC: American Psychological Association.

Chávez, T. A., Fernández, I. T., Hipolito-Delgado, C., & Torres Rivera, E. (2016). Unifying liberation psychology and humanistic values to promote social justice in counseling. *The Journal of Humanistic Counseling, 55,* 166–182. http://dx.doi.org/10.1002/johc.12032

Collins, P. H. (2001). *Black feminist thought: Knowledge, consciousness, and the politics of empowerment.* New York, NY: Routledge.

Crenshaw, K. (1991). Mapping the margins: Intersectionality, identity politics, and violence against Women of Color. *Stanford Law Review, 43,* 1241–1299.

D'Emilio, J. (2014). *In a new century: Essays on queer history, politics, and community life.* Madison: University of Wisconsin Press.

Ellison, J. M. (n.d.). Sylvia Rivera and Marsha P. Johnson, Guiding stars [Blog post]. Retrieved from https://jmellison.net/if-we-knew-trans-history/sylvia-rivera-and-marsha-p-johnson-guiding-stars/

Elsass, P. (1992). *Strategies for survival: The psychology of cultural resilience in ethnic minorities.* New York, NY: New York University Press.

Erich, S., Tittsworth, J., & Kersten, A. S. (2010). An examination and comparison of Transsexuals of Color and their White counterparts regarding personal well-being and support Networks. *Journal of GLBT Family Studies, 6*(1), 25–39. http://dx.doi.org/10.1080/15504280903472493

Feinberg, L. (1996). *Transgender warriors: Making history from Joan of Arc to Dennis Rodman.* San Francisco, CA: Beacon Press.

Figueroa, W. S., & Zoccola, P. M. (2015). Individual differences of risk and resiliency in sexual minority health: The roles of stigma consciousness and psychological hardiness. *Psychology of Sexual Orientation and Gender Diversity, 2,* 329–338. http://dx.doi.org/10.1037/sgd0000114

Finch, N. (Producer), & Livingston, J. (Director). (1990). *Paris is burning* [Documentary film]. United States: Academy Entertainment.

Folkman, S., & Lazarus, R. S. (1980). An analysis of coping in a middle-aged community sample. *Journal of Health and Social Behavior, 21,* 219–239. http://dx.doi.org/10.2307/2136617

Freire, P. (2000). *Pedagogy of the oppressed.* New York, NY: Continuum. (Original work published 1970)

Garza, A. (2016). A herstory of the #BlackLivesMatter movement. In J. L. Hobson (Ed.), *Are all the women still White? Rethinking race, expanding feminisms* (pp. 23–28). Albany: State University of New York Press.

Goodman, L. A., Liang, B., Helms, J., Latta, R., Sparks, E., & Weintraub, S. (2004). Training counseling psychologists as social justice agents: Feminist and multicultural principles in action. *The Counseling Psychologist, 32,* 793–837. http://dx.doi.org/10.1177/0011000004268802

Gossett, C., Gossett, R., & Lewis, A. J. (2012). Reclaiming our linage: Organized queer, gender-nonconforming, and transgender resistance to police violence. *The Scholar & Feminist Online.* Retrieved from https://psmag.com/social-justice/taking-freedom-claiming-our-lineage

Grothaus, T., McAuliffe, G., Danner, M., & Doyle, L. (2008). Equity, advocacy, and social justice. In G. McAuliffe & Associates (Eds.), *Culturally alert counseling: A comprehensive introduction* (pp. 45–70). Los Angeles, CA: Sage.

Hartling, L. M. (2008). Strengthening resilience in a risky world: It's all about relationships. *Women & Therapy, 31*(2–4), 51–70. http://dx.doi.org/10.1080/02703140802145870

Huang, C. (1995). Hardiness and stress: A critical review. *Maternal–Child Nursing Journal, 23*, 82–89.

James, S. E., Herman, L. L., Rankin, S., Keisling, M., Mottet, L., & Anafi, M. (2016). *The report of the 2015 U.S. Transgender Survey.* Washington, DC: National Center for Transgender Equality and National Gay and Lesbian Task Force.

Lewis, J. A., Ratts, M. J., Paladino, D. A., & Toporek, R. L. (2011). Social justice counseling and advocacy: Developing new leadership roles and competencies. *Journal for Social Action in Counseling and Psychology, 3*(1), 5–16.

Luthar, S. S. (2015). Resilience in development: A synthesis of research across five decades. In D. Cicchetti & D. J. Cohen (Eds.), *Developmental psychopathology: Vol. 3. Risk, disorder, and adaptation* (2nd ed., pp. 739–795). New York, NY: Wiley. http://dx.doi.org/10.1002/9780470939406.ch20

Martín-Baró, I. (1994). *Writings for a liberation psychology* (A. Aron & S. Corne, Eds.). Cambridge, MA: Harvard University Press.

Masten, A. S. (2001). Ordinary magic. Resilience processes in development. *American Psychologist, 56*, 227–238. http://dx.doi.org/10.1037/0003-066X.56.3.227

Meyer, I. H. (2015). Resilience in the study of minority stress and health of sexual and gender minorities. *Psychology of Sexual Orientation and Gender Diversity, 2*, 209–213. http://dx.doi.org/10.1037/sgd0000132

Moane, G. (2008). Applying psychology in contexts of oppression and marginalisation: Liberation psychology, wellness, and social justice. *The Irish Journal of Psychology, 29*, 89–101. http://dx.doi.org/10.1080/03033910.2008.10446276

Morris, B. J. (n.d.). *History of lesbian, gay, bisexual, and transgender social movements.* Retrieved from the American Psychological Association website: https://www.apa.org/pi/lgbt/resources/history.aspx

Motulsky, S. L., Gere, S. H., Saleem, R., & Trantham, S. M. (2014). Teaching social justice in counseling psychology. *The Counseling Psychologist, 42*, 1058–1083. http://dx.doi.org/10.1177/0011000014553855

Nadal, K. L. (2013). *That's so gay! Microaggressions and the lesbian, gay, bisexual, and transgender community* (pp. 15–37). Washington, DC: American Psychological Association. http://dx.doi.org/10.1037/14093-002

Nyland, D., & Waddle, H. (2016). Breaking out of the gender binary: Liberating transgender prisoners. In T. Afuape & G. Hughes (Eds.), *Liberation practices: Towards emotional wellbeing through dialogue* (pp. 140–148). New York, NY: Routledge.

Ratts, M. J., & Greenleaf, A. T. (2017). Multicultural and social justice counseling competencies: A leadership framework for professional school counselors. *Professional School Counseling, 21*(1b). Advance online publication. http://dx.doi.org/10.1177/2156759X18773582

Riemer, M., & Brown, L. (2019). *We are everywhere: Protest, power, and pride in the history of queer liberation.* New York, NY: Ten Speed Press.

Román, L. (2013). *The untold history of LGBT Latino activism.* Retrieved from the Lambda Legal website: https://www.lambdalegal.org/blog/the-untold-history-of-lgbt-latino-activism

Russell, G. M., & Bohan, J. S. (2007). Liberating psychotherapy: Liberation psychology and psychotherapy with LGBT clients. *Journal of Gay & Lesbian Psychotherapy, 11*(3–4), 59–75. http://dx.doi.org/10.1300/J236v11n03_04

Schlaffer, N. (2016, October 23). *The unsung heroines of Stonewall: Marsha P. Johnson and Sylvia Rivera.* Retrieved from https://sites.psu.edu/womeninhistory/2016/10/23/the-unsung-heroines-of-stonewall-marsha-p-johnson-and-sylvia-rivera/

Simon, K. (2016, April). Brief history of the LGBT movement in the United States. *Version Daily.* Retrieved from http://www.versiondaily.com/brief-history-of-the-lgbt-movement-in-the-united-states/

Singh, A. A. (2016a). Major contribution reaction: Yes! And let's move further toward trans-liberation. *The Counseling Psychologist, 47,* 1050–1061. http://dx.doi.org/10.1177/0011000016669435

Singh, A. A. (2016b). Moving from affirmation to liberation in psychological practice with transgender and gender nonconforming clients. *American Psychologist, 7,* 755–762. http://dx.doi.org/10.1037/amp0000106

Singh, A. A. (2018). *Queer and trans resilience workbook: Skills for navigating sexual orientation and gender identity.* San Francisco, CA: New Harbinger.

Singh, A. A., Hays, D. G., & Watson, L. S. (2011). Strength in the face of adversity: Resilience strategies of transgender individuals. *Journal of Counseling & Development, 89,* 20–27. http://dx.doi.org/10.1002/j.1556-6678.2011.tb00057.x

Singh, A. A., & McKleroy, V. S. (2011). "Just getting out of bed is a revolutionary act": The resilience of transgender People of Color who have survived traumatic life events. *Traumatology, 17*(2), 34–44. http://dx.doi.org/10.1177/1534765610369261

Singh, A. A., Meng, S., & Hansen, A. (2014). "I am my own gender": Resilience strategies of trans youth. *Journal of Counseling & Development, 92,* 208–218. http://dx.doi.org/10.1002/j.1556-6676.2014.00150.x

Stryker, S. (2008). *Transgender history.* Berkeley, CA: Seal Press.

Stulberg, L. M. (2018). *LGBTQ social movements.* Cambridge, England: Polity Press.

Tate, K. A., Torres Rivera, E., Brown, E., & Skaistis, L. (2013). Foundations for liberation: Social justice, liberation psychology, and counseling. *Revista Interamericana de Psicología/Interamerican Journal of Psychology, 47,* 373–382.

Tugade, M. M. (2011). Positive emotions and coping: Examining dual-process models of resilience. In S. Folkman (Ed.), *The Oxford handbook of stress, health, and coping* (pp. 186–199). New York, NY: Oxford University Press.

Ungar, M. (2011). The social ecology of resilience: Addressing contextual and cultural ambiguity of a nascent construct. *American Journal of Orthopsychiatry, 81,* 1–17. http://dx.doi.org/10.1111/j.1939-0025.2010.01067.x

Von Culin, K. R., Tsukayama, E., & Duckworth, A. L. (2014). Unpacking grit: Motivational correlates of perseverance and passion for long-term goals. *The Journal of Positive Psychology, 9,* 306–312. http://dx.doi.org/10.1080/17439760.2014.898320

Watkins, J. (2017). Keep on carryin' on: Recent research on the LGBTQ history of the American South. *History Compass, 15*(11). Advance online publication. http://dx.doi.org/10.1111/hic3.12428

Wilson, E. C., Chen, Y.-H., Arayasirikul, S., Raymond, H. F., & McFarland, W. (2016). The impact of discrimination on the mental health of trans*female youth and the protective effect of parental support. *AIDS and Behavior, 20,* 2203–2211. http://dx.doi.org/10.1007/s10461-016-1409-7

Zautra, A. J., Affleck, G. G., Tennen, H., Reich, J. W., & Davis, M. C. (2005). Dynamic approaches to emotions and stress in everyday life: Bolger and Zuckerman reloaded with positive as well as negative affects. *Journal of Personality, 73,* 1511–1538. http://dx.doi.org/10.1111/j.0022-3506.2005.00357.x

12

Transnational Feminist Liberation Psychology

Decolonizing Border Crossings

Kathryn L. Norsworthy and Ouyporn Khuankaew

Twenty-two years ago, we (Ouyporn Khuankaew and Kathryn Norsworthy) met in Bangkok, Thailand. Ouyporn described herself as a Thai feminist activist working at the grassroots level around the country on issues of violence against women and other social issues. Kathryn identified as a White U.S. feminist activist academic and counseling psychologist who also devoted attention to violence against women in her teaching, research, and practice. We had been introduced by a mutual Thai colleague who thought we had much in common and might appreciate connecting with one another. Since 1995, I (Ouyporn) have been facilitating workshops for groups of local women in Thailand, India, and Burma. These groups include Buddhist nuns from Thailand, Ladakh (India), and the Tibetan exile community in India as well as women from several ethnic minority communities of Burma (Karen, Shan, Mon, and Kachin). Many of these women live in refugee camps in Thailand, internally displaced camps in Burma, or without legal documentation in Thailand because the Thai government does not recognize them as refugees. The workshops topics have included empowerment and community-building, feminist leadership, and gender justice. Before meeting Ouyporn, I (Kathryn) spent 10 years visiting Thailand as a traveler, studying yoga and meditation. For the past 22 years, I have been collaborating with Ouyporn and groups from the Southeast and South Asia regions in social justice focused projects.

The coauthors extend deep appreciation and respect to our local collaborators and partners in Thailand, Burma, and to the Burma exile communities.

http://dx.doi.org/10.1037/0000198-013
Liberation Psychology: Theory, Method, Practice, and Social Justice, L. Comas-Díaz and E. Torres Rivera (Editors)

Shortly after our introduction, I (Ouyporn) invited Kathryn to collaborate in offering a workshop focusing on gender-based violence for a local Thai NGO. As I (Kathryn) entered this project, I lacked a deeper knowledge of the social, political, and cultural contexts of Thai people and had never had a friendship or meaningful relationship with a Thai person. Shortly after completing our first workshop, Ouyporn reported to me that she had encountered many "Westerners" who came to Thailand to "help," engage in "development projects," and otherwise "offer" their expertise, especially at the governmental level and through international aid organizations; thus, she wondered what kind of "Westerner" I would be. We had an honest conversation about centering mutuality and power-sharing in our relationship and the relationships with our local collaborators. From that point, we began a journey of inventing, refining, and articulating a decolonizing way of working together and with local partners in the region on a variety of social justice issues. One goal of this transnational feminist liberation methodological praxis is to disrupt the processes and effects of psychological colonization and neocolonialism often found in minority–majority world relationships.

In this chapter, we discuss key elements of a transnational feminist liberation psychology and bring it to life through examples drawn from the work in which we, along with our local partners, have engaged in Thailand and with the refugee communities of Burma over the past 22 years. Throughout this chapter, we use the terms *Global North* or *minority world* (often called "First World") and *Global South* or *majority world* (frequently referred to as "Third World" or "developing world") to subvert the hierarchical references often used when referring to these global regions. The use of minority and majority world references is consistent with Arnett's (2008) research demonstrating that approximately 96% of study samples in U.S. psychology are from Western industrialized countries, representing about 12% of the world's population. The research findings are then universalized, meaning generalized to the majority world. Finally, we refer to *Myanmar* (renamed by the dictatorship postcoup to mystify the military takeover of a government legally elected by democratic process) as *Burma* in solidarity with democracy movement advocates who continue their activism to this day.

UNDERSTANDING TRANSNATIONAL FEMINIST LIBERATION PSYCHOLOGY

Mainstream Western feminism has been critiqued because of its history of theorizing gender-based oppression based on the lives and experiences of Western, Educated, Industrialized, Rich, Democratic (WEIRD; Henrich, Heine, & Norenzayan, 2010) countries such as the United States. A further concern has focused on its tendency to center and privilege the experiences of White middle-class women, leaving out the voices and lived experiences of women holding target identities and social locations. Often, research results based on data generated by white Western feminist researchers with White under-graduate college students is universalized to women in the majority world; thus, perpetuating a hegemonic understanding of gender injustice that perpetuates the idea that majority world women are helpless and powerless (Grabe, 2016). This approach largely focuses on gender as the only variable rather than taking into consideration the multiple identities and power arrangements in play when understanding gender-based oppression. Further, as a minority world–centered framework, mainstream Western feminism is unlikely to recognize the global power structures across countries and cultures that contribute to gender injustice. There tends to be a lack of emphasis on how local contexts around the world vary in influencing the lives of women and contribute to their privilege or limit situations.

TRANSNATIONAL FEMINISM

Contesting a hegemonic mainstream Western feminism centered on the lives of White middle-class women in the minority world and critiquing the nation-state and the violence often perpetrated on its behalf, transnational feminism underscores the importance of recognizing multiple, contextually rooted feminisms and that local people on the ground need to define their own circumstances, issues, and challenges. Originally emerging from post-colonial and Women of Color feminisms, transnational feminist theorizing is multidirectional—emerging from local contexts while also understanding gender-based oppression from a multisystemic global perspective (Mohanty, 2003). Intersectionality is at the heart of a transnational feminist framework rather than focusing exclusively on gender as the central variable in gender-based oppression. This means that mutually reinforcing systems of inequality converge to form the complex web of injustice in which gender-based oppression, for example, intersects with economic inequities, racism, and homophobia in producing the variety of conditions in which women find themselves attempting to navigate, overcome, change, or survive. Thus, there is a recognition that limit situations experienced by women vary from one context to the next within and across countries and communities while some commonalities may also exist in terms of how gender-based oppression manifests.

Transnational feminism is concerned with power differentials and structural inequities spanning across cultures and national borders, particularly the impacts of social, political, and economic institutions and systems. Alexander and Mohanty (1997) emphasized that a transnational feminism involves challenging [Western] hegemonic perspectives such as generalizing about all women around the globe based on U.S. White, androcentric, heterosexist dominant standards. Further, they pointed out that to set the stage for trans-national feminist solidarity work, neoliberalism must be replaced with critical antiracist, anticapitalist frameworks for meaningful collaboration to take place. Finally, it is important to note that transnational feminism does not simply take a stance of cultural relativism (Grabe, 2016) without regard for how inequality might be at the root of some practices defined as "cultural." Feminist psychologist Laura Brown (2010) emphasized the importance of holding the tensions of diversity and antidomination values in making this assessment. Kurtiş and Adams (2015) underscored that transnational feminist psychology turns attention to often invisible or silenced majority world contexts for knowledge about human experience and struggles for collective liberation including but not exclusively geared toward gender justice. This framework includes a focus on social justice at the global level rather than a neoliberal emphasis on individual human rights. As Kurtiş and Adams (2015) pointed out,

> the goal is to generate knowledge from multiple sites, going beyond existing epistemological hierarchies, and dismantling the structures of domination that enable hegemonic feminisms and psychologies emanating from WEIRD spaces to claim their global "liberatory" status. In the process, a transnational feminist psychology analysis highlights the extent to which hegemonic forms of (feminist) psychologies—in their self-acclaimed role as liberators—might fail to see the ways in which they too require liberation. (p. 406)

FEMINIST LIBERATION PSYCHOLOGY

Liberation psychology is rooted in the participatory action methods and projects of Colombian sociologists Orlando Fals Borda (1985), Camilo Torres Restrepo (1971), and the "La Rosca" group, and was influenced by Brazilian educator and philosopher Paulo Freire (1972/2000), among others. Freire (1972) pushed against mainstream educational perspectives—the banking model of education—in which the expert deposits knowledge into the students, who are passive recipients in the process. He led a critical pedagogy movement in which people holding disenfranchised and subordinated positions in society became active participants in articulating and analyzing the challenging situations in which they found themselves and in developing and implementing solutions and social change strategies toward their own liberation.

Liberation psychology was articulated by the Spaniard social psychologist and Jesuit priest Ignacio Martín-Baró (1994), who lived and worked in El Salvador. He noted that psychological research served the interests of those with privilege and power in society and called for a change of focus whereby the lived experiences and needs of the majority of society would be addressed. For Martín-Baró, a psychology of liberation would center those in society who are oppressed; take into account their social, political, historical, and cultural contexts in understanding their lives and predicaments; and would value their collective knowledge and capacity for taking social action toward their own liberation, especially in building more empowered communities (de Oliveira, Neves, Nogueira, & De Koning, 2009). From this perspective, it is understood that "everyone is caught in the 'web of oppression' and that everyone has a stake in addressing our own internalizations of oppression as well as the external manifestations if we are all going to be truly free"

(Norsworthy, 2006, p. 431). Thus, liberation frameworks involve a praxis in which people engage in an ongoing, recursive process of critically reflecting on their experiences and circumstances and taking action toward social transformation. Through this process, critical consciousness develops whereby people increase and deepen their capacities not only to critically analyze their social realities but to engage in social action focused on changing oppressive systems and conditions revealed through their analyses. The agents in this work are the collective rather than the individual and often include members of the oppressed group as well as allies who accompany the group in their processes (Burton & Kagan, 2005).

Like transnational frameworks, feminist liberation psychology moves beyond WEIRD contexts to bring an understanding of how gender inequality is situated within global systems and particularly in terms of structural power differences and the status of women at interconnected levels, from the local to the global. With an emphasis on liberatory praxis and resistance to gender arrangements reinforced by contemporary globalization, feminist liberation frameworks focus on how women and their allies resist structural inequalities by accessing local knowledge and experience (Grabe, 2016). The focus is on the processes of gender-based oppression as they intersect with other identities and social locations at multiple levels, including the individual, institutional, and structural. Local people engage in a root cause analysis of these systems of inequality and their driving ideologies based on their specific limit situations. Thus, a feminist liberation psychology would guide minority world psychologists to form partnerships with local actors from the majority world rather than the power-holders in the countries and contexts in which we work.

POSTCOLONIAL AND DECOLONIAL INFLUENCES IN TRANSNATIONAL FEMINIST LIBERATION PSYCHOLOGY

Irish feminist liberation psychologist Geraldine Moane (1994) defined *colonialism* as "a system of domination characterized by social patterns or mechanisms of control which maintain oppression and which vary from context to context" (p. 252). Although colonization has historically involved physical occupation, with the rise of globalization, neoliberalism, and the uncritical exportation of minority world psychology, psychological colonization has been identified as a means of domination and influence within the majority world (Norsworthy, 2006, 2017). Colonization is enforced by imperialism, whereby a country or entity views itself as superior and thus justified in exercising domination and subordination (Said, 1993). Through this process of homogenizing countries and communities, the colonizers assert a profound psychological impact on the colonized, who begin to experience diminished agency as well as a shift in their belief in the world as just and safe (Comas-Díaz, 2008). Ever present are the insidious power structures upholding the European and American epistemologies situated as modernizing and as the universal standard. Thus, even postcolonization, *coloniality* (Quijano, 2007), the process by which the invisible hegemonic systems of power and control remain in place at every level of society, is upheld by global politics of domination and subordination (Grosfoguel, 2007) and by infiltrating the cultures, hearts, and minds of the colonized (Maldonado-Torres, 2007). "Coloniality perpetuates and sustains a dominant European/North American–centric epistemology claiming to be authoritative, universal, and based in science (Grosfoguel, 2007)" (Norsworthy, 2017, p. 1037). Moane (2010) noted the deleterious effects of colonization and colonialism on the colonized, including the undermining of trust and confidence in themselves and their ability to exert agency in their own lives. The colonizer is cast as an authority in relation to the colonized, who are viewed as incapable and in need of help and support (Nandy, 1983).

Decolonial and postcolonial frameworks have much to offer U.S. and other minority world psychologists who travel to communities and countries in the majority world to conduct research, activism, consultation, or other forms of practice. These frameworks, which inform transnational feminist liberation psychology, are particularly important considering the issue of false universalism in U.S. psychology, a system in which U.S. psychologists have been enculturated and trained. As previously discussed, false universalism occurs when sweeping claims are made based on knowledge and research representing WEIRD countries (Arnett, 2008; Henrich et al., 2010). With a strong emphasis on activism and liberation, decoloniality goes beyond exposing the influences of European American–dominating epistemologies, social and psychological theories and scholarship, Western colonialism, and imperialism. Decoloniality requires a democratization, de-Westernization, and dehegemonization of knowledge (Grabe, 2017; Ndlovu-Gatsheni, 2015). Of equal importance and in common with feminist liberation approaches, decoloniality involves bringing to light the experiences and wisdom of people whose voices have been erased and delegitimized (Norsworthy, 2017).

From a postcolonial perspective, those of us from the minority and majority worlds have internalized the colonizer–colonized mentalities and need to engage in decolonizing the mind as well as the attendant behaviors (Norsworthy, 2006). For minority world psychologists, this involves ongoing efforts toward recognizing our privilege globally and locally, understanding how it plays out, unlearning, and moving from power-over to power-sharing collaboration with local partners. Lillian Comas-Díaz (1994) discussed the project of decolonizing from the vantage point of those in the colonized position. She identified five steps in this process, including (a) increasing awareness of the colonial mentality by recognizing and understanding the systems of oppression and colonization; (b) correcting cognitive errors held by those experiencing colonization, including recognizing the ambivalence they experience in relation to the colonizers; (c) reclaiming racial, gender, and cultural identities as positive and worthy; (d) cultivating a sense of self-mastery and autonomous dignity; and (e) self-transformation through the release of the effects of colonization and movement toward a solid sense of one's self and one's community.

TOWARD A TRANSNATIONAL FEMINIST LIBERATION PRAXIS

During our initial project, we became aware that we had fallen into our own version of the global power arrangements. Without discussion, Kathryn, the White minority world member of the facilitation team, assumed the role of workshop "teacher" and Ouyporn, majority world Woman of Color, took on the role of translator. It only took 1 day for us to recognize that we were not comfortable with this hierarchical arrangement and to consciously decide that we would shift into cofacilitation within the context of a power-sharing partnership. We wanted to affirm that we each had important contributions to make to the project and to function accordingly. In retrospect, this was the beginning of the decolonizing process for us both, whereby we each engaged in our own critical consciousness development by unlearning and deinternalizing the colonizing–colonized mentalities connected to colonialism and imperialism. This included not only decolonizing our partnership but also our work with local collaborators through the development and ongoing refinement of a methodology informed by transnational feminist liberation values, principles, and practices.

THE METHODOLOGY

To subvert the ever-present processes of psychological colonization and colonialism, we agreed that we needed to bring a power analysis to our work. This included accounting for and regularly reflecting on the power differentials and enactments in our relationship as well as those emerging in our relationships with members of the groups with whom we partnered. We noted that we all hold sources of power connected to, for example, social and national identities, experience, and skills and that these can come into play in our partnership with one another and our groups, and among group members. Through our conversations and our collaboration, we realized that everyone had important contributions to make to our work with one another and resolved to consciously engage in power sharing and balancing the tensions of finding the most effective ways to maximize these contributions while remaining aware of power differentials that might undermine this process unless consciously acknowledged.

Thus, radical reflexivity was embedded into the process of each project, helping us elucidate and work to transform dynamics that might be undermining power-sharing and mutuality.

For example, during a workshop with a group of refugee women from Burma, during our end-of-day debriefing, I (Ouyporn) brought to Kathryn's attention a pattern developing in which participants systematically directed their comments to her as the White cofacilitator, rendering me invisible. Kathryn had not recognized this dynamic and was reinforcing it. After a candid discussion, we decided that Kathryn would sit and I would stand during the next segment of the workshop and that when participants looked at Kathryn, she would turn her attention to me so that I engaged with them and assumed the lead in the facilitation process. As the dynamic shifted, we resumed our cofacilitation process and later invited the group to notice what took place. Later we noted that our commitment to relational ethics, honest feedback, power-sharing, and a feminist liberation–based partnership and methodology provided the foundation for our successful negotiation of the situation.

As a White U.S. member of our team, I (Kathryn) have been on an ongoing journey in which I continue to learn how to partner effectively with Ouyporn and other local colleagues through embodiment of transnational feminist liberation values, principles, and practices. The following reflections illuminate elements of these efforts at meeting the inevitable challenges that arise:

> For the past two days, I have been very quiet in our workshop. I am struggling to find myself in my role as cofacilitator with Ouyporn. Upon reflection, I see that there were times when I could have used my skills to help clarify or move the conversation forward; yet I keep thinking about not wanting to come across as the [Western] "expert" or overshadow Ouyporn (Field note, July 2000). . . . The question of how to mindfully and consciously embody a decolonial stance in my work with Ouyporn and our local partners surfaced in the early years of our work together. After a period of struggle, I decided to mindfully and compassionately attend to, embrace, and investigate my interior and exterior experiences. Starting with Ouyporn, I shared my challenges with trusted feminist colleagues and friends. . . . Also, I noted some of the parallels with my personal journey of White racial/cultural identity development (Helms, 1995), particularly the process of waking up in more complex ways to my White privilege within the U.S. context, the effects of oppression on people of color, and how I am implicated and benefit. Reminded of the pattern of "White retreat," in which White people become overwhelmed, paralyzed, and then regress (Sue & Sue, 1999), I consciously decided to cultivate my critical consciousness development, the decolonizing of my own mind, and began to risk active, mindful engagement with our groups from a stance of cultural humility. Ouyporn and I reaffirmed our commitment to hold ourselves and one another accountable through open dialogue and feedback and the journey continued. (Norsworthy, 2017, p. 1040)

As is evident, my growth over these years has focused on "unlearning oppression and colonization" and, within the context of my relationships with Ouyporn and other local partners, cultivating critical consciousness and cultural humility as the foundation for power-sharing relationships and decolonializing the work.

The feminist liberation–based methodology also supports a reflexive praxis regarding how power is exercised among participants. In a workshop with a mixed-gender Thai group, we observed that men in the group were doing most of the talking and that women were ambivalently colluding by deferring to them, apart from a very senior woman in a governmental leadership position.

As part of a group reflection process, we asked the group to notice any patterns in participation. Who spoke and who did not? How did this get determined? The group members began to comment on the role of gender in relation to who contributed to the discussion and who held back. They also noted that the exception of the senior woman was linked to the power she held based on her privileged identities, including governmental rank and attendant social influence. Through the conversation, together we agreed that vital wisdom was lost in the exercise of male privilege and the privilege of institutional rank. The dynamic shifted toward increased participation by everyone, and the group later agreed that the benefits were immeasurable.

Another crucial element of our methodology involves creating structures and processes in which local knowledge, experience, and wisdom are centered and privileged (Norsworthy, 2006; Norsworthy & Khuankaew, 2004, 2008, 2012, 2014). To do this, we begin each project by offering the participants a description of a vision for our work together:

OUYPORN: Partnership culture can be created through power sharing among all of us. This is both the path and the goal. We are aware that social suffering caused by structural injustice exists everywhere and is overwhelming. But since it is created by the ignorance of human beings, it can be transformed or reduced through the wisdom and commitment of human beings. We are aware that changing these structures of inequality involves group members engaging in power-sharing with one another, including we as facilitators practicing power-sharing within our partnership and in our partnership with the group.

KATHRYN: Ouyporn and I view this workshop as an opportunity to accompany you in your work toward goals that you develop as a community. We see all members of the group, ourselves included, as teachers and students who will benefit from everyone's full engagement in the process. As we see it, our role as facilitators is to create and offer structure s and experiences in which the wisdom and skills of the group can emerge in identifying and defining the issues and problems you are facing, analyzing their root causes and their impact on the community, and in creating action plans for addressing them.

Through this methodological process, we aspire to create liberatory, decolonizing spaces in which participants are honored as experts on their own lives and circumstances and where they create indigenized and contextualized methods for social change and problem-solving (Smith, 2012). Group members, especially women without formal education who are directly impacted by, for example, violence and poverty, are centered, supported, and encouraged to speak their truths and share their wisdom. We recognize them as teachers for us all.

KEY THEMES AND LEARNINGS

Over the past 21 years, we have focused a significant portion of our work on a variety of social, peace, and justice issues in Thailand and with the refugee communities of Burma. Several themes have emerged when analyzing our experiences and reflecting on them with project participants, particularly in terms of our transnational feminist liberation framework.

Moving From Expert to Accompanier

Elsewhere, we have discussed in more detail the issues that arise when minority world people travel to the majority world to "help" (Norsworthy, 2006; Norsworthy & Khuankaew, 2004, 2012). Through extensive conversations with local collaborators, we heard many stories of Westerners arriving in Thailand, taking an expert position, and assuming they knew best the key issues and concerns of local people and how to address them. One of our local collaborators described his frustration with a U.S. professional who came to work with a refugee organization serving people of Burma in exile, reporting that the consultant never asked about what the members of the organization considered their most pressing problems and began to "teach" the group how to address issues he had predetermined to be most important. When our local colleague attempted to provide information about local contexts and cultures, his input was disregarded or minimized. The Western consultant was operating from a minority world–centered, universalizing narrative as previously discussed in this chapter. Recently, our local collaborators living in Burma have also reported that they are aware of international NGOs with significant financial resources, led by White Westerners, that are collaborating with the military government without input from people on the ground, thus directly disempowering the grassroots democracy movement and further contributing to systemic oppression.

Drawing from a transnational feminist liberation framework, Brinton Lykes (2013) and Geraldine Moane (2009) have reminded us to move to a stance of accompaniment of local groups in their context-centered efforts to define their limit situations and determine the best courses of action for change rooted in indigenous perspectives. Lykes (2013, p. 782) described the knowledge produced within this context of accompaniment as "hybridized," a blend she referred to as a "third voice" serving a function as local people continue their own journeys of self-determination and liberation.

Entry Points

As I (Ouyporn) pointed out to Kathryn early in our relationship, typically "Westerners" enter Thailand as experts via upper-level government offices or the university (Norsworthy, 2006). I explained that this can be problematic because of the hierarchy in Thailand in which development and knowledge are already centralized in the hands of upper-level government officers and university professors, particularly those in Bangkok or the other large cities. Many of these officers are ethnic Thai (the dominant ethnic group in Thailand), upper-middle-class, heterosexual, cisgender men, who tend to live in Bangkok. They tend to be insulated from injustice by their privilege; thus, their perspectives and ideas about development are less likely to be informed by the voices and experiences of the local people. I see the top-down, centralized governmental culture as a primary root cause of structural oppression in Thai society. The associated policies and practices connected with this culture create, perpetuate, and worsen many social problems in Thailand, such as poverty, environmental destruction, corruption, sexual violence, gender inequality, ethnic oppression, homophobia, and transphobia, and reinforce dominant-culture and structural oppression.

In the spirit of a transnational feminist liberation approach, we urge minority world psychologists traveling to majority world countries to consult, conduct research, and practice being aware of the points of entry and the implications of partnering with organizations, institutions, or other entities at the top levels of society. Whose interests are being served? Are local people and communities' voices centered and amplified when the work influences their lives and will impact them? Are local people viewed as experts on their circumstances or as victims in need of "help" or rescuing from above?

Establishing and Honoring Relational Ethics and Commitments

As we began to form relationships with local partners from Thailand and Burma, they shared their thoughts more freely. We learned of the frustration and disappointment that often came with their experiences with Westerners whom they allowed into their communities to conduct research or to offer training or consultation. For example, several local partners from one of the Burma ethnic minority exile communities revealed distress when a Western scholar conducted research with their group, had no further contact with them once the project concluded, and then published a research report without input from the participants (Norsworthy, 2006). One member of the group observed,

> We don't know where she got her information. She said things that were not true, and did not show what is happening as it really is. She didn't tell about the difficulties of the ethnic groups of Burma—how they are targeted by the SLORC [current military dictatorship] for torture and forced labor. The Westerners, they only want to come over and study us and go home and publish their article or get their degree. They benefit from our problems (personal communication, 1999). (Norsworthy, 2006, p. 427)

We recall an early conversation about this issue in which I (Ouyporn) disclosed to Kathryn that I was surprised when she continued to return to Thailand after her first visits (Norsworthy, 2006). I revealed that in my experience, Westerners typically come over once or twice, but then disappear and discontinue contact. Together we discussed the importance of forming and nurturing our relationship and our partnership, of committing to a process of radical reflexivity in terms of how it is working, and to addressing any issues that arise based on our mutual commitment to power-sharing and social justice. We agreed that equally important was doing the same with our local partners in the spirit of relational integrity and solidarity.

When working with local partners, we invite them to share their vision, goals, and the change they want to see, then accompany them in identifying the knowledge, skills, and other forms of support they need to develop action plans for social change. In this way, people on the ground define and direct their own visions, projects, and strategies. I (Ouyporn) see our role as one of good friends who, by invitation, collaborate with local people in identifying their concerns and needs within the context of a partnership culture. Partnership culture involves practices in which outside accompaniers and those in the community are true, good friends, where the accompaniers are neither fixer, teacher, nor expert believing they know how to "help" or "save" local people.

From a transnational feminist liberation perspective, minority world psychologists crossing borders into the majority world need to recognize our positions as situated outsiders (Fine, Weis, Weseen, & Wong, 2000). This framework guides us to engage with local partners in ways that support knowledge production based on their contexts and locations locally and globally, recognizing that Western-generated theories and practices are based on emic psychologies as well as social and political contexts of the minority world. For example, we accompanied a group of ethnic minority women from Burma (at their request) in their project of forming a women's organization. Early on, we shared a handout written in English and developed by a White, U.S. feminist, which outlined feminist and patriarchal principles and values guiding organizational structures and processes. The participants began engaging in a lively conversation during which it became clear that the handout content was not always translatable into their local language, that they had differing perspectives about what constituted feminism based on their cultures and contexts, and that their limit situations were specific to past and present events in Burma and globally. Because our local partner and translator had joined the group discussion, we were not privy to the details of the conversation until we inquired. At that point, she reported,

> The list you gave the group. . . . There are many words on it that are not part of our local language or even Burmese [the language of the dominant ethnic group of Burma]. There is no direct translation, and in some cases, nothing in our language that is even close, so they are trying to get the meaning through a discussion. A couple of the women speak English, so they are trying to help. The group is in the process of inventing their own terminology based on our cultural values and experiences. Also, we are not sure that we want a democratic organization (listed under feminist values). In a democracy, people's voices get left out. Small groups of people who are not part of the mainstream are not represented. We have lived in a dictatorship—a totalitarian system. We want something better than democracy! (Norsworthy & Khuankaew, 2012, pp. 226–227)

Through engagement in a reflexive praxis, the group members revealed their resistance to adopting the principles from our U.S.-generated handout and their process of claiming their own authority as they developed an organizational model based on their knowledge and experience. Recommitting to a transnational feminist liberation methodology, we accompanied participants in generating culture-centered principles for guiding the development of their organization, in their own language, based on their self-defined analysis of the impact of colonization and effects of the contemporary authoritarian regime. This process involved creating and articulating a feminism indigenous to their ethnic minority group's historical and contemporary social, political, and cultural contexts and language. The organization, Shan Women's Action Network (SWAN), developed based on principles of participatory leadership, power-sharing, and consensus, has provided important leadership in the Burma democracy movement. For example, SWAN gained the world's attention and influenced U.S. policy after the publication of a coauthored report documenting the Burma junta's use of rape as a weapon of war and genocide against the Shan ethnic minority group inside the country (Shan Human Rights Foundation & SWAN, 2002). This example illustrates the importance of cultivating relationships and group processes that support power-sharing and participants' claiming and embodying their authority to do what they believe is indicated based on their contexts and circumstances. These women, who were directly affected by the oppression, knew the root causes of their suffering and displayed their wisdom, courage, and self-designed strategies of resistance. A power-sharing model and culture within the group fueled their "power within" as a source of knowledge and energy in their work for social change. We, as outsiders and good friends, were inspired by and learned from their courageous actions.

Central to a transnational feminist liberation psychology is an understanding and interrogation of power at all levels, micro to macro. As illustrated in the previous example of our work with SWAN, creating conditions for and respecting the local group's resistance to a universalizing Western narrative and supporting their self-knowledge and skills in developing an organization based on their best judgment facilitated pluralizing epistemologies and ways of knowing previously silenced and distorted by colonialism and oppression (Ndlovu-Gatsheni, 2015).

Passing the Torch

Michelle Fine (2013) noted that engaging in projects as situated outsiders needs to involve creating the necessary conditions for local collaborators to continue the work without our involvement—that is, passing the torch. For example, we were invited to accompany a group of Thai mental health professionals in the development of a crisis-counseling model to be used in a newly formed national network of one-stop crisis centers for women survivors of gender-based violence. We assembled regularly with a team from around the country over a 3-year period to develop the model, which the local group decided would be grounded in Thai-centered feminist and social justice values, principles, and practices. At their request, we employed our feminist liberation methodology to support the group in their work, and they created a powerful social justice crisis counseling approach, deliberately subverting the dominant "medical model" of counseling. Once the model was completed, project participants needed to return to their home provinces and other parts of Thailand to build capacity. Within the context of developing these trainings, the group focused on equipping themselves in using a feminist liberation training–consultation methodology and in cultivating the knowledge and skills for building capacity with potential new workshop trainers and counseling staff.

To develop the workshops, participants deconstructed the methodology we had been using in our projects. They focused on defining the roles and stance of the facilitator(s) and the knowledge and skills required for liberatory facilitation and social justice crisis counseling for women survivors of gender-based violence, including the potential activities for supporting the group in their learning processes. Their analysis also included who was centered in the knowledge production and from whom the knowledge originated. Within the context of these participant-centered, experiential workshops, group members expanded their understandings of gender-based violence while cultivating the requisite awareness, knowledge, and skills for employing a feminist liberation–based methodology in their communities. Consistent with the principles and values of power-sharing, collaboration, and decolonization, the group engaged in radical reflexivity regarding the power dynamics among participants and with facilitators. On the basis of this ongoing praxis, they adjusted accordingly, embodying the empowerment they hoped would be cultivated by local facilitators, crisis counselors, and their women clients. Upon completion, participants developed and implemented a plan for continuing the work independently. They noted that the passing of the torch was successful.

A frequent question arises about the languages that are used in our work, given that we are each from different countries, we are working in Thailand with Thai groups, and that, as we shared previously, we also work with groups around the region, such as the Burma groups, where participants speak several languages depending on their ethnicities and cultures. This question points to the tensions that we hold in our efforts to employ a decolonizing, liberatory methodology in our work with local groups and in our relationship with one another. For example, although Kathryn has studied Thai and can converse conversationally, significantly advanced fluency is needed to conduct a workshop in the Thai language. Thus, when working with Thai groups, we each speak our first languages (Thai and English) and our local partners translate for Kathryn so that she can understand and communicate at the level of sophistication and nuance needed when complex cultural concepts and emotions are discussed. Because Ouyporn's English is much better than Kathryn's Thai, we speak English to one another. From a transnational feminist liberation perspective, the global politic is playing out in these situations; the language of the White U.S. member of the facilitation team is privileged, and special provisions are provided so that she can understand and communicate with Thai groups. Thus, it becomes important that Kathryn continue to make efforts to increase her Thai language fluency and cultural competence and that we continue to engage in our reflexive praxis about the tensions inherent in these situations.

In contrast, when we are working with our Burma groups, we encounter multiple languages spoken by participants who hold ethnic minority identities, such as Shan, Karen, Mon, and Karenni, in their home country. The dominant ethnic identity in Burma is Burman, the predominant identity of those holding leadership positions in the central government dominated by the military, a government that regularly targets ethnic minority groups around the country. When we work with a single ethnic minority group from Burma, local partners provide cofacilitation and translation from the local language to English (they do not usually speak Thai). In projects involving multiple ethnic minority groups and, at times, dominant-group Burmans, our cofacilitator translates between English and the dominant language, Burman, which is understood and spoken by many ethnic minority members. However, on numerous occasions multiple languages are being used within the group. For example, in one of our workshops, some Karen and Shan workshop participants did not speak Burman or English, so other Shan and Karen participants provided ongoing translation for them. In this case, the tensions were complex. Most of the ethnic minority group members were relying on translation into the Burmese language, considered the language of the oppressor. Kathryn and Ouyporn, both holding privilege in multiple ways, relied on English translation, the globally dominant language of the United States. In the spirit of our feminist liberation values and principles, regular reflexive praxis about the power dynamics in play, ongoing efforts on our part and with the groups to avoid exacerbation of these dynamics, and efforts to support participants in using their local languages regularly were inherent in our workshop processes in these situations.

CONCLUSION

A transnational feminist liberation psychology has much to offer the processes of research and practice involving minority and majority world partners. Starting from a foundation of centralizing activism and social change (Grabe, 2016), this approach subverts the global politic in which hierarchical power dynamics can set the stage for universalization and domination of Western psychology and minority world feminist narratives and the undermining of authority of majority world women over their own lives. With a focus on addressing structural inequality and intersectionality, transnational feminist liberation frameworks guide minority world psychologists to accompany people on the ground in their conscientization, the process of cultivating a critical consciousness regarding one's social, political, and cultural reality through an ongoing process of reflection and action (Freire, 1972/2000). This involves accompanying local actors in defining the issues of most concern, analyzing the root causes of their limit situations systemically using local and global lens, and developing and implementing action plans to change unjust social conditions. In other words, those who are most affected by structural inequality, women of the majority world, exercise their resistance and engage in social justice within and on behalf of their communities. As transnational feminist Chandra Mohanty (2003) noted, "Sisterhood cannot be assumed on the basis of gender; it must be forged in concrete historical and political practice and analysis" (p. 24). Western feminist psychologists often need to engage effectively in horizontal collaboration (Leung, 2003) with local actors who are not psychologists to support those most affected by oppression, colonization, and imperialism in solidarity work.

I (Ouyporn) encourage minority world partners to participate in transnational projects with a "humble mind," recognizing that everyone involved in these social justice projects will be learning from one another, that local people are the experts on their own lives and circumstances, and that they have the wisdom to address their own problems drawing from Indigenous knowledge and change strategies (Norsworthy & Khuankaew, 2012). When grassroots groups gather and share their suffering collectively, they feel less isolated and invisible, and out of these discussions solutions emerge. We, the accompaniers, play an important role of bearing witness as group members share their suffering and their wisdom. In this way, we are all together in encountering the injustice and in creating strategies for change. This process and methodology speaks to the goal of the deuniversalization and pluralization of ways of knowing, knowledge itself, and its applications (Ndlovu-Gatsheni, 2015), particularly in the case of knowledge and epistemologies that have been silenced and delegitimized by colonizing entities and influences.

As a minority world psychologist living the questions connected to articulating and applying a transnational feminist liberation psychology in my work in Southeast Asia, I (Kathryn) resonate with Brinton Lykes's (2013) challenge to decenter ourselves to the margins, as part of a "third voice" embracing "epistemic uncertainties" (Sholock, 2012, p. 701) participating in the development of hybridized, transitional knowledge to be owned and implemented by local people themselves.

As the Thai collaborator in this partnership, I (Ouyporn) am keenly aware that local people know the root causes of their suffering and can see the ways to end it; yet the power to change their circumstances is often not completely in their hands. Thus, I see my role as important in witnessing the struggles of local people. As the same time, when they can share the struggle from their own lived experiences and social locations, such as in dealing with racism or gender oppression in their own cultures, local people may come to see themselves not as poorer or more unfortunate than the third voice location but as human beings with the shared experience of living in a male dominated, patriarchal social structure. A transnational feminist liberation framework has the potential to foster a sense of connectedness among local groups and partners and to build a more powerful global movement across Global South and North devoted to resisting the structural inequality and creating more just societies and communities.

In accompanying partners from Thailand and Burma in their journeys of liberation, we have witnessed and experienced the transformations we all undergo as our critical consciousness expands and empowerment is elevated, particularly within the context of sustained, power-sharing relationships. Further, we (Norsworthy [with Khuankaew], 2006) discovered that using a decolonizing framework involves simultaneously deconstructing and trans-forming "our own "colonial mentality," ethnocentrism, cultural encapsulation, power and privilege" (p. 438) and challenging and supporting our partners in the same interrogation and change processes. We have witnessed the mean-ingful and important social change projects as well as the powerful outcomes that have grown out of many of these peace and justice projects, from the micro to the macro levels. Through this chapter, we, in solidarity with our local partners, have offered a *testimonio* (Smith, 2010) of how the practice of transnational feminist liberation psychology is emancipatory for everyone involved and how our struggles and liberations are truly interconnected locally and globally. In this spirit, we hope readers are inspired to continue this transnational feminist liberation work for peace and justice around the globe.

REFERENCES

Alexander, M. J., & Mohanty, C. T. (1997). *Feminist genealogies, colonial legacies, democratic futures*. New York, NY: Routledge.

Arnett, J. J. (2008). The neglected 95%: Why American psychology needs to become less American. *American Psychologist, 63*, 602–614. http://dx.doi.org/10.1037/0003-066X.63.7.602

Brown, L. S. (2010). *Feminist therapy*. Washington, DC: American Psychological Association.

Burton, M., & Kagan, C. (2005). Liberation social psychology: Learning from Latin America. *Journal of Community & Applied Social Psychology, 15*, 63–78. http://dx.doi.org/10.1002/casp.786

Comas-Díaz, L. (1994). An integrative approach. In L. Comas-Díaz & B. Greene, *Women of Color: Integrating ethnic and gender identities in psychotherapy* (pp. 287–318). New York, NY: Guilford Press.

Comas-Díaz, L. (2008). 2007 Carolyn Sherif award address: *Spirita*: Reclaiming womanist sacredness into feminism. *Psychology of Women Quarterly, 32*, 13–21. http://dx.doi.org/10.1111/j.1471-6402.2007.00403.x

de Oliveira, J. M., Neves, S., Nogueira, C., & De Koning, M. (2009). Present but un-named: Feminist liberation psychology in Portugal. *Feminism & Psychology, 19*, 394–406. http://dx.doi.org/10.1177/0959353509105631

Fals Borda, O. (1985). *Knowledge and people's power: Lessons with peasants in Nicaragua, Mexico and Colombia*. New Delhi, India: Indian Social Institute.

Fine, M. (2013). Echoes of Bedford: A 20-year social psychology memoir on participatory action research hatched behind bars. *American Psychologist, 68,* 687–698. http://dx.doi.org/10.1037/a0034359

Fine, M., Weis, L., Weseen, S., & Wong, L. (2000). For whom? Qualitative research, representations, and social responsibilities. In N. K. Denzin & Y. S. Lincoln (Eds.), *Handbook of qualitative research* (2nd ed., pp. 107–131). Thousand Oaks, CA: Sage.

Freire, P. (2000). *Pedagogy of the oppressed.* New York, NY: Continuum. (Original work published 1972)

Grabe, S. (2016). Transnational feminism in psychology: Moving beyond difference to investigate processes of power at the intersection of the global and local. In T. Roberts, N. Curtin, L. E. Duncan, & L. M. Cortina (Eds.), *Feminist perspectives on building a better psychological science of gender* (pp. 295–318). Switzerland: Springer International. http://dx.doi.org/10.1007/978-3-319-32141-7_17

Grabe, S. (2017). *Narrating a psychology of resistance: Voices of the Campeneras in Nicaragua.* New York, NY: Oxford University Press. http://dx.doi.org/10.1093/acprof:oso/9780190614256.001.0001

Grosfoguel, R. (2007). The epistemic decolonial turn: Beyond political-economy paradigms. *Cultural Studies, 21,* 211–246. http://dx.doi.org/10.1080/09502380601162514

Helms, J. E. (1995). An update of Helm's White and People of Color racial identity models. In J. G. Ponterotto, J. M. Casas, L. A. Suzuki, & C. M. Alexander (Eds.), *Handbook of multicultural counseling* (pp. 181–198). Thousand Oaks, CA: Sage.

Henrich, J., Heine, S. J., & Norenzayan, A. (2010). The weirdest people in the world? *Behavioral and Brain Sciences, 33*(2-3), 61–83. http://dx.doi.org/10.1017/S0140525X0999152X

Kurtiş, T., & Adams, G. (2015). Decolonizing liberation: Toward a transnational feminist psychology. *Journal of Political and Social Psychology, 3,* 388–413. http://dx.doi.org/10.5964/jspp.v3i1.326

Leung, S. A. (2003). A journey worth traveling: Globalization of counseling psychology. *The Counseling Psychologist, 31,* 412–419. http://dx.doi.org/10.1177/0011000003031004004

Lykes, M. B. (2013). Participatory and action research as a transformative praxis: Responding to humanitarian crises from the margins. *American Psychologist, 68,* 774–783. http://dx.doi.org/10.1037/a0034360

Maldonado-Torres, N. (2007). On coloniality of being: Contributions to the development of a concept. *Cultural Studies, 21,* 240–270. http://dx.doi.org/10.1080/09502380601162548

Martín-Baró, I. (1994). *Writings for a liberation psychology* (A. Aron & S. Corne, Trans. & Eds.). Cambridge, MA: Harvard University Press.

Moane, G. (1994). A psychological analysis of colonialism in an Irish context. *The Irish Journal of Psychology, 15,* 250–265. http://dx.doi.org/10.1080/03033910.1994.10558009

Moane, G. (2009). Reflections on liberation psychology in action in an Irish context. In M. M. Montero & C. C. Sonn (Eds.), *Psychology of liberation: Theory and practice* (pp. 135–154). New York, NY: Springer Science+Business Media.

Moane, G. (2010). *Gender and colonialism: A psychological analysis of oppression and liberation.* London, England: Palgrave Macmillan.

Mohanty, C. T. (2003). *Feminism without borders: Decolonizing theory, practicing solidarity.* Durham, NC: Duke University Press. http://dx.doi.org/10.1215/9780822384649

Nandy, A. (1983). *The intimate enemy.* Oxford, England: Oxford University Press.

Ndlovu-Gatsheni, S. J. (2015). Decoloniality as the future of Africa. *History Compass, 13,* 485–496. http://dx.doi.org/10.1111/hic3.12264

Norsworthy, K. L. (2017). Mindful activism: Embracing the complexities of international border crossings. *American Psychologist, 72,* 1035–1043. http://dx.doi.org/10.1037/amp0000262

Norsworthy, K. L., & Khuankaew, O. (2004). Women of Burma speak out: Workshops to deconstruct gender-based violence and build systems of peace and justice. *Journal for Specialists in Group Work, 29,* 259–283. http://dx.doi.org/10.1080/01933920490477011

Norsworthy, K. L. (with Khuankaew, O.). (2006). Bringing social justice to international practices of counseling psychology. In R. L. Toporek, L. H. Gerstein, N. A. Fouad, G. Roysircar, & T. Israel (Eds.), *Handbook for social justice in counseling psychology: Leadership, vision, and action* (pp. 421–441). Thousand Oaks, CA: Sage.

Norsworthy, K. L., & Khuankaew, O. (2008). A new view from women of Thailand about gender, sexuality, and HIV/AIDS. *Feminism & Psychology, 18,* 527–536. http://dx.doi.org/10.1177/0959353508095534

Norsworthy, K. L., & Khuankaew, O. (2012). Feminist border crossings: Our transnational partnership in peace and justice work. In J. Kottler, M. Englar-Carlson, & J. Carlson (Eds.), *Helping beyond the 50-minute hour: Therapists involved in meaningful social action* (pp. 222–233). New York, NY: Routledge.

Norsworthy, K. L., & Khuankaew, O. (2014). Models of trauma in the Global South and the Global North (Interviewer: Michelle Clonch). *Oppositional conversations: After catastrophe.* Retrieved from http://cargocollective.com/OppositionalConversations_Iii/Models-of-Trauma-in-the-Global-South-and-Global-North

Quijano, A. (2007). Coloniality and modernity/rationality. *Cultural Studies, 21,* 168–178. http://dx.doi.org/10.1080/09502380601164353

Restrepo, C. T. (1971). *Revolutionary priest: The complete writings and messages of Camilo Torres.* New York, NY: Random House.

Said, E. W. (1993). *Culture and imperialism.* New York, NY: Knopf.

Shan Human Rights Foundation, & Shan Women's Action Network. (2002, May). *License to rape.* Retrieved from https://www.shanwomen.org/images/reports/licensetorape/Licence_to_rape.pdf

Sholock, A. (2012). Methodology of the privileged: White anti-racist feminism, systematic ignorance, and epistemic uncertainty. *Hypatia, 27,* 701–714. http://dx.doi.org/10.1111/j.1527-2001.2012.01275.x

Smith, K. M. (2010). Female voice and female text: *Testimonio* as a form of resistance in Latin America. *Florida Atlantic Comparative Studies Journal, 12,* 21–38.

Smith, L. T. (2012). *Decolonizing methodologies: Research and indigenous people* (2nd ed.). London, England: Zed Books.

Sue, D. W., & Sue, D. (1999). *Counseling the culturally different* (3rd ed.). Hoboken, NJ: Wiley.

V

LIBERATION PSYCHOLOGY
SOCIAL ACTION

13

Liberation Psychology, Creativity, and Arts-Based Activism and Artivism

Culturally Meaningful Methods Connecting Personal Development and Social Change

Ester R. Shapiro

This chapter draws from critical–emancipatory and cultural developmental perspectives to explore the unique role of creativity and participatory creative arts–based methods in catalyzing the experientially grounded, emancipatory knowledge leading to collective social justice actions sought by liberation psychology. The chapter reviews theory and methods articulating how liberation psychology (and related disciplines; Teo, 2015) uses creative arts–based research methods within equitable community-engaged collaborations as methods of inquiry, particularly toward elevating contributions to knowledge production offered by those most oppressed or excluded by society. The review of critical cultural and developmental perspectives highlights how creative arts offer experientially grounded, emotionally meaningful critical, ethical, and spiritual insights promoting personal and collective growth and change. The review of emancipatory arts–based research methods draws on transdisciplinarity, bricolage, and participatory action research (PAR) as offering theory and philosophy of methods advancing liberation psychology's goals. By building bridges between these approaches, the chapter argues that creativity catalyzes shared communication leading to new insights and empowered personal and collective action, illuminating pathways for personal wholeness and collective action toward equitable change (Cohen-Cruz, 2005; Shapiro & Modestin, 2013; Zittoun et al., 2013).

This author is also known as Ester Rebeca Shapiro Rok.

http://dx.doi.org/10.1037/0000198-014

Liberation Psychology: Theory, Method, Practice, and Social Justice, L. Comas-Díaz and E. Torres Rivera (Editors)

The chapter reviews creativity and creative arts-based practices formally linked to liberation psychology as well as to other emancipatory movements, including Brazilian Augusto Boal's *Theater of the Oppressed* (1974/2008) and *The Aesthetics of the Oppressed* (2006), and Chela Sandoval's (2000) *Methodologies of the Oppressed*. Chicana and Latinx feminists have historically offered arts-centered, spiritually based revisionings of home, families, and communities grounded in Indigenous cosmologies and ways of knowing as alternative transformational pedagogies mobilizing the power of arts in promoting wholeness and healing in everyday life—*lo cotidiano* (Calderón, Bernal, Huber, Malagón, & Vélez, 2012; Espinoza & Blackwell, 2018; Shapiro & Alcantara, 2016). Sandoval was among the first to use the term *artivism* to describe arts-based participatory youth pedagogy from a critical race and youth development perspective (Sandoval & Latorre, 2008). The term is now widely used in a range of fields, including communications, education, and interdisciplinary cultural studies (Aladro-Vico, Jivkova-Semova, & Bailey, 2018; Awad & Wagoner, 2017; Zaccaria, 2014, 2017). This chapter also reviews arts-based PAR, designed to collaboratively create knowledge leading to social change (Cammarota & Fine, 2008; Torre, Fine, Stoudt, & Fox, 2012; Leavy, 2011, 2017; Lykes, 2013).

This chapter's review is guided by gender sensitive, culturally informed, systems-minded theories of complexity and equity promoting positive shared human development across generations, by Paulo Freire's education for critical consciousness, and by participatory methods of social justice inquiry within psychology and across disciplines. Sharing experiential learning from my life as an immigrant woman, I have partnered to create knowledge instigating change in clinical, community health and educational settings (Shapiro, 2018; Shapiro et al., 2018). Expanding my appreciation of relationships and environments promoting wellness through equity, I work as a "cultural practitioner." I apply critical–participatory pedagogies to appreciate how cultural and spiritual creative resources promoting both continuity and innovation during life course transitions support positive development and wellness or *bienestar* (Shapiro & Alcantara, 2016). Holistic cultural and human rights–oriented frameworks for wellness recognize our fundamental connections across generational time in communities and settings where we live and work, producing and protecting what indigenous communities view as a web of life, interdependent human and nonhuman elements sustaining life and increasingly endangered by ideologies celebrating individual mastery over other humans, nonhumans, and environments sustaining life.

LIBERATION PSYCHOLOGY AND CREATIVE ARTS: THEORY AND METHODS

Culturally centered creative arts, arts-based activism. artivism, and arts-based PAR can generate new knowledge for transformative responding even to conditions of psychopolitical oppression, material scarcity, and suffering

(Cohen-Cruz, 2010; Fine, 2018; Fox, 2015; Lykes, 2013; Shapiro, 2014; Shapiro & Alcantara, 2016; Watkins & Shulman, 2008). Liberation psychology and related disciplines argue that oppressed individuals and communities are taught to view themselves as inferior compared with a dominant individual and sector of society as the optimal standard and to understand their conditions of oppression as inevitably emerging from their inferiority rather than from the web of social policies, practices, and governing ideologies such as White supremacy, colonization, patriarchy, social class privilege heteronormativity, or caste protecting privilege and maintaining oppression. Methodologically, liberation psychologists apply PAR and other social justice centered approaches to inquiry, whose primary goal is to include the voices of those most disparaged and marginalized, toward recognizing, resisting and refusing oppressive social ideologies while generating new knowledge contributing to greater equity. To achieve these goals, methods are centered on community or collectively engaged, experiential, multimodal testimonials and dialogues, including shared oral and digital storytelling, Photovoice, and other arts-based research methods, tools developed to democratize the process of asking questions and build knowledge for action. Colombian sociologist Orlando Fals-Borda is most directly associated with PAR as an experiential emancipatory method (Fals-Borda & Rahman, 1991). However, educator Paulo Freire and psychologist Ignacio Martín-Baró also emphasized research conducted with disadvantaged communities as necessary to building knowledge from shared, direct experiences. At La Universidad de Centro America, El Salvador, Martín-Baró founded the Instituto de Opinión Pública (Institute of Public Opinion), a research center focused on direct surveys of community knowledge. Martín-Baró (1994) in "Public Opinion Research as De-ideologizing Instrument," argued that direct public polling offered a highly effective method of *deideologizing*, or uncovering and countering the taken-for-granted ideologies devaluing the knowledge and experience of the poor and excluded. These deideologizing methods included conducting systematic research documenting changes over time, sensitivity to participant representativeness with primary focus on the historically excluded, and a holistic, dialectical approach drawing from multiple perspectives to understand the whole. Working from this legacy, Fine and colleagues (Fine, 2018) reviewed PAR public opinion research in which urban youth of color and queer youth document their constant confrontations with subordination and social danger through experiences of targeting and criminalization in schools and on the streets.

Emancipatory approaches emphasize popular "arts" in everyday life settings, rather than "Art" by recognized experts displayed on stage or in museums, although both can help instigate social change partnerships. Drawing from cultural, aesthetic, and spiritual rituals and traditions such as household altars, textile arts, gospel call-and-response, or coming-of-age celebrations, popular arts are at the same time culturally patterned yet improvised and imaginatively re-interpreted, enriching our everyday lives. At the productive intersections of artivism, cultural organizing, and participatory inquiries, creative methods of shared learning and collaborative affirmation and discovery offer valuable accessible tools for critical participatory teaching and learning (Adams, Salter, Kurtiş, Naemi, & Estrada-Villalta, 2018; Awad & Wagoner, 2017; Cohen-Cruz, 2005; Kuttner, 2016; Switzer, 2018; Teo, 2018). These include storytelling, hip-hop and spoken word, graphic novels and telenovelas, choreography and performance, photography, video, embroidery and fabric arts, graffiti, and public murals. When linked to liberation psychology, creative methods facilitate deep reflection on lived experiences sensitive to social contexts, emotional engagement in equitable relationships based on trust, and collaborative learning re-visioning possibilities while inspiring social action (Fine, 2018; Fox, 2015; Gallagher, 2018; Lykes, 2017; Torre et al., 2012). Using the language of Chicana feminists, arts-based collective learning helps us use everything we know toward new movements "*movidas*/moves" (Espinoza & Blackwell, 2018).

TRANSDISCIPLINARITY AS TRANSFORMATIVE SOCIAL JUSTICE INQUIRY

To better connect critical, decolonizing, and emancipatory with work on culture, creativity, artivism and transformative human development, I turn to transdisciplinary critical cultural studies (Espina Prieto, 2005). Transdisciplinarity in critical social sciences is an approach to research that recognizes limitations of deterministic predict-and-control research methods designed to reduce complexity to measurable narrow, isolated variables for hypothesis testing. Transdisciplinarity offers a complexity/systems-science based, politically and historically contextualized, social justice–oriented research approach emphasizing collaborative production of knowledge for community impact toward greater equity. Calling on relevant sources of expertise within and outside academia, transdisciplinary research critiques power inequalities both within and outside the work group, requires reflexivity regarding participant disciplinary and personal subjectivities, collaboration toward inclusive knowledge creation, and application of systems-minded contextualized perspectives. Finally, this approach emphasizes accountability to participants and local settings in taking action on knowledge gained (Espina Prieto, 2005; Leavy, 2011). Social justice–oriented transdisciplinary research uses accessible methods including digital or narrative storytelling and creative arts to holistically understand, communicate with coresearchers, and take actions addressing complex, real-world problems.

Complexity sciences recognizing multifinality, contingency, and emergent outcomes are widely used in developmental, environmental, and organizational change studies, although in these fields too often lacking a critical, intersectional social justice lens. Cultural developmental psychologists study how individuals imaginatively engage and represent their multifaceted, complex social environments to emerge with novel solutions (Zittoun et al., 2013). However, lacking a critical race analysis, celebrations of culture can collude with inequality by obscuring legacies of oppression (Yosso & Burciaga, 2016). Critical cultural perspectives go further, challenging health and other outcomes of shared development associated with power inequalities, recognizing realistic, enduring consequences of deprivations we both live materially and internalize. Critical cultural perspectives challenge social science research emphasizing normativity of affluent lives and viewing "damaged," nonnormative marginalized groups as targets of decontextualized scientific regard (Teo, 2015). Lacking a critical emancipatory perspective, seemingly compassionate but ultimately collusive approaches accept social conditions of inequality while helping construct the psychological component of oppression by blaming urban adolescents, women experiencing sexual assault or suicidal queer youth for their own "risky behaviors" and failures of personal resilience, offering only expert treatment for private maladies (Fine & Cross, 2016; Fox, 2015). Participatory inquiry allows novel, more just solutions to emerge (Espina Prieto, 2005; Linds, 2006; Teo, 2018; Torre et al., 2012).

Communication and cultural studies scholar–activist Appadurai (2006) argued that cocreative representations of lived experiences, especially for those confronting inequalities, offer methods of systematic inquiry forming the right to research as a human right: to ask questions about problems we face yet don't have answers for, knowledge we need for living. Appadurai proposes that globalization, disenfranchising the poor especially youth from feeling they belong in their own cities, can be countered with arts-based "documentation as intervention" (Appadurai, 2006, p. 174; see https://www.pukar.org.in for arts-based work with youth organizing in Mumbai, India). Building on critical transdisciplinarity as ethically informed participatory inquiry, a cultural developmental approach within liberation psychology connects learning grounded in everyday lives—lo cotidiano—with arts-based inquiry designed for personal development, collaborative consciousness raising, and societal transformation.

TRANSITIONS AND TRANSFORMATIONS: INQUIRY AS BRICOLAGE

Emancipatory scholars, artists, and activists often use the vocabulary of the world of transition and transformation or the in-between: *metaxis*, in Boal's (2008) *Theater of the Oppressed* (discussed in more depth later in this chapter), describes a state of belonging, at the same time, to the world of reality and to the images we have created of that world (Linds, 2006); *nepantla*, the indigenous word for the in-between world of materiality and spirituality, which Gloria Anzaldúa (2015) described as the space for transformation of self from oppression to possibility; and *liminality*, which comes from anthropology of transitions or life course rituals, used by Latinx feminists to describe creative transformation during periods of crisis (Lugones, 2003; Shapiro & Alcantara, 2016). Boal, Anzaldúa, and Lugones combine their scholarly writing with images, poetry, and performance to inspire knowledge for transformation.

Participatory education and critical health/qualitative research use the term *bricolage* for multimethod research, following anthropologist Lévi-Strauss's description of improvisational cultural practices using materials at hand. Researchers using a bricolage approach pose questions, then work with coresearchers in selecting the most relevant methods, permitting novel and creative connections to emerge (Kincheloe & Berry, 2004; Leavy, 2017). Michelle Fine's Public Science Project uses multigenerational PAR to better understand the lives of targeted and marginalized youth of color and queer youth. Arts-based methods are "knowledge equalizers" cultivating youth perspectives disrupting normative assumptions, while allowing emergence of critical perspectives on lived experiences of schooling, policing, or sexualities (Fine, 2018; Torre et al., 2012). Applying knowledge gained from lived experiences to challenge injustices and take action offers powerful tools for change. Working with Muslim students at UMASS Boston, I shared Fine and Sirin's (2008) arts-based depictions of Muslim immigrant youth's social targeting and cultural pride in hyphenated lives. Inspiring their own exploration of gendered social constraints, fears, and safe harbors in Boston's racialized anti-Muslim climate, intensified after the April 19, 2013, Boston Marathon bombing, Muslim students successfully advocated for reconfiguring the Interfaith chapel as a fully inclusive campus prayer space.

INCITING CREATIVE MALADJUSTMENT IN SHARED DEVELOPMENT: CRITICAL HISTORIES AND COUNTER-STORIES AS CULTURAL AFFORDANCES PROMOTING CHANGE

Critique of psychology's focus on adjustment or adaptation to unjust social conditions of racism and poverty, and invitation to creative rebellion, was offered in 1967, when the Society for the Psychological Study of Social Issues invited Martin Luther King, Jr., to address the American Psychological Association Annual Convention (see https://www.apa.org/monitor/features/king-challenge). In the midst of societal upheaval, a few months before his courageous calls for mobilization resulted in his assassination, King challenged psychologists to conduct research on the urgent questions of refusing White supremacy. Speaking to psychologists as experts too often using the term *maladjustment* to encourage adjustment to the status quo, King offered *creative maladjustment* as principled refusal to adjust to the beliefs and norms of an unjust society. King believed psychologists should play a central role in civil rights and antipoverty movements, one we struggle and strive to fulfill. In a special issue of *Journal of Social Issues* commemorating the 50th anniversary of King's speech, Allen and Leach (2018) argued that King's call is particularly difficult for U.S. and Anglophone Psychology to study or theorize because of the field's strongly imposed belief that adjustment to the world that exists, with its multilevel enforced power hierarchies producing inequalities, represents the highest accomplishment of psychological development. Adams and colleagues (2015, 2018) have suggested that a decolonizing psychology, founded on the emancipatory work of Black Caribbean psychiatrist Frantz Fanon, the critical consciousness pedagogy of Paulo Freire, and the liberation psychology of Ignacio Martín-Baró, offers a starting point for an alternative psychology recognizing and refusing its role in normalizing social dominance.

Adams and colleagues (2018) applied the construct of *cultural affordances*, a theoretical approach to the social ecology of developmental cognition based in complex adaptive–developmental systems theories of culturally and relationally scaffolded learning (Ramstead, Veissière, & Kirmayer, 2016). Using this construct within a critical historical perspective on understanding racism, they described the very different representations of Black History Month in Historically Black Colleges and Universities, which emphasized histories of slavery and Jim Crow, compared with those at Predominantly White Institutions, presenting a White-washed "diversity" narrative emphasizing "celebrations of culture" rather than histories of racism. For participants of all backgrounds, exposure to Black History Month celebrations incorporating critical historical awareness was associated with better understanding of contemporary, everyday racism. Following Martín-Baró (1994), methods for recapturing erased histories, while elevating subordinated communities' marginalized knowledge toward detecting and denouncing ideologies infusing everyday life and protecting inequality, offer guiding principles toward creative maladjustment, as refusal and righteous anger regarding the entangled ideologies, policies, and practices enforcing racism and other forms of inequality.

Without a critical sociopolitical perspective, the psychological construct of "adaptation" invokes acceptance of what is and a view of change that makes it possible to conform to new conditions without questioning what is. Developmental systems sciences have been slow to recognize sociopolitical inequalities, although work bridging societal stressors and their biological impacts through multilevel analysis currently begins to offer this critique although not (yet) a guide toward social accountability (Juster et al., 2016). Zittoun and colleagues (2013), in a collaborative six-author "dialogue" on human development, explored the centrality of every individual's unique creativity in designing a signature response to lifelong challenges they termed "Melodies of Living." They argued that imagination allows individuals to revisit past experiences, perceive and negotiate current social realities, and consider possible futures through a semiotic/meaning-making process creating a unique perspective on the present and opening up new possibilities in their own lives. However, their focus was more on individual enrichment and less on collective efforts to ensure these enriched opportunities are equitably distributed. Critiquing this decontextualized developmental approach through research using collaborative performance, Gallagher, Starkman, and Rhoades (2017) reported on a multicity Canadian arts-based research project on sheltered youth experiences of urban gentrification and exclusion. They argued against the customary youth development language of "resilience" demanded of "at-risk" youth living precarious lives as colluding with and reinforcing both actual structural inequalities and the multiple systems for their enforcement, and they argued for a critical perspective on "creative resilience" as ensemble practice, recognizing the power of theater as a forum in which targeted youth can build collective knowledge toward greater justice in cities.

ARTS-BASED METHODS IN LIBERATION PSYCHOLOGY: BOAL AND *THEATER OF THE OPPRESSED*

Augusto Boal's (2008) *Theater of the Oppressed*, named as an homage to Paulo Freire's (1970/1994) *Pedagogy of the Oppressed*, is the artistic emancipatory practice most directly related to liberation psychology (Cohen-Cruz & Schutzman, 2006). Boal, similarly facing the Brazilian dictatorship of the 1960s and 1970s, described his own process of confrontation and transformation when, after staging a performance of a play where oppressed peasants took up armed insurrection, audience members asked him and his actors to join their revolutionary movement. Appreciating that traditional theater failed to directly address realities of injustice, he developed "Forum Theater" as a means of directly involving audience members. Coining the terminology and methods supporting audiences as actors, he created a role for "Spect-actors." In Forum Theater and evolving innovations, audiences are invited to identify social problems, present them dramatically in theater form, then stop the action so participants can debate potential solutions. Boal productions identify a "Joker," a position derived from the Joker's role in a deck of cards to be whatever value is needed. In Forum Theater, the Joker's job it is to ensure performances flow so that an initially dramatized topic is opened to the audience, who become actors and participants who debate, reenact, and revise the theater piece, exploring possible consensus and potential solutions and actions both within and subsequent to the performance. Exiled from Brazil first to Argentina and then to Europe (1976–1986), Boal spent time in Scandinavia where, appreciating that even affluent communities experienced challenges such as social isolation or mental health distress, he developed a form of Therapeutic Theater he called *Cop in the Head/Rainbow of Desire*. Returning to Brazil in 1986, he was elected to Rio de Janeiro's City Council, developing "Legislative Theater" for community members to identify problems and enact policy solutions.

Theater of the Oppressed (Boal, 2008) became highly influential in Latin America, Europe, and the United States during his years of exile. Initially focused on the history, poetics, and politics of theater as an art form, he came to appreciate performance more broadly as an avenue for representation of human experience, and self-discovery in community. In *Aesthetics of the Oppressed*, Boal (2006) presented both a broader theory of performance within and beyond theater as methods for nurturing creativity foundational to discovery leading to collective action. Boal described the step-by-step exercises encouraging creative use of embodied senses, depicting a Tree of Theatre of the Oppressed (TO), Modeled on a Tree of Life (p. x). The soil nourishing the Tree of TO consists of the aesthetic of the oppressed and an ethics of solidarity, feeding roots made of images, sounds, and words, each developed through workshop activities he called games designed to open up creative expressions of one's own embodied experiential understanding. The Tree of TO grows within a context of history and philosophy of theater and arts for social change on one side and political participation on its other. The tree's branches and leaves represent forms of TO evolving over time in multiple settings, including image theater, Forum Theater, Newspaper Theater, Rainbow of Desire, Invisible Theater, and Legislative Theater. Social Actions, at the tree's crown, must be concrete and continuous, using organized forms of multiplication, represented by a bird nesting on the upper branches, ready to take flight.

Boal developed and inspired highly practical theater projects empowering individuals to reclaim themselves as subjects through their own creativity—art offering a means of self-discovery connected to collective social action. These actions of "symbolic trespass" help transcend imposed limits of silencing cultural norms in collusion with oppression, greatly expanding self-knowledge, self-respect, and freedom of thought and action. Boal's work has evolved both as specific theater technique and as broader performative public art (Cohen-Cruz, 2005; Cohen-Cruz & Schutzman, 2006). Cohen-Cruz and Schutzman (2006) noted that Boal's deeply theorized and highly practical evolving practice moved as he did through decades forced by exile to work in multiple settings including political theater, pedagogy, activism, therapy, and legislation. After returning to Brazil, Boal worked as a legislator, continuing to develop performance as offering communal opportunities to re-vision selves, connect through dialogues developing critical consciousness, solidarity, and active planning toward transforming realities.

Cohen-Cruz (2005, 2010) described community-based performance in the United States as both grounded in Boal's work and moving beyond it by incorporating multiple arts-based practices. She described four principles resulting in community cultural development: sensitivity to and partnerships within the communal context; reciprocity; multiplicity of purpose open to "boundary jumping," such that performances can at the same time operate as art, ritual, therapy, and politics; and active culture rather than passive observation. She used anthropological theory of cultural ritual in rites of passage to conceptualize community performance as a liminal–transformational space in which ritual represents both continuity–stability and flexibility–capacity for imagination, improvisation, and invention. She and others have argued that arts-based community practices require evaluation of authentic, engaged participation, so they do not perpetuate power relations of inequality, for example, between arts foundations or museums creating community partnerships and the communities they serve. Arts-based community engaged practices offer opportunities for impactful cultural organizing.

In this spirit, I highly recommend U.S. African American artist Nick Cave's Shreveport, Louisiana, project, *As Is*, and the film (Falbaum, 2016) depicting development of this multimedia performance in collaboration with arts funders, local artists, and six local social service agencies with participants of all ages impacted by social disadvantage. Cave described his artistic practice as transformed by Rodney King's 1992 beating by Los Angeles police and subsequent protests. As a queer Black man, he wanted his art to include his holistic experiences of creatively confronting vulnerability and standing up to power while having a social impact. Soundsuits, his best-known works, emerged from his determination to transform vulnerable Black bodies into power through collective rituals of transformation. Soundsuits are simultaneously African all-body masks, protective shelters, ornate colorful sculptures made of fabric or found objects, and sound and dance performances when in motion, conveying ritual's power to invent new forms. In *As Is*, Cave joined local spoken-word artists, gospel and country musicians and singers, and textile weavers in working with youth, disabled veterans, and other community members to create unique artworks representing their life experiences while becoming part of a larger collective artwork. Individually created quilts were then interwoven into the performance, representing unique and communal visions of facing challenges and arising. Musicians, singers, and dancers learned to move within the magnificent constraints and invocations of Cave's Soundsuits. The collective weight of dozens of woven bead quilts representing participant stories of suffering and resilience became especially impactful when Cave himself carried their visibly heavy burden across the stage, inviting participants into a space of compassionate communal witnessing. *As Is* culminated in a traditional performance, yet the thousands of people who contributed to and viewed this representation of Shreveport's community life, both creators and audience, found their lives reflected in a magnificent representation of the beauty found within community.

ARTS-BASED METHODS OF TRANSFORMATION: ARTIVISM AS METHODOLOGIES OF THE OPPRESSED

Chicana feminists pioneered the centering of the arts as exemplary tools for oppositional representation of devalued lived experiences (Blackwell, 2016; Espinoza & Blackwell, 2018). Their work interweaves emancipatory theories with creative arts, doing so in line with ancestral archetypes; with culturally meaningful, revolutionary popular arts traditions such as mural art; and increasingly with digital age activism. In this spirit, I recommend Chela Sandoval's landmark book *Methodologies of the Oppressed*, her coauthored paper on artivism in the work of Judith Baca, and the 5-minute video depicting Sandoval as a Chicana super-heroine by video graphic artist and animator Rafael Solorzano (Sandoval, 2000; Sandoval & Latorre, 2008; Solorzano, 2014). Sandoval began work in the 1970s within Chicana and Women of Color critiques of second-wave feminism, offering the term *U.S. third world feminisms* as recognition of U.S. oppressions and early expression of intersectional feminisms. She wrote *Methodologies of the Oppressed* while working in Chicana activist spaces, where arts were central to creating oppositional, alternative representations of women's experiences. Methodologies of the oppressed challenge dominant ideologies through five "technologies of resistance": first, reading of cultural signs, what she called *semiotics*; second, deconstructing these signs by disentangling their physical forms from the ways they communicate dominant–oppressive meanings; third, the oppressed appropriate and transform these dominant ideological forms, what she termed *meta-ideologizing*; fourth, these methodologies require "democratics," or a moral commitment to equality; finally, they reappropriate space and boundaries through "differential movement" or self-shifting, recognizing when survival requires recognition and seeming adherence to dominant power while also resisting these constructions. For Sandoval, methodologies of the oppressed as techniques of resistance specifically target the transformation of cultural signs imposing rules of the dominance game, offering alternative modes of representation—representation in the form of artistic-symbolic material as well as representation through democratic inclusion.

Sandoval and Latorre (2008) introduced the term *artivism* in their paper on Judith Baca's digital participatory work with youth of color in Los Angeles. Baca founded the Cesar Chavez Digital Mural Lab within the Social and Public Art Resource Center (SPARC), a production facility creating large-scale digitally generated murals, educational DVDs, animations, community archives, and digital art. The authors viewed artivism as cultivating what Anzaldúa (2015) termed *mestiza consciousness*, an indigenous feminist-critical race perspective on knowledge gained by deciphering life on society's marginalized borderlands. The authors argued that access to one's own cultural complexity and ability to negotiate multiple worldviews with consciousness of their messaging regarding power and values permits youth as artists working in community to create new ways to see and challenge oppression while seeking equitable alliances across differences. In defining artivism as a tool of youth development in a digital age, Sandoval and LaTorre celebrated both the college classroom experiences of creating and sharing activist art and community-engaged digital mural work involving community youth, many of them deemed "at risk" and irredeemable, documenting the transformative nature of these collective alternative visions actualized in public spaces. Baca's work incorporates young women and queer sensibilities in the digital domain, which too often remains exclusively male. The authors described the work of seeing others and being seen empathically against the grain of stereotypes as "active witnessing." Young student-artivists share their images of Los Angeles life experiences, asking youth participants to share what the images mean to them. They identify this pedagogy as a ritual generating emotionally and spiritually intense learning, pushing artistic and intellectual boundaries, appreciating how collective histories can be expressed uniquely.

PAR AND MULTIGENERATIONAL PAR

PAR, emerging from multiple emancipatory projects, incorporates ideas regarding coconstructed or dialogic inquiry committed to social understanding in the service of ethical accountability to communities (Lykes, 2013). Fals-Borda's work has been most directly associated with development of this research method. However, both Freire's participatory pedagogy and Martín-Baró's liberation psychology have made discovery and inquiry central to their understanding of knowledge creation centered on those most marginalized who have the greatest understanding of their own lived experiences. Within psychology, the work of Michelle Fine and her team at CUNY's Public Science Project and of Brinton Lykes at Boston University's Center for Mental Health and Human Rights are most closely connected to PAR within liberation psychology. Additionally, the work of community-based participatory research in community psychology and public health also draws from participatory pedagogy and community engaged knowledge production accountable to changing conditions toward health with equity (Wallerstein, Duran, Oetzel, & Minkler, 2017; Wandersman, 2003). Working with disempowered groups including youth of color living in urban poverty, communities of color experiencing health disparities, or communities displaced by armed conflict all over the world, PAR strives toward collaboration and power-sharing in all phases of inquiry, including selecting questions and research methods that will best answer those questions, emphasizing community participation in data collection and analysis and in decisions about how best to use knowledge gained for the benefit of those most impacted.

M. Brinton Lykes has worked in settings of humanitarian crisis, using methods of PAR based in creative arts to provide opportunities for targeted communities to reflect on and testify to their experiences and support accompaniment, witnessing, and resilient recovery (see Chapter 6, this volume). Constituting what she has termed *a people's psychosocial praxis*, these projects recognize erased histories, offer alternative visions of trauma and recovery placing historical and contextual responsibility on social oppression, and demand a better future for themselves, their families, and their communities. A dedicated collaborator and transdisciplinary community psychologist, Lykes connects her work to participatory community economic development, a field that rejects the exploitative, savage capitalist models of globalization development economics and centers economic development on the self-defined needs and cultural preferences of displaced and targeted communities.

The transdisciplinary work of Michelle Fine and partners in the Center for Public Science is located as applied social psychology and conducts multigenerational PAR (Fine, 2018; Torre, Fine, Stoudt, & Fox, 2012). Fine, Torre, and their collaborators offer three principles for multigenerational PAR. First, expertise is shared, and power relationships in sharing expertise are carefully monitored. Arts-based methods are particularly important as "knowledge equalizers" and are used in their multigenerational training through, among other spaces, a "research camp" for research methods. Second, their work emphasizes cultivating a critical lens, encouraging participants to question their assumptions, trust their lived experiences, and consider contexts, particularly the way adults and youth from different intersecting locations navigate public spaces differently. Working with queer youth, Muslim youth, youth of color, and urban youth, Fine and her collaborators have supported participants in composing, drawing, and mapping spaces of school push-out, violent policing, gender surveillance, and religious persecution based on visible signs such as wearing a hijab, cultivating the empowerment that only contributing to new knowledge can bring to those who have internalized oppressive categories as elements of self-regard.

Visual methods, including Photovoice, digital storytelling, and participatory film and performance projects, offer meaningful opportunities for democratizing inquiry, particularly with highly targeted, deeply stereotyped, and excluded communities. Like all participatory methods, arts-based methods require careful, consistent attention to inclusive practices (Liebenberg, 2018). Gubrium and colleagues have developed digital storytelling as an empowerment health promotion strategy with Latinx teen mothers living in western Massachusetts (Gubrium & Harper, 2013). Rhoades (2012) described the work of the nonprofit organization Youth Video OUTreach (YVO), which taught LGBTQ youth skills to create a documentary about their lives that they could use for outreach and advocacy efforts by and for LGBTQ youth. She conceptualizes this work as artivist PAR promoting critical civic praxis, arguing that research designed to counter destructive stereotypes and offer alternative images and counter-stories for self-representation is enormously powerful and destigmatizing, healing hurtful social experiences. Walker (2014) conducted a quantitative dissertation, "Black Beauty, White Standards," exploring the role of Black feminist consciousness in protecting Black women from negative effects of White beauty standards. On our Health Promotion Research Team, a work group of Black undergraduate women helped culturally adapt measures of skin color, facial characteristics, and body image while exploring these themes in their own lives. Finding this mixed-methods research to open an inviting gateway to learning from lived experiences, subsequent classes continued this work. Using dialogues, family photographs with narratives, and collaborative auto-ethnographies, they studied and taught impacts of family-centered colorism, particularly for Boston's Black and Latinx immigrant families including Dominican, Puerto Rican, and Cape Verdean. In partnership with Yvette Modestin's Encuentro Diaspora Afro, we invited Magia, of the Cuban hip-hop group Obsesion, whose music video "Mis pelos/My hair" shares her pride in her natural hair within Cuba's culture of hair-straightening, for campus and community performances and dialogues. I share one of many meaningful moments: Jada Evans (personal communication), an African American undergraduate research coordinator, now studying social work, responded to a dialogue group member who asked, "How are we supposed to wear our hair?" Her answer: "Once you have Black feminist consciousness, you wear your hair any way you want to."

CARIBBEAN AND CREOLE COUNTERPOINTS: CULTIVATING KNOWLEDGE BEYOND IMPOSED OPPRESSIVE CERTAINTIES

Cuban anthropologist Fernando Ortiz trained as a lawyer and criminologist at the turn of the 20th century, within Lombroso's European, colonial White supremacist criminology, which insisted on the innate criminal tendencies of African and other subordinate races. Although Ortiz's early ethnographic work imposed these racist and colonial theories, his direct observations allowed him to challenge his training. Ortiz emerged as a lifelong appreciator of African cultures, developing a decolonizing theory of transculturation (Ortiz, 1995). Challenging Malinowski's theory of "acculturation" arguing that "newcomers" (glossing over enslavement, indentured servitude, and indigenous genocide) become part of the new culture, Ortiz proposed that even under conditions of severe inequality of power, both communities emerge mutually transformed in valuable ways. In *Contrapunteo de Tabaco y Azucar/Counterpoint of Tobacco* (representing Black lives) and *Sugar* (representing European Whiteness and global capitalism), Ortiz used a genre-crossing metaphor to tell the story of lives officially organized by a dominant colonizing racial order while creating spaces of privacy, creativity, and resistance. Ortiz's work was especially powerful in elevating the understanding of Afro Cuban religions as the artistic and spiritual legacies of African slaves maintaining their valued traditions and in the process transforming Cuban society. Similarly, Martinican Psychiatrist Frantz Fanon's 1952 publication of *Black Skins, White Masks* offered a revolutionary discipline and genre-crossing work exploring the Black experience of internalizing the White colonial gaze. Ortiz was able to observe beyond imposed categories and report back with field-changing scholarly work, made more impactful by deliberate use of creative, genre-crossing narrative and aesthetic methods.

Caribbean and Creole decolonizing methods using creative arts continue to contribute novel ways of seeing cross-cultural encounters. Zaccaria (2014, 2017) has suggested that the European immigration crisis hardening nationalistic borders while obscuring the role of colonization in creating worlds of inequality can be reframed using Caribbean critiques and methods of decolonization. She highlights the work of European artivists who reimagine Europe's racialized borders. At the University of Massachusetts–Boston, where immigrants and refugees from the world's conflict zones meet to advance their education and actualize their families' dreams, I teach graduate students in the Critical Ethnic and Community Studies Masters in Science program where capstone projects require community-engaged inquiry toward transformative goals. Graduate students Jeannette Mejia and Mirlande Thermidor, working independently on transdisciplinary capstone projects designed to challenge and question Dominican anti-Haitian attitudes, practices, and policies, joined me at the 2018 Dominican Studies Conference at Hostos College in Queens in a session titled "Healing Hispaniola." Together with participants, we explored the ways Caribbean-centered, decolonizing, creative arts–based inquiry, including poetry, testimonial, and dance, helped Dominicans confront internalized racism resulting from anti-Black and anti-Haitian attitudes and policies while appreciating and elevating the many commonalities of Transnational Hispaniola. Mejia and Thermidor (2019) completed their own mixed-methods capstone projects while working collaboratively with student and community coresearchers to present their continuing inquiry. *Sak Pase/Que lo Que*, a campus–community educational project, convened more than 150 students who viewed, responded to, and expanded their arts-based inquiry exploring Haitian–Dominican division and unity as a model for exploring how Pan-African Diaspora communities can heal wounds of colonization and racism.

CONCLUSION

In an unjust world structured to promote complicity with our own oppression, convincing ourselves that conditions of unequal power are what we desire and deserve, redeeming us as "normal" or "successful," how do we discover alternatives? Within liberation psychology's emancipatory framework, creative arts and arts-based activism and artivism offer compelling methods for developing generative, ethically informed (rather than predictable and controlled) ways of knowing, and using the knowledge gained to achieve greater justice. These critical–creative–collaborative methods of action-oriented inquiry, tools for ethically informed systematic study of everyday lives, can catalyze powerful and empowering culturally and spiritually rooted knowledge. These creative inquiry methods recognize both our complex, unique human development and our capacity to build solidarity in community. Creativity, cultivated through arts-based expression and inquiry within liberation psychology, defies imposition of inequality by discovering abundance and beauty even in spaces of scarcity, by elevating marginalized or subordinated lived experiences, making environments and their consequences visible, and invoking a world of culturally, aesthetically, spiritually, and ethically meaningful resistance and resilience. Both in private spaces and public engagement, creative arts allow us to transgress oppressive rules, illuminating alternative pathways and instigating new opportunities on shared journeys toward affirming social justice values and taking action allowing us to live by these most cherished values.

REFERENCES

Adams, G., Salter, P. S., Kurtiş, T., Naemi, P., & Estrada-Villalta, S. (2018). Subordinated knowledge as a tool for creative maladjustment and resistance to racial oppression. *Journal of Social Issues, 74*, 337–354. http://dx.doi.org/10.1111/josi.12272

Adams, G. E., Dobles, I., Gómez, L. H., Kurtiş, T., & Molina, L. E. (2015). Decolonizing psychological science: Introduction to the special thematic section. *Journal of Applied Social and Political Psychology, 3*, 213–238. http://dx.doi.org/10.5964/jspp.v3i1.564

Aladro-Vico, E., Jivkova-Semova, D., & Bailey, O. (2018). Artivism: A new educative language for transformative social action. *Comunicar: Media Education Research Journal, 26*(57), 9–18. http://dx.doi.org/10.3916/C57-2018-01

Allen, A. M., & Leach, C. W. (2018). The psychology of Martin Luther King Jr.'s "creative maladjustment" at societal injustice and oppression. *Journal of Social Issues, 74*, 317–336. http://dx.doi.org/10.1111/josi.12271

Anzaldúa, G. (2015). *Light in the dark/Luz en lo oscuro: Rewriting identity, spirituality, reality.* Durham, NC: Duke University Press. http://dx.doi.org/10.1215/9780822375036

Appadurai, A. (2006). The right to research. *Globalisation, Societies and Education, 4*, 167–177. http://dx.doi.org/10.1080/14767720600750696

Awad, S., & Wagoner, B. (Eds.). (2017). *Street art of resistance.* Singapore: Springer. http://dx.doi.org/10.1007/978-3-319-63330-5

Blackwell, M. (2016). *Chicana power! Contested histories of feminism in the Chicano movement.* Austin: University of Texas Press.

Boal, A. (2006). *The aesthetics of the oppressed.* New York, NY: Routledge.

Boal, A. (2008). *Theater of the oppressed.* London, England: Pluto Press. (Original work published 1974)

Calderón, D., Bernal, D. D., Huber, L. P., Malagón, M., & Vélez, V. N. (2012). A Chicana feminist epistemology revisited: Cultivating ideas a generation later. *Harvard Educational Review, 82*, 513–539. http://dx.doi.org/10.17763/haer.82.4.l518621577461p68

Cammarota, J., & Fine, M. (2008). *Revolutionizing education: Youth participatory action research in motion.* New York, NY: Routledge.

Cohen-Cruz, J. (2005). *Local acts: Community based performance in the United States.* New Brunswick, NJ: Rutgers University Press.

Cohen-Cruz, J. (2010). *Engaging performance: Theatre as call and response.* New York, NY: Routledge.

Cohen-Cruz, J., & Schutzman, M. (Eds.). (2006). *A Boal companion: Dialogues on theatre andculturalpolitics.*NewYork,NY:Routledge.http://dx.doi.org/10.4324/9780203300794

Espina Prieto, M. (2005). *Complejidad y pensamiento social* [Complexity and social thought]. *COMPLEXUS, Journal of Complexity, Science and Aesthetics*, 77–114.

Espinoza, D., & Blackwell, M. (Eds.). (2018). *Chicana movidas: New narratives of activism and feminism in the movement era.* Austin: University of Texas Press.

Falbaum, E. (Producer and Director). (2016). AS IS by Nick Cave—Art documentary [Motion Picture]. United States: Moviesauce. Retrieved from https://www.youtube.com/watch?v=wVdIGBSQy78

Fals-Borda, O., & Rahman, M. A. (Eds.). (1991). *Action and knowledge: Breaking the monopoly with participatory action research.* New York, NY: Apex Press. http://dx.doi.org/10.3362/9781780444239

Fine, M. (2018). *Just research in contentious times: Widening the methodological imagination.* New York, NY: Teachers College Press.

Fine, M., & Cross, W. (2016). Critical race, psychology, and social policy: Refusing damage, cataloging oppression, and documenting desire. In A. N. Alvarez, C. T. Liang, & H. A. Neville (Eds.), *The cost of racism for People of Color: Contextualizing experiences of discrimination* (pp. 273–294). Washington, DC: American Psychological Association. http://dx.doi.org/10.1037/14852-013

Fine, M., & Sirin, S. R. (2008). *Muslim American youth: Understanding hyphenated identities through multiple methods.* New York, NY: NYU Press.

Fox, M. (2015). Embodied methodologies, participation, and the art of research. *Social and Personality Psychology Compass, 9*, 321–332. http://dx.doi.org/10.1111/spc3.12182

Freire, P. (1994). *Pedagogy of the oppressed.* New York, NY: Seabury Press. (Original work published 1970)

Gallagher, K. (Ed.). (2018). *The methodological dilemma revisited: Creative, critical and collaborative approaches to qualitative research for a new era.* New York, NY: Routledge. http://dx.doi.org/10.4324/9781315149325

Gallagher, K., Starkman, R., & Rhoades, R. (2017). Performing counter-narratives and mining creative resilience: Using applied theatre to theorize notions of youth resilience. *Journal of Youth Studies, 20,* 216–233. http://dx.doi.org/10.1080/13676261.2016.1206864

Gubrium, A., & Harper, K. (2013). *Participatory visual and digital methods.* New York, NY: Routledge.

Juster, R. P., Seeman, T., McEwen, B. S., Picard, M., Mahar, I., Mechawar, N., . . . Lanoix, D. (2016). Social inequalities and the road to allostatic load: From vulnerability to resilience. In D. Chichetti (Ed.), *Developmental psychopathology* (pp. 381–434). New York, NY: Wiley.

Kincheloe, J., & Berry, K. (2004). *Rigour and complexity in educational research: Conceptualising the bricolage.* Berkshire, England: Open University Press.

Kuttner, P. J. (2016). Hip-hop citizens: Arts-based, culturally sustaining civic engagement pedagogy. *Harvard Educational Review, 86,* 527–555. http://dx.doi.org/10.17763/1943-5045-86.4.527

Leavy, P. (2011). *Essentials of transdisciplinary research: Using problem-centered methodologies.* New York, NY: Routledge.

Leavy, P. (Ed.). (2017). *Handbook of arts-based research.* New York, NY: Guilford Press.

Liebenberg, L. (2018). Thinking critically about photovoice: Achieving empowerment and social change. *International Journal of Qualitative Methods, 17*(1), 1–9. http://dx.doi.org/10.1177/1609406918757631

Linds, W. (2006). Metaxis: Dancing (in) the in-between. In J. Cohen-Cruz & M. Schutzman (Eds.), *A Boal companion* (pp. 124–134). New York, NY: Routledge.

Lugones, M. (2003). *Pilgrimages/peregrinajes: Theorizing coalition against multiple oppressions.* New York, NY: Rowman & Littlefield.

Lykes, M. B. (2013). Participatory and action research as a transformative praxis: Responding to humanitarian crises from the margins. *American Psychologist, 68,* 774–783. http://dx.doi.org/10.1037/a0034360

Lykes, M. B. (2017). Community-based and participatory action research: Community psychology collaborations within and across borders. In M. A. Bond, I. Serrano-García, C. B. Keys, & M. Shinn (Eds.), *APA handbook of community psychology: Methods for community research and action for diverse groups and issues* (pp. 43–58). Washington, DC: American Psychological Association. http://dx.doi.org/10.1037/14954-003

Martín-Baró, I. (1994). *Writings for a liberation psychology.* Cambridge, MA: Harvard University Press.

Mejia, J., & Thermidor, M. (2019). *Sak pase/Que lo que: Healing Hispaniola.* University of Massachusetts–Boston, Transnational Cultural and Community Studies Program.

Ortiz, F. (1995). *Cuban counterpoint: Tobacco and sugar.* Durham, NC: Duke University Press.

Ramstead, M. J., Veissière, S. P., & Kirmayer, L. J. (2016). Cultural affordances: Scaffolding local worlds through shared intentionality and regimes of attention. *Frontiers in Psychology, 7,* 1090. http://dx.doi.org/10.3389/fpsyg.2016.01090

Rhoades, M. (2012). LGBTQ youth+ video artivism: Arts-based critical civic praxis. *Studies in Art Education, 53,* 317–329. http://dx.doi.org/10.1080/00393541.2012.11518872

Sandoval, C. (2000). *Methodologies of the oppressed.* Minneapolis: University of Minnesota Press.

Sandoval, C., & Latorre, G. (2008). Chicana/o artivism: Judy Baca's digital work with youth of color. *Learning race and ethnicity: Youth and digital media,* 81–108.

Shapiro, E. R. (2014). Translating Latin American/U.S. Latina frameworks and methods in gender and health equity: Linking women's health education and participatory social change. *International Quarterly of Community Health Education, 34,* 19–36. http://dx.doi.org/10.2190/IQ.34.1.c

Shapiro, E. R. (2018). Transforming development through just communities: A lifelong journey of inquiry. In L. Comas-Díaz & C. Vazquez (Eds.), *Latina psychologists* (pp. 158–175). New York, NY: Routledge.

Shapiro, E. R., & Alcantara, D. (2016). Mujerista creativity: Latin@ sacred arts as life-course developmental resources. In T. Bryant-Davis & L. Comas Diaz (Eds.), *Womanist and* mujerista *psychologies: Voices of fire, acts of courage* (pp. 195–216). Washington, DC: American Psychological Association Press. http://dx.doi.org/10.1037/14937-009

Shapiro, E. R., Andino Valdez, F., Bailey, Y., Furtado, G., Lamothe, D., Mohammad, K., & Wood, N. (2018). Teaching health and human rights in a psychology capstone: Cultivating connections between rights, personal wellness, and social justice. In E. Choudhury & R. Srikanth (Eds.), *Interdisciplinary approaches to human rights* (pp. 312–330). New York, NY: Routledge. http://dx.doi.org/10.4324/9781351058438-20

Shapiro, E. R., & Modestin, Y. (2013). Women of color and the arts: Creativities in everyday life as wellsprings of resistance and resilience. In L. Comas-Diaz & B. Greene (Eds.), *Psychological health of women of color: Intersections, challenges, and opportunities* (pp. 317–336). New York, NY: Prager.

Solorzano, R. (2014). *Chela Sandoval: The nuts and bolts of Chicana feminist theory.* Los Angeles, CA: UCLA Chicano Studies Center. Retrieved from https://player.vimeo.com/video/122843854

Switzer, S. (2018). What's in an image? Towards a critical and interdisciplinary reading of participatory visual methods. In M. Capous-Desyllas & K. Morgaine (Eds.), *Creating social change through creativity* (pp. 189–207). Cham, Switzerland: Palgrave Macmillan. http://dx.doi.org/10.1007/978-3-319-52129-9_11

Teo, T. (2015). Critical psychology: A geography of intellectual engagement and resistance. *American Psychologist, 70,* 243–254. http://dx.doi.org/10.1037/a0038727

Teo, T. (2018). *Outline of theoretical psychology: Critical investigations* (pp. 241–266). London, England: Palgrave. http://dx.doi.org/10.1057/978-1-137-59651-2_11

Torre, M. E., Fine, M., Stoudt, B. G., & Fox, M. (2012). Critical participatory action research as public science. In H. Cooper, P. M. Camic, D. L. Long, A. T. Panter, D. Rindskopf, & K. J. Sher (Eds.), *APA handbook of research methods in psychology: Vol. 2. Research designs: Quantitative, qualitative, neuropsychological, and biological* (pp. 171–184). Washington, DC: American Psychological Association. http://dx.doi.org/10.1037/13620-011

Walker, S. T. (2014). *Black beauty, White standards: Impacts on Black women and resources for resistance and resilience.* Boston: University of Massachusetts.

Wallerstein, N., Duran, B., Oetzel, J. G., & Minkler, M. (Eds.). (2017). *Community-based participatory research for health: Advancing social and health equity.* New York, NY: Wiley.

Wandersman, A. (2003). Community science: Bridging the gap between research and practice with community-centered models. *American Journal of Community Psychology, 31,* 227–242. http://dx.doi.org/10.1023/A:1023954503247

Watkins, M., & Shulman, H. (2008). *Towards psychologies of liberation.* New York, NY: Palgrave. http://dx.doi.org/10.1057/9780230227736

Yosso, T. J., & Burciaga, R. (2016, July). *Reclaiming our histories, recovering community cultural wealth* (Center for Critical Race Studies at UCLA Research Brief, No. 5).

Zaccaria, P. (2014). Mediterranean and transatlantic artivism. Counter-acting neo-colonialisms in the public sphere. *Journal of Cross-Cultural Studies and Environmental Communication, 1*(1), 41–51.

Zaccaria, P. (2017). A breach in the wall: Artivist no-border atlases of mobility. *Journal of Mediterranean Studies, 26*(1), 37–53.

Zittoun, T., Valsiner, J., Vedeler, D., Salgado, J., Gonçalves, M. M., & Ferring, D. (2013). *Human development in the life course: Melodies of living.* Cambridge, MA: Harvard University Press. http://dx.doi.org/10.1017/CBO9781139019804

14

Liberation, Inspiration, and Critical Consciousness

Preparing the Next Generation of Practitioners

Carrie L. Castañeda-Sound, Daryl M. Rowe, Nahaal Binazir, and Marlene L. Cabrera

Worse yet, it [the banking model of education] turns them [students] into "containers" to be "filled" by the teacher. The more completely she fills the receptacles, the better a teacher she is. The more meekly the receptacles permit themselves to be filled, the better students they are.

—PAULO FREIRE (2000, p. 53)

Liberation psychology compels mental health practitioners to address the systemic and structural influences in the lives of clients so that we do not inadvertently perpetuate the oppression in their lives (Martín-Baró, 1994). The praxis of liberation psychology for students training to be psychologists can be elusive within the structure of accredited doctoral programs due to the constraints of dominant professional perspectives and discourse. This chapter presents the development of a yearlong multicultural specialty track for clinical psychology doctoral students, many of whom are working with underserved communities in the greater Los Angeles basin that seeks to position liberation psychology as a grounding perspective for making applied psychology more accessible and relevant to communities of color. The liberatory frameworks guiding the curriculum development and pedagogy of the specialty track are grounded in African, Indigenous, and Latinx paradigms, which seek to privilege marginalized voices. The course also introduces students to developing theories such as *mujerista* psychology, a theory infused with a spiritual-feminist liberatory approach (Bryant-Davis & Comas-Díaz, 2016). The voices

http://dx.doi.org/10.1037/0000198-015
Liberation Psychology: Theory, Method, Practice, and Social Justice, L. Comas-Díaz and E. Torres Rivera (Editors)

and experiences present in this chapter are the developers of this specialty track, Drs. Daryl Rowe and Carrie Castañeda-Sound, and two previous doctoral students, Nahaal Binazir and Marlene Cabrera, who have completed this training and now are working in pre- and postdoctoral clinical settings. We provide examples of conceptual and structural concerns for developing this track; share our growth in critical consciousness as professors, students, and clinicians; and reflect on continuing areas for improvement.

CONTEXT OF THE MULTICULTURAL SPECIALTY TRACK

The Multicultural[1] Specialty Track transpires over the course of two semesters and is an optional two-course sequence within a generalist clinical psychology PsyD program in a very ethnically diverse part of the United States. The program is a post–master's degree program and embraces a practitioner–scholar model, which means that science and practice are integrated with an emphasis on evidence-based treatment approaches in the curriculum and clinical training. This clinical psychology doctoral program is housed within a private, Christian university with multiple campuses in the Los Angeles area. Christian religion is not specifically integrated into the professional training; rather, the program is inspired by the biblical teachings of inclusivity, compassion, and justice. Further, the university includes in its strategic goals that "diversity does not simply enrich the educational endeavor, it is central to it" (Pepperdine University, n.d., "Goal 4," para. 1). Critical to promoting an appreciation of science has been the inclusion of an understanding of context involving the historical and cultural origins and assumptions embedded in psychological theory and practice in clinical psychology. This strategic goal notwithstanding, there are many areas for growth in the implementation of diversity and social justice within the broader university and specifically within the doctoral program.

The PsyD program is shaped by a variety of forces, but the most powerful is its accreditation by the American Psychological Association's (APA's) Commission on Accreditation, which sets voluntary standards for the curriculum and outcomes, student selection processes, and faculty qualifications for professional education and training programs in psychology. Another force is the state licensing board, which defines the coursework and training required for our students to become licensed psychologists within the state of California. Finally, with the rising cost of tuition, particularly at private universities such as ours, the desire to lower the number of units required to graduate while still meeting the aforementioned expectations is valued by the faculty and students. Unfortunately, these broad forces, coupled with faculty worldviews

---

[1]We use *multicultural* as pragmatic shorthand for the complex constellation of human difference factors that have been historically neglected in clinical psychology, within a faculty of generalist psychologists located at various points along a continuum of individualists to contextualists.

informed by privilege and power, make teaching from a liberation psychology framework challenging, even as the program advances a more inclusive approach to training students in professional psychology. After significant advocacy within the faculty, the broad umbrella of multiculturalism has been used because it best reflects the degree of comfort for the full faculty and is consistent with the language APA uses in its accreditation processes.

HISTORY AND REBIRTH OF THE SPECIALTY TRACK

Washing one's hands of the conflict between the powerful and the powerless means to side with the powerful, not to be neutral.
—PAULO FREIRE (1985, p. 122)

Historically, the PsyD program has had five specialty tracks—Cognitive Behavioral, Humanistic, Psychodynamic, and Family Systems—with several attempts to develop and sustain a Multicultural Track. Over the course of 2 years, PsyD students choose two track specializations. The first attempt to broaden the training of PsyD students was a two-unit elective offered in summer 2006 titled "Culturally Affirmative Approaches to Interventions With Multicultural Populations," developed and taught by Daryl Rowe. The seminar had 10 students but was offered only once due to limited student interest. The next iteration was a Multicultural Track developed and taught by Drs. Miguel Gallardo and Shelly Harrell, both experts in the field of multicultural psychology. At that time, the track was informed by community-ecological and liberation psychology frameworks. This was a rigorous track sequence, but over time, enrollment dwindled, so the last cohort was in 2009–2010.

In 2010, Carrie Castañeda-Sound joined the faculty and immediately developed a professional relationship with Daryl Rowe grounded in teaching classes that explored the sociocultural dimensions of clinical psychology consumers. In the first semester of the program, students take a required course titled "Sociocultural Bases of Behavior." The cohort is divided into two sections, one with Daryl and the other with Carrie. This introductory course does not allow enough time to delve deeply into the broad field of cultural psychology, much less areas of our personal interest, Latinx and liberation psychology, and African and Indigenous perspectives; it does, however, provide students with an overview of the confluence of factors that both mitigate against and provide insight into why the consideration of sociocultural variables are critical in providing efficacious treatment of diverse clients. Students with similar interests requested that a specialty track, grounded in perspectives that privilege members of marginalized communities, be revived in 2015. Daryl helped these students navigate the departmental requirements to "rebirth" the class, the most important being a minimum of nine students. The students began recruiting students for the track, and in the fall 2015 semester, the Specialty Track was reborn. It continued to use Multicultural as its primary descriptor because that course sequence had previously been approved administratively. Since then, four cohorts have completed the revitalized track.

SCOPE AND ASSUMPTIONS OF THE SPECIALTY TRACK

> The problem we still have today in thinking well about the rich diversity of humankind is expressed by the observation that, at the beginning of the dominant Western tradition, a particular group of privileged men took themselves to be the inclusive term or kind, the norm, and the *ideal for all*, a 'mis-taking' that is locked into our thinking. (Minnich, 1990, p. 2)

In 1967, Gordon Paul urged researchers to adjust their central question of "what treatments work?" to "*what* treatment, by *whom*, is most effective for *this* individual, with *that* specific problem, and under *which* set of circumstances?" (p. 111). This was a call to emphasize a more emic versus an etic approach to understanding human psychology. Indeed, in the study of human psychology, an attempt to establish efficacious treatment protocols with limited consideration of the person, and in turn, a person's context, would serve as nothing more than an argument for the perfect symmetry of the human experience; although neat and superficially convenient, it reflects a rather simplistic understanding.

Conceptualizing optimal training in psychology for addressing the needs of a broader cross-section of the human family has been a long-standing challenge for Western psychology. The challenge occurs across at least three dimensions: methodological issues, value-based issues, and conceptual issues (Allwood & Berry, 2006). It has been the introduction of the salience of culture into the discipline that has ushered in a more humanitarian study of psychology. We argue that it reflects a flattening or *humanizing* influence because a cultural perspective seeks to include the full range of humans into our theorizing about human beingness, delineating the broad features of human functioning, and authorizing a fuller scope of the various ways to restore balance when humans are determined to be out of balance (Rowe & Webb-Msemaji, 2004).

Thus, the word *cultural* has modified psychology throughout its history: (a) Edward Sapir saw cultural psychology as "a promising theoretical framework" (Levine, 2007, p. 44); (b) Shweder (2007) as a "psychological diversity, rather than psychological uniformity" (p. 827); and (c) Miller (1999) argued that psychology "always has been cultural" (p. 90). Despite the terminology debate, whether one prefers *multicultural, cross-cultural, cultural, psychological anthropology,* or *sociocultural,* the increased attention, focus, and interest reflects a significant development in the evolution of the field (Triandis, 2007). Notwithstanding all of the conceptual overlap and ambiguity, its historical elusiveness and empirically challenging strategies, people and their social worlds are inseparable: They require each other (Shweder, 1990). Because there have been significant gaps in contemporary psychology, and because of its lag in cultural knowledge, its underpinnings of cultural approaches to professional psychology, and its rationale for adopting a bottom-up application of professional psychology, the aim of the reborn Multicultural Specialty Track was to examine theories that emerge out of the lived cultural or socio-cultural contexts that reflect non-Western locations. Liberation psychology fills these gaps by addressing historical, political, and cultural influences on people's lives.

DEFINING CULTURE

Although culture is an elusive construct to define and there have been countless definitions offered (Kroeber & Kluckhohn, 1952; Lonner & Malpass, 1994; Nobles, 1986), Kleinman's (1996) definition provides a powerful, elegant framing: "Culture is constituted by, and in turn constitutes, local worlds of experience" (p. 16). In other words, that which we know as culture emerges out of everyday experience: It is not something that is esoteric and mysterious— it literally reflects our personal and collective or communal everyday patterns of daily life experiences. Culture reflects our *common sense*(s), communication with others, *routines* (rhythms, rituals, roles), and *responsibilities* of everyday community or communal life that we take for granted as commonplace, normal, and natural (although these aspects are natural only within specified bounds of place and time). Thus, cultural influences lead persons to develop specific belief or value systems, common language, and norms. Further, direct or vicarious experiences of oppression moderate how persons may or may not choose to honor cultural influences or seek to change influences judged not to be positive.

The United States was born out of a mixed history. The articulation in the Bill of Rights and the U.S. Constitution of the fundamental rights of human beings—including the exercise of individual freedoms as long as such exercise does not infringe on the fundamental rights of others—continues to serve as an anchor for democratic debate and represents one of the finest social experiments in human history. At the same time, we cannot ignore the gross contradictions that were in play during the formation of these foundational documents. An African in the United States was legally considered to be three fifths of a human being; women could not vote or own property; men who did not own property could not vote; indentured servitude was legal; the mass genocide of the Indigenous people of this land mass was sanctioned policy; and persons of Asian ancestry were considered second-class aliens (Lee, 2008). Whiteness, as the normative framing to understand human behavior, served to justify all these forms of discrimination against those who were classified as non-White. Given these historical realities within our society, cultural competence must be approached as a process—a way of thinking about students as therapists, the client, the client's context, and theoretical approaches that center the understanding of populations with multidimensional identities in the complex transactional spaces that inform everyday living.

CONCEPTUAL IMPLICATIONS OF A CULTURAL LENS

As Lee (2008) further argued, when we study culturally distinct communities of practice, there are at least two critical issues to explore: (a) the *uniqueness* of each community that reflects the *interior perspective* of its members and (b) the community consistencies that can be *generalized across* cultural communities. Lee extends these critical issues to advance four fundamental propositions for understanding cultural or contextual complexities of culturally distinct communities of practice, as follows: (a) cultural membership is based on *shared routine practices and beliefs* that are *transmitted through generations*, across time and space (Gutiérrez & Rogoff, 2003); (b) although people can and do live in multiple cultural communities of practice, the *meanings and functions* of these different cultural communities differ (Gutiérrez, 2004); (c) often (although not always), the sense of identity associated with ethnicity as it is embodied in the practices of the family in which one grows up will serve as an important psychological anchor for the developing person (Cross, 1991; Sellers et al., 1998); and (d) cultural communities are communities precisely because of *what they share*, but at the same time, there is *always significant variation* within communities (Spencer, 2000). Thus, according to Lee (2008), researchers who seek to examine or generate fundamental theories about how and what human beings learn and the psychosocial processes entailed in such learning need to consider these propositions from the beginning, when deciding how to formulate their inquiries, sampling processes, what kinds of data to collect, the validity of instruments, the assumptions underlying the variables articulated, and the potential limitations of their findings (Lee, Spencer, & Harpalani, 2003).

Therefore, to generate robust and generative theories about how and what people learn to function effectively, we must attend to issues of diversity based on conceptually complex frameworks that position diversity as essential to the human experience and not as some wayward pathology. Thus, our aim is to expose students to theories that emerge out of the lived cultural–sociocultural contexts that reflect non-Western locations. Professional psychology's future must be tied to its ability to transform its defining features and structures to account for how humans around the world understand the systems of meaning of human beingness—features of human functioning and systems for restoring order with imbalance occurs (Rowe & Webb-Msemaji, 2004).

We believe that liberation psychology, broadly defined, can serve to operationalize a sociocultural psychological perspective in the training of professional psychologists better equipped to work with members of our diverse human family. Sociocultural psychology advances the notion that humans are mutually constituted—that is, the psychological and the cultural "make each other up" (Shweder, 1990, p. 24), and they are most productively understood and analyzed together (Adams & Markus, 2003). Indeed, according to Markus and Hamedani (2007), the increased interest in how human behavior is socially and culturally constituted is driven by three factors:

(a) a set of empirical findings that challenge many of Western psychology's signature theories—findings that are not easily interpreted by Western frameworks; (b) growing realization among Western psychologists that the capacity for *culture-making* and *culture-sharing* is at the core of what is means to be human and that this capacity is a clear evolutionary advantage of the human species; and (c) an increasing sophistication in how to conceptualize both the cultural and psychological, such that the nature of their mutual constitution or reciprocal influence can be examined and grasped. Furthermore, they argued that resistance to this idea is promoted primarily by a minority perspective of human functioning that originated in the strongly individualist framing of the West, especially in North American–Western psychology (Arnett, 2008; Henrich, Heine, & Norenzayan, 2010). Thus, the foundational idea in Western psychology is that it's what's *inside* the person, and not the *context* that envelops the person, that matters most (Markus & Hamedani, 2007). Despite unprecedented access to information and diffusion of knowledge across the globe, the bulk of the research and theory development in mainstream psychological science still reflects and promotes the interests of a privileged minority of people in affluent centers of the modern global order (Adams, Dobles, Gómez, Kurtiş, & Molina, 2015).

As Martín-Baró (1994) put it,

> The prevailing discourse puts forth an apparently natural and ahistorical reality, structuring it in such a way as to cause it to be accepted without question. This makes it impossible to derive lessons from experience and, more important, makes it impossible to find the roots of one's own identity, which is as much needed for interpreting one's sense of the present as for glimpsing possible alternatives that might exist. . . . The recovery of historical memory supposes the reconstruction of models of identification that, instead of chaining and caging the people, open up the horizon for them, toward their liberation and fulfillment. (p. 30)

COCONSTRUCTION OF THE DECOLONIZED CLASSROOM

Toscano Villanueva's (2013) article chronicling the decolonization of her classroom inspired me (Carrie) to intentionally incorporate liberation psychology principles in my classes. *Decolonization* refers to the decentering and shedding of paradigms of Eurocentric epistemology and pedagogy that further the agenda of Whiteness. Toscano Villanueva sees the classroom "as a space of hopeful resistance where minds are cultivated, ideas are nurtured, identities emerge, and convictions coalesce" (p. 27). The Specialty Track classes thus become a space for developing critically conscious mental health practitioners and change agents in the field of clinical psychology.

The first semester of the Specialty Track sets the theoretical foundations of Indigenous and African-centered perspectives and essentially involves shifting (e.g., decentering Whiteness) and widening the lens of students' worldviews both personally and professionally. The majority of the students work with youth and adults in underserved communities in the Los Angeles area and are seeking support for culturally responsive approaches. Moreover, many students who select the Specialty Track classes have experiences with oppression in their personal or professional lives due to a variety of social identities—racial, ethnic, religious, sexual orientation, socioeconomic status, immigrant status, disability, gender, or a combination of these. Exposure to Indigenous and liberation psychology approaches often raises students' own critical consciousness and awakens them to conceptualizations congruent with their clients' lives as well as their personal lives. This *conscientization* is explained by Montero (2009) as

> a mobilization of consciousness aiming to produce historic knowledge about oneself and about the groups to which one belongs, thereby producing a different understanding, and giving sense to one's temporal and spatial place in the society, and in one's specific life-world. (pp. 73–74)

This requires students to engage in self-reflection about their positionality in relation to their peers and clients, the professor, and the authors of the readings and videos shown in class.

Important to this decolonized approach is a departure from the banking system of education (Freire, 2000), in which the teacher expects students to receive, memorize, and repeat dominant discourses. For example, authentic dialogue in the classroom contributes to the process of *deideologizing* (Martín-Baró, 1994) the labels of client, student, and professor. Deideologization questions the taken-for-granted assumptions of teaching, learning, and healing in psychotherapy. This process interrogates power and privilege within each of these roles and centralizes life experiences and historical memory as a source of knowledge and expertise.

Humanization (Freire, 2000) of individuals from disenfranchised communities is an important component of the class. Often this process happens when we discuss the students' clients and reflect on the systems of oppression that maintain their dehumanization. Students contribute to their own humanization by sharing their ancestral history and current experiences with oppression. This process of humanization increases empathy and connection among the students and contributes to a collective critical consciousness in the class.

Teaching from a liberation psychology framework requires flexibility and creativity. The semester preceding my course, I (Carrie) ask students what they would like to learn more about in the next semester. Before entering my class, they already know they have a voice in their education. After reviewing the syllabus the first day of class, we have another conversation about the topics and assignments and their vision for their learning. I again invite them to be coconstructors of their education. Examples of requests include adding topics relevant to their current training sites (e.g., working with incarcerated youth of color or LGBT youth), adding content that prepares them for the oral clinical competency exam at the end of their second year, and changing assignments to be more in line with their professional interests. I ask them to help me develop the language for proposed assignment changes so that I can insert it into the revised syllabus. We also engage in a conversation about how the assignment should be graded and what the criteria will be. I have been pleasantly surprised at the level of rigor these students bring to the table.

The second semester of the Specialty Track addresses the different "voices" and perspectives in cultural psychology, including intersectionality and decolonial perspectives. The interdisciplinary resources and materials that comprise this class include scholarly literature, clinical case studies, videos, think pieces and blog posts, podcasts, art in the community (e.g., murals and graffiti), music, children's literature, and social media discourse. Further, I regularly invite guest speakers to give voice to the topics from the class. In the past, we have heard from psychologists working in state hospitals, correctional facilities, counseling centers, and private practice who integrate liberation psychology ideas in their clinical work. I also invite community activists engaged in community healing practices.

The assignments and activities for the course include reflection papers, role-playing in class, development of a multidisciplinary program to address a social issue, and case presentations. Students also have taken ideas from the course to write blogs and conduct outreach on campus and in the community. They also take liberation psychology concepts to their training sites by advocating for their clients—and for their own education by asking for more cultural training. More creative activities include creating a theater of the oppressed (Boal, 1979) on campus to engage passersby in a dialogue about social issues that affect mental wellness. For more in-depth discussion of this theatrical form, see Chapter 13 (this volume), and the work of Dr. Jason Platt (2016) with students in Mexico City for a detailed description.

The following section includes reflections from two students, Nahaal and Marlene, who completed the Specialty Track. Their stories reflect the systemic challenges for students choosing to enroll in this training. Finally, they illustrate how the track classes have shaped their personal and professional development.

SUPPORTING OTHERS TO FIND THEIR VOICES HELPED ME FIND MY OWN

In my second year of graduate school, I (Nahaal) opted for the specialized Multicultural Track—certainly not the standard choice when considering the more traditional orientations available (e.g., psychodynamic, humanist, cognitive behavior therapy). I was drawn to this track for seemingly obvious reasons—because I am a cultural being (as many of us are). To provide context: I am South African born and raised, I am of Iranian heritage, and I have been nurtured within the Bahá'í community. I am also an immigrant who continues to pursue my studies in the United States. And finally, I am an advocate. My upbringing inevitably impacted my worldview about the role of multiculturalism in my life and the lives of those whom I serve.

Studying undergraduate psychology in South Africa, I was encouraged to explore the impact of the application of Eurocentric frameworks on various traditional South African cultural groups. This experience unearthed my passion to explore and unpack the collision between traditional psychology practice and the various people, cultures, and communities with which it comes into contact. When moving on to graduate studies, I eagerly sought out more spaces where I could continue to critically reflect on my own assumptions, biases, and position as a burgeoning professional. This was a taste of the realization of how little I knew about others and myself; I was yearning for more opportunities to learn and further humble myself. As such, the Multicultural Track felt like less of a choice and more of a necessity. I cannot say I impulsively selected this track without reflecting on my own professional goals, however. I considered how multicultural classes would assist me on my road to internship and licensure as a well-rounded and fully competent psychologist. I took the time to reflect on my professional trajectory and engage in detailed consultation with peers, colleagues, family, supervisors, and professors alike. To describe the feedback I received as varied would be an understatement.

One aspect that was common across opinions was clear: There was widespread appreciation for multicultural psychology, an endorsement of its importance and necessity, and, at times, relief that this was finally becoming a primary area of focus in a field whose reputation is sometimes perceived as one of tunnel vision. Many individuals I spoke with outside of the psychology field were not even aware that this was a consideration of psychologists and expressed appreciation that it was gaining traction. Overtly, it was apparent that multiculturalism needed to become a priority and was completely necessary in our practice. Covertly, there were more nuanced messages that necessitated further exploration.

Although multiculturalism was described as "indispensable," I also witnessed how often others insinuated that it was more of a subsidiary or subordinate to more widely recognized and respected therapeutic techniques. This was a view that I felt pervaded many of the spaces I was in—primarily among my peers and colleagues, but sometimes even among select supervisors. This message singlehandedly relegated multicultural theory's importance to that of a mere accessory and peripheral to more widely recognized therapeutic methods. I also encountered commentary that "everything is cultural, culture is everywhere." This oversimplification suggested that culture could be studied in any class or site and, as a result, did not necessitate focused and concerted effort in its own specialized track. I felt this was a careless "one size fits all" blanket statement that severely underestimated the complexity of human experience and the role of culture and context therein.

However, surely if the study of culture is "everywhere" and central to everything, that would indicate that it is fundamental to study and that it should be mandatory rather than optional? Even with this thought in mind, I became apprehensive about whether I was placing myself at a disadvantage among my peers and colleagues. Was multicultural psychology not recognized work? Was it really at the periphery of more in-demand orientations and therapies? Was culture really just "everywhere" and "easy" to explore? Reflecting back on this experience, I have no doubt that my choice not only enriched my learning experience as a clinician but completely transformed who I am as a person. I learned that the intensive and intentional study of multicultural psychology has the capacity to shake up the core of who we are as people and how we view ourselves.

I cannot stress enough how disempowered I felt at times when I was initially exposed to the flawed, prejudiced, and often unjust history on which the profession of psychology (and most professions) was built. This feeling of helplessness intensified when I realized that our field was not exempt from the corruptions of ego, hierarchy, status, and materialism. My pursuit for truth and justice increased with every sobering realization.

My hope for the track itself had initially been simple: to gain competency, knowledge, and skills. But soon, it developed into a necessary pursuit of cadres of colleagues who shared similar aspirations—a desire to serve and empower our marginalized communities, a passion for social justice, and a recognition and appreciation of the complexities of human experience.

Needless to say, the concepts explored in this track were able to transfer into practice more seamlessly than I had anticipated. I hold particularly dear the first case in which I was able to translate liberatory concepts and theories into practice with a client. This client was unresponsive to other treatment modalities and demonstrated a limited buy-in to the function of therapy. Through advocacy for multicultural techniques and exploration of the literature with my supervisor, I was eventually able to use liberation theory to validate and address this client's experiences of oppression. I was also able to rule out redundant diagnoses through relevant information gathered in our deeper dialogue, as well as enrich our therapeutic alliance through deep exploration of our power dynamic.

Within multicultural work, I was almost instantly drawn to liberation psychology. Following continuous suggestions from others to explore this theory (as a result of my interests in community empowerment and critical consciousness development), I eventually adopted this theory to inform clinical cases where relevant, and even used it for my clinical competency examinations. This was particularly nerve-racking because popular opinion appeared to point toward using more prevalent and "clear-cut" theories. I nonetheless left my examination with a particularly rich experience in which the selected framework was supported as relevant to the client. It was particularly influential in breaking down the client's hesitation to engage in therapy and invited him on a path of critical consciousness development and social action that was deemed age-appropriate, culturally appropriate, and ultimately empowering— empowering for my client in his daily life and empowering for my own confidence and voice as a growing professional. While liberation psychology presents many strengths; the challenge is undoubtedly that it is in early stages of adaptation and thus does not present a uniform approach. Nevertheless, this did not deter me from implementing it with my client.

In line with liberation theory, my client and I explored three tasks outlined by Martín-Baró (1994) in session. In the act of "politicizing" the client's memories and narrative, I supported him in exploring his story not as an isolated event, but rather that he continually connect these memories to context—historical, social, community, political, and otherwise. What were the messages he received from the media, family, school, his community, and his country about his experience and who he was? How had he internalized these narratives and begun to believe them as reality? How did he view himself in contrast? This exploration was supported through the use of tools such as concept mapping and his own music to dissect messages he had received about who he was and what he was destined for.

Once the client was able to place his own experiences (e.g., feeling ridiculed by specific school staff) 'in the greater context of societal messages about people who looked like him (e.g., "People who look like me are perceived as troublemakers"), I elicited his views about the messages and systems that sought to dehumanize him. The resulting narrative shed light on his experience (e.g., "People like me are considered guilty, people who look like me are often sent to prison, and thus assumptions are made by staff about who I am—even when I'm innocent"). This involved a process of *sensitization*—supporting the client in recognizing that some experiences are, in fact, not okay. I asked questions and engaged the client in deconstructing the ideas and messages that existed in society about "people like [him]," and encouraged him not only to break away from the stories told by dominant culture but to develop his own narrative ("How do you view yourself? Who do you want to be?")

Finally, I encouraged the client to explore methods of social action to channel his newfound understanding and to use his values and capacity to directly address the issues outside of the therapy space. The client was able to organize meetings with school staff to discuss the reality of being a student of color in his school and then explore options to create increased safety for students of marginalized groups in such environments.

The client's counselor observed his increased ability to take ownership for his actions, and his caregiver was adamant for continued treatment in the next year after observed changes. My supervisor also expressed appreciation for suggesting a different framework and method for a client who had historically been unresponsive to treatment. Because I primarily work with adolescents, I find more and more space for liberatory concepts to be implemented, allowing young people to find their voices and truly feel empowered.

In reflecting back on my experience, I recognized a significant change within my thinking patterns and my ability to reflect on myself and the world—both professionally and personally. I wasn't just learning about how to facilitate critical consciousness with the clients I served; I was also developing my own critical consciousness as I progressed through the track's elements. That knowledge now deeply influences, on a daily basis, the other techniques and theories that I learn. What is most encouraging is how it has shaped my confidence and ability to advocate on behalf of my clients and their needs and, in turn, has allowed me to learn how to advocate for the things that matter to me as well—to find my voice.

MARLENE CABRERA'S *TESTIMONIO*

I am a first-generation Salvadorian American Latina descendent from Pipil ancestry and the first in my family to graduate from a university and pursue a doctoral degree in clinical psychology. For the majority of my training in psychology, I rejected my Latinx heritage by tailoring my education to reflect Western values. I studied and valued research of human behavior based on Western, educated, industrialized, rich, and democratic (aka "WEIRD") science and applied that training to treat diverse populations. I avoided most forms of cultural studies for fear that I would become the token Latina. I feared that professors, peers, and community members would perceive me as the student who was admitted to the program by using her "race card." I wanted to be valued as a "legitimate" psychologist, and I rejected any professional reminders that I was other. This perspective ultimately led to my adherence to "pure" evidence-based treatments in sessions. During my first and second years of training, I was successful when working with populations that represented Western culture, but I found myself struggling in connecting and making significant improvements with clients from diverse backgrounds, including those from my own culture and ethnicity. This awareness that my lack of culturally focused training was negatively affecting my clients led me to enroll to the Specialty Track during the third year in my training program.

When I vocalized my decision to pursue a multicultural orientation, many of my peers were concerned that I would be shortchanging my education by not pursuing a mainstream theory. "All that work, for what? Of course, culture is part of one's identity, but you have to learn how to treat them; you need to learn a 'real' scientific theory," or "That should be your elective, not your major. Don't you think it will hurt your chances of getting a strong internship site?" or "You're throwing this opportunity away." The consensus was that the track included "grueling" course work in an area that should be a consideration in treatment, but not necessarily the primary focus when providing psychological services. My insecurities that I would fail to realize my professional aspirations of becoming an effective, competent, and respected psychologist were triggered. For the entirety of my academic career, I was taught that the Western psychological norms were the most evolved and that to practice outside of that hierarchical standard meant I would be providing subpar treatment to my field and the community at large. However, my goals when entering the field of psychology were to provide mental health services for the historically marginalized and underrepresented populations from my diverse community that include the low- and middle-socioeconomic class Latinx population. I knew that I had to learn about the struggles and challenges they faced.

When I entered the Specialty Track, my hopes were initially to learn about subtle behaviors and symptoms that different populations may display in sessions to avoid overdiagnosing, including behaviors that I should display or avoid when providing treatment to solidify rapport. I quickly learned that this was an oversimplified objective. Instead, I learned how to facilitate a collaborative process, where my clients and I negotiate ways to work together. Specifically, I began to incorporate a reflexivity process to my therapeutic treatments to assist my clients in tapping into their own cultural unconsciousness. I cultivated a sacred environment where my clients began to identify their own cultural schemas, cultural scripts, and stereotype primers. While I bared witness to my clients' cultural consciousness, I learned how to understand them through a holistic perspective. It was through this holistic practice that I experienced the power of the human condition; I was continuously moved and humbled by the rich and complex work my clients processed in session. I became a vessel in therapy where the power differentials between my clients and me were explored and scrutinized.

The Specialty Track has forever changed me. I jokingly liken my experience to that of the character Neo from the movie *The Matrix*. Similar to the character, I have been awakened, and I am now aware of the overt and covert cultural information that drives our everyday experiences. My own cultural identity as a heterosexual, Salvadorian American Jewish female from a low-resource community has shaped my passion for understanding sociocultural factors that affect clients' lives. My personal experiences of marginalization have highlighted the importance of having affirming spaces. To understand not only the distress patients are presenting but also experiences of differences they currently or historically have encountered have become my personal and professional goals. In efforts to safeguard against cultural blind-spot syndrome (Lin, 1983) and stereotypical assumptions, when working with individuals who share or do not share dimensions of my identity, I am mindful and aware of my own biases and preconceived notions informed by my positionality in society.

It was in the Specialty Track that I was initially exposed to *mujerista* psychology, which evolved from a feminist and liberation psychology framework. This framework highlights the daily lives (*la cotidiana*) of Latinx womxn. Inspired by Isasi Diaz, mujerista psychology calls for Latinaxs to develop their inner voice, resist oppression, chart their journey, and advocate for social justice (Comas-Díaz, 2012). Further, mujeristas fight the established domination that oppresses individuals based on gender, race, class, and sexual orientation. Mujeristas acknowledge and give honor to their ancestral legacy; recognize their cultural values, norms, and rituals; and affirm their historical trauma and soul wounds. As a mujerista therapist, I join with my client's perception of her environment and assist her in reconnecting with her spiritual gifts as healer, social justice warrior, holder of wisdom, teacher, and more. Through this theoretical orientation, I was changed, and I found that as I learned about my rich culture as a Latina woman, not only were my clients becoming more empowered, but I was as well.

I used the mujerista framework for my clinical competence exam in my doctoral program. The process was challenging because I was the first student to be examined in this framework. My journey in learning and implementing it was demanding, and I was forced to face and acknowledge my own biases and privilege with my client. My Latina client and I worked to analyze the intersectional factors that interacted with her symptoms of distress (e.g., loneliness, binge eating, and lethargy). In comparing our respective areas of oppression and privilege, we were able to connect and solidify a strong therapeutic alliance. By identifying cultural schemas, scripts, and primers, we created cultural and community genograms. The process was crucial to providing treatment and ultimately solidified and charged our sacred space.

Amid my practicum training, I was fortunate to work in settings with clients from diverse ethnic populations (e.g., European American, Asian, Middle Eastern, Latinx, and African American). Although certain sites were more critically conscious than others, they were all open to discussing cultural factors that they were and were not aware of. I was fortunate that my supervisors and peers were eager to discuss and implement changes to treatment that were culturally congruent and centered justice. As I became more confident as a clinician, I was able to identify various instances when diverse clients were being overdiagnosed and were provided with ineffective treatments that resulted in little change in treatment outcomes. As an example, at my first externship, I provided treatment to a Latino adolescent male who had recently migrated to the United States and had experienced severe neglect for most of his childhood. He was initially diagnosed with conduct disorder. However, as we worked together and processed his experience in his home country and the nature of his migration to the United States, it was evident that he was exhibiting culturally congruent behaviors that suggested an understandable reaction to trauma, and he was eventually diagnosed with posttraumatic stress disorder. Typically, systemic forces thwart changes that challenge the status quo, but I was fortunate that my proposed changes were embraced and valued. I owe this to the cultural humility of my supervisors.

I continue to seek training in which cultural integration is valued with the hope of expanding culturally responsive interventions. As I continue to develop as a clinician, it is my personal and professional goal to maintain practicing from a perspective that acknowledges the centrality of individual and collective identities, considers specific care needs of diverse communities, and challenges the status quo to make systems of oppression visible. Currently, I am an extern at a cultural neuropsychological site that prioritizes culturally congruent symptoms and creating innovative bilingual training models. The training site values a multidisciplinary team to develop models of clinical service, training, and research focused on culturally and linguistically proficient care aimed at reducing disparities in treatment outcome. I hope to continue on this journey and make a meaningful impact in my community.

CONCLUSION

The narratives of Marlene and Nahaal illustrate systemic forces that attempt to dismantle an empowered, decolonial psychology. Questioning liberation psychology's legitimacy and value is a tool of colonization. It decenters the focus from the voices of our communities to a never-ending battle of "proving" legitimacy. The resulting internalization of doubt and fear drains the physical, psychological, and spiritual energy of psychologists and students in training who work from a liberation psychology framework. The communities we work with are ultimately hurt by the lack of responsive and socially ethical care.

Liberation psychology is not a uniform and manualized approach to working with disenfranchised communities; instead, it strives to unearth the complexity of individual and collective voices. The goal is to deideologize and develop critical consciousness about the current structures and processes that maintain the status quo of oppression. This critical consciousness is translated into action to dismantle social processes of oppression in many ways. As a result, therapists empower clients and communities to reengage with ancestral foundations for healing and wellness, while empowering themselves to make changes to systems that maintain oppression.

The title of this chapter includes the word *inspiration*. This word has tremendous meaning for the instructors of this Specialty Track. We both have experienced numerous challenges in professional psychology, yet we have sought inspiration from our ancestors and elders, our brothers and sisters. Most important, the courage and energy of our students ultimately inspires us to persevere giving voice to the clients we serve.

REFERENCES

Adams, G., Dobles, I., Gómez, L. H., Kurtiş, T., & Molina, L. E. (2015). Decolonizing psychological science: Introduction to the special thematic section. *Journal of Social and Political Psychology, 3*, 213–238. http://dx.doi.org/10.5964/jspp.v3i1.564

Adams, G., & Markus, H. R. (2003). Toward a conception of culture suitable for a social psychology of culture. In M. Schaller & C. S. Crandall (Eds.), *The psychological foundations of culture* (pp. 335–360). Mahwah, NJ: Erlbaum.

Allwood, C. M., & Berry, J. W. (2006). Origins and development of indigenous psychologies: An international analysis. *International Journal of Psychology, 41*, 243–268. http://dx.doi.org/10.1080/00207590544000013

Arnett, J. J. (2008). The neglected 95%: Why American psychology needs to become less American. *American Psychologist, 63*, 602–614. http://dx.doi.org/10.1037/0003-066X.63.7.602

Boal, A. (1979). *The theatre of the oppressed*. London, England: Pluto Press.

Bryant-Davis, T., & Comas-Díaz, L. (Eds.). (2016). *Womanist and mujerista psychologies: Voices of fire, and acts of courage*. Washington, DC: American Psychological Association. http://dx.doi.org/10.1037/14937-000

Comas-Díaz, L. (2012). *Multicultural care: A clinician's guide to cultural competence*. Washington, DC: American Psychological Association.

Cross, W. (1991). *Shades of black: Diversity in African American identity*. Philadelphia, PA: Temple University Press.

Freire, P. (1985). *The politics of education: Culture, power, and liberation*. London, England: Macmillan. http://dx.doi.org/10.1007/978-1-349-17771-4

Freire, P. (2000). *Pedagogy of the oppressed*. New York, NY: Continuum.

Gutiérrez, K. (2004). *Rethinking education policy for English learners*. Washington, DC: Carnegie Foundation and Aspen Institute.

Gutiérrez, K., & Rogoff, B. (2003). Cultural ways of learning: Individual traits or repertoires of practice. *Educational Researcher, 32*(5), 19–25. http://dx.doi.org/10.3102/0013189X032005019

Henrich, J., Heine, S. J., & Norenzayan, A. (2010). The weirdest people in the world? *Behavioral and Brain Sciences, 33*, 61–83. http://dx.doi.org/10.1017/S0140525X0999152X

Kleinman, A. (1996). How is culture important for *DSM–IV*? In J. E. Mezzich, A. Kleinman, H. Fabrega, Jr., & D. L. Parron (Eds.), *Culture and psychiatric diagnosis: A DSM–IV perspective* (pp. 15–25). Washington, DC: American Psychiatric Association.

Kroeber, A. L., & Kluckhohn, C. K. M. (1952). *Culture: A critical review of concepts and definitions* (Papers of the Peabody Museum, no. 47). Cambridge, MA: Harvard University.

Lee, C. D. (2008). 2008 Wallace Foundation Distinguished Lecture—The Centrality of Culture to the Scientific Study of Learning and Development: How an Ecological Framework in Education Research Facilitates Civic Responsibility. *Educational Researcher, 37*, 267–279. http://dx.doi.org/10.3102/0013189X08322683

Lee, C. D., Spencer, M. B., & Harpalani, V. (2003). "Every shut eye ain't sleep": Studying how people live culturally. *Educational Researcher, 32*(5), 6–13. http://dx.doi.org/10.3102/0013189X032005006

LeVine, R. A. (2007). Anthropological foundations of cultural psychology. In S. Kitayama & D. Cohen (Eds.), *Handbook of cultural psychology* (pp. 40–58). New York, NY: Guilford Press.

Lin, E. H. (1983). Intraethnic characteristics and the patient–physician interaction: "Cultural blind spot syndrome." *The Journal of Family Practice, 16*(1), 91–98.

Lonner, W. J., & Malpass, R. (1994). *Psychology and culture*. Needham Heights, MA: Allyn and Bacon.

Markus, H. R., & Hamedani, M. G. (2007). Sociocultural psychology: The dynamic interdependence among self systems and social systems. In S. Kitayama & D. Cohen (Eds.), *Handbook of cultural psychology* (pp. 3–46). New York, NY: Guilford Press.

Martín-Baró, I. (1994). *Writings for a liberation psychology* (A. Aron & S. Corne, Eds.). Cambridge, MA: Harvard University Press.

Miller, J. G. (1999). Cultural psychology: Implications for basic psychological theory. *Psychological Science, 10*, 85–91. http://dx.doi.org/10.1111/1467-9280.00113

Minnich, E. K. (1990). *Transforming knowledge*. Philadelphia, PA: Temple University Press.

Montero, M. (2009). Methods for liberation: Critical consciousness in action. In M. Montero & C. C. Sonn (Eds.), *Psychology of liberation: Theory and applications* (pp. 73–91). New York, NY: Springer. http://dx.doi.org/10.1007/978-0-387-85784-8_4

Nobles, W. W. (1986). *African psychology: Towards its reclamation, reascension and revitalization*. Oakland, CA: Institute for the Advanced Study of Black Family Life and Culture.

Paul, G. L. (1967). Strategy of outcome research in psychotherapy. *Journal of Consulting Psychology, 31*, 109–118. http://dx.doi.org/10.1037/h0024436

Pepperdine University. (n.d.). *Goals—Pepperdine 2020: Boundless horizons*. Retrieved from https://www.pepperdine.edu/about/our-story/strategic-plan/goals.htm

Platt, J. J. (2016, September). Pedestrians as professors: Theatre of the oppressed in Mexico City. *Psychology International, 27*(3), 6–7. Retrieved from https://www.apa.org/international/pi/2016/09/pedestrians-professors

Rowe, D. M., & Webb-Msemaji, F. (2004). African-centered psychology in the community. In R. Jones (Ed.), *Black psychology* (4th ed., pp. 701–721). Hampton, VA: Cobb & Henry.

Sellers, R., Shelton, N., Cooke, D., Chavous, T., Rowley, S. J., & Smith, M. (1998). A multidimensional model of racial identity: Assumptions, findings, and future directions. In R. Jones (Ed.), *African American identity development* (pp. 275–303). Hampton, VA: Cobb & Henry.

Shweder, R. A. (1990). Cultural psychology: What is it? In J. E. Stigler, R. A. Shweder, & G. Herdt (Eds.), *Cultural psychology: Essays on comparative human development* (pp. 1–43). New York, NY: Cambridge University Press. http://dx.doi.org/10.1017/CBO9781139173728.002

Shweder, R. A. (2007). An anthropological perspective: The revival of cultural psychology—Some premonitions and reflections. In S. Kitayama & D. Cohen (Eds.), *Handbook of cultural psychology* (pp. 40–58). New York, NY: The Guilford Press.

Spencer, M. B. (2000). Identity, achievement orientation and race: "Lessons learned" about the normative developmental experiences of African American males. In W. Watkins, J. Lewis, & V. Chou (Eds.), *Race and education* (pp. 100–127). Needham Heights, MA: Allyn & Bacon.

Toscano Villanueva, S. (2013). Teaching as healing craft: Decolonizing the classroom and creating spaces of hopeful resistance through Chicano-Indigenous pedagogical practice. *The Urban Review: Issues and Ideas in Public Education, 45*(1), 23–40.

Triandis, H. C. (2007). Culture and psychology: A history of the study of their relationship. In S. Kitayama & D. Cohen (Eds.), *Handbook of cultural psychology* (pp. 40–58). New York, NY: Guilford Press.

Conclusion

Liberation Psychology—Crossing Borders Into New Frontiers

Lillian Comas-Díaz and Edil Torres Rivera

*If you have come to help me, please go away. But, if you have come because your libera-
tion is bound up with mine, let us work together.*
—LILLA WATSON, ABORIGINAL ARTIST-ACTIVIST

In this conclusion, we aim to integrate this volume's content, discussing
liberation psychology's essential concepts. We comment on the chapters'
similarities, as well as their singularities. Moreover, we discuss how the
contributors crossed disciplines to expand liberation psychology's scope into
new frontiers. Finally, we envision liberation psychology's evolution into
upcoming contributions. To achieve these goals, we follow a developmental
process as we discuss liberation psychology's origins, current contributions,
and future directions.

BEGINNINGS: LIBERATION PSYCHOLOGY'S ROOTS

Born in Latin America, a member of the Global South, liberation psychology
is often perceived as a lesser discipline compared with European and American psychologies. The concept of Global South is an empowering and less
hierarchical notion developed to identify diverse geopolitical regions of the
world (Kloß, 2017). Within this context, the architect of liberation psychology, Ignacio Martín-Baró, although fluent in English and holding a PhD in

http://dx.doi.org/10.1037/0000198-016
Liberation Psychology: Theory, Method, Practice, and Social Justice, L. Comas-Díaz and E.
Torres Rivera (Editors)

community psychology from the University of Chicago, made a conscious decision to write his work in Spanish. This act seemed consistent with the liberation psychology principle of recovering historical memory—a necessary process in the coconstruction of new types of knowledge. Moreover, writing in Spanish was an act of resistance and subversion against the repression of non-English languages in academia (see Chapter 8). With its emphasis on addressing the needs of the marginalized and a preferential option for the poor, liberation psychology emerged to address oppression, power dynamics, and trauma and to promote social justice.

The contributors in this volume enacted a paradigmatic shift within liberation psychology. As Mark Burton and Raquel Guzzo (Chapter 1) provided a rich description of liberation psychology's origins, including liberation theology (Gutiérrez, 1973) and pedagogy of the oppressed (Freire, 2000), and Edil Torres Rivera (Chapter 2) defined liberation psychology concepts, articulating an emancipatory language. These two chapters illustrated liberation psychology's interdisciplinary focus and envisioned its adherence to syncretism. Moreover, in an exciting historical revelation, Daniel Gaztambide (Chapter 4) analyzed how psychoanalysis aligned itself with a social justice commitment during its early development. In his brilliant integration of Freud, Fanon, and Freire's work, Gaztambide quoted Erich Fromm, who described Freire's method as "a kind of historical–sociocultural and political psychoanalysis." Consequently, Daniel Gaztambide identified psychoanalysis as a liberation method and constructed an epistemological bridge connecting liberation psychology with early psychoanalysis. In the next section, we examine liberation psychology's contemporary developments.

CROSSING BORDERS: THIRD VOICES

This edited book followed an interdisciplinary approach elucidating an integration of multicultural, feminist, womanist/*mujerista* (Latina womanism), trauma, decolonial, postcolonial, Indigenous, community, transcultural, antiracist, intersectional theory, and LGBTQ+ approaches (among others) into liberation psychology. Therefore, a dialogue between liberation psychology and other psychologies resulted in the emergence of *third voices*. The concept of *third voices* refers to a coconstructed position that works toward a collective, liberatory, and transformative change (Lykes, Terre Blanche, & Hamber, 2003). As M. Brinton Lykes and Gabriela Távara (Chapter 6) asserted, a third voice approach entails an interaction of multiple understandings where the whole emerges greater than the sum of its parts. We recognize our third voices as signs of paradigmatic shifts within liberation psychology. Given that history is written from the position of the oppressor (Martín-Baró, 1994), Smith (2012) described history as being patriarchal, local (not universal), and complicit (not innocent) with an oppressive status quo. Likewise, we extended Smith's observations to dominant psychology, acknowledging that it is heterocentric, patriarchal, local, and supportive (explicit or implicit) of the status quo. To illustrate, Chakira M. Haddock-Lazala (Chapter 8) discussed how to challenge dominant psychology's collusion with an oppressive status quo. She remarked on the need for liberation psychologists to consciously navigate being agents of the status quo, as well as being agents of social change and liberation. To describe this condition, Haddock-Lazala coined the term *double agency*. Within this context, we believe that examining our positionality helps us to navigate our double agency.

As third voices, we engaged in a self-reflection of our positionality and thus acknowledged the centrality of historical, contemporary, and systemic oppression, context, life experiences, and intersectionality in peoples' lives. Positionality, a feminist and queer concept, refers to how our social intersecting identities and social positions influence the understanding of our realities (Alcoff, 1988). Therefore, when we embody our positionality, we counteract the myth that psychological theory, practice, and research are neutral and innocent. Thus, reflecting on positionality helps to avoid colluding with cultural and psychological imperialism. As an illustration, Lykes and Távara (Chapter 6) shared how they reflected on their positionality while working alongside Maya Ixil (Guatemala) and Andean (Perú) *campesinas* (peasant women) using feminist participatory action research (PAR). In this fashion, they expanded feminist PAR's scope by adding an action–reflection dialectic. Such dialectical process fostered new ways of thinking and alternative cultural practices, including multiple and differing Indigenous beliefs and perspectives.

While grounded in positionality, we aimed to accompany those we work with. A central liberation psychology concept, accompaniment, is an intentional act of being while working alongside oppressed people (Watkins, 2015). In this volume, we envisioned how accompaniment could be helpful to mainstream psychology and thus be incorporated into psychological research and practice. To illustrate, Jesica Siham Fernández (Chapter 5) offered a luminous description of accompaniment, demonstrating its utility while engaging in PAR. Similar to Alejandro Cervantes's discussion on *testimonio* (Chapter 7), Fernández highlighted the relevance of autoethnography, a qualitative research method, to liberation psychologists' critical reflexivity on their personal and political experiences. She concluded that accompaniment facilitated the interrogation of power, offered counter-hegemonic storying, and fostered collective healing within community–researcher relationships.

Likewise, Kathryn L. Norsworthy and Ouyporn Khuankaew (Chapter 12) embarked on accompaniment while coconstructing knowledge with Thai and Burmese women during a transnational feminist liberation psychology project. In doing so, these contributors promoted the recovery of historical memory by using the name Burma, the country's native appellation, instead of Myanmar, the name imposed by a dictatorship. Hence, this act exemplified how the recovery of historical memory fostered the cocreation of new knowledge, leading to a development of a psychopolitical consciousness. Similarly, therapists, counselors, and clinicians could adopt accompaniment into a socially conscious clinical practice. For instance, Lillian Comas-Díaz (Chapter 9) incorporated accompaniment into the psychotherapeutic relationship. She encouraged psychotherapists to expand their professional roles to express mirroring, witnessing, compassion, respect, and positive regard toward their clients. By promoting therapist flexibility, she articulated a third-voice approach, engaging in radical empathy while accompanying clients.

A mutual accompaniment among liberation psychologists is crucial, particularly during social justice activism. For example, M. Brinton Lykes and Gabriela Távara (Chapter 6) accompanied each other during their feminist participatory action research. Their mutual accompaniment facilitated the coparticipation and coconstruction of knowledge with Mayan and Andean women. As such, these contributors grounded new *conocimiento* (knowledge) in the lived experiences of these Indigenous women. Given that accompaniment is related to the awareness of positionality, when liberation psychologists critically reflected on their positionality, they accompanied their clients in an authentic way. Next, we discuss how we applied liberation psychology to clinical practice, specifically to trauma treatment.

Liberation psychology is a trauma psychology because it originated in the Central American context of war, armed conflict, and state-sponsored genocide. Certainly, trauma is not circumscribed to Latin America. Severe conflicts at both the national and international levels frequently give birth to trauma. For instance, racial trauma arises in the United States from the cumulative attacks that People of Color and Indigenous individuals receive (or perceive) within an oppressive racist climate (Comas-Díaz, Hall, & Neville, 2019). Unfortunately, dominant psychotherapy is limited in the treatment of sociopolitical trauma (see Chapter 9). To give a concrete example, sociopolitical and racial traumas differ from post-traumatic stress disorder in that they are caused by historical, intergenerational, and contemporary sociopolitical oppression (Comas-Díaz, 2000). Moreover, the definitions of trauma and trauma therapy are infused with European American individualistic cultural values (Hernández-Wolfe, 2013). As a result, applying a dominant psychology medical model of trauma therapy is limited to address the systemic and environmental sources of sociopolitical and racial trauma (see Chapters 9 and 10). With its emphasis on people's lived experiences, context, recovery of historical memory, critical consciousness, and social justice action, liberation psychology is better equipped to address sociopolitical trauma (Comas-Díaz, in press). In this regard, liberation psychologists focus on personal and collective trauma within socially conscious and holistic therapeutic approaches. What is more, liberation trauma therapists emphasize antioppression, decolonial, postcolonial, and antiracist practices.

At the heart of liberation psychology is the need to address racism, a major oppression throughout most of the world. Raúl Quiñones-Rosado (Chapter 3) discussed how liberation psychology, anchored in an antiracist, decolonial, and empowering approach, can be an effective approach to treat racial trauma. Using an integral model of well-being, he presented the principle of *buen vivir* (living well/well-being), an Indigenous decolonial framework of personal and communal wellness (see also Chapter 9). Similarly, focusing on Black Americans, Thema Bryant-Davis and Shavonne Moore-Lobban (Chapter 10) presented a Black liberation psychology—a combination of Black theology with liberation psychology aimed at empowering and emancipating Black Americans. As third voices, these contributors illustrated how a Black liberation psychology (see Chapter 2) addresses the oppression of racism and gendered racism to promote holistic freedom among Black Americans. Given that racism is a form of colonization (Fanon, 1967), Bryant-Davis and Moore-Lobban attested that Black liberation psychology addresses internalized racism and oppression among Black Americans. In a similar fashion, Anneliese A. Singh and her colleagues (Chapter 11) applied liberation psychology to queer and transgender communities. They examined the effects of colonization and postcolonization on these communities, affirming the recovery of historical memories and asserting their trans resistance and resilience. Due to Ignacio Martín-Baró's background as a Jesuit priest, early liberation psychological literature was silent regarding queer and trans individuals and groups (see Chapter 11). Therefore, Singh and her collaborators used a third voice to incorporate queer and trans mental health issues into liberation psychology. Significantly, they stated that problematizing psychology from a queer and trans liberation psychology demands the removal of cisgender and heterosexual normative conceptions of mental health. As liberation psychologists, we are in full support of this position.

Other antioppression and trauma healing practices include testimonio, urban liberation, and liberation psychotherapy. To illustrate, Alejandro Cervantes (Chapter 7) discussed testimonio (testimony), a therapeutic intervention born out of the structural violence, oppressive systems, and institutional racism prevalent in Latin America (Cienfuegos & Monelli, 1983). To become familiar with this approach, read the impressive testimonios of Nahaal Binazir and Marlene L. Cabrera in Chapter 14. While discussing testimonio therapy, Cervantes highlighted the relevance of sharing the *papelitos guardados*—suppressed memories and lived experiences—as a means of promoting liberatory practices for both client and therapist. He recommended that therapists ask clients if they want their therapist to create a testimonio with them. Thus, when appropriate, therapists can engage in self-reflection and share their testimonio with clients. According to Cervantes, this practice fosters a positive therapeutic alliance grounded in mutuality. For instance, he discussed a Latinx male adolescent group therapy wherein members shared their testimonios, resulting in the building of solidarity. Likewise, client–therapist reciprocal sharing enhanced authenticity within the therapeutic relationship (see Chapters 8 and 9). Certainly, liberation psychology's emphasis on mutuality highlights the interdependence and mutuality between client and therapist. In other words: Your client's healing is connected to your own healing.

In a similar spirit, Haddock-Lazala (Chapter 8) offered a third voice into socially conscious psychotherapy. She introduced urban liberation, an integration of intersectional feminism and postcolonial psychology, into a socially conscious therapeutic practice. In her excellent discussion of postcolonial theory, Haddock-Lazala identified urban liberation as an antidote to the color-blind and decontextualized mainstream trauma therapies. Anchored in the belief that social identity needs to be understood within a collective context, she highlighted therapists' need to recognize the impact of power dynamics, oppression, and conflict in clients' lives. In this manner, Haddock-Lazala showed how to oppose a Western medical model in a capitalist stratified society by having therapists exhibit radical openness (authenticity) and helping clients to be motivated to become liberated. Additionally, she advocated for the use of multiple languages, cultural healing traditions and creativity as therapeutic interventions at the individual, couple, group, and community levels. Likewise, Comas-Díaz (Chapter 9) conceptualized liberation psychotherapy as an integration of alternative forms of knowledge and methods into healing, such as ethnic and anticolonial postcolonial psychotherapies, including *dichos* (proverbs used as flash therapy), testimonio, Indigenous healing, liberatory arts, and psychospirituality, among others. Specifically, she articulated a third voice through the syncretism of holistic healing and liberation psychology.

SOCIAL JUSTICE ACTION

As previously indicated, social justice action is at the center of liberation psychology. Indeed, the chapters in this volume articulated an urgent need for social justice. Therefore, we discuss specific social justice methods including liberatory arts, liberatory education/training, and liberatory spirituality in the following section.

Creativity is an avenue for healing, liberation, and transformation. Ester R. Shapiro (Chapter 13) identified liberatory arts as culturally centered creative arts, arts-based activism-artivism (art for the purpose of social justice), arts-based PAR, storytelling, and photovoice (an empowering method combining photography with grassroots to promote social justice action; Lykes & Scheib, 2015). Indeed, Lykes and Távara (Chapter 6) used creativity in the form of photovoice with Mayan women and knitting with Andean women, to generate new understandings of issues relevant to these Indigenous women. Similarly, Shapiro discussed popular arts as a vehicle for liberation. She used a transdisciplinary approach to offer a complex/systems, politically and historically contextualized, and social justice–oriented approach to psychological inquiry. Moreover, she emphasized a collaborative coproduction of knowledge for equity. A self-defined "cultural practitioner," Shapiro applied critical–participatory pedagogies to identify how cultural, spiritual, and creative resources promote continuity and innovation during life course transitions. Similar to Quiñones-Rosado (Chapter 3) and to Comas-Díaz (Chapter 9), Shapiro supported clients' positive development and wellness/*bienestar* (buen vivir) through liberatory arts. Likewise, Haddock-Lazala (Chapter 8) suggested taking therapy off of the couch and into the streets. She identified creative expression such as spoken word, poetry, rap workshops, and other urban arts as healing and liberating approaches. In this fashion, she advised therapists to collaborate with community artists and professionals to promote clients' use of liberatory arts to heal trauma and promote social justice action. In this vein, Bryant-Davis and Moore-Lobban (Chapter 10) identified hip-hop psychology and liturgical dance as creative means to promote social justice.

Advancing social justice, Carrie L. Castañeda-Sound and her colleagues (Chapter 14) developed a liberation psychology training with a focus on an integration of feminism, antiracism, and decoloniality. They followed a critical education method, with a deideologization of the roles of client, student, and professor. Moreover, they fostered students' engagement in the humanization of individuals from marginalized communities. According to Castañeda-Sound and her collaborators, these approaches helped to cultivate empathy among the trainees. Throughout these processes, these contributors found that conducting liberation psychology training required flexibility and creativity. Following a similar line of reasoning, Singh and her colleagues (Chapter 11) encouraged graduate students to reflect on their positionality, as well as on the positionality of the other students, to develop mutual empathy. Moreover, they invited students to actively coconstruct their education.

Contrary to dominant psychology's lack of focus on spirituality, liberation psychology emphasizes spirituality in social justice action. From this perspective, liberation psychology is a psychology of hope because oppression and violence corrode hope. What is more, hope annunciates visions of a just and egalitarian future among the oppressed (Neville, 2017). Consequently, liberation psychologists explore and nurture clients' sources of hope (see Chapters 9 and 10). Equally important, Martín-Baró (1998) contrasted religion with faith in his chapter titled "From the Religious Opium to the Liberating Faith." He described *liberating faith* as sustaining hope, resistance, subversion, healing, empowerment, and transformation. Liberating faith is a psychospiritual method, similar to Latina feminist Gloria Anzaldúa's concept of spiritual activism— a combination of a social activism with a spiritual vision (Keating, 2006).

As stated before, engagement in social justice action is at the heart of liberation psychology. Accordingly, Haddock-Lazala (Chapter 8) described social justice action as attending to (a) real economic conditions; (b) state-sponsored violence, including police attacks on People of Color and Indigenous individuals; and (c) issues related to civil rights. Certainly, engaging in social justice action can be gratifying and rewarding. However, social justice activism can also be emotionally and physically exhausting. In fact, it can result in compassion fatigue among social activists. For these reasons, we believe that it is imperative for those working in social justice action to practice self-care. In fact, Martín-Baró (1994) stated that before we can liberate others, we must liberate ourselves. Indeed, he was also referring to self-care. In other words, self-care constitutes an integral aspect of liberation. For instance, Sloan (2013) indicated that activists are faced with feelings of intense fear, anxiety, despair, frustration, and isolation, among other severe feelings that can be debilitating. Thus, he suggested using a number of approaches to maintain a healthy well-being. The primary tools Sloan recommended for self-care include small psychoeducational support groups. Additionally, dialogue and constant communication among activists are helpful ways to maintain a healthy life balance. Finally, personal psychotherapy can also be a fountain of self-care.

To summarize this section, we created a diagram of liberation psychology, following the Native American Medicine Wheel. We focused on the liberation psychology's concepts of decolonization, healing, action, and transformation. We placed liberation psychology's elements in a cyclical progression to denote their constant evolution. Much like the Native American Medicine Wheel, the Liberation Psychology Wheel can be an instrument for learning, teaching, healing, and transformation. You can see the Liberation Psychology Wheel in Figure 15.1.

FIGURE 15.1. Liberation Psychology Wheel

Healing
• Indigenous wisdom— *Buen Vivir*
• *Testimonio, Autohistoria*
• Syncretistic healing (ethnic and psychological)
• Spirituality/ Interdependence
• Creativity

Decolonization
• Historical memory
• Deideologization
• Dialogue
• Critical Consciousness

Liberation

Action
• Accompaniment
• Solidarity
• Social Justice
• Liberatory arts

Transformation
• Psychological
• Sociopolitical
• Environmental
• Global

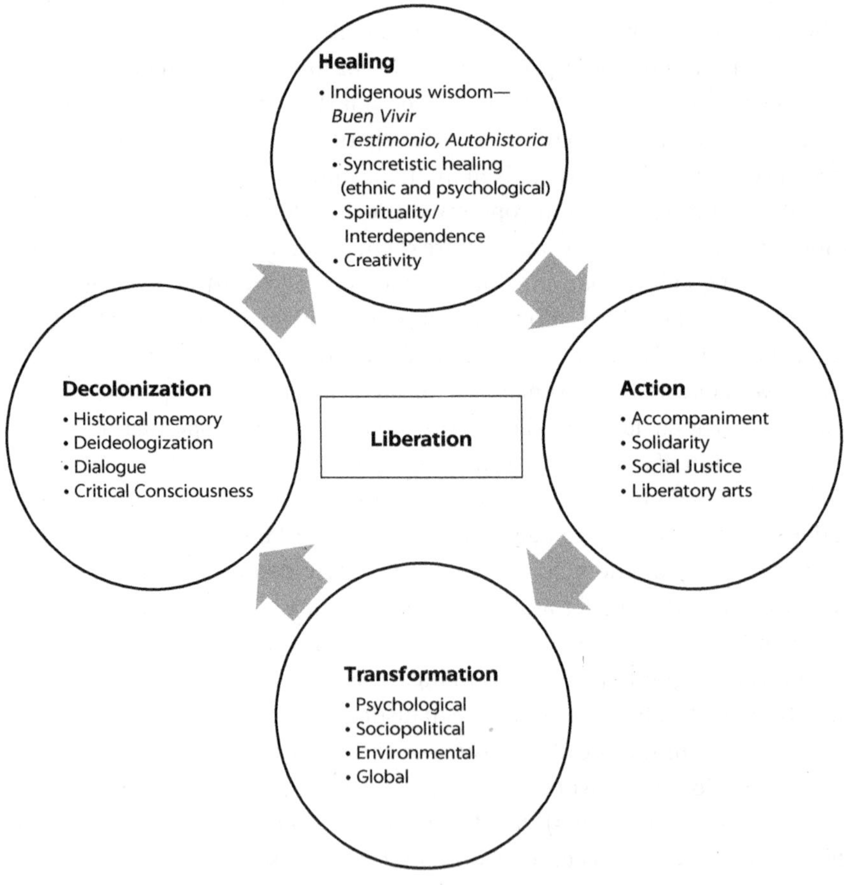

NEW FRONTIERS: RADICAL LIBERATION

Liberation is the horizon of psychology.

—IGNACIO MARTÍN-BARÓ

In this section, we examine liberation psychology's potential future contributions. As we recover our historical memories, we envision the future. Liberation psychology offers a blueprint for psychology's new frontiers. Therefore, we augur psychology's next paradigmatic shift through a radical approach. For this reason, we conceive radical liberation as an inclusive, interconnected, collective, and global emancipation. Rooted in holism and wellness, specifically in buen vivir (Indigenous wellness; see Chapters 3 and 9), radical liberation is an antioppressive, antiracist, decolonial, postcolonial, and intersectional feminist approach toward social justice. In short, the goal of radical liberation is to achieve liberation for all. As such, radical liberation embodies structural competency. A health care concept, structural competency refers to the recognition of how oppressive social and economic structures affect physical, mental, and public health, coupled with a commitment to eradicate such oppressive structures (Metzl & Hansen, 2014). However, to attain radical liberation, we require radical healing. According to Bryana French and her colleagues (2019), radical healing integrates liberation psychology, Black psychology, ethnopolitical psychology and intersectionality theory. As conceived by Comas-Díaz (2007), ethnopolitical psychology expands liberation psychology's scope to include decolonization, ethno-racial-cultural identity reformulation, and racial reconciliation. For these reasons, radical liberation embraces an ethnopolitical perspective, one that cultivates the development of a sociopolitical consciousness and nurtures fundamental social justice action.

We subscribe to the belief that individual liberation ignites collective liberation resulting in the advancement of society's welfare. From this standpoint, radical liberation psychology has potential national and international applications (Dykstra, 2014; Steele, 2008). For instance, it can be applied to individuals with racial privilege. To illustrate, when White individuals cope with poverty, liberation psychologists could help by promoting their critical consciousness of the systemic factors that created economic inequality (Dykstra & Moane, 2017). A critical awareness of systemic economical oppression could enable members of the low socioeconomic class to engage in deideologization, construct new narratives, and participate in a collective socioeconomic justice action. It is instructive to note that Martín-Baró (1998) identified unemployment and underemployment as endemic problems in Latin America. He asked psychologists to redefine these endemic problems as arising from oppressive systems and exhorted them to work toward changing such oppressive systems.

Radical liberation psychology could also be applied to gender issues, specifically to gender inequality. For instance, women of all colors may find in feminist liberation psychology a source of empowerment to address gender economic disparities. Moreover, liberation psychology's ethics of mutual respect, communality, solidarity, and conviviality (Martín-Baró, 1994) could potentially ameliorate sexual harassment in work environments. Indeed, as indicated in this book's Introduction, the American Psychological Association's (APA; 2018a) revised *Guidelines for Psychological Practice With Girls and Women* included numerous liberation psychology precepts. Similarly, boys and men of all colors may find in liberation psychology a refuge from toxic masculinity socialization. As an illustration, the APA *Guidelines for Psychological Practice With Boys and Men* (APA, 2018b) included a liberation psychological approach (Guideline 3) that urged psychologists to understand the impact of power, privilege, and sexism on the development of boys and men and on their relationships.

Radical liberation psychology could infuse psychological research with a much-needed emancipatory and social justice orientation. To illustrate, the ongoing application of qualitative research to oppressed populations (Nagata, Kohn-Wood, & Suzuki, 2012) could impart emancipatory methods into quantitative approaches. Indeed, emancipatory qualitative research reduces the possibility of the oppressed to remain marginalized (Behar-Horenstein & Feng, 2015). For example, within a liberation psychology framework, research is conducted with and for the benefit of the groups being studied. Therefore, researchers move from experts to coparticipants and advocates and do not speak "for" the group members studied; instead, they speak "with" the research participants. Even more, when research participants own the study's findings, the research agenda becomes an instrument of collective welfare (Smith, 2012).

An area of potential radical liberation psychology's contribution is at the United States' national political arena. Emphasis on conscientization regarding power dynamics and differences, development of a psycho-socio-political consciousness, in addition to the value of equality and justice, could impart national politics with a sense of wellness and peaceful relations (Freire, 2000). For example, Haddock-Lazala (Chapter 8) advised liberation psychologists to run for public office to change the culture of politics, promoting the advancement of our nation's collective well-being. To elucidate this point, having a liberation psychologist at a high governmental level could bear significant societal benefits. Similar to the Surgeon General position in the U.S. government, a Psychologist General position could help improve our national public health and well-being. APA's Council of Representatives considered an Action Item, presented by K. Schneider, titled "A Call to Investigate the Creation of a Psychologist General of the United States," but at this point the organization has declined to move forward with the initiative (K. Schneider, personal communications, June 23, 2019, February 20, 2020).

Another area of radical liberation's potential impact is at the international level. In this arena, radical liberation psychology could offer effective ways of negotiating international differences (e.g., cultural, national, political, religious), focusing on the value of global conviviality and wellness. Without a doubt, national, international, and transnational, populations could benefit from liberation psychology's focus on social justice action.

Last, but not least, radical liberation psychology needs to be taught in schools. Children, parents and community members could learn to recover their historical memories, engage in liberatory arts, develop sociopolitical consciousness, and cultivate a thirst for social justice action. As an illustration, Watts, Williams, and Jagers (2003) described sociopolitical development as a process of acquiring knowledge, critical skills, emotional aptitudes, and a capacity for social justice activism among African Americans. Likewise, Castañeda-Sound and her colleagues (Chapter 14) showed how to effectively train college students in liberation psychology.

The potential examples described here are just a few illustrations of how radical liberation psychology could contribute to the development of a future society where justice, freedom, and wellness prevail.

CONCLUSION

As liberation psychologists, we do not "come to help"; rather, we accompany others in a mutual healing and liberation journey. Along these lines, we conceived this edited book as a dialogue and accompaniment among the chapters' contributors. We created a space to dialogue about liberation psychology. We have found this space to be a home for our collective identity as liberation psychologists and a source of sustenance for our work. Therefore, feel free to join us in this effort. We reiterate the invitation we offered you in this book's Introduction—join us in the growing numbers of liberation-minded psychologists. We welcome your ideas, concerns, and comments via e-mail (NLPA-L@LISTS.UFL.EDU). In addition to this edited book, and its list of references, there are several online resources available to expand your knowledge and commitment to liberation psychology. Following is a list of such resources.

ONLINE RESOURCES ABOUT LIBERATION PSYCHOLOGY

1. Liberation Psychology: English language Liberation Psychology Network: http://libpsy.org/sources-on-liberation-psychology/
2. Cátedra Libre Martín-Baró (in Spanish): http://www.catedralibremartin-baro.org/
3. Fondation Frantz Fanon (in French): http://fondation-frantzfanon.com/
4. Colección Digital Ignacio Martín-Baró (in Spanish): http://www.uca.edu.sv/coleccion-digital-IMB/

Finally, we believe that radical liberation could ignite the future of psychology. With its commitment to collective healing and social justice, radical liberation envisions psychology's horizon: the cocreation of a global society characterized by reconciliation, solidary, conviviality, and wellness for all.

REFERENCES

Alcoff, L. (1988). Cultural feminism vs. post-structuralism: The identity crisis in feminist theory. *Signs: Journal of Women in Culture and Society, 13*, 405–436. http://dx.doi.org/10.1086/494426

American Psychological Association. (2018a, February). *APA Guidelines for Psychological Practice With Girls and Women.* Retrieved from https://www.apa.org/about/policy/psychological-practice-girls-women.pdf

American Psychological Association, Boys and Men Group. (2018b). *APA Guidelines for Psychological Practice With Boys and Men.* Retrieved from https://www.apa.org/about/policy/boys-men-practice-guidelines.pdf

Behar-Horenstein, L., & Feng, X. (2015, May–June). Emancipatory research: A synthesis of quantitative evidence. *IOSR Journal of Research & Method in Education, 5*(3), 46–56.

Cienfuegos, A. J., & Monelli, C. (1983). The testimony of political repression as a therapeutic instrument. *American Journal of Orthopsychiatry, 53*(1), 43–51. http://dx.doi.org/10.1111/j.1939-0025.1983.tb03348.x

Comas-Díaz, L. (2000). An ethnopolitical approach to working with People of Color. *American Psychologist, 55*, 1319–1325. http://dx.doi.org/10.1037/0003-066X.55.11.1319

Comas-Díaz, L. (2007). Ethnopolitical psychology: Healing and transformation. In E. Aldarondo (Ed.), *Promoting social justice in mental health practice* (pp. 91–118). Mahwah, NJ: Erlbaum.

Comas-Díaz, L. (in press). Sociopolitical trauma: Ethnicity, race and immigration. In P. Tummala-Narra (Ed.), *Racial minority immigration and trauma.* Washington, DC: American Psychological Association.

Comas-Díaz, L., Hall, G. N., & Neville, H. A. (2019). Racial trauma: Theory, research, and healing: Introduction to the special issue. *American Psychologist, 74*, 1–5. http://dx.doi.org/10.1037/amp0000442

Dykstra, W. (2014). Liberation psychology—A history for the future. *The Psychologist, 27*, 888–891. Retrieved from https://www.academia.edu/9188465/Liberation_psychology_A_history_for_the_future

Dykstra, W., & Moane, G. (2017). Liberation psychology. In B. S. Turner (Ed.), *The Wiley Blackwell encyclopedia of social theory* (pp. 1–3). London, England: Wiley. http://dx.doi.org/10.1002/9781118430873.est0214

Fanon, F. (1967). *Black skins, White masks.* New York, NY: Grove Press.

Freire, P. (2000). *Cultural action for freedom.* Boston, MA: Harvard Education Press.

French, B. H., Lewis, J. A., Mosley, D. V., Adames, H. Y., Chavez-Dueñas, N. Y., Chen, G. A., & Neville, H. A. (2019). Toward a psychological framework of radical healing in Communities of Color. *The Counseling Psychologist, 48*, 14–46. http://dx.doi.org/10.1177/0011000019843506

Gutiérrez, G. (1973). *A theology of liberation.* New York, NY: Orbis.

Hernández-Wolfe, P. (2013). *A borderlands view on Latinos, Latin Americans, and decolonization: Rethinking mental health.* Lanham, MD: Aronson.

Keating, A. (2006). From borderlands and new *mestizas* to *nepantlas* and *nepantleras*: Anzaldúan theories for social change. *Human Architecture: Journal of the Sociology of Self-Knowledge, IV*, 5–16.

Kloß, S. T. (2017). The Global South as subversive practice: Challenges and potentials of a heuristic concept. *Global Society, 11*(2), 1–17. http://dx.doi.org/10.2979/globalsouth.11.2.01

Lykes, M. B., & Scheib, H. (2015). The artistry of emancipatory practice: Photovoice, creative techniques and feminist anti-racist participatory action research. In H. Bradury-Huang (Ed.), *Handbook of action research* (3rd ed.; pp. 130–141). Newbury Park, CA: Sage. http://dx.doi.org/10.4135/9781473921290.n14

Lykes, M. B., Terre Blanche, M., & Hamber, B. (2003). Narrating survival and change in Guatemala and South Africa: The politics of representation and a liberatory community psychology. *American Journal of Community Psychology, 31*(1–2), 79–90. http://dx.doi.org/10.1023/A:1023074620506

Martín-Baró, I. (1994). *Writings for a liberation psychology* (A. Aron & S. Corne, Trans. & Eds.). Cambridge, MA: Harvard University Press.

Martín-Baró, I. (1998). *Psicología de la liberación* [Liberation psychology] (A. Blanco, Ed.). Madrid, Spain: Editorial Trotta.

Metzl, J. M., & Hansen, H. (2014). Structural competency: Theorizing a new medical engagement with stigma and inequality. *Social Science & Medicine, 103*, 126–133. Retrieved from https://www.ncbi.nlm.nih.gov/pmc/articles/PMC4269606/

Nagata, D. K., Kohn-Wood, L., & Suzuki, L. A. (Eds.). (2012). *Qualitative strategies for ethnocultural research*. Washington, DC: American Psychological Association. http://dx.doi.org/10.1037/13742-000

Neville, H. A. (2017, February). *The role of counseling centers in promoting wellbeing and social justice*. Keynote address presented at the Big Ten Counseling Centers Conference. Champaign, IL.

Sloan, T. S. (2013). Activist support as a form of critical psychology praxis. *Annual Review of Critical Psychology, 10*, 952–963.

Smith, L. T. (2012). *Decolonizing methodologies: Research and Indigenous people* (2nd ed.). London, England: Zed Books.

Steele, J. M. (2008). Counselor preparation: Preparing counselors to advocate for social justice: A liberation model. *Counselor Education and Supervision, 48*, 74–86. http://dx.doi.org/10.1002/j.1556-6978.2008.tb00064.x

Watkins, M. (2015). Psychological psychosocial accompaniment [Special thematic section on decolonizing psychological science]. *Journal of Social and Political Psychology, 3*, 324–341. http://dx.doi.org/10.5964/jspp.v3i1.103

Watts, R. J., Williams, N. C., & Jagers, R. J. (2003). Sociopolitical development. *American Journal of Community Psychology, 31*, 185–194. http://dx.doi.org/10.1023/A:1023091024140

GLOSSARY

Acompañamiento ("accompaniment") An intentional act of being and experiencing social conditions alongside those who are affected by these and interconnected systems of oppression (Goizueta, 2009; Sepúlveda, 2011; Watkins, 2015).

Artivism Art for social justice purposes (Sandoval & Latorre, 2008).

Autoethnography A qualitative research method in which psychologists engage in critical reflexivity on their personal and political experiences (see Chapter 5); similar to *testimonio* (see Chapter 7).

Autohistoria A creative process of integrating a fragmented identity (Anzaldúa, 2002).

Buen vivir ("well-being") An Ayamara concept of living in balance; a contemplative, decolonial, and emancipatory principle that grounds humans into their sociopolitical and ecological contexts (Chapters 3 and 9).

Colonial mentality An internalized attitude of ethnic or cultural inferiority felt by people as a result of colonization; in the United States, colonial mentality has been associated with internalized oppression and internalized racism.

Coloniality The process of becoming colonized; also the understanding that

> colonization is not a simple matter of real estate and political control. Rather, it is a complex process that also involves colonizing the psychological and social worlds of the colonial subjects. These subjects include both the original inhabitants of particular geographic areas and also those who come thereafter, subjugated by the colonizers' sociopolitical system. (Tate, Torres Rivera, & Edwards, 2015, pp. 41–54)

Coloniality of gender The "analysis of racialized, capitalist, and gender oppression" (Lugones, 2003, p. 111).

Coloniality of power The interconnected practices of epistemic and socio-cultural hegemony that maintain systems of oppression within the social order (Quijano, 2000).

Concientização/Concientización/Concientization The process of acquiring a critical consciousness, meaning the conscious construction and reconstruction of an understanding of one's reality, as part of a totality of one's experience (Montero, 2009).

Conocimiento ("knowledge") A holistic understanding developed through self-reflection, imagination, rational thought, and social justice action (Keating, 2012).

Decolonialization The process of decentering the power and influence of the social researcher over the research processes and outcomes.

Deideologization The process in which people do not take their truth as simply everyday occurrences, based on sociopolitical ideology that may be seen as biased or limited.

Dialoguing A process asserting that community members and researchers coconstruct a new knowledge (Montenegro & Pujol, 2003).

Dicho ("proverb") An ethnic flash therapy (see Chapter 9).

Double agency Psychologists' conscious management of being agents of the status quo and of social change and liberation (see Chapter 8).

Facultad Spiritual intuition that allows the oppressed to see accurately, especially power dynamics (Anzaldúa, 2002).

El pueblo The people.

Global South Africa, Latin America, and developing parts of Asia and the Middle East; an empowering and less hierarchical term developed to identify diverse geopolitical regions of the world (Kloß, 2017; see the Conclusion).

Intuitive inquiry Analysis of objective and subjective data through data collection and reflection.

Mestizaje The process through which Indigenous and European ancestry becomes mixed and creates *mestizo/a* people (see Chapter 8).

Mujerista/muxerista Latinx womanist, that is, a conceptual and spiritual alliance of womanist and *mujerista* psychologies (Comas-Díaz, 2016; see Chapter 8).

Mulataje The mixing of African and European ancestry, creating *mulato/a* people (see Chapter 8).

Muxerista A concept aimed at being inclusive of transgender and gender-nonconforming people who identify as women (see Chapter 8).

Neocolonization The use of new methods to colonize other countries through economic, political, cultural, or other pressures to control or influence, especially former European or American colonies; the use of new methods to (re)colonized members of subaltern groups.

Participatory action research (PAR) An approach to conducted studies in communities that emphasizes community and research participation as well as action by both the community and the researchers.

PhotoPAR or photovoice Photography used to document daily life of marginalized groups to analyze the photos and narratives and to generate community survival and resilience.

Positionality A concept that describes how our social intersecting identities and social positions influence the understanding of our realities (Alcoff, 1988).

Postcolonial theory A theory that aims to account for the effects of European imperialism and colonization on most cultures and practices around the world and acknowledges that some peoples have been affected more than others; importantly, some people continue to live under colonial rule (e.g., Palestinians, Puerto Ricans; see Chapters 8 and 12).

Postcolonization stress disorder The result of coping with cultural imperialism and the imposition and internalization of mainstream culture as superior (Comas-Díaz, 2007).

Problematización ("problematizing") The process of critically analyzing life circumstances and the role(s) they play on the person or people; it questions the explanations and typical considerations of a situation (see Chapters 2 & 11).

Radical liberation An inclusive, interconnected, collective, and global emancipation rooted in holism and wellness, specifically in *buen vivir* (Indigenous wellness; see Conclusion).

Realismo crítico A theory stating that reality, although independent of the people, cannot be known in an absolute manner and can only be known as an approximation of what it is.

Sabiduría Spanish word for wisdom knowledge.

Sensuous knowledge A form of knowing and doing that comes from being socially situated within a particular embodiment, leading to different ways of being and living in our bodies within society (Shotwell, 2009; see Chapter 8).

Spiritual activism Engagement in social justice action with a spiritual vision.

Structural competency A health care concept advocating for the recognition of how oppressive social and economic structures affect physical, mental, and public health, coupled with a commitment to address such oppressive structures (Metzl & Hansen, 2014; see the Conclusion).

Testimonio A first-person testimony of significant experiences in which the narrative voice is that of a typical or extraordinary witness or protagonist (see Chapter 7).

Testimoniando (giving *testimonio*) The act of sharing one's testimonio with others.

Transnational feminism Analysis of power differentials and structural inequities spanning across cultures and national borders, focusing on the impacts of social, political, and economic institutions and systems.

Urban liberation The integration of intersectional feminism and postcolonial psychology into a socially conscious therapeutic practice (see Chapter 8).

Zambo/a/xs People of mixed Indigenous and African ancestry (see Chapter 8).

REFERENCES

Alcoff, L. (1988). Cultural feminism vs. post-structuralism: The identity crisis in feminist theory. *Signs: Journal of Women in Culture and Society, 13*, 405–436.

Anzaldúa, G. (2002). now let us shift . . . the path of *conocimiento* . . . inner work, public acts. In G. E. Anzaldúa & A. Keating (Eds.), *This bridge we call home: Radical visions for transformation* (pp. 540–570). New York, NY: Routledge.

Comas-Díaz, L. (2007). Ethnopolitical psychology: Healing and transformation. In E. Aldarondo (Ed). *Advancing social justice through clinical practice* (pp. 91–118). Mahwah, NJ: Lawrence Earlbaum Associates.

Comas-Díaz, L. (2016). *Mujerista* psychospirituality. In T. Bryant-Davis & L. Comás-Díaz (Eds.), *Womanist and* mujerista *psychologies: Voices of fire, acts of courage* (pp. 149–169). Washington, DC: American Psychological Association.

Goizueta, R. (2009). *Christ our companion: Toward a theological aesthetics of liberation.* New York, NY: Orbis Books.

Keating, A. (2012). Making face, making soul: Spiritual activism and social transformation. In K. M. Vaz & G. L. Lemons (Eds.), *Feminist solidarity at the crossroads: Intersectional women's studies for transracial alliance* (pp. 205–219). New York, NY: Routledge.

Lugones, M. (2003). *Pilgrimages/peregrinajes: Theorizing coalition against multiple oppressions.* New York, NY: Rowan & Littlefield.

Metzl, J. M., & Hansen, H. (2014). Structural competency: Theorizing a new medical engagement with stigma and inequality. *Social Science & Medicine, 103*, 126–133. Retrieved from https://www.ncbi.nlm.nih.gov/pmc/articles/PMC4269606/

Montenegro, M., & Pujol, J. (2003). *Conocimiento situado: Un forcejeo entre el relativismo construccionista y la necesidad de fundamentar la acción* [Situated knowledge: A struggle between constructivist relativism and the need to substantiate action]. *Revista Interamericana de Psicología, 37*, 295–307. Retrieved from https://www.redalyc.org/articulo.oa?id=28437209

Montero, M. (2009). Methods for liberation: Critical consciousness in action. In M. Montero & C. C. Sonn (Eds.), *Psychology of liberation: Theory and applications* (pp. 73–91). New York, NY: Springer.

Quijano, A. (2000). Coloniality of power and Eurocentrism in Latin America. *International Sociology, 15*, 215–232.

Sandoval, C., & Latorre, G. (2008). Chicana/o artivism: Judy Baca's digital work with youth of color. In A. Everett (Ed.), *Learning race and ethnicity: Youth and digital media* (pp. 81–108). Cambridge, MA: MIT Press.

Sepúlveda, E., III. (2011). Toward a pedagogy of acompañamiento: Mexican migrant youth writing from the underside of modernity. *Harvard Educational Review, 81*, 550–573. http://dx.doi.org/10.17763/haer.81.3.088mv5t704828u67

Shotwell, A. (2009). A knowing that resided in my bones: Sensuous embodiment and trans social movement. In S. Campbell & L. Meynell (Eds.), *Embodiment and agency* (pp. 58–75). University Park: The Pennsylvania State University Press.

Tate, K., Torres Rivera, E., & Edwards, L. M. (2015). Colonialism and multicultural counseling competence research: A liberatory analysis. In R. D. Goodman & P. Gorski (Eds.), *Decolonizing "multicultural" counseling through social justice* (pp. 41–54). New York, NY: Springer.

Watkins, M. (2015). Psychosocial accompaniment. *Journal of Social and Political Psychology, 3*, 324–341.

INDEX

ABOUT THE EDITORS

Lillian Comas-Díaz, PhD, is a clinical psychologist in private practice and a clinical professor at George Washington University Department of Psychiatry. A past faculty member at Yale University Psychiatry Department, she directed the Yale Hispanic Clinic. She is a former director of the Office of Ethnic Minority Affairs at the American Psychological Association (APA). The founding editor of the journal *Cultural Diversity and Ethnic Minority Psychology*, Dr. Comas-Díaz is an associate editor of the *American Psychologist*. She is the author or editor of over 175 scholarly publications, including *Multicultural Care: A Clinician's Guide to Cultural Competence*; *Latina Psychologists: Thriving in the Cultural Borderlands* (coedited with C. Vazquez); *Womanist and* Mujerista *Psychologies* (coedited with T. Bryant-Davis); and *Psychological Health of Women of Color* (coedited with B. Greene). A former president of Psychologists in Independence Practice (APA Division 42), Dr. Comas-Díaz is the recipient of the American Psychological Foundation and American Psychological Association 2019 Gold Medal for Life Achievement in the Practice of Psychology.

Edil Torres Rivera, PhD, is a professor and director of the Latinx Studies program at Wichita State University, Kansas (https://www.wichita.edu/academics/applied_studies/CLES/People/people_page.php). He holds a doctorate in counseling psychology from the University of Connecticut. His primary research focuses on complexity and how Indigenous healing techniques are a necessary ingredient when working with ethnic minority populations in the United States. His work has appeared in the *Journal of Multicultural Counseling and Development*; the *Journal of Counseling and Development*; the *Radical Psychology Journal*; the *Journal of Humanistic Counseling, Education and Development*; the

Counselor Education and Supervision Journal; the *Journal for Specialists in Group Work*; the *Journal of Psychological Practice*; the *Counseling and Values Journal*; the *Journal of Technology in Counseling*; and the *Canadian Journal of Counselling*. Presently he serves on the editorial board of the *Journal for Social Action in Counseling and Psychology* and is the editor of the *Interamerican Journal of Psychology*.